A History
of Hand Knitting

To Joan

She sayd as her whytte hands
whytte hosen were knyttynge,
What pleasure ytt ys to be married.

Richard Rutt

A History
of Hand Knitting

B T Batsford Ltd, London

© Richard Rutt 1987
First published 1987
Reprinted 1987 and 1989

ISBN 0 7134 5118 1

Typeset by Tek-Art Limited, Kent
and printed in Great Britain by
Anchor Press Limited
Tiptree, Essex
for the publishers
B.T. Batsford Limited.
4 Fitzhardinge Street
London W1H 0AH.

Contents

Preface

William Turner, my grandfather, was the village blacksmith of Langford in Bedfordshire. He taught me to knit when I was 7 years old, to keep me quiet indoors on a rainy day. The year was 1932 or 1933. He himself had learned to knit in about 1873, when he was a little boy in the neighbouring village of Henlow.

So far as I know, he did not knit garments. He was a craftsman in iron and wire, who understood and respected a craft that used yarn, and conveyed to me the fascination of fabric construction by interlooping rather than weaving. I learned more by pestering my mother and studying *Woolcraft*, and before long had mastered the turning of a sock heel. My shop-bought woollen gloves never fitted, so I designed myself better fittings with ribbed fabrics and longer fingers. Fair Isle knitting was again in fashion, and, like most children, I preferred pictures to patterns: struggling to knit a picture of a pet guinea-pig, I discovered by rule of thumb the principles of intarsia knitting.

When the war came I was positively encouraged to knit because of the clothing shortages. I was called up into the navy (though I never went to sea), where knitting was still acceptable as a craft for men, and I remember knitting through long slow journeys to Plymouth in darkened trains. I worked an Aran jumper from the famous picture in Mary Thomas's book, and for long used fawn bathing trunks that I had made to fit; but knitting was by no means my only hobby.

From 1954 to 74 I gave it up completely. During those years I was working in Korea, where knitting yarn was then unobtainable. Not until I returned to Britain and found myself depressed by 'return culture shock' did my wife suggest that I resume knitting as a gently therapeutic craft. It worked; but two decades of having Oriental history as my principal hobby made me question the history of knitting. For the past ten years seeking out the history of hand knitting has given me as much pleasure as has the craft itself.

This book is the first monograph on hand knitting history. It has the weaknesses to which pioneer writing is liable: it is incomplete and uneven, it is an amateur work, it asks questions it is not able to answer. I hope that by giving a general survey and indicating the various types of source for further research, it will be useful in stimulating others to write in greater detail and with greater accuracy.

Because this is not an academic thesis I have forsworn the full delights of notes and page references. Where it may be helpful I have given page numbers in brackets after quotations.

In most of the quotations I have modernised the spelling and punctuation for the sake of clarity and to avoid the risk of quaintness.

Some charts have been deduced from photographs.

in festo BMV 21.8.1987 ✠ Richard Leicester

Acknowledgements

The quotation from Queen Victoria's unpublished journals is given by gracious permission of Her Majesty the Queen. The tune of 'Tarry wool' is printed by permission of Mrs Ralph Vaughan Williams.

I should never have undertaken the labour of preparing this book had I not been encouraged by Kathleen Kinder, that inspired enthusiast for machine knitting as a craft, who persuaded Batsford to persuade me. Dr Helen Bennett, professional historian of costume and textiles, has been generous with materials and advice.

Members of the Knitting and Crochet Guild have helped enthusiastically: especially Montse Stanley, Sue Leighton-White, Edna Treen, Olga Edwards, Mavis Walker, and Paul Cochrane.

Numerous people have helped me with special knowledge and experience. These include: Professor Denis Munden of Leicester Polytechnic School of Textile and Knitwear Technology; Sheila MacGregor, Mary Wright, Alexandra Rowlands; Margaret Meikle, keeper of Cowichan knitting at Vancouver University; Jane Forsyth of Sanquhar; Howard W. Ayles, Beatrice Dennis, Alma Wilcox and Lilian Bursey, who all know Ringwood and its gloves; Benjamin G. Cox of Blandford Museum; Clara Sedgwick of Dent; Kathy Goostrey of Wilkinson's Cornish Knitwear; Bishop Daniel Pina de Cabral and his wife, other Portuguese friends and Miss Edith Miller; deacon George Bebawi of the Coptic Church, his wife Carol, and Jane Handford, on knitting in Egypt; Michael Harvey, historian of Patons; Aldyth Cadoux, generous in lending books and specimens; Bernard T Lee, archivist of Needle Industries; Stowell Kenyon, former manager for Patons and Baldwins in Shanghai; sons and daughters of Marjory Tillotson, Mary Thomas, Jane Koster and Margaret Murray; Alec Dalglish of the Knitting Craft Group; Susan Raven of *The Sunday Times*; Tessa Lorant; and Rohana Darlington.

Librarians rarely receive their due. Jack Smirfitt of the Hosiery and Allied Trades Retail Association in Nottingham gave me much guidance, as well as help with books; Aubrey Stevenson, Local History Librarian of Leicestershire, worked hard and patiently for me; Leslie O'Connell Edwards of Aberdeen University helped me over some rare items. The British Library Reference Division, the National Art Library, the School of Oriental and African Studies, Leicester University and the Amateur Swimming Association at Loughborough have all been indispensable. The staff of Stamford Public Library has coped weekly with requests for the recondite.

Museum staffs have given generous help, especially at the Victoria & Albert, the Museum of London, the National Museum of Ireland, the National Museum of Scotland, Bankfield Museum, the Ashmolean, York Castle, Gawthorpe Hall, Lerwick, the Royal Maritime Museum, the Mary Rose Trust, the Wordsworth Museum, the Newarke Houses and Jewry Wall Museums in Leicester, and Textilmuseum, St Gallen.

Acknowledgements for black and white photographs

Halberstadt Domschatz 8, 52, 53; Gwynedd County Council 14, 122, 123; Bernard T Lee 17; Yale University Art Gallery 21; Victoria & Albert Museum 55, 57, 70, 71, 72, 75, 108, 156; Leicestershire Museums Service 23, 83; Detroit Institute of Arts 26; Metropolitan Museum of Art, New York 27; Kulturhistoriska Föreningen, Lund 31, 32; Ministerio de Cultura, Madrid 35, 39; Abegg Stiftung, Riggisberg 42; Museo Poldi-Pezzoli, Milan 43; Pinacoteca Nazionale di Bologna 44; Hamburger Kunsthalle 45; Musées de Sens 54; Museum of London 56, 58, 67; The Mary Rose Trust 59, 60, 61, 62; Soprintendenza Beni Artistici e Storici, Firenze 63, 64; Museum Narodowe, Szczecin 65; Grimsthorpe and Drummond Castle Trust 68; Deutsche Fotothek, Dresden 69; Museum Narodowe, Wroclaw 74; Castle Museum, York 84, 85, 86, 120; Hispanic Society of America 89, 90; Mrs R Leighton-White 91; Dove Cottage Trust, Grasmere 95; Michael Harvey 100, 119; Scottish Fisheries Museum Trust, Anstruther 102; Norfolk Museums Service 103; *Punch* 104, 107, 130; Patons and Baldwins 106, 111, 113, 117; BBC Hulton Picture Library 109, 154; Costume Museum, Bath 110; Mrs C Fraser-Smith 112; Richard Thomas 116; David Koster 118; Knitting Craft Group 121; Royal Museum of Scotland 124, 125, 126, 127, 129; *Illustrated London News* 132; Howard W Ayles; National Museum of Ireland 140; International Broadcasting Trust 144; Margaret Meikle 147; Peloponnesian Folklore Foundation 155, 156, 157.

Introduction

The first English records of the history of knitting lie in Edmund Howes's two famous stories, published in 1615, of the knit hose seen by William Rider in the Mantua merchant's house, and the stockings made for Queen Elizabeth by Mrs Montague. Howes believed these were the first worsted stockings and silk stockings made in England. (See below page 67.)

The next recorded reference to the history of knitting was an unacknowledged quotation from Howes. William Howell, a fellow of Magdalene College, Cambridge, published in 1680 and 1685 two magnificent volumes on the history of Greek and Roman civilization entitled *An Institution of General History: or the History of the World*. In describing the encouragement of silk production under the Emperor Justinian at Byzantium in the sixth century, Howell digressed:

> Silk is now grown nigh as common as wool and become the clothing of those in the kitchen as well as the court . . . even that magnificent and expensive prince Henry the Eighth wore ordinarily cloth hose, except there came from Spain, by great chance, a pair of silk stockings . . . (II 222)

The theme did not attract other writers until the beginning of dictionary writing, two generations after Howell. Ephraim Chambers, who died in 1740, published in 1728 *Cyclopaedia . . . or Dictionary of Arts and Sciences* in two volumes. He drew on a French source, the *Dictionnaire Universel de Commerce* of Jacques Savary des Bruslons, published in 1723.

Under the heading 'Bonneterie', Savary des Bruslons described the foundation in Paris in 1527 of a capknitters' guild under the patronage of St Fiacra, guessing that St Fiacra was chosen because he was a Scot and the Parisians thought that knitting came to them from Scotland. It was a bad guess in more ways than one – St Fiacra was actually Irish – but Ephraim Chambers copied the story and the mistake goes on being repeated to this day. I have discussed it further in the section on cap-knitting. (See page 60.)

Chambers's reference to knitting was picked up and further developed by Malachy Postlethwayt, who produced in 1751 an English version of Savary des Bruslons's work and called it *A Universal Dictionary of Trade and Commerce*. This was not a translation, but a book modelled on the French one, in which references to English hand knitting were entered under the various county names.

The whole question of knitting history suddenly became of interest to all educated Englishmen in 1782 when controversy over the Rowley poems was rife. These poems were supposed to be the work of a fifteenth-century priest of Bristol named Thomas Rowley, discovered in the 1760s by Thomas Chatterton, who was the son of a lay-clerk at Bristol cathedral and nephew of the sexton of the church of St Mary Redcliffe. Chatterton claimed to have found Rowley's poems in St Mary's muniment room.

Chatterton was a gifted poet in his own right – Wordsworth called him 'the marvellous boy' – and in April 1770 he set off to seek fame and fortune in London. His quest was fruitless. He remained squalidly poor, and on 25 August was found dead at his lodging in Holborn, having taken arsenic. He was 17 years old.

Chatterton's early death gave him romantic

appeal. Some citizens of Bristol believed his story about the Rowley manuscripts, and the poems were published in 1778 and 1782. Immediately some scholars suspected they were forged and denied their authenticity. The controversy raged for some time, in pamphlets and in the columns of *The Gentleman's Magazine*. One of the central points of the argument was a reference to knitting in one of the poems.

The masterpiece of the Rowley collection is a verse tragedy 'Ælla', which tells of a Saxon hero's struggles against the Danish horde threatening Bristol. In it are the lines:

As Elynour bie the green lesselle was syttynge,
As from the sone's hete she harried,
She sayde as her whytte hands whytte hosen
were knyttynge,
What pleasure ytt ys to be married.

The anti-Rowleians claimed that this was anachronistic, because Howes's stories of William Ryder and Mrs Montague showed that knitting was unknown in England before 1560. The Dean of Exeter retorted that Chambers's story of the guild of St Fiacra showed that knitting was older than 1560, for if the French had learned it from the Scots before 1527, the English must have known it at least half a century before that, which meant that knitting was known in England in the reign of Edward IV (1461-83), when Thomas Rowley was supposed to have lived. The controversy rumbled on till it was decisively settled by Walter William Skeat's 1871 edition of Chatterton's works, which proved that Chatterton himself wrote all the poems in mock Middle English.

This controversy explains why so many subsequent writers, including Adam Smith in *The Wealth of Nations* (1776), were anxious about whether or not the English could knit stockings in the reign of Edward IV.

The anonymous scholars, dilettanti and anti-quarians who discussed the Rowleian controversy in the pages of *The Gentleman's Magazine* in 1778 published further snippets of knitting history. *The Gentleman's Magazine* (the first periodical to be called a 'magazine') was widely read, and the 11 articles that appeared in it before the middle of

1783 brought the subject of knitting history before the educated public.

The first serious scholarly monograph on knitting history was the work of Johann Christoph Beckmann (1739-1811), professor of oeconomy in the University of Göttingen. It appears in volume IV of his *Beytrage zur Geschichte der Erfindungen*, published in parts from 1780 to 1805. This compendious work was translated into English and published in several editions between 1797 and 1846 as *A History of Inventions, Discoveries and Origins*. Beckmann had read Howell, Howes, *The Gentleman's Magazine*, Holinshed, Palsgrave and more besides, but had much less material from France or Germany.

Beckmann brought Germanic scholarship to his work, offering a definition of knitting and gently criticizing some of his sources. He noted, for example, that Savary des Bruslons's conjecture as to the Scottish origin of knitting 'rests only on a very slight foundation'. Referring to Henry VIII's garments with 'every cut knit with points of fine gold', he adds: 'What the word *knit* here signifies might perhaps be discovered if we had an English journal of luxury and fashion for the sixteenth century'. In two sober judgements he says it is 'more than probable that the art of knitting was first found out in the sixteenth century'; and 'did the invention belong to the Spaniards, I should be inclined to conjecture that these people obtained it from the Arabians.'

In 1831 Gravenor Henson (1785-1852) published his *History of the Framework Knitters*, which has become a classic in that field. Henson was a Nottingham framework knitter who moved into lace-making. He became a trade unionist at 23 and developed into a legendary figure of the movement, once imprisoned for Luddite complicity. He was self-educated and much influenced by Methodism. In a period when free trade was gaining ground, he argued for government control and protectionism. His book was inspired as a tract for his political doctrine, rather than as an essay in history for its own sake.

The first chapter contains a brief account of knitting before the invention of the knitting frame. The devout Henson here published for the first time the myths of knitting in the Odyssey and the

Bible, saying that Penelope knitted, and giving a reverent account of Christ's seamless garment. Both these stories have been often and uncritically repeated.

William Felkin (1795-1874), a younger acquaintance of Gravenor Henson, and like Henson largely self-educated, published his *History of the Machine Wrought Hosiery and Lace Manufactures* in 1867. Felkin was born in the mining and hosiery village of Ilkeston in Derbyshire to the family of a framework knitter who in the year of William's birth became an Evangelical Baptist minister. During the Luddite disturbances William was an apprentice in Nottingham. In his late twenties he (like Henson) transferred to the lace trade, eventually becoming a man of some influence in Nottingham affairs; but he was an intellectual rather than a politician. His book, which is better planned than Henson's, begins with 20 pages on the history of hand knitting, highly speculative and much informed by his nonconformist faith. He draws on Beckmann and Henson for details, and perpetuates Henson's legends without adding anything new.

The next contribution was by Sophia Frances Anne Caulfeild and Blanche C. Saward. The brief historical introduction to the section on knitting in *The Dictionary of Needlework*, which they published in 1882, introduces the Spanish Armada into the history of British knitting; gives a romantic account of the women knitting round the guillotine during the French Revolution; and mentions some details about Shetland knitting.

Little more was published about the history of knitting for another 50 years. Then Mary Thomas, a leading fashion journalist, published *Mary Thomas's Knitting Book* (1938) and *Mary Thomas's Book of Knitting Patterns* (1943). The historical matter in them has been influential. Some of it is misleading and some wrong, but the illustrations from items in continental museums, the first publication in England of the Buxtehude Madonna, and the first account of Aran jerseys are only a few of the features of these books that have deeply influenced subsequent approaches to knitting history.

James Norbury (1904-72) was a friend of Mary Thomas and chief designer for the spinning firm Patons and Baldwins, a television lecturer and pioneer in travelling to discover local knitting traditions. From about 1951 till he retired in 1967, he frequently lectured and published on historical questions, contributing the article on knitting in *A History of Science and Technology* for Oxford University Press in 1957. He too was untrained as a historian and drew broad conclusions from slender evidence. Yet he was in his lifetime second only to Mary Thomas in the influence he exercised on thought about knitting history.

More serious work was done by Marie Hartley and Joan Ingilby of Askrigg. They have written only one book on knitting, but its influence has been great and good: *The Old Hand-Knitters of the Dales* (1951). It is a specialist study of a local industry, with an introductory section on general knitting history.

The next historian of knitting was the American Milton Grass, whose *History of Hosiery* appeared in America in 1955. Milton Grass was an executive in the textile industry, writing out of curiosity and interest in the history of his industry. Much of his work is unreliable, though it has useful pictures of artefacts in American museums. In 1966 Mr Grass collaborated with his wife Anna in writing *Stockings for a Queen*, a life of William Lee, inventor of the knitting frame. This is a better book. It contains some general history of knitting, but often reaches wrong conclusions because the sources have not been completely examined. The Grasses, like so many writers on knitting, have a distinct bias towards the romantic.

The most romantic writer of all in the mid-twentieth century was Heinz Edgar Kiewe. I have written more about him in my chapter on Aran knitting. He described himself as a textile journalist, and it was in that role that he wrote his rhapsodic *The Sacred History of Knitting* – a book which has not won the approval of scholars.

The next essay on knitting history – and the best so far – was the first chapter of *Patons Book of Knitting and Crochet* by Patience Horne and Stephen Bowden (1973) who worked for Patons and Baldwins. Their essay, though unpretentious, draws on a wide range of books and was the first to call attention to the importance of Daniel Defoe in the chronicles of the knitting trade; the backbone of their material, however, is still Beckmann's account of 1800.

The same firm published the next account of knitting history: Michael Harvey *Patons: a Story of Handknitting* (1985), celebrating the firm's bi-centenary. Professor Harvey was commissioned to write a history of the company. He interlaced it with a general history of knitting, notably critical about legends and romances, but nevertheless lively and stimulating.

Academic historians have been discouraged from writing about hand knitting for several reasons. Hand knitting has relatively little to show in museum collections; books about it are in the main either journalistic or amateur; the domesticity of the craft has reduced its attractive-ness to historians; and there is no outline of the subject to which monograph studies can be related. Other textile and costume studies have wider support from industry. Machine knitting attracts local interest and loyalty, especially in the East Midlands; hand knitting has not yet received the attention it deserves from professional historians.

Irena Turnau *Historia Dziewiarstwa Europejskiego do Poczatku XIX Wieku* ('*The History of Knitting in Europe till the Beginning of the Nineteenth Century*') Warsaw (1979), has not been translated into English, save for the first chapter. It is to date the only work that covers the history of knitting throughout Europe, and it concentrates on the industrial aspect of the subject. A rich mine of references to works in European languages, it gives no attention to literary references, depending largely on academic writers and museum collections. I find some of Dr Turnau's conclusions rather bolder than the evidence would allow me to be, but anyone with an opportunity to ferret out all her references could greatly improve on parts of what I have written about knitting in continental Europe.

Words for 'knitting'

Just as there is no ancient Greek word for knitting, so there never has been an accurate Latin word for it, not even in mediaeval and Renaissance times. Even in the sixteenth century, when knitting was widespread in western Europe, the saintly cardinal-archbishop of Milan, Carlo Borromeo (1538-84), in his Latin regulations on ecclesiastical dress used *contextus*, 'interwoven', to describe the fabric of bishops' gloves. He had no accurate Latin word for 'knitted', so he was driven to use a slightly unusual word meaning 'woven'.

An eighteenth-century French scholar, Louis Poinsinet de Sivry, thought he had discovered a Latin word for 'knitting'. In 1771–82 he published a three-volume edition of Pliny the Elder's *Natural History*, which was completed shortly before Pliny died in AD 79. Chapter 73 of the eighth book of the *Natural History* deals with wool, and describes sheep whose fleece is more like hair than wool. Such sheep were found, Pliny said, in Croatia, Narbonne, Egypt and Portugal, where their fleece was used for making *scutulatum textum*. Later in the chapter he said that *polymita*, a cloth woven of many threads (probably damask) was first made in Alexandria, but cloth decorated with *scutula* was first made in Gaul. Poinsinet de Sivry, noticing that elsewhere Pliny speaks of a spider's web as *scutulatum*, quite illogically deduced that the word meant 'knitted', gave himself credit for discovering the Latin word for 'knitting' and demanded that Latin dictionaries should be revised accordingly.

The dictionaries were never revised. Poinsinet de Sivry was wrong. *Scutulum* means a little shield or plate, usually square, perhaps lozenge-shaped. A pattern of little squares or patches, or a chequered pattern, was described as *scutulatum*. Pliny used the same word to describe an ornamental pavement; other writers use it to describe the colour of certain horses, as well as of clothes. When applied to a spider's web it refers to the quadrangular spaces between the threads of the web. Pliny's reference to Gaul probably indicates a primitive Celtic check or tartan. There is no justification for Poinsinet de Sivry's guess that Pliny knew about knitting.

Not until the Renaissance do we find words that mean 'to knit'. At first they are confused. Words related to 'mesh', 'net' or 'knot' were tried. At the same time words related to the commonest knitted objects – caps and stockings – were used.

French in the early sixteenth century used *lasser*, 'lacing' and *bonneterie*, 'cap-making'. The modern French word *tricot* is not known before 1660. It is probably from the same root as the German *strikke*, from a word meaning 'rod' or 'stick'. The Italian *maglia*, 'mesh' and Spanish *punto di media* 'stocking point' are not known to be older. Scandinavian words have similar short histories. In Norway the modern word is *strikke* (as in Denmark, *sticke* in Sweden) from the German, but before the mid-nineteenth century Norwegians used *binde*, 'binding'. Russian has *vyazat'* 'to interlace' or 'to twine', and lacks a precise word: the common word in modern use comes from French: *trikotazh*. Even Arabic, in whose region the oldest pieces of knitted fabric have been found, has no true word for knitting: *hayyak* is used, but it also means weaving and plaiting. Many Arabs prefer to use the French word. China, Japan and Korea use words borrowed from weaving and netting.

The contrast with words for 'weaving' is striking. In most languages there is a precise, ancient and well developed vocabulary for weaving. Weaving is older than history. The apparently simple process of knitting turns out to be much less ancient.

The English word 'to knit'

In modern English the verb 'to knit' still has several meanings. Besides meaning 'to make a fabric with knitting needles or knitting machine', it means 'to fuse' (as when a broken bone knits), or 'to draw together' (as in knitting the brows). We can push the history of the word itself back to Old English (formerly called Anglo-Saxon), in which *cnyttan* means 'to tie in or with a knot', and is closely related to *cnotta*, 'a knot'; but in Old English there is no known case of the word being used to mean what we now mean by knitting. The Anglo-Saxons did not knit. They used the word for 'fasten' or 'attach' (as in a famous leechdom book that tells how to 'knit' coriander seeds to a linen cloth used in assuring easy childbirth) or for 'marry'. Attempts to go further back and connect the Sanskrit *nahyat* (to tie) with knitting are unreasonable.

In Middle English the word, often spelt *knytt*, had broadened its meaning. It still meant 'to tie in or with a knot', as when William Langland in the prologue to *The Vision of Piers Plowman* told the fable of rats belling a cat by taking a bell to 'knytt upon his colere'. An extension of the meaning came in the more general sense of 'drawing close together', which is found in the fourteenth century; but not until the end of the fifteenth century do we find it used to mean making a fabric. Then it occurs first in relation to cap-making.

The older meanings survived, and many new ones developed by the Tudor period. A mid-fifteenth-century proverb, *Know well or thou knyt to fast, for ofte rathe rewythe at last*, shows 'knit' meaning 'marry'. It is an early version of *'Marry in haste, repent at leisure'*. Further meanings include: to twine, weave, or plait; to clench (of the fist); to pack hard or solidify; to set fruit (or blossom); to swarm (of bees); to join by a pact; to cement or join together; to congeal. By the eighteenth century two further meanings at least can be found: to conceive offspring (of a female animal); and to ferment. It is only from the late sixteenth century onwards that the word is frequently used to mean the textile craft we now call knitting. More than one writer has been misled into thinking that 'to knit' always meant what we mean by it today, and therefore to claim that knitting was known in England during the fourteenth century or earlier.

Shakespeare

Nothing shows more clearly how wary the reader must be of the meaning of the word 'knit' than study of the way Shakespeare used it between about 1590 and 1610. The word occurs in his plays 38 times. In 18 places it means simply 'join' and is used of broken bones, of hands, hearts, souls, persons and scattered ships after a naval battle. Four times it refers to knitted brows. In *Romeo and Juliet* it means wedding, as it does once in *A Midsummer Night's Dream*. In *Timon of Athens* it means gathering corn into a sheaf; and in the workmen's play in the *Dream* Thisbe speaks to the wall of its 'stones with lime and hair knit up'. The same meaning is found in *Othello*. In five cases 'knit' means 'tie' or 'knot', as when in *King John* Hubert knits a handkerchief on Arthur's brow because Arthur has a headache. In *Timon of Athens* a man making a noose is said to 'knit' a cord to hang himself.

In *The Taming of the Shrew* the servants wear 'garters of an indifferent knit', which, although some scholars assume this means the garters were of knitted fabric, more likely means tied in simple (not ornamental) knots; Macbeth speaks of 'sleep, that knits up the ravelled sleeve of care', where 'knit' clearly means repair, and would as easily refer to netting as to knitting. Then in *Twelfth Night* Orsino speaks of the 'spinsters and the knitters in the sun' and 'the free maids that weave their thread with bones', which many commentators understand as a reference to lacemaking, though it may refer to knitting.

In only one place (where the word occurs twice) does Shakespeare unequivocally use 'knit' to mean knitting as we now understand it. At the beginning of *Two Gentlemen of Verona* the comic servants Launce and Speed have a punning conversation about the girl Launce loves, and he says that she can knit him a stock (that is a stocking).

The 'knitting cup'

An inappropriate drawing in *Mary Thomas's Knitting Book* has led to a mistaken idea that there was a knitting cup at mediaeval marriage feasts. The phrase 'knitting cup' is not mediaeval. It occurs in Ben Jonson's play *The Magnetic Lady* (IV. i or ii), which was written in 1632, the last but one of his plays, during the reign of Charles I. A scholar and a lawyer are planning a wedding. The scholar says: '. . . mind the parson's pint, to engage him in the business: a knitting cup there must be.' The parson's pint and the knitting cup are the same thing: the lawyer means there must be drink for the wedding guests. There is no evidence of ceremoniousness, such as attends the 'loving cup'. Here 'knitting' simply means marriage and has no reference to hand knitting.

1 Definitions and techniques

The definition of knitting

It is surprisingly difficult to say what knitting is. The International Standards Organization has defined many knitting terms, but not knitting itself. The difficulty springs partly from the necessity to define the structure of knitted fabric rather than the techniques of making it. Simply to determine the scope of this book, it is necessary to attempt a temporary definition.

Knitted fabric is a fabric consisting solely of parallel courses of yarn, each course meshed into the fabric by being looped into bights of a course above. Only in the last course are the loops locked by being laterally looped into the same course.

This definition allows for a great variety of fabric structures and methods of working. It is based upon the definition given by Irene Emery in *The Primary Structures of Fabrics* (1966).

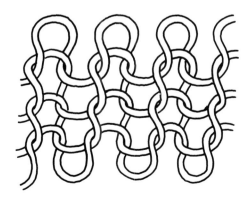

1 A non-knitted mesh, with parallel courses twisted, not looped. After Max Schmidt 'Die Paressi-Kabisi' *Baessler Archiv* 4.1 (1914). From Matto Grosso, Brazil.

Knitting differs from weaving in that all the courses (usually called rows or rounds) of knitting lie parallel, in one plane. In weaving there are at least two sets of yarn, normally at right angles to each other. The courses of knitting are secured to one another by the bights of the yarn, not by weaving the whole length of the yarn as in basketry, woven textiles, and certain rare primitive fabrics that bear a superficial resemblance to knitting, but in which the whole length of the yarn passes through the loops. (See figs 1 and 3b, the latter for the same principle in some forms of nalbinding.)

The yarn of a knitted fabric is not necessarily continuous throughout the piece. Since the yarn can be carried from one course to another, a piece of knitted fabric can be made of a single continuous piece of yarn; but each course may consist of separate pieces of yarn, especially in coloured work or in fancy work employing different qualities of yarn.

A course may also consist of two or more yarns, either to produce a denser fabric or to produce coloured patterns. These yarns may or may not be meshed into the next course by a similar pattern of loops: thus stranded-colour knitting and slip-stitch effects can be obtained. The yarn can also be changed in the midst of a course, and either spliced or otherwise secured (as in intarsia knitting).

The number of stitches in a course can be increased or decreased by the method of looping the bights of the previous course. In any case every loop will finally be meshed by one or more loops in a course above; equally, a loop may mesh one or more loops from the course below. Loops may be slipped or twisted before being meshed by a loop in a succeeding course. The meshing may be affected by a loop in a course two or more above the course of the loop that is meshed. This is the principle of the slipped stitch, of 'mosaic' knitting and certain fancy lace stitches. Loops may be open (as in plain knitting) or twisted (as in 'crossed knitting' or 'knitting through the backs of the loops'). Twisted stitches are often described as 'closed'. They are typical of hand knitting and cannot be made by machine.

The courses in a flat piece of fabric are usually called 'rows' by hand knitters. In tubular fabric the courses become a spiral and are known to hand knitters as rounds. The vertical columns of loops are known to machine-knitters as 'wales' – a term that could be used with advantage by hand-knitters. In tubular knitting the wale of the first stitch made can be identified throughout the work and its position enables the knitter to divide the spiral accurately into courses. In stranded-colour knitting and some plain-and-purl fabrics this wale is easily seen, but in stockinet it can be detected only at the beginning and end of the fabric.

There has been almost no scientific study of hand knitting. Mrs Thuc-Nghi Arnold-Baker wrote a thesis on shrinkage for Leeds University in 1979: 'The dimensional characteristics of fabrics knitted from wool hand knitting yarns'. Her work is based on Professor Dennis Munden's studies of fabric geometry in machine knitting, published in *The Journal of the Textile Institute* (1959, 1960 and 1962), in which he established that the dimensions of knitted fabrics in relaxed states are determined solely by their stitch lengths. (See below p. 15.)

Structures readily confused with knitting

The study of historical specimens has been so restricted that other fabric structures have been mistaken for knitting even by careful students. Many a textile keeper in a museum willingly admits to ignorance of knitting and to doubt about whether some specimens are knitted or not. It is helpful to know what the fabrics are which sometimes have a superficial resemblance to knitting.

(1) Netting

Netting includes a variety of fabric structures. Although the yarn of netting is worked in parallel courses, it differs from knitting in that the end of the yarn is drawn through the loops and locked in a knot for each unit or 'mesh' of the net. Unlike knitting, netting will not unravel. Netting is of such high and universal antiquity that its origins cannot be guessed.

(2) Nalbinding

In Africa, Scandinavia and other places there is an ancient method of producing a looped fabric using an eyed needle loaded with a relatively short length of yarn. The result may be knitted fabric, usually,

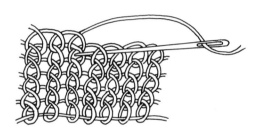

2 Nalbinding: method of work.

though not necessarily, composed of cross-knit stitches (the effect achieved in hand knitting by 'knitting into the backs of the loops', but often twisting the loop in the opposite direction). In the making, however, the 'knitted' stitch appears with the loop at the bottom. In knitting the loop is formed at the top. Detecting whether a piece of fabric has been made this way can be difficult. The spliced joins between each two needlefuls of yarn are useful indications. Increases and decreases help to identify nalbinding (see p. 29) and definitively distinguish it from knitting.

Some writers prefer to call this kind of fabric by such names as looping, needle-knitting, eyed-needle knitting, knotless netting, vantsom or other Scandinavian terms. I follow Dr Helen Bennett, our most distinguished professional historian of knitting, in using the Norwegian term.

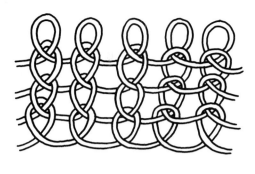

a

b

3 Simple nalbinding structures that resemble knitting: (*a*) a structure identical with knitted fabric; (*b*) a non-knitted nalbinding fabric.

Useful descriptions of nalbinding can be found in O. Nordland *Primitive Scandinavian Textiles in Knotless Netting* (Oslo 1961) and D.K. Burnham 'Coptic knitting; an ancient technique' *Textile History* III (1972, 116-24). African techniques are described in E.W. Dendel *African Fabric Crafts* (1974).

This technique has been used for footwear (in the Middle East and Europe), gloves (throughout Europe), bags and carriers (Africa) and even whole-body cat-suits for young male dancers (West Africa). Because the fabric produced is sometimes a true knitted fabric, I have given it some attention in this book, but I have not dealt with nalbinding fabrics that are not structurally knitted fabrics, nor with nalbinding after the invention of knitting on rods.

(3) Sprang

Sprang is, strictly, a method of creating fabric rather than a fabric structure. The classic description is Peter Collingwood *The Techniques of Sprang* (1974). He defines sprang as 'a method of making fabric by manipulating the parallel threads of a warp that is fixed at both ends'. The fabric is formed at both ends of the warp simultaneously with corresponding but contrary plaited structures, growing towards the centre, which must always be locked by a central linking line.

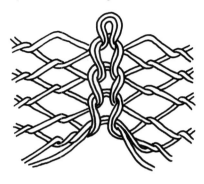

4 The 'casting off' or locking of a piece of sprang.

Following Irene Emery *The Primary Structure of Fabrics* (1968), Collingwood describes the three fundamental structures produced by sprang as interlinking, interlacing and intertwining. None of these three has the same structure as knitting. When a sprang fabric is closely made it may bear a superficial resemblance to knitting, especially in vertical rib fabric of 'over three, under three, interlaced' sprang, which has a herringbone effect somewhat similar to stockinet. Close examination shows that the courses of yarn run vertically up the wales, not horizontally across them. Loops that are truly of the same structure as knitting are used for the essential central finishing line or cast off edge of a piece of sprang (fig. 4); and some openwork sprang can look like knitting from a distance. Tubular sprang fabrics may at first sight appear to be knitting done in the round.

Sprang fabrics are much older than knitting. The oldest known example is from the Danish Bronze Age circa 1400 BC. Sprang is also known from pre-ceramic Peru circa 1100 BC, and has been done in practically every part of the world. It was a precursor of knitting as a stretch fabric, but because it was always made on a frame and produced such very different structures from knitting, it is unlikely that sprang and knitting have any historical or prehistorical connection.

(4) Crochet

Crochet fabric resembles knitting in that it is usually made with a single thread running in horizontal courses, but differs in that the loops are locked laterally as well as vertically. The structure of crochet is usually readily identifiable, but there is a form of simple crochet fabric made in the round which looks disconcertingly like stockinet. It is not hard to distinguish with care. This crochet fabric is always worked in the round, and what look like stockinet wales on the smooth side run at right angles to the apparent 'reverse stockinet' side of the fabric. If the fabric is worked in two colours, it is even easier to distinguish from knitting.

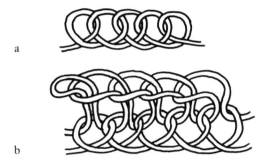

a

b

5 (*a*) The fundamental structure of crochet, with lateral interlocking of the loops. (*b*) A second row of chain worked in the opposite direction.

The history of crochet has not been much studied. The fundamental technique was known by the end of the eighteenth century in Britain, where it was known as 'shepherd's crook knitting' and used for shawls and comforters. The word 'crochet' is French for 'a small hook', and is not known to have been used as a name for this craft before 1840 in either Britain or France. The great variety of modern crochet stitches seems to have been created in Victorian England.

So-called Tunisian crochet, which can produce a very bulky fabric looking like stockinet on one side, is worked with a long hooked needle. Whole rows of loops are alternately kept on the needle and worked off on the next row. The resulting fabric retains the essential crochet structure, with lateral locking of alternate rows of yarn. Whether it came from north Africa or not is unknown. It appeared in England about 1860 and was then claimed as a new

6 Tunisian crochet: alternate rows of knitting and crochet.

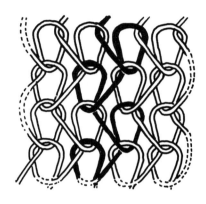

7 The structure of warp knitting, a machine technique.

invention, *crochet à tricoter*, by Mee and Austin in an advertisement in *The Knitter's Companion* (1861).

There is no reason to believe that crochet preceded knitting or that knitting developed from crochet. The superficial resemblance of one form of Tunisian crochet to stockinet is deceptive: the fabrics are of fundamentally different structure.

(5) Warp knitting

My definition of knitting applies only to what are known in industry as 'weft-knitted fabrics'. Industry also produces looped fabrics called 'warp-knitted fabrics', made by a machine carrying a separate thread for each wale of the fabric. Warp knitting resembles crochet in that each loop is meshed laterally (by the stitch in the next wale) as well as vertically (by a stitch in a course above), but the resulting structure differs from both knitting and crochet because the yarns run vertically up the fabric, not horizontally across.

(6) Tablet weaving

Tablet weaving is a method of weaving bands of cloth in which the warp threads run lengthwise from end to end of the band and the weft runs across the band. The warp threads are passed through holes in one or more perforated tablets or cards, which are twisted to produce the shed, or space between the warp threads for the shuttle to go through.

8 Tablet weaving. Detail of the belt section of the Halberstadt girdle. Warp of green silk and weft of green linen, with gold brocading. 1.7 cm (²⁄₃ in.) wide. See also figs 52 and 53.

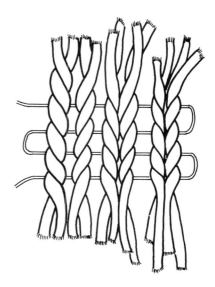

9 The structure of a tablet-woven fabric that superficially resembles stockinet.

This technique was known in Spain early in the fourth century BC and is probably even older. It is well attested in western Europe during the Iron Age and the Anglo-Saxon period. During the mediæval period it was much used for priests' girdles and stoles. Some of the patterns produced look deceptively like knitted stockinet, and it may be necessary to use a magnifying lens to ascertain that the fabric is actually woven and not knitted. There is also no purl effect on the reverse of the fabric. The central section of the fourteenth-century Halberstadt girdle is tablet woven in a manner that produces a knitted effect (see fig. 8).

Tablet weaving has been done in nearly all the civilized world, and discoveries of ancient fabric thought to be knitting can turn out to be tablet weaving. The subject is exhaustively treated in Peter Collingwood's *The Techniques of Tablet Weaving* (1982).

(7) Other techniques

A number of other techniques, less common than those listed above, have a superficial resemblance to knitting. Although Peter Collingwood does not make this point, he illustrates several such fabrics in *Textile and Weaving Structures* (1987).

Plain and Purl

The interlooping of the courses has two aspects: the side where the bight of the loops stands, called 'purl'; and the other side, called 'plain'. Strictly speaking, these are not different stitches, but obverse and reverse of the fundamental interlooping or 'stitch'. Which side is the obverse or 'right side' is an arbitrary decision by the knitter or the user. Because the 'plain' side is smooth, showing the wales as close herringbones (or columns of Vs with the points open) it has come to be regarded as the right side, and is most frequently used in this way.

The simplest method of knitting produces the plain side towards the knitter as he works. When knitted in the round, as in stocking making, the same face of the fabric is towards the knitter throughout the working. If the same fabric is to be obtained in working a flat piece, it must have alternate rows, when the reverse of the fabric is towards the knitter, purled. Because of the tension of the bights on the purl side, the resulting flat fabric will not lie flat, but will curl concavely, laterally (at the sides) on the purl face and meridionally (at the top and bottom) on the plain face. Tubular knitting will curl at the cast-on and cast-off edges, concavely on the plain side only, because it has no sides or selvedges.

This fabric is known in the British Isles as 'stocking stitch', a clumsy name including the imprecise word 'stitch'. It was formerly known as 'stockinet', which was probably derived from 'stocking-net'. In America it is called 'stockinette', with a fancy Frenchification of the spelling which is curiously at odds with the rationalism of received American spelling. The older English word has much to recommend it, and I have used it freely in this book.

Plain and purl aspects of the knitted stitch can be mixed to good effect. Alternate courses of plain and purl produce a fabric that does not curl. The tension of the bights causes the purled faces to stand proud as horizontal ridges across the fabric; the fabric is meridionally more elastic than stockinet; and is fully reversible. This is 'garter-stitch', so called probably because a few rows of it

were used at the tops of stockings to prevent the curling already described. It was also the simple stitch used for making knitted garters.

Instead of alternate plain and purl courses, alternate plain and purl wales can be made. This produces a fabric called ribbing, that is laterally more elastic than stockinet or garter-stitch. Like garter-stitch it is fully reversible and does not curl, but whereas in garter-stitch the purl faces stand proud, in ribbing it is the plain faces that stand proud.

A third basic mixture of plain and purl is that in which the alternation of plain and purl occurs both in the course and in the wale: what in the British Isles is called 'moss stitch'. As with garter-stitch and ribbing, the equalizing of the plain and purl faces on each side of the fabric creates a fabric that does not curl; but it has no pronounced elasticity and neither aspect of the stitches is predominant, because the plain faces stand proud horizontally and the purl faces stand proud meridionally.

The decorative possibilities of mixed plain and purl faces were realized very early. The third-century Dura-Europos fragments exploit the qualities of ribbing and the closely allied cabling. By the middle of the sixteenth century European knitters were using mixed plain and purl in stockings, and beginning to develop geometric and floral designs in which plain and purl faces were used to imitate the effects of woven damask. The basic principle of these designs was that the purled areas should stand proud of the plain ground; but this was no more than half true. A square in purl on a plain ground will stand proud of the ground at the top and bottom of the square but sink below it at the side. In elaborate floral designs this fact can lead to muddled effects, such as can be seen in some white cotton knitting. The solution to that problem was found in composing the design with moss-stitch motifs on a plain ground. The separated purls each stand proud and give a distinctive surface to the moss-stitch areas. King Charles I's shirt in the Museum of London is a good example of this technique. (See fig. 7.)

Casting on and binding off

The creation of the first course of loops, the foundation of a piece of knitted fabric, is the initial problem in knitting. In theory, the first course can be a simple piece of thread, with no twists in it, and in practice this method is sometimes used, especially if work is subsequently to be done from the same course in the opposite direction. More often, however, the first course is given extra stability and firmness by the twisting or crossing of the loops.

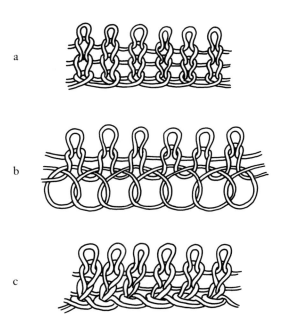

10 Three ways of casting on: (*a*) the commonest European method before the nineteenth century – often called the 'thumb method' in Britain; (*b*) the crochet chain in its simplest form, often inaccurately called 'knitting on'; (*c*) the 'cable cast on' or 'knitting between the loops'.

The simplest way of doing this is by using the left thumb to twist the yarn in loops on to a needle held in the right hand. When the required number of loops has been put on the needle, the needle is transferred to the left hand and the knitting begins in the normal way. According to James Norbury in C. Singer *A History of Technology* (1958) (III 183-4)

this was the method used by knitters in rural districts throughout Europe until the beginning of the twentieth century. In England it is now called the 'thumb method'. It is performed in many ways, usually combining the first row of knitting with the creation of the initial loops, in what is also called a 'two-strand cast-on', or 'double-ended cast-on'. In this method, work begins at a point well along the yarn, and the initial crossed loops are made in the section towards the beginning of the yarn, which is passed round the left thumb and at the same time knitted off with the yarn from the continuing supply (or ball). There are many methods for handling the yarn, of which the Scandinavian or 'continental' is most efficient.

Norbury did not justify his statement that this was the older and universal method of casting on. There are several reasons for thinking he was right. First, there is the evidence of pieces of Tudor knitting that have been examined from this point of view; then there is the evidence of various writers who have examined the knitting of rural communities with a knitting tradition; lastly, there is the evidence of nineteenth-century writers on knitting.

Victorian knitting books rarely include descriptions of casting-on technique. When they do, the early books usually give a method for the construction I have described, using one needle. Examples can be found in *The Workwoman's Guide* (1840), Miss Watts (1845), Mlle Riego (1848), Bohn's *Ladies' Worktable Book* (1852).

Other methods, using two needles and sometimes described as 'knitting on', are described by *The Workwoman's Guide*, Miss Watts and Mrs Mee in her *Companion* (1844). Two-needle methods are, however, sometimes given exotic names. Miss Watts calls them 'German', Mlle Riego, 'Spanish'.

Casting on with two needles gained in popularity in Britain from Victorian times. It tends to produce a lax edge, even a looped edge. As a cast-on for ribbing, it produces an edge that lies awkwardly. Its popularity in England must depend solely on its simplicity of execution, which led to its being taught in schools. In structure it is a crochet chain.

A better way of casting on with two needles is to draw each new loop not from within the previous loop, but from beween the two previous loops. I

a

b

11 Casting off: (*a*) as it appears in the making; (*b*) when stretched to show its structure as a crochet chain.

have not found this method described in print before *Myra's Knitting Lessons* (circa 1889), and it does not seem to have become popular until well into the twentieth century. It gives a good tension, but a bulky edge.

The expression 'cast on' is not recorded before 1838, when *The Ladies' Knitting and Netting Book* used it interchangeably with 'put on'. 'Cast' must have been used in the sense of 'make a knot', recorded from the sixteenth century (see OED 'cast' XII.58), though it does not occur in the earliest extant knitting pattern, printed in 1655.

Nor does 'cast off', for which the 1655 pattern uses 'bind' – a word that survives as standard American usage. *The Workwoman's Guide* (1840) speaks of 'finishing off' or 'fastening off', and uses 'bind' for casting off two pieces of fabric together as in the then common method of making a stocking heel. *The Ladies' Knitting and Netting Book* uses 'cast off'.

Binding or casting off means locking a wale so that it will not unravel, and is achieved by passing a

loop over its neighbour. When this is done over a number of loops or along a whole course, the resulting structure is a crochet chain.

Increasing and Decreasing

Increasing

Whatever technique is used for increasing the number of loops in a course, there are only two structural possibilities, both of which employ two techniques.

The first is to knit more than once into one loop. This is commonly done in one of two ways: by knitting and purling into a loop, or by working into the front and back of a loop. Both methods disturb the surface of the plain side of stockinet; the first by producing a purl, the second by twisting the loop. Both methods also tend to strain the loop which is worked into twice, and produce a small hole.

Another method of working twice into a loop is to knit again into a loop that has once been knitted into an earlier (usually the immediately preceding) course. This method causes less superficial interruption to the surface of stockinet, though it strains the loop twice worked and elongates it. There is usually no hole created. Early knitters, working in tubular stockinet naturally adopted this way of increasing, which is similar to a method used in nalbinding. (See below page 29.)

The second structural possibility is to create extra stitches by taking up new loops between those already worked. Again there are two techniques. The simplest is to cast the yarn over the right-hand needle between two knitted loops. This 'over' becomes a loop for knitting in the next course. A hole or eyelet is created, which can be used to produce lace patterns or decorative eyelets.

The other way is simply to knit under the yarn between two loops. This is often called 'raised increase' or 'bar increase', because it lifts the running thread or 'bar' between two wales. Like the 'over', it tends to make a hole, though a smaller one. The hole is reduced by working the lifted loop through the back. This method has been used for gussets and gores, and is part of the traditional technique of British glove-knitting.

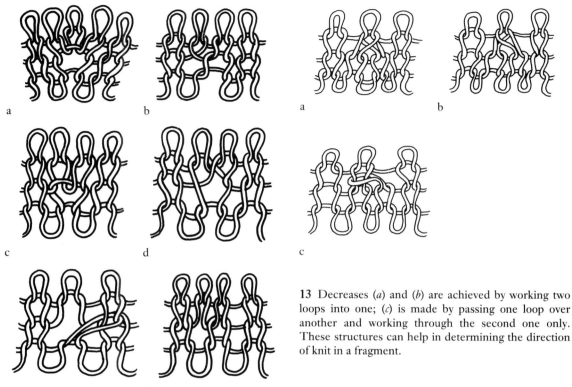

a b

c d

e f

a b

c

13 Decreases (*a*) and (*b*) are achieved by working two loops into one; (*c*) is made by passing one loop over another and working through the second one only. These structures can help in determining the direction of knit in a fragment.

12 Increases:
(*a*) three stitches worked in one loop;
(*b*) a stitch worked in the bar between two stitches of the previous row;
(*c*) two stitches worked in one loop;
(*d*) a stitch worked in a loop from the course below the course being worked (a method found in sixteenth-century work);
(*e*) two stitches worked together and accompanied by an over, producing an eyelet but no increase;
(*f*) an over producing an eyelet and an increase. These structures help in determining the direction of knit.

Decreasing

Decreasing is simpler. All decreases are made by knitting once only through two or more loops. The techniques for this are various, but the principle is always the same.

All these methods were in use by the beginning of the sixteenth century.

Tension and gauge

'Tension' is the word commonly used by British knitters to mean the size of the loops, measured by number of loops to the linear unit laterally and number of courses to the linear unit vertically. (Today the usual linear unit is the decimetre.) Americans use 'gauge' for this sense. The American word is preferable, for tension is more correctly used to denote the stress which the fabric structure puts on the yarn. Tension is controlled by several factors: the calibre of the needles and of the yarn; the elasticity of the yarn, including the effects of the spinning and plying; the tension put on the yarn by the knitter while working, whether by 'knitting tightly' with the fingers, or by creating tension through the way in which the yarn is fed to the working finger. Gauge is determined by tension, fabric structure ('geometry') and the degree of relaxation in the yarn after the work leaves the needles.

The shape of the stitch, by whatever method it is

created, will always be the same. Given lack of obstructive friction on the surface of the yarn, equilibrium of forces will eventually relax a course of knitting to a state of even tension. This is why old pieces of knitting normally look so regular. Knitters of the past get praised for even working, but hand knitters know that any piece of knitting will improve with time, and only wildly irregular stitches will fail to fall into evenness. Lubrication of the yarn by wetting the fabric hastens the process. As Elizabeth Zimmerman puts it, 'Time is a great leveller'. At this stage, gauge is determined solely by the length of yarn used in each stitch.

Tension is the only crucial manual skill in hand knitting. Once the method of creating the fabric has been mastered, the acquisition of new stitch patterns is not difficult. Design of fabric and garment calls for knowledge of simple arithmetic and geometry, and an inkling of topology. No further mathematics are required. Tension is theoretically measurable, but the hand knitter's knowledge of it must be intuitive and expressed chiefly through his fingers. This is the point of technique at which experience counts.

Surprisingly, writers of knitting recipes rarely mentioned gauge before the 1920s. Miss H.P. Ryder in *Cycling and Shooting Knickerbocker Stockings* (1896) was among the first to write carefully. She prescribed garter stitch of 8 stitches and 8 rows to the inch with Alloa yarn on size 12 (2¾ mm) needles, and noted that for associated Fair Isle work 3 ply fingering should be used on size 10 (3¼ mm) needles.

Knitting needles

The majority of knitting needles have been made of metal: steel for Europe, brass for north Africa and some countries of the Levant. Alfred Bel and Prosper Ricard, in their article on Algerian knitting in 1913, mentioned hooked brass needles as the normal knitting tool of the Tlemcen district.

Spaniards believe that Toledo steel was the material of early Spanish needles. There is no doubt that British needles were normally of steel until the end of the eighteenth century. By 1842,

however, Miss Lambert was noting that knitting needles were obtainable in boxwood, ivory and whalebone.

In the twentieth century various plastics, especially casein, were used. Mary Thomas in 1938 mentioned briar, bone, steel, erinoid, galalith, vulcanite and tortoiseshell. With such materials the colour of the needle could be chosen to contrast aptly with the colour of the yarn. The only colour choice in steel needles was the 'blueing' sometimes used for lace needles, occasionally with gilding of the tips. Nickel plating was applied to needles to prevent rusting. Steel needles are heavy. Aluminium has now generally replaced it, but many Shetlanders still work with heavy steel 'wires'. Very large sizes were made of wood until it became possible to make them of plastic. Today needles of 5 mm and above are made of plastic. Smaller sizes are also made in plastic for use by arthritic knitters. Since 1983 bamboo needles have been imported from Japan.

Early needles often had blunt ends. It is said that in many villages the blacksmith would cut lengths of steel wire, temper them and smooth the ends. Some museums, such as Hawes, have specimens of these blunt-ended needles. Drawing room knitters of the mid-nineteenth century preferred points to their needles, because the new method of inserting the needle through the loop instead of putting the loop over the needle, and the practice of 'holding the needle like a pen' concentrated attention on the point of the needle. Two shapes of point were evolved: the 'roach-back' with a convex contour, introduced by Milwards in the 1960s, and the straight tapered point. Within five years Milwards had to lengthen the roach-back point, and in the early 1980s customer reaction was such that the roach-back point was abandoned. Today all British knitting needles have straight tapering.

Miss Lambert in 1842 also noted that a knob was sometimes put on one end of a knitting needle to prevent the work being pushed off. The idea was clearly still new at that date. Caulfeild and Saward's *Dictionary of Needlework* (1882) calls the knobbed needle as a 'pin'; but this distinction, though it has appealed to others, is indefensible. Mrs Gaugain tended to reserve 'pins' for sets of two needles not made of steel, but she was not consistent. Historically the words 'knitting needle' and 'knitting pin' have been interchangeable.

Needles were always made straight. Using them with the knitting sheath often bent them into an arc, which is why old knitting needles in museums appear to be bent or curved. The twentieth century has seen the introduction of the 'circular knitting needle', a double-ended needle with the central section made of flexible material. The needle is not strictly circular: it is straight, but can be bent into a circle. Since the 1970s it has been called a 'twin pin'. Many knitters, especially in Germany, use the twin-pin for flat knitting as well as for round knitting, because it has the advantage of keeping the weight of the knitted fabric towards the knitter's own centre of gravity.

The circular needle was probably developed in Norway. It was advertised as 'Flexiknit, patent applied for', in *'Ladies' Field' Jumpers* (Book 1) in 1924. The flexible part was then made of steel wire cable, and the rigid ends were crimped on. The join would, with use and wear, tend to snag the knitted yarn, and this feature contributed to the slow success of the circular needle. Improved methods of joining the elements in plastic or aluminium needles have eliminated this problem.

The gauge or calibre of knitting needles has traditionally been different in each country, even for each manufacturer. The gauges, called *filières*, made in the nineteenth century were not all the same. Mary Thomas noted that in the 1930s American needle gauges differed according to the manufacturer. British sizes were based on the British Standard Steel Wire Gauge, but were not always strictly to the standard. When metrication came in 1975, British sizes were given the nearest approximate metric designation (not always accurate to the second decimal place) but vulgar fractions such as $3\frac{3}{4}$ mm were adopted. This oddity is partly due to the distinction between the standard scale of German sizes, which goes in half-millimetre steps, and the British scale, which keeps the quarter and three-quarter millimetre steps between 2 and 4 millimetres. Needles of $2\frac{1}{2}$ mm and $3\frac{1}{2}$ mm are not used in Britain. This tends to discourage the import of German needles. The German company, Rump (with the trade name Inox), is the world's largest producer of knitting

needles, though British production is fast catching up.

By the 1920s needle-making in Britain was centred in Redditch in Worcestershire and the nearby village of Studley in Warwickshire. Needles of all descriptions, including gramophone needles and surgical needles, as well as knitting needles were manufactured. A series of amalgamations had reduced the industry to three major concerns: William Hall, Henry Milward, and Abel Morrall. Hall and Milward amalgamated in 1930, continuing to make knitting needles under the name of Milward. In 1973 this firm was taken into the Coats Patons group, and in 1983 Abel Morrall, whose needles were sold under the Aero trademark, came into the group, now known as Needle Industries. Today 60 per cent of the knitting needles produced by the firm are exported.

Needles hooked at one end are still used in the country districts of Portugal in round knitting. Some young people in towns are preserving or reviving this kind of knitting, which also survives in Peru and some Balkan areas. The yarn is kept in tension by being passed behind the knitter's neck, or drawn through a hook pinned on the knitter's clothing.

Handling the needles

By the beginning of Queen Victoria's reign (and perhaps for a while before) English ladies, as distinct from working knitters, had abandoned the older way of holding knitting needles. Instead of holding the right-hand needle under the palm of the right hand they began to hold it like a pen, grasping the point between the thumb and index finger, and allowing the shaft to lie over the outside of the thumb joint. Before long, working class knitters, especially in southern England, began to emulate the new fashion, which is inefficient and limits the speed of knitting, but is to this day the commonest way of knitting in England.

Holding an instrument pen-wise is natural and appropriate when accurate movement of the tip of the tool is the main object. Thus it is right for delicate work with a pencil or scalpel. Drawing

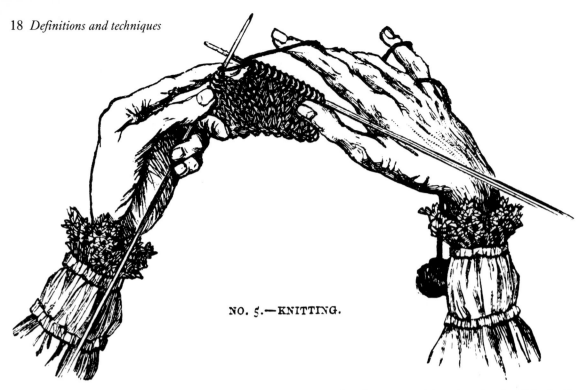

NO. 5.—KNITTING.

14 The nineteenth-century English manner of holding the needles; adopted for 'drawing room' knitting. From *The Young Ladies' Journal. Complete Guide to the Worktable* (1884). As seen by the knitter.

room knitters did not wish to emulate hard-working cottage knitters. The cottagers could 'knock off the loops' of their coarse stockings, but the ladies usually worked with silk or fine Berlin wool to produce delicate objects. They thought of their work as artistic and refined. Although the cottagers placed the loop over the tip of the right-hand needle, the ladies inserted the tip of the needle into the loop. They thought of the tip of the needle doing delicate work; and not unnaturally held it like a pen or a water-colour brush.

These same ladies were anxious to deport themselves elegantly. Cottage knitting was efficient, but it offered little opportunity for graceful or languid gestures. The shaft of the needle held in the ladies' fashion moved in an agreeably elegant manner. What was more, the little finger could be delicately crooked in the air. There is an interesting parallel in the handling of a table-knife. The socially non-acceptable way of holding a table-knife like a pencil developed in a quest for elegance and in using the tip of the knife as a food-pusher rather than the edge of the blade for cutting. The airing of the little finger occurs also in the more affected way of holding a teacup.

Annie S. Frost, an American, in the *Ladies' Guide to Needlework* (1877) was insistent that the needle should not be held under the left palm because 'no feminine employment is better calculated to display a pretty hand and graceful motions than knitting'. (75)

Nineteenth-century writers rarely commented on extravagant daintiness in knitting. The suggestion is there, however, in a note in *The Hosiery Review*, 20 June 1888, where a writer observes that knitting at concerts is 'a new freak'. He had seen a lady knitting in the Prince's Hall; 'the hands were white and covered in jewels, and I have a suspicion that the knitting was intended to display these beauties and to show a taste for the industry'. He was right: ladylike knitting was an example of Thorsten Veblen's 'conspicuous leisure', however much the protestant work ethic was advanced to

15 A card for tourists, published about 1895, showing a Welsh knitter holding the needles in the traditional British fashion, under her palms. See page 165.

ANN DAFYDD,

95 years of age.   Now living at Pandyrodyn,
Dolgelley, and has never worn glasses.

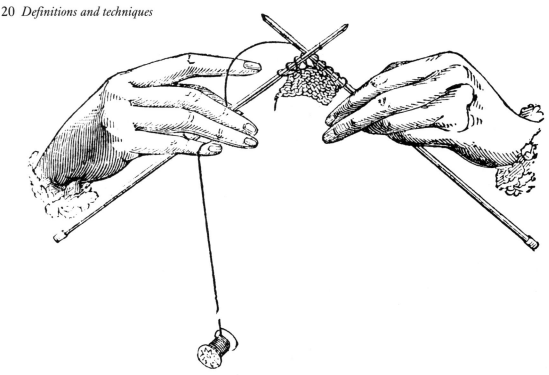

excuse it as an industrious employment of leisure.

The ladies did not suffer much from the new elegance so long as they made purses, pincushions, muffatees and other small objects. When they came to knit coats and guernseys the weight of the growing work was ill placed over the thumb. Yet generations of English women have persisted with this bad practice. Some of them achieve remarkable speed, though at great waste of energy, and never so fast as a Shetlander working in the older fashion. Books printed in the 1980s nearly all teach the bad way and knitters in films invariably knit in the inefficient way, waggling the ends of the needles at ear-level.

Ideally, only one needle should move. Tools are extensions of the hands and when two are used with maximum efficiency (such as chopsticks, knife-and-fork, hammer-and-chisel) one tool extends the hand's power to hold, the other the hand's power to move. If the right-hand needle is anchored under the arm by a sheath or a belt, the left-hand needle alone need move. The right hand holds the needle in the palm naturally and efficiently. This was the older way to knit. The oldest dated sheath (1628) is in The Newarke Houses Museum, Leicester.

16 The traditional way of holding the needles. From Mlle Riego de la Branchardiere *The Knitting Book* 3rd edition, 1848. Seen from a viewpoint facing the knitter.

Holding the yarn

Carrying the yarn on the right hand seems to be the oldest way, at least in western Europe. It can be seen in the pictures of knitting madonnas. In Britain, at least, it has remained the normal way of knitting.

Carrying the yarn over the left hand seems to have originated in Germany. An article in *Vestlandske Kunstindustrimuseum Årbok 1954-7* (Bergen 1958) states that this practice was introduced to Norway by upper-class knitters during the nineteenth century and passed to the artisan class. At the same period the Norwegian word *binde* gave way to the German *strikke* as the usual word for knitting. English books of the 1840s call carrying the yarn on the left hand 'German' or 'Dutch' – 'Dutch' perhaps meaning *deutsch*. In

17 A Greek woman knitting with yarn kept in tension through a hook attached at the neck of her clothing, throwing the yarn with her left thumb, *c.* 1983.

1854 Anne Stephens in her *Complete Guide* published in New York noted that this method was typical of Russia as well as of Germany. Since the time of Catherine the Great, German cultural influences had been strong in Russia, so perhaps the German method of hand knitting was well established in Russia by the end of the eighteenth century.

This German method requires its own way of manipulating the needles. If the right-hand needle is kept inert, as in a knitting sheath, the left hand is forced to perform two functions: moving the needle and throwing the yarn. Efficient knitters in the German fashion avoid this by holding the left-hand needle still. The effect is simply to reverse the action of the traditional English knitter. Though it is often thought that the German method is faster than the English method, this is not strictly true. Even a fast knitter in the German style rarely achieves the speed of a Shetland knitter in the older method.

Measuring the speed of knitting has not been done scientifically. Claims of knitters who achieved 300 stitches a minute (5 per second) are exaggerated. Knitting 100 stitches a minute is working faster than most eyes can follow. Sponsored-knitting organizers reckon that the average knitter working with double knitting yarn on 4 mm needles across 16 stitches will average 35-40 stitches a minute.

The reason for working fast was clear when people knitted for income. When the knitter works for pleasure, the desire to complete the work quickly has more to do with impatience. Very fast knitters tend to work in short stabs, with frequent pauses. For most knitters it is more important to knit rhythmically and with economy of effort – and therefore with pleasure – than to knit at high speed.

Since World War II the German method of holding the yarn has been adopted by some knitters in England, usually in the belief that it is quicker. In Japan since World War II it has been widely adopted, but not in China. In America, both methods are in use.

Working with the yarn in the left hand is also common in Portugal, Greece, Turkey, Bolivia and Peru, and perhaps in other countries too. In these countries the yarn is carried round the nape of the neck to ensure a working tension, and if two yarns are being used for colour-knitting, one yarn will pass behind the neck from left to right, the other from right to left. In Portugal, at least, the yarn is carried on the left thumb, not the forefinger. Hooked needles are used, held horizontally. No claim of high speed is made for this method of knitting. Indeed Peruvian men, knitting caps with geometric and animal designs, work with the floats and the purl side of the fabric towards the knitter and have to keep looking at the further side to check the progress of the pattern.

Peg frame knitting

A knitting-frame is a range of pegs on a fixed base. The pegs may be arranged in a row or a ring. The 'knitting reel' or 'knitting nancy', such as is sometimes used as a children's toy or for making tubular girdles, is a simple form of round knitting-frame. Stitches are made by treating each peg as the needle for one wale of the fabric. The loops are formed by winding the yarn round the ring twice and lifting the first course of yarn over the peg and the second course of yarn. The same process is followed with each successive course.

If the pegs are set in two parallel rows, with a slit in the base between the two rows of pegs, through which slit the fabric can drop as it grows, a double-sided flat fabric can be made. Complex knitted structures can be produced, as well as elaborate colour-patterns. Such a frame is called *dassenplank*, 'scarf-board', in Germany.

Peg frames exist in some museums but are hard, if not impossible, to date and they therefore do not fall within the scope of this book. Work done on them is hand knitting in that the peg frame is a tool, not a machine, and the peg frame probably belongs with the knitting-pin in the prehistory of machine-knitting. The only clear evidence for the early existence of the peg frame is in Gustav Schmoller *Die Strassburger Tucher- und Weberzunft* (1879), an account of textile guilds in Strasburg. He mentions evidence for the *stühl* or *gestell*, a knitting frame, in 1535 and regulations drafted in 1618 about the number of *stühl* to be allowed in a master-knitter's workshop. Thus it is at least possible that the

Silesian and Alsatian carpets of the seventeenth and eighteenth centuries (see p. 90) were made on peg frames.

The origins of knitting

Many people assume that all knitting must be derived from invention at a single time and in a single place. This assumption is unjustifiable and improbable. We cannot even accurately relate the earliest datable pieces of knitting: thirteenth-century Spanish cushions (see p. 39) and Egyptian mediaeval fragments (see p. 32).

The evidence that crochet and Tunisian crochet are more recent inventions than knitting is so strong that theories suggesting that these crafts are the origin of knitting must be discounted. They resemble knitting in that knitting has often been done with a hooked implement, and that both crafts work with the bight, not the end, of the yarn. Beyond that there is no resemblance. The structures are quite different. Similar considerations apply to suggestions that knitting was derived from sprang or netting.

Nalbinding can produce a true knitted structure, but by a different method of manufacture. We have evidence of nalbinding much older than our evidence for knitting; and we know that knitting was at an early point used to make footwear, in the cultural region where nalbinding was earlier used for the same purpose. To say that knitting developed from nalbinding, probably in Egypt, is conjectural, but reasonable. It is not reasonable to attribute knitting to the Arabs or Arabia.

In Roman Egypt socks were made in nalbinding. The work was tubular, starting from the point of the toe. The process was laborious, and involved repeated splicing of the yarn. Eventually someone may have realized that the new loops could be pulled through the earlier loops with a hooked rod. The beginning of hand knitting with hooked 'knitting needles' is thus simply, though conjecturally, reconstructed. Hooked needles are used to this day in Egyptian villages.

Eventually someone may have realized that the hooks were not necessary, and discovered that plain knitting rods were more efficient. It is equally reasonable to suppose that the plain needle was earlier.

In another part of the world knitted fabric is produced in a different way. The Fritz Iklé collection contains knitting from the Taulipang Indians of the Roraima Mountains between Venezuela, Guyana and Brazil (the setting of Conan Doyle's 'lost world'), which is made with a separate rod or skewer for each wale of the fabric. In effect this means a knitting-frame in which the needles are not anchored to a common base. Thus headbands are knitted. Knitted structures were also discovered by Walter Edmund Roth among the Warrau people of the Orinoco delta in 1916-17.

Roth describes the Warrau craft in 'An introductory study of the arts, crafts and customs of the Guiana Indians' (1924). He describes a rich repertoire of yarn crafts, defining crochet and knitting, not by the structure of the fabric, but by the nature of the tools used. Hence Warrau work done on two rods he calls 'knitting', though the fabric produced is a kind of braiding (107). He describes true crochet worked on a single hook (103), but he also defines as 'crochet' a fabric made on two hooked needles, which is in fact knitting (105-6). It was used for making belts.

Annemarie Seiler-Baldinger published a detailed compendium of previous ethnological accounts of South and Central American Indian yarn crafts in *Maschenstoffe in Süd- und Mittelamerika* (Basle 1971). She noted seven races of Indians knitting with skewers: the Arecuna, Macushi, Patamona and Taulipang making headbands; the Palikur, Uaça and Warrau making belts. All these races live in a single region covering parts of Venezuela, Guyana and Brazil. They do not make piece fabric. It may be concluded that their discovery of knitting is unconnected with the Eurasian tradition.

Purling and flat knitting

Surviving artefacts suggest that tubular stockinet was the first form of knitting and that the purl stitch was a later invention. The earliest verifiable purled stitches are on the stockings of Eleanora of Toledo, 1562 or earlier (see p. 71). There is good reason to suppose that purling had been used in turning the heels of stockings earlier than this, but no clear evidence. From the mid-sixteenth century onwards the purl was used as decorative stitch – as, indeed, its name, often spelt 'pearl', suggests.

Mediaeval and earlier knitting that survives is nearly all done in the round. A number of fragments must be regarded as doubtful, but some that are now flat can be shown to be remains of round knitting. The number of needles used is doubtful. Late mediaeval paintings of the Madonna knitting show her with work on four needles, but they are not photographs, and cannot be taken as conclusive evidence that either four or five needles were used. We know, however, that by 1655, when the pattern in *Natura Exenterata* was printed, it was normal for English stockings to be worked on four needles. By contrast Turkish and Portuguese knitters, among others, use five needles to this day.

Knitting on two needles may first have been developed for turning the heels of stockings. Some knitters in Dagestan, Turkey and other places east of Suez work a pouch heel in garter stitch, which avoids purling.

Three-dimensional shaping of round knitting was well understood by the cap-knitters of the sixteenth century, and is beautifully illustrated by the light-coloured fragment from the wreck of the *Mary Rose* in 1545 (see p. 63).

When was flat knitting on two needles first done? The answer is hard to find. Some mediaeval Egyptian knitting was flat, but in Europe flat knitting was probably influenced by framework knitting and the desire to imitate clothes tailored in cloth. The undatable 'brocade' jackets are made of flat pieces. By the nineteenth century flat knitting was commonplace.

The careful shaping of knitted pieces for tailored garments did not reach its apogee until the 1930s . Seamed garments were increasingly made as the nineteenth century passed, but the early ones were crudely shaped. Marjory Tillotson was probably the most important influence in developing skilled shapings (see p. 143). There has

been a marked return to simpler shapes in British knitting since the 1960s. The growing preference for comfort rather than style, the fashion for more casual clothing and the neglect of technical training for designers have all contributed to this development.

Knitted metal

Metal wire or strips can be bent and intertwined into a knitted structure. When fine and decorative, this is sometimes called trichinopoly work, from its resemblance to the gold and silver wirework and filigree jewellery made at Tiruchirapalli (traditionally known to the British as Trichinopoly) near Madras in South India.

The most famous piece of trichinopoly 'knitting' in Britain is the decoration on the base of the Ardagh chalice in the National Museum in Dublin. The chalice dates from the eighth century and is ornamented with strips of fine gold wire work, that superficially resemble stockinet. In fact they are more complex, each course passing through the two previous courses. Similar structures have been found in metal artefacts from many periods and places: Viking relics at Croy and Ballinaby in Scotland, the ninth-century Trewhiddle hoard in Cornwall and Irish finds at Tara and Clonmacnoise. There is also a train of evidence showing that this metal knitting, usually in the form of a hollow and flexible rope or cord, was popular in the Byzantine world and must eventually have derived from Greece in the millenium before Christ. The same work is found in Nepal, Tibet and the Yemen, and at Dura-Europos in Syria.

Braham Norwick has discussed these pieces in his articles on knitting history, but, as Helen Bennett points out, the method by which they were made is far from clear. Recognizing their knitted structure does not give them a place in the history of hand knitting, unless some direct connection can be shown between the techniques of bending metal and of manipulating yarn.

Art or craft?

The distinction between art and craft is practical rather than logical. It is useful in education and in museums, but essentially blurred. Unhappily it is coloured by intellectual snobbery, as though art were in some way intrinsically higher, greater, or better than craft.

Eric Gill (1882–1940) the sculptor and typographer, insisted that art is simply making things. Etymologically, 'art' has a Latin root, and 'craft' an Old English root. Both words mean the same thing: skill. The distinction between 'artist' and 'artisan' is modern. It was not fixed till the end of the eighteenth century, during which the idea of 'fine arts' first emerged, and the cult of 'artistic inspiration' was developed.

The modern distinction can be summarized using four contrasts. Material and technique dominate in craft, but are subservient in art. Reproduction is acceptable in craft, but not in art (except as a training exercise). Craft contributes to living, practically or ornamentally; art reflects or comments on living and may admonish. Craft may perpetuate the past objectively by reproducing what has previously existed; art can record, revive and communicate reminiscences, subjective memory and recalled emotions.

Some educationists distinguish craft as the exercise of skill, and art as the playful development of selfhood, or as creative. But the simplest crafts can be exercises in self-expression, and creative is a word of little meaning.

Creation means making what has not previously existed. Therefore, if creative means anything, it must mean 'original'. Originality is a concept that has dominated European ideas about art since the eighteenth century. Modern attitudes to community art may eventually succeed in eroding what is false in our restless quest for originality and creativity.

Knitting is best called a craft. It serves life and is relatively ephemeral. It gets worn and wears out (hence museum collections are sparse). It can be expensive, but is almost never precious. Its structure is more limiting than the structures of tapestry and embroidery. Therefore knitting is widely practised by non-professionals and tends to be a people's craft. Therein lies much of its interest and the fascination of knitting history.

Fashion and folk dress

Though fashion in dress springs from craving for display and for novelty, it is nurtured by wealth. New fashions are promoted by the rich and powerful. Early knitting was neither showy nor costly: hence knitting played no part in fashion until expensive and ostentatious silk stockings became the *dernier cri*. High fashion soon proved its innate obsession with exaggeration: young bloods of the 1580s wore the longest possible stockings with the shortest possible trunkhose – an Elizabethan male equivalent of the 1960s female mini-skirt.

The extreme fashion simmered down, as it always does, and was moderated into standard fashion. Silk stockings remained standard menswear until trousers gained ground after the French Revolution. Thereafter, wealth found a new interest in fashion: money could now be made by encouraging and selling fashionable clothes; but until the First World War no one thought of exploiting knitwear. The fashionable silhouette, though it changed, remained crisp and clear. Knitted fabric was useful only for some of the softening detail of women's dress, such as clouds, fascinators and canezous; and since these played little part in high fashion, knitting was allocated a modest role in standard fashion.

The comfort and warmth of knitted garments began to attract the less wealthy classes, and even the rich, on occasions when high fashion was not important. Sports jumpers and cardigans entered standard fashion before the First World War. High fashion often amuses itself by making expensive versions of cheap things, so the jumper craze of the 1920s broke into high fashion. Since then knitted clothes have steadily increased in importance in standard fashion and repeatedly come into high fashion.

The social picture of western fashion changed in the 1960s when young people, even teenagers, emerged as a class with enough money to indulge in frequent changes of exaggerated dress, but not enough to pay for high fashion. Street fashion evolved, and cheap, comfortable, sometimes zany, knitwear plays an important role in it, differing from the knitwear of high fashion chiefly in that the latter is overpriced. Veblen's law of conspicuous consumption is in full operation; but hand knitting today is kept vigorous by the two strains of standard fashion and street fashion.

Folk dress was the creation of a section of society that was not rich or powerful enough to keep up with high fashion, but was wealthy enough to preserve standard fashion (usually of the late eighteenth or early nineteenth century) in an ostentatious and sometimes exaggerated form. Folk dress was subject to change in detail, but was characterized by sumptuous ornament. Knitwear has little place in such costume, except for providing splendid stockings, of which the elaborate Balkan designs provide notable examples.

Folk dress, in this sense, is strictly not the same as regional dress. Knitwear has its place in regional dress, as in Shetland jumpers and Scandinavian sweaters. Here again hosiery is significant: the *guêtres* or footless stockings worn over wooden clogs in the French Pyrenees, the footless half-socks or calf-bands of men on Gran Canaria, and the leggings of some Greeks. The nineteenth-century fishermen's jersey, though strictly endemic to an occupation, was effectively regional. Where there is a local or national knitting tradition, it belongs to regional dress or standard fashion rather than to folk dress.

2 Before 1500

Myths and Legends

A myth is a story with archetypal characters, usually gods or great heroes, that explains some fact or phenomenon of life or culture. The truly ancient crafts, such as smithery and weaving, have a place in myths the world over, but there is no ancient myth about knitting. Myths are older than knitting, which finds its way only very sparingly into legend, and then usually romantically and trivially. The supposed Yemeni story, mentioned by Mary Thomas, of Eve in the Garden of Eden knitting the pattern on the serpent's back, illustrates the point. Mary Thomas gave no verifiable source or proof of the origin of the story, but even had she done so, we should have had no more than a trivial legend appended to a great religious myth.

The ancient Greek language contained no word for 'to knit', but that did not stop Gravenor Henson in his *History of the Framework Knitters* (1831) from suggesting that Homer's stories of Helen and Andromache weaving (in the Iliad) and of Penelope weaving her father-in-law's shroud (in the Odyssey) were really about knitting. The story of Penelope unravelling her work at night by the light of torches to deceive her unwelcome suitors was, Henson thought, easier to understand if the fabric was not woven but knitted on pegs attached to a beam. He went too far in asserting that the Greek words *histon uphaine* must mean 'knitting on a pegged bar'. The words more obviously mean 'weaving on a loom', and, even if a modicum of doubt be allowed, they cannot be claimed certainly to mean any knitting process.

The pious William Felkin in his *History of the Machine-Wrought Hosiery and Lace Manufacture* (1867) took up two references that Henson had given to knitting in the Bible. Henson had claimed that the description of Sisera's battle-spoils in the song of Deborah (*Judges* v. 30) referred to knitted fabrics. In fact all the Bible mentions is the colour of the materials, perhaps embroidered or, more likely, striped.

Felkin also took from Henson the idea that the coat of which Christ was divested at his crucifixion may have been knitted. He argued that the 'coat wrought without seam from the top throughout' (*John* xix 23), for which the soldiers threw dice rather than cut it, would be hard to weave but easy to knit.

We can be quite sure it was woven. The garments which were taken from Christ at Calvary were the *himation*, an outer garment, and the *khitōn*, an undergarment or shift. The *khitōn* was the seamless one. It was the distant ancestor of our modern priest's alb and man's shirt, a garment worn next to the skin, usually made of an oblong piece of stuff, wrapped round the body and pinned over one or both shoulders. It was left open at the side, or might be belted. It would be knee-length or longer, was naturally made of woven stuff, and had no sleeves. The best modern translations call it simply an 'undergarment'.

The evangelist was concerned to record this point about Christ's clothes because it fulfilled the psalm verse (*Psalms* xxii 18):

They divided my garments among them:
and cast lots upon my vesture;

and also because the Jewish high priest wore a seamless *khitōn*. This detail reinforced St John's view of Christ as the supreme high priest. Knitting

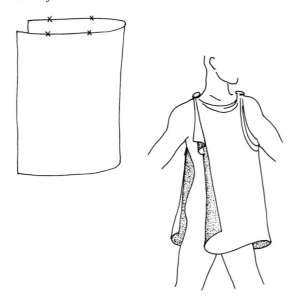

18 The 'seamless garment' or khitōn. It was fastened on one or both shoulders, and might be girded.

does not come into the story at all. It was quite possible in Roman times to weave a single piece of cloth big enough to make a shift for a man without seaming it.

The Esch fragments

The oldest datable pieces of what is claimed as knitted fabric were found by L.J.A.M. Van der Hurk in the late second-century grave of a woman at Esch in southern Holland. There were two of them, each about 2 cm (¾ in.) square, made of woollen yarn about 1 mm (¹⁄₂₅ in.) thick, in stockinet of very close gauge, 8 stitches to the centimetre. Each was backed by another material, possibly leather. Near them were two bronze rods, 20 cm (7¾ in.) long, in a box. They were examined in 1966 by the textile technologist J.E. Leene, who declared that they had the structure of stockinet. In the course of the examination one of the fragments was practically destroyed; in 1973 the other fragment was also crumbling.

We do not know how they were made. Because both fragments were attached to something stronger than themselves, they were almost certainly ornamental. They appear not to have been hosiery, nor the basic fabric of any garment. The two rods may have belonged to jewellery. It has never been shown that the rods were of the right size to have produced such fine knitting. Van der Hurk says the pieces could have been made by bobbin work.

Further investigation seems impossible. Only if similar knitted fabric of similar date is discovered elsewhere shall we be able to assess the significance of the Esch fragments. They may be unique examples of one person's work at one time, which never spread to others and have no connection with knitting found elsewhere. They must have been made by hand, but we cannot say what tools were used.

There was a suggestion in the late 1960s that a bronze knitting needle had been found at Silchester and kept in Reading Museum, mentioned by Mary Andere in *Old Needlework Boxes and Tools* (1971). A similar rod found at Corinium and seen by Heinz Kiewe in Cirencester Museum was identified by him as 'Britain's first', a Roman knitting needle. These 'identifications' were pure guesswork, and both have now been abandoned.

Nalbinding from the Middle East

The city of Dura was an ancient Babylonian foundation in Eastern Syria on the right bank of the Euphrates, an important border post between Syria and Mesopotamia. Before the time of Christ it had become a great caravan centre on the trade routes from East to West. In AD 256 it was destroyed by the Sasanian Persians. The site of Dura (usually called Dura-Europos from its honorific Greco-Roman title), near the modern village of Qal'at-es-Salihiye, was excavated after 1922 and proved rich in cultural finds, including the site of a third-century Christian church. There were also three fragments of knitted fabric, which were discovered by Rudolf Pfister in 1933. These fragments are now kept at Yale University Museum in America.

Two of the pieces are very small scraps of

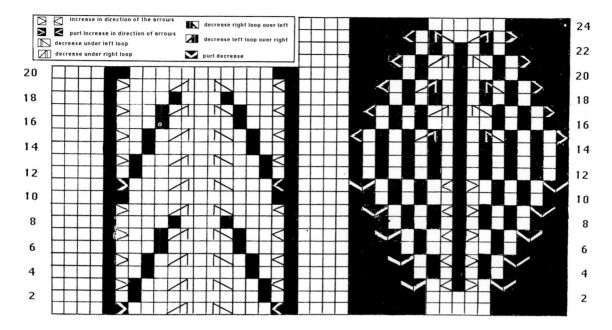

19 Chart for a knitted simulation of the Dura fragment as reconstructed by Barbara Walker, with the technical details noted by Louisa Bellinger. Black squares represent purl, white squares plain. Work in eastern crossed knitting throughout.

ribbing (knit 3, purl 2) with bands of tan, red, grey, purple and green on a natural fawn ground. The larger piece is about 14 cm (5½ in.) square, though so distressed that precise measurement is scarcely possible. It is made entirely of undyed wool with crossed loops (left over right), both purl and plain. The pattern is in three bands. The central band has a vertical stem with parallel rhomboid leaves springing diagonally from it. The outer bands have a large ovoid figure, resembling a pomegranate, repeated vertically. These patterns are created by ingenious placing of decreases and increases to create areas of plain and rib on a purl ground.

Louisa Bellinger, in the official publication of the find (1945), not unnaturally assumed that this was a fragment of flat knitting. She noticed the peculiar techniques of increase and decrease, and composed a recipe for reproducing the fabric. Her instructions are laborious and hard to understand.

a

b

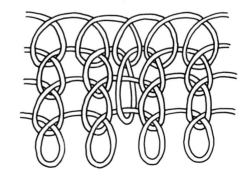

20 (*a*) Nalbinding decrease, which cannot be simulated in knitting; (*b*) nalbinding increase, which can be simulated by knitting, but only with difficulty.

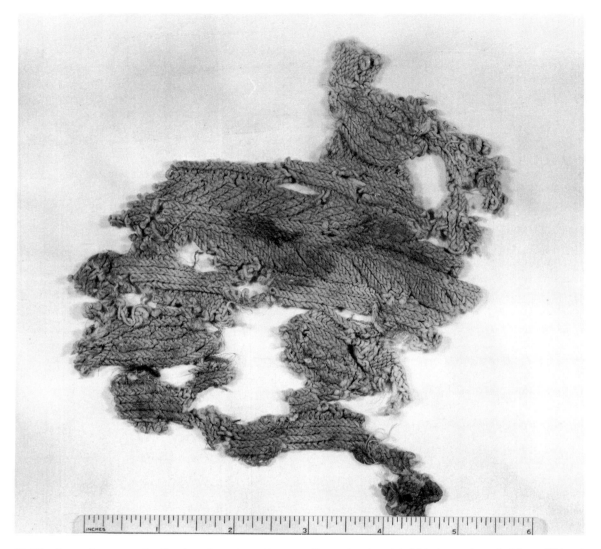

21 The larger fragment of nalbinding from Dura-Europos, Syria, dated to AD 256. Approximately 14 cm (5½ in.) across.

Barbara Walker in *A Second Treasury of Knitting Patterns* (1970) gave a simplifed recipe with a different and much better version of the pomegranate.

Neither writer thought of nalbinding, yet there can be little doubt that the Dura fragment is nalbinding. The peculiar techniques described by Louisa Bellinger are easy and natural in nalbinding, impractical in knitting. The work was probably done in the round and may be part of a sock. We cannot guess where it was made. Artefacts from anywhere in the world might turn up at a trading centre like Dura. Only the date is certain.

For a map of Syria and Egypt, see page 218.

Romano-Egyptian socks

Several museum collections, notably in Paris (the Louvre), Prague, Toronto (Royal Ontario Museum) and Leicester, and above all the Victoria & Albert Museum in London, possess what are frequently called 'Coptic socks'. This title has caused much misunderstanding because 'Coptic' has been taken to refer to the Coptic Church. In fact 'Coptic' simply means 'Egyptian', and is particularly used to refer to Egypt of the Hellenic period before Islam arrived in the country. As the socks date from the later Roman period, it is better to call them Romano-Egyptian.

'Sock' too, is an imprecise word. The items in question reach above the ankle and have a division for the big toe. This division was probably intended to accommodate the thong of a sandal.

These socks are now generally dated from the fourth or fifth century after Christ. They are made of wool, in a fabric resembling knitting, which Dorothy Burnham has shown was produced by nalbinding, not by knitting on rods.

Romano-Egyptian socks in the Victoria & Albert Museum, which possesses four pairs, two complete and two broken, were all found in the burial grounds of ancient Oxyrhynchus, a Greek colony by the Nile in central Egypt, which by the fifth century was a notable monastic centre. The modern village on the site is El Bahnasā. The larger socks are each from 20 to 24 cm (7¾-9½ in.) long. One pair is dull red; the others are one brown, one purple. A child's sock, 12.5 cm (5 in.) long, is red with three yellow bands. The purple sock has lacing at the instep, and a dozen courses of ribbing (3 plain, 1 purl) at the ankle.

22 Romano-Egyptian socks in red wool made by nalbinding. Fifth century. From Oxyrhynchus.

In the Jewry Wall Museum at Leicester is another child's sock. It was found in the town rubbish pit at Shaikh Abāda, the ancient Antinoöpolis or Antinoë, south of Oxyrhynchus, on the right bank of the Nile. This was the city founded in AD 130 by the Roman emperor Hadrian. From the beginning it was a centre of Hellenized culture, where Greeks and Egyptians intermarried. The sock has unequal bands of colour: blue, red, violet, yellow, and green. The colours are changed at random points in the round, according to the place where each coloured length came to an end.

The Victoria & Albert Museum also possesses two other objects made in the same way as the socks. One is a tiny bag, 7.5 x 2.5 cm (3 x 1 in.), with a drawstring top, horizontally banded, purple, green and red. The other, a little brown woollen

piece about 6 x 3.5 cm (2⅜ x 1⅜ in.), is labelled 'doll's cap', but is in fact the toe section of an incomplete sock.

The collection of similar socks in the Royal Ontario Museum at Toronto contains some that came from El Faiyum, the ancient Crocodilopolis, or Arsinoë, about 50 miles south-east of Cairo. Some are for adults, some have darned or grafted repairs, and some are children's size, with coloured bands. It was the study of this group by Dorothy Burnham, published in *Textile History* in 1972, that established the fact that they were made by nalbinding (called by Mrs Burnham 'single-needle knitting'). In fact, the Austrian Luise Schinnerer had made the same conclusion in *Antike Handarbeiten* in about 1905. All these socks are worked in the round from the toe upwards. Romano-Egyptian socks were not made on rods, and may have no connection with the knitted socks of mediaeval Europe. Their rarity may be due simply to the fact that wool is not durable in tombs and other archaeological sites. We do not know where they were made, only that they come to us from Roman Egypt. We do not know anything of the social status of the people who wore them. It is unlikely that they had any connection with monks. There is no reason to think that they came from Arabia; and, strictly speaking, they are not knitting.

Mediaeval Egypt

Amr ibn al-As, representative of the Khalif of Medina, conquered Egypt for Islam in AD 641, and set up his administrative capital at Fustat, now part of modern Cairo. What are probably the earliest pieces of true hand knitting now known to us come from Islamic Egypt.

None of these pieces is more tantalizing than a fragment in the collection of the Swiss textile expert Fritz Iklé (1877-1946) at Basle. According to his family it has now been lost, but fortunately a half-tone illustration from a photograph of it appears in *Mary Thomas's Knitting Book* (1938 p. 91). It was approximately 6.5 cm (2⅝ in.) wide, made of crossed stockinet with a gauge of 36 stitches to the inch (about 15 to the centimetre), in

23 Child's sock from Antinöe, Egypt, in red, blue, green, yellow and violet wool. Sixth century. Foot 12 cm (4¾ in.) long.

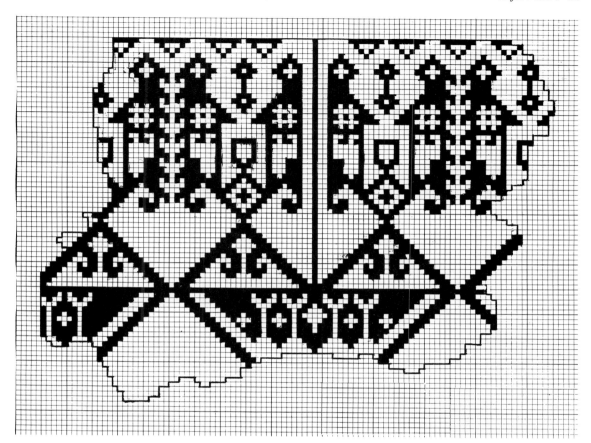

24 Chart of a fragment of Egyptian knitting in maroon and golden yellow. Egyptian, 600-800. See page 32.

deep red and golden yellow silk, stranded from colour to colour at the back of the fabric. A reconstructed chart of the pattern, which is elaborately geometrical, is given in figure 24.

This fascinating specimen came from Fustat and was dated by Iklé to the seventh to ninth centuries. Now that it has been lost, the difficulty of assessing its significance has become perpetually insoluble. It may even be of later date. The other pieces of Islamic knitting are hardly any easier to understand, but at least they can still be seen and examined. None of them is thought to be earlier than the twelfth century.

Louisa Bellinger claimed that some of the several blue and white knitted cotton stockings now in the Textile Museum at Washington, D.C.

were made in the twelfth century, possibly in India. Dr Bellinger was a most careful student, but she did not recognize that the Romano-Egyptian socks were made by nalbinding. She also wrongly asserted that they were worked from top to toe, and therefore thought that these blue and white stockings, which are knitted from the toe upwards, must have belonged to a different tradition. Knowing that Indian cotton prints of this period had been found in quantity at Fustat, she further suggested that the blue and white cotton socks were made in India. The foundation of her argument for their origin falls away now we know that all old Egyptian stockings were made from the toe upwards. There is no positive indication that these stockings came from India: it is safer to refer to them simply as Egyptian.

The new development represented by these stockings lies in the fact that they are made in plain

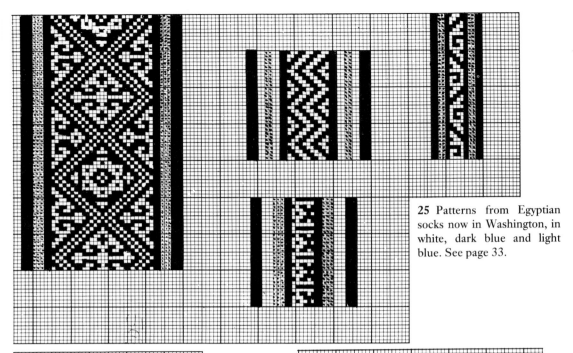

25 Patterns from Egyptian socks now in Washington, in white, dark blue and light blue. See page 33.

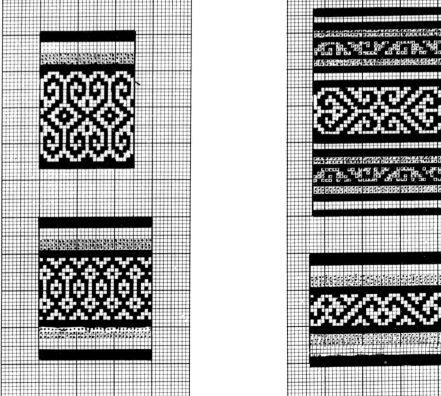

26 A fragment of knitted cotton. Egyptian of the Fatimid Dynasty; AD 1000-1200.

stockinet, hand knitted, almost certainly with rods. The rods may have been hooked. Dr Bellinger noticed that the construction of the heel is different from that of the Romano-Egyptian nalbinding heels. The difference is explained by the difference in the two techniques of manufacture. The 'seam' wale of these stockings runs up the side of the leg, not the back.

Blue-and-white Islamic stockings and fragments of knitting are to be found in many museum collections. They are mostly knitted in cotton, and all worked from the toe up. Most of them are known to have come from Egypt. Dating such stockings is very risky, and for the most part museum authorities are content to approximate 1200-1500.

Several of these stockings have bands of Arabic script on them, used ornamentally. The script is

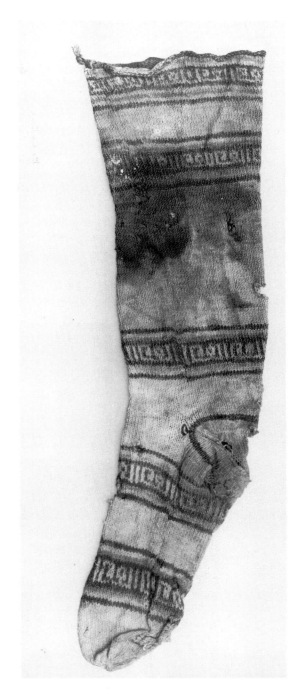

27 Sock knitted in blue and white cotton, with Kufesque inscription 'Allah'. Of unknown origin, possibly thirteenth century. Length 50 cm (20 in.), width 15.5 cm (6⅕ in.).

simplified and conventionalized, resembling the early form of Arabic script known as Kufic. Richard Ettinghausen distinguishes it as Kufesque, and convincingly shows that the inscriptions are a form of *Allah*, the name of God.

Another form of decoration consists of what appears to be the Roman capital letter 'N' together with its mirror image. This also is an Islamic motif, common in south-west Asian carpet designs.

Some fragments, such as those in the Victoria & Albert Museum (fig. 28) and the Detroit Institute of Arts (fig. 26), are puzzling. They may be pieces of stockings or bags. There is no proof that they were knitted as flat pieces, but no convincing evidence that they were not.

Carl Johann Lamm's collection in the

28 Fragment of Egyptian blue and white knitted cotton. Date uncertain, but not earlier than the twelfth century.

Kulturhistoriska Museet at Lund contains three fragments of Egyptian knitting from the Ayyūbid and Mamlūk periods, fourteenth and fifteenth century. One of them, perhaps earlier and even of thirteenth century date, is in écru, mid-blue and turquoise cottons, with engaging errors in the Kufesque script. The 'seam' wale in the round knitting shows and proves that the knitting was not done flat. The other two pieces are more colourful, and knitted in wool. One, 16 cm (6⅜ in.) square, is of clear red, salmon pink, dark blue, yellow, brown and turquoise; the other, 8 by 13 cm (3¹⁄₁₆ x 5¹⁄₁₆ in.), is predominantly red, with motifs in fawn, dark blue, green and light blue. Both these pieces have white elements in the design, knitted in undyed cotton. (Figs 31 and 32.)

In the Victoria & Albert Museum there is a fragment, numbered T87-1939, that resembles this colourful piece at Lund. It is roughly 17 cm

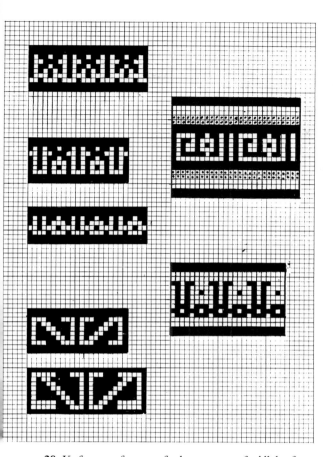

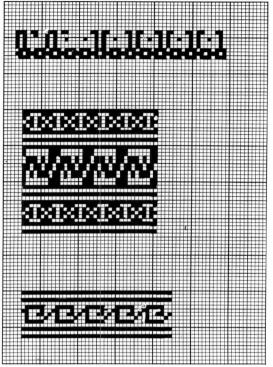

30 Pattern elements from mediaeval knitted fragments from Egypt, now in the Lamm collection at Lund, including the Kufesque band with 'Allah' correctly worked only once in six repeats.

29 Kufesque forms of the name of Allah from mediaeval Egyptian stockings, and a non-calligraphic design.

(6¾ in.) square, knitted in fine two-ply wool at 7 stitches to the centimetre (³⁄₈ in.). The colours are much faded and the fragment much damaged, but the richness of the pattern can still be seen. The ground colour is predominantly reddish brown, with broad dark indigo bands. The reddish part is decorated with separated chevrons of indigo, outlined in undyed white, and adorned with coloured crosses, the spaces being filled with square clusters composed of coloured crosses and diamonds, with occasional tiny camels, all coloured indigo, fawn, olive and turquoise. On the indigo bands the red-brown and other colours are used for cartouches with conventionalized foliage within them and several linear motifs. There is a coloured illustration in Eve Harlow *The Art of Knitting* (1977

p 90), but an accurate description must wait until the structure of the knitting has been examined under a microscope.

The provenance of this beautiful piece is unknown. As in Lamm's fragment, the whitish yarn may be cotton, and the back of the fabric shows a mixture of stranding and intarsia that argues strongly for this group of fabrics having been knitted flat, on two needles. If so, they are probably the oldest known pieces of flat knitting.

Mediaeval Egyptian fragments are kept in other museums too. All are impossible to date accurately, and we cannot tell for what purpose they were made. Several of them show an interesting design peculiarity: the unit of design is not the single stitch, roughly square (as in Fair Isle knitting), but, because the stitches are much broader than they are deep, it is a unit of two stitches, one above the other in the same wale. (This feature is clearly evident in fig. 33.)

31 *(facing page, above)* A fragment of knitting from Egypt from the Lamm Collection. Ayyūbid or Mamlūk period AD 1300-1400. 8 x 13 cm (3⅛ x 5⅛ in.). Red wool decorated in fawn, dark blue, light blue and green wools, and undyed cotton.

32 *(facing page, below)* Reverse of Egyptian fragment shown in fig. 31, showing that the work was knitted flat, not in the round.

No independent literary or iconographic evidence is available to help us evaluate these pieces. It seems that nalbinding had given way to knitting between AD 500 and 1200 and that knitting was used chiefly for footwear, mostly in the round, though flat knitting had begun. The decorative possibilities of stranded-colour knitting were developed, but not 'damask' ornament of plain-and-purl.

We shall find that mediaeval European knitting also was stranded-colour stockinet, worked in the round, but no connection with Egypt can be established. What role the conquering Arabs played in the development of Egyptian knitting is also beyond discovery. The most that can be said is that there are small indications that knitting had connections with Muslim culture in Spain.

Chain mail

Historians who are not specialists in textiles or armour have sometimes assumed that chain armour was knitted. Their mistake is understandable, because of the modern theatrical convention of simulating chain mail for the stage by garter stitch coloured with silver paint. Chain armour was true chain-work, made of small interlaced steel rings, usually with each ring linked into the four rings surrounding it. Coats of mail draped and moved on the wearer's body almost like liquid, in a way that knitted fabric never could.

33 Pattern of a mediaeval Egyptian fragment from Fustat in the Museum für Völkerkunde at Basel, showing a design with units of two stitches in one wale. 15 x 13 cm (6 x 5⅟16 in.). Red, patterned in dark and light blue, ochre, white, pink, green and brown.

34 The structure of chain mail.

The cushions of Las Huelgas

The monastery of St Mary of Las Huelgas, near Burgos in northern Spain, still houses a community of Cistercian nuns. It was founded by King Alfonso VI of Leon and Castile and his wife

Eleanor of Aragon in 1187 as a royal monastery for nuns of high birth, and the abbey church was designated as the royal mausoleum of Castile.

The contents of the tombs were conserved in 1944-5 and published by Manuel Gomez-Moreno y Martinez in *El Panteon Real* (Madrid 1946). Much important mediaeval textile material was discovered, including cushions that are knitted.

The first cushion came from the tomb of Fernando de la Cerda, heir of Alfonso X of Castile. Prince Fernando died in 1275, and the cushion doubtless dates from that time. It is knitted in close stockinet, at a tension of about 80 stitches to 10 centimetres (roughly 20 to the inch), and is 36 cm (14¼ in.) square. It is the better preserved of the two cushions, dark brown with straw yellow patterning on both sides. Perhaps it was originally

36 The diaper pattern from the cushion in the tomb of Fernando de la Cerda, c. 1275.

35 Cushion from the tomb of the Infante Fernando de la Cerda. 36 cm (14¼ in.) square. Late thirteenth century.

crimson, decorated with golden-yellow. There is a pendant green tassel on each of the four corners.

One side has a diamond diaper of yellow lines dividing the field into lozenges, each of which contains an eagle or fleur-de-lys. Diagonal rows of each of these two designs alternate, running downwards towards the left. Some of the eagles face left and some right, with no discernible pattern in the direction of the heads.

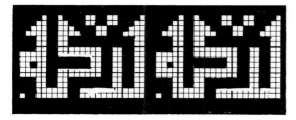

37 The Arabic word *baraka*, 'blessing', repeated round the borders of the cushion of Fernando de la Cerda.

38 The pattern of the reverse of the cushion of Fernando de la Cerda.

The other side of the cushion is covered with a more complicated trellis or web that divides the field into octagons interspaced with small squares. Each octagon contains a golden castle with three towers, or an eight-petalled golden rosette. The bands of castles alternate with bands of rosettes, all running diagonally from top left to bottom right. Each small square contains a swastika.

The horizontal bands alternate between bands of regular octagons (21 rows high and 21 stitches across; 9 rows on the vertical sides and 9 stitches on the horizontal sides) and bands of irregular octagons (with the same maximum measurement but 13 rows on the vertical sides and 13 stitches on the horizontal sides). The motifs are not adapted to the differing shapes of the octagons, but remain the same. The four edges of each side have an Arabic inscription knitted both sideways and lengthways. This inscription consists of repetitions of the word *baraka*, meaning 'blessing', with three dots in the form of a V. The dots are a *vacat* mark, a meaningless ornament. *Baraka liṣāḥibihi*, 'blessing to the owner (or *ṣāḥib*)' is the commonest secular

inscription in Islamic art. Its abbreviated presence on the cushion of a Spanish Christian prince makes it clear that the cushion is *mudéjar* work: the work of a Muslim craftsman in a reclaimed Christian area.

The second cushion is smaller, 28 cm (11 in.) square, and came from the tomb of Mafalda, Alfonso VIII's little daughter, but is thought to have come from the burial of another Fernando, infant bastard of Alfonso X and half-brother of Fernando de la Cerda, who died some years earlier. The pattern is a rectangular gridiron on both sides of the cushion. Bands of alternate coloured stitches (dark and light chequer) 6 stitches or 6 rows wide, divide the field into 36 squares. Each square contains a motif, light motif on dark ground in one square being counter-changed with dark motif on light ground in another square. Two colour combinations are used: dark red and cream, dark green and warm fawn

39 The reverse of the cushion in figure 35.

40 A chart showing the disposition of the pattern elements on the cushion from the tomb of Mafalda (the coffin of the bastard prince). The border is not to scale and the finely chequered divisions are not shown. Horizontal colour-bands: A = brownish-red and cream; B = blackish-green and pale fawn.

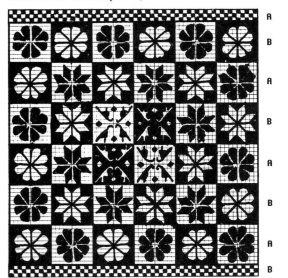

Obverse   Reverse

■ black
✗ red

ground: cream with red;
     yellow with black

41 The elements of the pattern on the cushion from the tomb of Mafalda, together with the border and divisions. The left-hand column refers to the obverse, the right hand column to the reverse of the cushion.

(originally possibly red, white, black and yellow). The colour-combination changes at midpoint in each of the horizontal chequered bands.

On one side the motifs are: a spread eagle in the central four squares; a fleur-de-lys in 12 squares surrounding the central four; and a lion passant guardant in the 20 squares around the outside edge. On the other side of the cushion the central four squares have four birds; the surrounding 12 have an eight-pointed star; and the outside 20 have an eight-petalled rosette.

The dark and light backgrounds are arranged as on a chessboard. On the side with eagles and lions they face towards the centre, except for two lions in the top and bottom borders which are arranged so that the lions in those two horizontal bands face alternately left and right. It is a subtle and precise design.

The edges of the cushion are surrounded by bands of square check, each square 2 stitches by 2 rows. There are 3 rows of squares (6 stitches all told) edged with a row of dark colour and a row of light. The hues are those of the main motifs, maintaining the alternation of colour bands.

Both cushions are in stockinet. They must have been made on steel pins, which were probably hooked. The photographs suggest they were knitted in the round.

The cushion from the tomb of Prince Fernando has heraldic elements: the castle of Castile and the eagle of Aragon; the eagles and lions on the little bastard's cushion could have heraldic reference, but neither cushion is strictly heraldic. The designs were in common use. Most striking is the resemblance of the cushions to woven brocade fabrics in half-silk from thirteenth-century Regensburg, in Bavaria, illustrated by Ernst Flemming in his *Encyclopaedia of Textiles* (1926, p 48). They show diaper and octagonal grids like the cushions of Las Huelgas, and similar rosettes, eagles, stars and birds.

It is tempting to say that the cushions represent the heritage of Muslim knitting, assisted by Hispano-Arab skill in steelwork that made the necessary fine knitting-needles. We can say little more for certain than that they are works of the highest craftsmanship.

Knitting madonnas

During the fourteenth century both art and literature became increasingly concerned with the human and emotional elements in the life of Christ. Paintings of the Madonna and Child began to emphasize the tenderness of the mother-and-baby relationship, and to introduce imaginative suggestions of the domestic background of the Holy Family. A few of them show Saint Mary knitting.

The brothers Lorenzetti painted in Siena. Ambrogio Lorenzetti, active about 1319 to 1347, was the brother, probably the elder brother, of Pietro, and both are thought to have died in the Black Death which ravaged Siena in 1348. The knitting madonna, now in the Abegg Collection at Berne, was probably painted at the very end of Ambrogio's life. It belongs to the type of painting known as *Madonna dell'umiltà*, 'Madonna of humility', because it portrays the Blessed Virgin seated, not on a chair or throne, but on the floor. The 'knitting madonna' shows a domestic interior. St Joseph sits at the righthand side looking at Mary and the little boy Jesus, who sits with one hand on his mother's arm. She is knitting in the round with four needles and purple yarn, but it is impossible to see what she is making. The needles are held under the palm. She carries the yarn over her right forefinger, and yarn of various colours is wound on a dozen or so spools or bobbins. The spools stand upright on pegs on a circular board which may possibly be a revolving 'lazy susan', set on the floor before her. The yarn could be either silk or wool.

The evidence must not be over-interpreted. It shows that knitting was known in northern Italy before 1350, and that the Lorenzetti brothers knew how knitting was done. It suggests that knitting was done at home by women, but does not tell us whether it was an occupation for ladies of leisure or a common pursuit, whether it was cheap or expensive.

A second knitting madonna is in the Poldi-Pezzoli Museum in Milan. It is the work of Vitale

42 A painting of the Holy Family attributed to Ambrogio Lorenzetti (c. 1345) of Siena. Size 54.5 x 25.5 cm (21⅔ x 10¹⁄₁₆ in.).

43 Madonna of humility with St Catherine and another virgin martyr, by Vitale degli Equi (also called Vitale of Bologna) 1308-59. Size 41 cm x 24 cm (16¼ x 9½ in.).

44 Our Lady knitting. Detail of a polyptich by Tommaso da Modena (1325-?75).

degli Equi and dates from the second quarter of the fourteenth century, possibly a little earlier than the Lorenzetti picture. Our Lady is shown sitting on the ground before a bench covered with a red fabric patterned with blue flowers. She is dressed in a blue robe, brocaded with gold. Behind the seat are St Catherine and another woman martyr. The little boy Jesus sits at her left side, putting out his left hand to pick up a spool of yarn from a two-tiered table. He looks at his mother and grasps her free needle with his right hand. She holds her knitting in her left hand and with the index finger of the same hand tickles his chin as though coaxing him not to play with the spools. Her knitting is on three, four or more needles and has a floral pattern in two colours, too wide for a stocking, too narrow for a child's vest. It may be a bag like the knitted relic bags of the same period now kept in Switzerland.

Yet another northern Italian painter of the same period, Tommaso da Modena (1325–? 1375) has left a knitting madonna, probably painted in Bologna between 1345 and 1355 and now in the Pinacoteca Nazionale at Bologna. This picture is one of three panels, each of which shows Mary seated on a chair or throne. In one she is without the child and has a book on her knee; in one she is suckling him; and in one he sits in the chair beside her as she knits. She is knitting in the round on needles (apparently five) held under her palms, carrying the light-coloured yarn on the right hand. Only a few inches of knitting have been completed, and she holds it in front of her as she works so that we see the work forming a hollow square, slightly rounded. The yarn is on spools on a round board like the ones in the Lorenzetti pictures, but here the board is on Mary's lap. All three pictures have the golden backgrounds of Byzantine ikons and early Italian paintings of saints.

The best known of the knitting madonnas, however, is the one painted by Master Bertram of Minden, probably a little before 1400 – about 50 years after the three northern Italian pictures already described – for the benedictine nuns of Buxtehude. It is on the right-hand side of a triptych altar-piece, and is significantly different from the Italian pictures. Bertram had a long career in Hamburg (where the picture is now in the Kunsthalle) from 1367 to about 1415. He was a forerunner of fifteenth-century realism and the tender style of German painting called the Soft Style or International Gothic.

In this picture St Mary sits in an elegant room, knitting a little crimson shirt on four needles held out to view. She has almost finished the garment, and is ready to cast off round the neck. Three balls of yarn lie in a straw basket beside her, and she is using two yarns, apparently both carried over her right hand. The boy Jesus lies on the grass in the garden with an open book before him and a whip and top at his side. He does not look at his mother but turns his head to look over his shoulder at two angels who stand behind him, one carrying a cross and three nails, the other a spear and a crown of thorns – the so-called 'instruments of the Passion'. The whip and top too are doubtless a reference to the scourging of Christ by order of Pontius Pilate.

Although this picture is commonly called 'The visit of the angels' it is really an example of a 'madonna of the Passion'. It belongs to the same iconographic family as the Russian ikon called *Strástnaya* or the Greek *Kardiótissa*. This ikon is a development of the much older Greek ikon called *Hodigítria* (usually translated as 'our Lady of the Way') and well known from the Russian example called the Smolensk Mother of God. In the Smolensk ikon the archangels Michael and Gabriel are painted in the upper corners of the ikon. At a later period the archangels were shown bearing the instruments of the Passion of Jesus, and the face of the child was turned to look at them over his shoulder. This was being painted as the ikon of Our Lady of the Passion in Serbia by 1400, which is the probable date of the *Kardiótissa* ikon that has become most widely known in the West – the so-called 'Our Lady of Perpetual Succour' (now kept in the Church of St Alfonso in Rome). It is believed to emanate from the Creto-Venetian school of ikon painters and was probably painted shortly before Master Bertram's picture.

This iconographic and theological background to Master Bertram's picture explains the little garment that Mary is making. Such a coat was frequently included among the instruments of the Passion by fourteenth-century artists, who assumed that the seamless robe stripped from Christ before his crucifixion must have had

45 The Buxtehude Madonna by Master Bertram of Minden. An example of Madonna and Child with instruments of the Passion, painted probably shortly before 1400.

sleeves. Here we have the earliest occurrence of the idea, which I have above shown to be mistaken, that the seamless robe may have been knitted.

One other picture has been treated as a knitting madonna. It is an engraving of the Holy Family by the German sculptor Veit Stoss (1440/50–1533), and shows our Lady dressing a child's vest on a cross-shaped frame. The engraving dates from 1480 or soon after. The Passion symbolism is again evident, but it is not at all clear how Mary is dressing the vest, or even whether the vest is knitted or woven.

The 'knitting madonnas' show that knitting was known in Italy and Germany during the fourteenth century. Beyond that, little can be said. The Passion symbolism means that the pictures cannot be taken as social records of the time. We cannot even assert that knitting was done in Siena, Bologna, or Hamburg – the artists could have known of knitting because it was done elsewhere. It may have been done much or rarely, by the wealthy or the poor, by housewives or by nuns.

The pictures suggest that knitting was done in the round on four needles (though some of them could be interpreted as showing five-needle knitting); that the working needles were held under the palms of each hand; that the needles were not hooked; that the yarn was carried on the right hand; and that more than one yarn could be used. We cannot be certain what the needles were made of.

The search for mediaeval pictures of knitting has only just begun. More will doubtless be found, not only of the Madonna. Some of the virgin saints surrounding the Madonna and child in a Spanish painting on wood in St Mary's Church at Borja, near Zaragoza, are performing textile crafts, and one of them is knitting a stocking with coloured patterns on five needles. The painting is attributed to Jaume Lana, 1492. It adds little to knitting history, but is of great charm.

Relic purses in Switzerland

In the treasury of the ancient cathedral at Sion (Sitten) in western Switzerland are five knitted purses or bags for holding the relics of saints. There is a sixth in another ancient cathedral at Chur, in the German-speaking east of the country. They are considered to be of fourteenth-century origin and are notably similar. Doubtless all six came from one source, but where that source was is beyond conjecture.

Each is knitted in the round in multi-coloured stranded stockinet, of spun silk at a tension of about 7 stitches to the centimetre ($\frac{3}{8}$ in.). The cylinder of knitting has been flattened to a rectangle, ranging from 20.5 to 34 cm ($8\frac{1}{8}$–$13\frac{3}{8}$ in.) in height, and 16 to 26 cm in breadth ($6\frac{1}{4}$–$10\frac{3}{8}$ in.). The bottom edge is closed and adorned with a row of nine to fourteen tassels, each 13 to 17 cm ($6\frac{3}{4}$ in.) long. The opening is finished with drawstring, usually with two tassels on it. All the purses are patterned in horizontal bands, using red, green, blue, violet, beige and white silks. The top and bottom have narrow borders of horizontal chevron or diagonal patterns. The main patterns differ on each bag. The first is covered with an all-over pattern of bi-coloured stars in horizontal bands staggered by a half drop. The stars are green and beige or blue and white on a red ground. The second is an all-over design of squat crosses, with

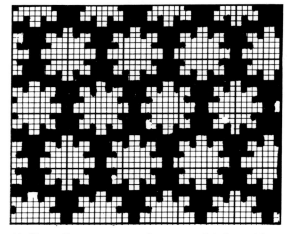

46 Sion relic-purse pattern I: green-and-beige or blue-and-beige on a red ground.

47 Sion relic-purse pattern II: blue-and-white and green-and-white on a red ground.

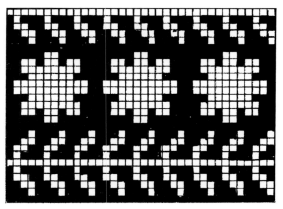

49 Sion relic-purse pattern IV: white-and-beige stars, and white line with green leaves, all on a violet ground.

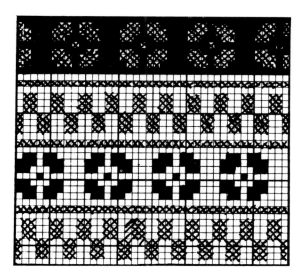

48 Sion relic-purse pattern III: beige-and-blue checks; red rosettes on green and green rosettes on violet.

50 Sion relic-purse pattern V: blue on beige and green on red, with central narrow bands counter-changed. Sawtooth design in violet and white.

rectangles between the short arms of the crosses. Each cross is charged with a large eight-pointed star, and at the centre of each star is a tiny cross or fleur-de-lys of five stitches. Although it is an all-over pattern, it appears horizontally striped because it is worked in stripes of blue-and-white and green-and-white on a red ground. The third has two bands of quadratic rosettes alternating with bands of chequered squares. The checks are beige and blue, the rosettes red on a green ground or green on a violet ground. Narrow red and white lines divide the chequers from the rosette bands.

The fourth also has two types of pattern band: rows of large eight-pointed stars and a horizontal line with leaves above and below it. The stars are not staggered. The ground is violet, the stars white and beige, the line white and the leaves green. The fifth is heraldic. Each band is composed of identical shields, with a small star at the bottom of the space between each two shields. The bands of shields are staggered by a lateral half drop; each carries a bird. The bands alternate: one band of beige with the shields outlined and decorated in blue, one band of red with shields in green; all bands counter-changed with stripes across the middle of the shields in which the colours are reversed. The bands of shields are separated by a narrow saw-toothed design in violet and white.

The purse at Chur, the finest and largest of them all, is also heraldic. It is made of wool and silk and is believed to have been made at Regensburg. The five bands are alternately red and beige. Two shield designs alternate on each band. The shields on the red band are charged, respectively, with a lion rampant and narrow chevrons, all worked in light blue. The shields on the beige band are

changed, respectively, with an octagonal rosette and indented chevrons, worked in red. The shields are separated laterally by a long stalked fleur-de-lys with leaves. Tiny open diamonds are used to break the large triangular areas of background at the base of each shield. The shields are vertically above one another, but the chevronny designs are staggered.

Between the bands of shields and flowers are narrow dividing stripes, composed of two rows each of green, white, red, white and blue. Through the centre of each band run three rows of contrasting colours. On the red band they are green for the ground and beige for the motif; on the beige band, they are green for the ground and white for the motif.

In the cathedral treasury at Sens in France is a knitted bag that has been thought to belong to the thirteenth century, probably another relic purse. It is only 12.5 cm high and 14.5 cm wide (5 x 5¾ in.), of four sections, fawn in colour, with human-headed peacocks, small birds, flowers and foliage in white, green and brown. The upper border has traces of black lettering on a white ground. The flowers are the same motif as the Sion 'stars', but in other respects the Sens style is quite unlike the Swiss. (See colour plate 2.)

51 Chur relic-purse pattern: lion band in light blue on red, with central line of beige on green. Rosette band red on beige, with central line of white on green.

Knit girdles

Several writers have claimed that mediaeval monks wore knitted girdles. That claim cannot be substantiated. The chief evidence adduced to support the theory comes from the record of Marco Polo's journeys to and from China in the last quarter of the thirteenth century. At Tabriz, in Kurdistan, now in northern Persia, Marco Polo found the Nestorian monastery of St Barsauma, where the monks were employed in making woollen girdles, which they laid on the altar during the liturgy and then gave to the benefactors of the monastery. The girdles were much sought after because they were believed to be efficacious in relieving bodily pain.

Some important translators of Marco Polo's book, such as Sir Henry Yule (1903) and Aldo

Ricci (1931), translate the word used for 'making' the girdles as 'knitting'. Others translate it as 'weaving'. Most scholars are agreed that Marco Polo's story was first written down by Rustichello of Pisa in Italianate French about 1298. Luigi Foscolo Benedetto in his great diplomatic edition of Marco Polo, called *Il Milione* (1928), shows that the earliest version of the account of the monastery of St Barsauma is in the Italian-language version of Giambattista Ramusio, published in 1553, some 300 years after Marco Polo's time. The story may be genuine or may not. In any case the word used

by Ramusio is *lavorano*, which means simply 'make'. Girdles can be twisted, braided, plaited, woven or otherwise made, and the meaning of *lavorano* would cover any technique of girdle making. There is no proof of knitting in this story.

Another reference to a mediaeval knitted girdle, given by some modern writers, is in the *Acts of the Chapter of the Collegiate Church of St Peter and St Wilfrid, Ripon* (now Ripon Cathedral) published by the Surtees Society in 1874. The will of John Gregson in 1488 contains the obscure sentence *lego Willelmo Rayner capellano j knytt gyrdyll et harnest cum argento*. This appears to mean 'I bequeath to William Rayner the chaplain one knitted girdle with silver appurtenances'.

Costly girdles decorated with silver appear in other wills of the period, and there is no reason to suppose that they were restricted to ecclesiastical

52 Priest's or bishop's mass girdle. Tablet-woven 108 cm (43 in.) long. Late thirteenth century. Made of green silk decorated with blue, gold and red. See also figs 8 and 53.

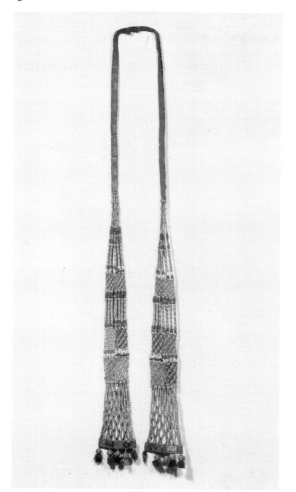

53 Detail of a priest's or bishop's mass-girdle, tablet-woven and decorated with plaited work. Gold, blue and green (see figs 8, 52).

wear. The word 'knytt' also meant plaited or braided, and is more likely to indicate some such technique rather than what we now call knitting.

Today the word girdle suggests a cord, but mediaeval girdles looked very different. Monks' girdles were what we should now call leather belts. Some orders used cloth cinctures. In the thirteenth century the Franciscans introduced their girdles of cord or rope as a dramatic sign of humility.

Priests wore a girdle over the white alb at mass. For the past couple of centuries the mass girdle has been a cord or rope, sometimes crocheted or peg-knitted, and usually white. The jesuit writer Father Joseph Braun in his classic book on ecclesiastical vestments *Die Liturgische Gewandung* (1907) says that such knitted girdles were first made in the sixteenth century in Italy and began to be popular in Rome. The mediaeval mass girdle was a woven band, sometimes lined with leather, fastened at the front with short cords or tapes. Narrow ribbons hung from the front, sometimes three on each side. One such girdle has the hanging bands richly decorated with plaiting, braiding and fringes – what in England would then have been called a 'knit girdle', but we should call a woven belt.

Most interestingly the churches of northern Persia, where Marco Polo's monastery of St Barsauma was, have never adopted knit or rope girdles. To this day their priests wear cloth belts tied with tapes, very like the mass girdles of mediaeval Europe.

54 Girdle from the tomb of St Edmund Rich, (1170-1240) Archbishop of Canterbury, dating from the translation of the relics in 1247. Tablet-woven red silk, mistakenly called 'knitting' by the nineteenth-century writer Louis de Farcey.

Asian spinning men

Another mediaeval traveller in Asia is also occasionally quoted as providing evidence for

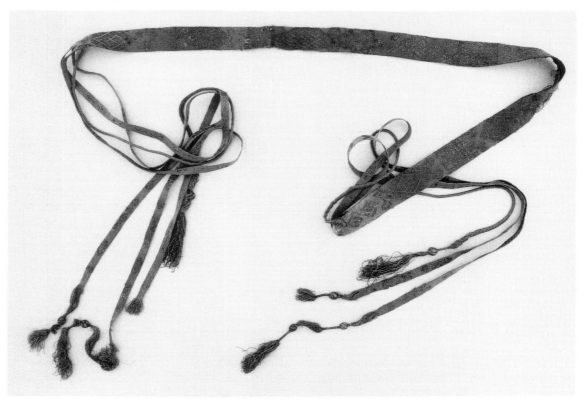

mediaeval knitting in the Middle East. Again it was Sir Henry Yule who used the word 'knit' in a translation. In 1886 he translated the *Itinerarium* of Odoric of Pordenone, an Italian franciscan friar who lived in Asia from about 1316 to 30. Odoric journeyed to China, and when he returned to Italy one of his fellow friars wrote down his travel memoirs in simple Latin. In describing the region of Huz in Persia he says *homines nent et filant, mulieres vero non*, which Sir Henry Yule translated as ' 'tis the custom there for the men to knit and spin, and not the women', noting this was still true of men in the Himalayas. The obvious meaning of *nent* is 'they spin', though it could mean 'they weave'. It is most unlikely that it means 'they knit'. Odoric's scribe was not a skilled Latinist – he may even have misused *filant* to mean 'they weave'.

The probability that Odoric meant spinning and weaving is increased by statements made by travellers in the Himalayas in the nineteenth century. That doughty Englishwoman, Isabella Bird Bishop, records in *Among the Tibetans* (1904) what she saw at Nubra in Ladakh, the so-called 'Little Tibet' of the western Himalayas:

> In the capacious breast of his coat he (the Tibetan) carries wool for spinning – for he spins as he walks – balls of cold barley dough and much besides . . . . Whether in the house or journeying, the men are never seen without the distaff. They weave also and make the clothes of the women and children.

The same point was made by the American explorer William Woodville Rockhill in his *Diary of a journey through Mongolia and Tibet in 1891 and 1892*, recording his passage through the Arundo district in eastern Tibet:

> When at home they (the men) weave the variegated stuff used for making boot tops, gun cases and suchlike things. They also weave their pretty garters. Weaving is, I consequently infer, not a drudgery among these people. If it were, it would be left to the women.

Rockhill was too readily disillusioned about Tibetan male attitudes. These were regions where polyandry was practised. A woman could scarcely make all the clothes for several husbands, and male spinning and weaving are doubtless linked to the marriage customs. Even as late as the 1920s, according to Thubten Norbu, brother of the Dalai Lama, cloth was woven by itinerant male weavers, and his father always had his hands occupied, usually spinning thread for sewing. That too was in the Arundo region (*Tibet is my country* 1960: 40).

Nuns' work

Mediaeval nuns are occasionally portrayed as early knitters, but there is no reliable evidence. The distinguished historian Eileen Power in her book *Mediaeval English Nunneries* (1922), quoted the thirteenth-century archbishop of Rheims, the Franciscan Eude Rigaud, as forbidding nuns to give presents of knitting to people outside their convents. Eude Rigaud was a strict and holy man who constantly strove to improve the religious life of his diocese. The original reports of his visits to convents were edited and published by Theodore Bonnin in 1852. They show that on several occasions between 1254 and 1267 the archbishop forbad nuns in Rheims and Evreux to do handwork except for use in church. The words used vary in spelling from one year to another, but the standard forms are *acuaria* and *frisella*. *Acuaria* means 'needlework'. *Frisella* means 'fringes', which Eileen Power quite reasonably took to include tassels, and may have included galloon or braid.

We cannot reasonably argue from these accounts that knitting was known in thirteenth-century France. No other evidence supports the idea. Eileen Power made an unjustifiable translation of *acuaria* as 'knitting'.

Mediaeval gaiters

Another much repeated claim for mediaeval knitting in England is no more than wishful thinking. This stems from a reference to two pairs of *caligae de wyrstede* at 11½d listed in an Oxford inventory of 1320. Thorold Rogers said in *A*

History of Agriculture and Prices in England (1866-87) that they seemed to be knitted goods.

There is no reason to suppose that these 'buskins of worsted' were knitted. There are ample references in mediaeval sources to lengths of worsted cloth for making buskins. Ecclesiastical buskins were a kind of gaiters made of woven woollen cloth. Bishops in full pontifical vestments wore silk buskins until 1968 when they were made optional. They were made of silk cloth and were tied with ribbons, or thongs, as *caligae* were in Roman times.

Joseph Braun in his classic work mentions the buskins of Konrad von Sternberg, bishop of Worms, who died in 1192. Braun does not prove that they were knitted. He shows pictures of buskins which were true socks, not gaiters, that do not appear to be woven. Perhaps they were made by a form of netting or *nalbinding*. In the absence of proof we can only conclude that there is no other evidence of knitted buskins and that it is most unlikely that bishops' socks were knitted when no one else's were.

Liturgical gloves

The Romans had no word for 'glove'. Gloves must have originated in the early Middle Ages. In mediaeval Latin they were called either *manica*, meaning 'wristlet' or 'cuff'; or by new words based on a Germanic root, such as *wanto* or *guantus*; or a word based on Greek, *chirotheca*, 'hand-case'.

In practice *chirotheca* meant a bishop's liturgical glove. It is possible that some bishops began to wear gloves, as insignia of rank or dignity, as early as the seventh century – certainly some were doing so by the middle of the ninth. By the twelfth century most bishops had adopted liturgical gloves, and from that time onwards gloves were increasingly mentioned in service books. By the fourteenth century all bishops were wearing them. Gloves for travelling and other occasions were then distinguished, and made of stuff or skin.

Liturgical gloves were worn only by bishops and certain abbots and other prelates. They were worn when the mitre was worn, but were taken off when

the bishop went to the altar to consecrate the bread and wine of the mass. (Thus they should not be called 'altar-gloves'.) They were very early treated as emblems of purity, and were made of undyed or white silk. Only in *Ordo Romanus XI* of 1271 was it first allowed that the gloves should be of the same colour as the bishop's chasuble or cope. Since the colour most frequently used for solemn episcopal functions, apart from white, was red, most extant liturgical gloves are red. Blue, purple, rose-coloured and green gloves can be found, but black gloves were never used. (On Good Friday and in services for the dead bishops did not wear gloves.) The bishop's ring was worn outside the glove.

The earliest decoration used on bishops' gloves was a medallion, usually a plaque of precious metal or enamel, sewn on the back of the hand. Later the cuffs were decorated. Finally, simulated rings were embroidered or otherwise placed on the fingers. The earliest examples are hand knitted or made in nalbinding. The gloves of Abbot Peter de Courpalay, who died in 1334, now kept one in the Cluny Museum in Paris and one in the municipal library of Amiens, are made of écru silk in a beautiful pattern of nalbinding.

The gloves kept in the Cathedral of St Sernin at Toulouse are confidently attributed to the thirteenth century. They are knitted in fine white stockinet, quite plain, with clumsy fingers and thumbs. Each has an embroidered medallion sewn on the back: a cross on the left hand and a lamb on the right hand. A similar glove in the Cathedral of St Vitus at Prague may be of fourteenth-century date.

Two fragments of gloves from the tomb of Bishop Siegfried von Westerburg, who was buried in Bonn in 1297, show that the wrists of gloves were by that time being decorated with stranded-colour knitting. They have blue and gold eagles, eight-petalled rosettes, and saltires, reminiscent of the cushions from the royal Spanish tombs at Las Huelgas, of similar date, but the fragments are very small.

In the Cathedral of Moutiers-Tarentaise in Savoy there is a pair of white knitted gloves with embroidered decoration that probably dates from the fifteenth century.

The red-and-gold knitted gloves now kept at

55 Two liturgical gloves in red and gold, believed to be Spanish and of the sixteenth century.

Saint-Bertrand de Comminges have much in common with the gloves in the Victoria & Albert Museum, usually described as sixteenth-century Spanish work, though the reasons for believing that they came from Spain are not fully convincing. They belong to a group of gloves kept in various collections, all red or white and all having an octagonal medallion of the sacred monogram knitted into the back of the hand. The IHS of the monogram is surmounted by a cross and surrounded by floriate rays. There is a similar white pair in Barcelona. Another pair of red liturgical gloves with such a medallion is kept at New College, Oxford, where it has long been thought of as having belonged to Bishop William of Wykeham, founder of the college. He died in 1404, leaving some of his pontificalia to the college. He undoubtedly wore liturgical gloves, but these are

more likely to be of later date. They have around the wrist a band of octagons enclosing eight-petalled rosettes, worked in green and gold. Similar gloves exist elsewhere, notably in the Spence Collection, owned by the Glovers' Company and kept in the Museum of London; and more are illustrated in Irena Turnau's Polish book on European knitting.

The Society of Antiquaries of Scotland in 1854 described the fragments of fabric found in the tomb of a bishop at Fortrose. Two tiny scraps of knitted fabric made in 2 ply cream-coloured silk at 11.5 stitches to the centimetre (3/8 in.), one 7.5 cm (3 in.) long and the other 5 cm (2 in.) long, are all that remains. The gloves belonged either to Bishop Fraser, who died in 1507, or Bishop Cairncross, who died in 1545.

It is difficult to describe the true history of these knitted liturgical gloves. Only one or two of them can be dated with certainty. We know where none of them were made, though it is probable, in view of the similar features (the rosettes-in-octagons patterns and the floriated monogram) shown by some of them, that they came from specialist workshops or groups. There is no reason to suppose that any of them were made by nuns. They give us no idea how well established was the craft of knitting, because they could all have come from a very small group of sources, even from one place.

Fifteenth-century Pomerania

Sophia, daughter of Procopius, Margrave of Moravia, was married to Duke Bogislaus VIII of Pomerania. She died in 1417. According to the Lutheran divine, Johannes Micraelius, in his *Altes Pommerland* (1640, p 389), when she grew old, her eyesight was too poor for embroidery or sewing and *nie die knütte von ihren Handen geleget*, 'she never put the knitting needles down'. Beckmann thought it probable that Micraelius had committed an anachronism and, in order to show the duchess's industry, named an occupation of his own time. Yet Sophia may even have learnt to knit in Moravia, and nalbinding was known in Pomerania. The meaning of *knütte* is not clear.

In her 1986 article Irena Turnau refers to six knitted fragments of the twelfth or thirteenth century found in a grave near Ketrzyn in Poland, and a cap and four pairs of gloves of the fourteenth or fifteenth century found in Latvia, near Riga. These pieces have been described only in Polish and Latvian respectively, so we cannot yet know their significance.

Cap knitting

Caps seem to have been the first things to be knitted in England, though perhaps there were other articles of early date and we simply lack the evidence of records and remains. Coventry cappers can be traced to the thirteenth century, and were established by 1424. Cappers are mentioned in the roll of the Hundred Court at Monmouth in 1449. Marjorie Claton of Ripon was

a cap-knitter in 1465, and the records of Nottingham show that Joan and Isabella Capper sought licences to trade as cap-knitters in 1478. In 1488 the Cappers' Act fixed prices in an effort to stop cappers profiteering, and the Coventry Leet Book recorded the rules of the Cappers' Company in 1496. The verse satire *Cock Lorell's Boat*, printed by Wynkyn de Worde, in 1515, includes cap-knitters in its catalogue of rogues and tradesmen.

Kirstie Buckland, in an article published in *Costume* in 1979, traces the story of the Monmouth cap. The Welsh border town of Monmouth was a centre for cap-making from the 1520s to about 1585. Monmouth caps were of peculiar design and were sold far and wide, becoming well known throughout England. They were also made at Bewdley in Worcestershire as early as the 1540s, and towards the end of that century Bewdley seems to have been the chief centre of the industry. Daniel Defoe in his *Tour through Great Britain* (1712) still referred to 'Monmouth caps, sold chiefly to the Dutch seamen and made only at Bewdley'. Shakespeare mentions the Monmouth cap in *Henry V* when at Agincourt the Welsh officer Fluellen describes the Welsh soldiers wearing leeks in their Monmouth caps. *Henry V* was written in 1599, when Monmouth caps were at the height of popularity, especially for wear under military steel helments. They remained in military and sailors' use for two centuries more, and were often regarded as the typical headgear of Welshmen.

Little has been recorded of their appearance, except that they were round, brown, and topped with a button. A cap found in an old house in Monmouth about 1969, and thought perhaps to be of sixteenth-century date, is probably in the classic form. It is now in the Monmouth local history collection. It was knitted in the round on four needles, entirely in stockinet, felted and shorn. The dark wool is coarse, thick 2 ply, knitted at a tension of 1 stitch to a centimetre (3/4 in.) The knitted structure is obscured by the felting, but the work seems to have begun with 59 stitches. First a hem or brim of double fabric was shaped by increase or decrease at the end of each needle on the third round inside and outside the hem. The hem was eight rounds deep. Above the hem the cap was shaped by decreasing three times in every tenth round, at the end of each needle in the tenth and thirtieth round, the middle of each needle in the twentieth round. After the thirtieth row the remaining fifty stitches were decreased after every third and second stitch in alternate rounds till eight stitches remained. These were drawn together and topped with the button. A loop of fourteen stitches was added at the back. The resulting cap is a close-fitting deep skull-cap, hard-wearing and warm, about 20 cm (8 in.) deep and 55 cm (22 in.) in circumference.

'Welsh wig' appears to have been another name for the Monmouth cap, but this is not certain, for a finely knitted nineteenth-century cap at St Fagan's Folk Museum, which was knitted in Bangor as a specimen for supply to the army in the Crimea in 1854, has woollen loops down at the nape. Some of the Welsh wigs mentioned by Dickens and other nineteenth-century writers however, were almost certainly skull caps of the Monmouth type.

Another form of skull cap was coarse, sometimes

56 Sixteenth-century woollen cap with earflaps, found with others in Moorfields.

nearly as coarse as the Monmouth cap, but with ear-flaps or lappets that may have been secured under the chin. Such caps have been found particularly in the city of London, and are believed to have been worn by artisans, and to date from the first half of the sixteenth century. The extant examples are black. They were knitted from the centre of the crown outwards and downwards.

The other sixteenth-century type is that familiar from Holbein's portraits, a flat cap with a narrow brim. Knitted caps of this kind have been found in quantity in London, but also in Newcastle, in the wreck of the *Mary Rose*, and in two places in Scotland. The London finds are well represented in the collection at the Museum of London, but examples have been distributed to provincial museums such as Platt Hall in Manchester, and Newarke Houses in Leicester.

Audrey Henshall has described the Scottish caps in the *Proceedings of the Society of Antiquaries of Scotland*. One of them came from the burial of a young man on Dava Moor, Cromdale, in Morayshire, and is dated as seventeenth century though it may be older. It is similar to the English Tudor caps, but has two pieces of cloth knotted through the brim, presumably for tying under the chin. The knitting starts at the inside under edge of the brim; increases to the outer edge of the brim; decreases again to the inner top edge of the brim; and doubles back to produce a flat ring of double fabric forming the brim. Further increasing provides the fulness for the crown, which is then decreased towards the centre of the cap.

The other two Scottish caps came from Tarvie near Garve in Ross-shire, where they were found three feet below the surface of a peat bog. The brim of each cap is very narrow indeed, and the crown protrudes well beyond it. These caps are green. One is kept in the Scottish United Services Museum and the other in Inverness Museum.

The shapes of the London caps vary considerably. Most of them are black or dark brown, though one is dyed crimson with madder and another has a stockinet lining of red. Some are as coarse as 15 stitches to 10 cm (4 in.), though 24–28 stitches to 10 cm is commoner. One type has the brim decoratively slashed; some have no brim, but a deep downward extension to cover the ears and nape of the neck; some are cut and moulded into an irregular concertina of several soft brims, one above the other. Some are knitted from the brim to the centre of the crown, some are begun at the top of the crown and worked outwards and downwards. All have been moulded and felted after knitting, then napped. The nap on most of them has worn away, but a tiny baby's hat in the Museum of London, knitted in very dark indigo blue, nearly black, retains a perfect nap. On the outside the knitted structure is completely obscured. Only on the inside can it be seen.

The Newcastle caps, found in the castle ditch in 1974–6, are fragmented but resemble other early sixteenth-century caps. We do not know exactly how these caps were made. The process was called 'knitting' and the structure of the caps that survive is what we define as knitting, but there is no record as to the number of needles used or their shape. So far as we can ascertain, cap-knitting was restricted to licensed professionals. If, as is probable, they used steel needles, these will have been tools in short supply. The knitting process would be connected in the popular mind with the whole of

the industry of cap-making, including dyeing, shrinking, fulling and raising the nap. Domestic knitting would not enter the public imagination. It was work for a 'mistery', that is to say, a professional 'mastery'. Caps were not knitted at home.

British records of guilds of capmakers are scarce and concerned with legalities. We know little of the rest of Europe, though Irena Turnau claims evidence for a Paris knitters' guild going back to 1268, others in Tournai in 1429 and Barcelona in 1496; and fuller evidence for confirmation of guild statutes in France, Alsace and Germany after the beginning of the sixteenth century.

Patron saints

In popular writing about the history of knitting the Guild of St Fiacra in Paris, established in August 1527, is a commonplace. All references to this guild derive from Savary des Bruslons *Dictionnaire Universel de Commerce*, published in 1723, two hundred years after the supposed event. Savary des Bruslons says that the *Corps de la Bonneterie* had its own arms, a silver fleece on an azure field, superimposed with five silver ships, three at the top and two at the bottom. He also says that this

57 A sixteenth-century cap of reddish-brown wool, 27.5 cm (11 in.) in diameter. Found in an old house in Worship Street (just north of Bishopsgate and Moorgate).

58 Knitted cap of brown wool, with slashed brim, 1560-70. Found in Finsbury.

confraternity was established at the church of St Jacques de la Boucherie (or le Majeur) and that its patron saint was St Fiacra. According to Savary des Bruslons, St Fiacra was chosen as patron because he was the son of a Scottish king, and it was believed that knitting first came to France from Scotland.

Beckmann took up this story and it has become part of the legendary history of knitting. Fiacra was in truth a wandering Irishman of the seventh century, a hermit who was welcomed by the bishop of Meaux, in whose diocese he built a hermitage. He became a patron of gardeners and was much invoked for the sick. A hospital in Paris was named after him. It is not now possible to give a reason why the cappers chose him for their patron. He was very popular, and they may have chosen him because he was already well known. According to René de Lespinasse *Les métiers et corporations de Paris* (1898) (III, 154) St Fiacra was already patron saint of the cotton-cap makers in 1387. One thing is clear, whyever he was chosen, St Fiacra was the patron of cappers rather than of knitters.

Patron saints for craftsmen were chosen for accidental reasons, such as the name of the guild church or altar, or a saint's day that provided a winter holiday. The later reason may explain why in Barcelona the silk knitters chose St Lucy and St Ursula, while the wool-stocking knitters chose St Sebastian – though St Sebastian's arrows may have suggested knitting needles.

There was another Parisian guild of *bonnetiers*, established at the church of St Martin in the Faubourg Saint Marcel. St Michael the Archangel, their patron, was certainly not chosen because he had any close connection with either caps or knitting.

Stockings

It is difficult to say when the first stockings were knitted. Irena Turnau quotes fragments of French documents, recorded in Victor Gay *Glossaire Archéologique* (1887) and elsewhere, which mention stockings and mittens *faits a l'aiguille* from 1387 onwards. Whether these were knitted or made in some sort of nalbinding is not clear. Nor is it clear whether they were professional or tradesmen's work. Much study remains to be done on this period.

3 Henry VIII to the Commonwealth

Henry VIII (1509–47)

The reasons for the slow growth of knitting can be guessed. In a society where weaving was widespread in small as well as large centres of population, where hose were customarily cut from cloth, and hats were made of cloth or felt, the need for knitted fabric would not be readily experienced. Perhaps more importantly, knitting needles could not easily be made. Steel rods required a high degree of skill from a whitesmith hammering away to produce them. Fine metal rods could be easily produced only after the art of drawing steel through perforated plates was perfected. This happened in England during Elizabeth's reign.

We have seen that caps were the first items to be produced on a large scale by knitting; stockings were next. The oldest knitted stockings known to us now are coarse knee-stockings. Well-dressed people went on wearing cloth hose long after knitted stockings were first made, and it seems likely that before Elizabeth's reign knitted stockings were worn only by children, and perhaps some artisans.

Evidence from Henry VIII's reign shows the word 'knit' simply meant 'tied', even in relation to hose. Edward Hall in his *Chronicle* described a party during a tournament at Richmond in November 1511 when the 20-year-old king and five others were

> . . . disguised in white satin and green, embroidered and set with letters and castles of fine gold in bullion. The garments were of strange fashion with also strange cuts, every cut knit with points of fine gold and tassels of

> the same, their hosen cut and tied in likewise . . . (1805 ed. 516)

This was the passage that, in Holinshed's transcription from Hall, puzzled Beckman (above p 2).

We can now clearly see that this contains no reference to knitted stockings. 'Hose' in the sixteenth century included breeches as well as stockings. 'Cuts knit with points of fine gold' means that the slashes in their clothes were fastened with gold cord or gold-tipped laces or 'points'. The words 'tied in likewise' show that the word 'knit' referred to the knotting of these cords. It is often thus used by Hall.

Henry's household accounts for 1529–32 were transcribed and edited by Nicholas Harris Nicolas in 1827. Christopher the milliner appears in them frequently, providing hose for the king; but the word 'knit', where it appears, is always ambiguous. In December 1532 Parker, of the robes, is recorded as receiving seven shillings and sixpence for a pair of 'nyte hosen' for the king. (279). 'Nyte' may mean 'knit'; but the lack of the initial *k* is suspicious. It could mean 'night'; but the lack of the *gh* is also suspicious. Even if it does mean 'knit', it gives no clue as to whether the hose were made in England or not.

Yet it is almost certain that silk stockings were occasionally imported into England before 1547. Howes, editing Stow only two generations later, wrote in his *Annals* that 'King Henry the Eighth did wear only cloth hose, or cut out of ell-broad taffeta, or that by great chance there came a pair of Spanish silk stockings from Spain'.

There were also woollen stockings in Henry's

reign. Credence has long been given to the household accounts of Sir Thomas l'Estrange of Hunstanton in which his wife Ann noted 8 shillings spent on a pair of knit hose for him in September 1533 and a shilling spent on two pairs for their children in 1538. This reference was given in *The Gentleman's Magazine* in 1782 (liii 229) during the Rowley controversy, and has often been repeated but not recently verified.

The 1530s

Of similar date is the use of the word 'knit' in a book for teaching the French language, *L'esclarcissement de la langue Françoyse* (1530) written by John Palsgrave, chaplain to Henry VIII and tutor to Princess Mary. He gives eight different meanings for 'knit' in French, including 'I knyt bonnets or hosen: *Je lasse*. She that sitteth knitting from morrow to night can scantly win her bread: *Elle qui ne fait que lasser despuis le matin jusques au soyr a grant payne peut elle gaigner son payn*'. He not only gives a word for knitting that means 'to lace' or 'to interlace' and mentions bonnets and hose, but notes that knitting is financially unprofitable – as it has been ever since.

A puzzling word of the period is 'knitter'. It occurs several times in the collection of *Wells Wills* published by F.W. Weaver in 1890. These Somerset wills record how Agnes Smythe of Minehead on 15 January 1532 bequeathed to John Hyll's eldest daughter 'a cape and a knytter', and to his second daughter 'an apron and a knitter'. On 19 October 1530 William Everard made a bequest of his wife's 'best cap, and her best gown and her best knytter'. 'Best knytter' occurs in at least one more will in the collection. There is no way of telling what a knitter was, though it was probably an article of women's dress.

The Mary Rose

On 19 July 1545 Henry VIII's flagship, the *Mary Rose* sank with all hands off Spithead. In all, 700 men were lost. The accident was sudden, and the contents of roughly half the ship were preserved anaerobically in the silt of the sea bottom until they were raised over 400 years later. Among them were

59 Shaped fragment from the *Mary Rose* 1545.

several pieces of knitting. Two of the pieces were flat caps with brims all round – the simplest type of Tudor bonnet, already described. Another was a fragment, roughly triangular, about 15 cm (6 in.) across the bottom edge, now light khaki in colour, and made of fine wool knitted in stockinet. Like all the pieces, except for one cap, it was found with other scraps and rags and a leather jerkin on the orlop deck, slightly to the stern of the galley. Though only a mutilated scrap, it shows excellent craftsmanship and knowledge of knitted shaping.

The fourth piece is a tube 30 cm (12 in.) long and 28 cm (11¼ in.) in diameter, of heavy black stockinet with a tension of 12 stitches and 19 rows to 5 cm (2 in.). It was probably knitted on four needles, for it has fairly regular decreases made by knitting two stitches together at the ends of each of three needles in a single round, the decrease rounds being set at regular intervals down the tube. The cast-on end is clear, but the other end is frayed. It could be a stocking leg, but is just as likely to have been a scogger (a detached sleeve worn on the forearm during work for protection and

O _____ 10cm

60 A cap from the *Mary Rose* 1545.

warmth) or a hogger (a gaiter or footless stocking).

As these pieces were found on the orlop deck, they probably belonged to soldiers or seamen rather than to the officers and noblemen of the upper deck; yet, because they were found among miscellaneous fabric pieces, this conclusion cannot be certain. They may be noblemen's throwaways. We cannot say whether the knitting was done in England or elsewhere. All we can say is that we have some idea of the knowledge of knitted shaping by 1545, and that there were knitted objects, besides hats, in England by that date.

Knitted pieces similar to those found on the *Mary Rose* have been recovered from sixteenth-century levels in several places in the city of London. The Museum of London has the principal collection of these pieces. They include sleeves or gaiters with rows of purl stitches at the ends. These rows are not of garter stitch, but single rows of purl separated by two rows of plain. There are also socks with garter stitch heels of a simple pouch type, and decreases distributed all round the leg with no defined seam-line at the back of the leg – this is the same construction as that of the

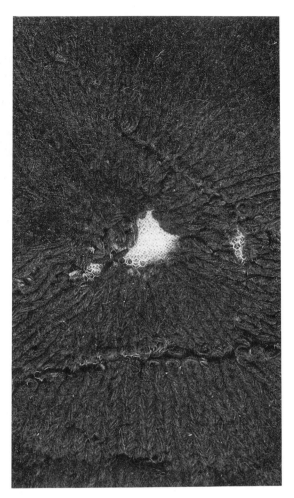

61 Detail of the centre of the cap from the *Mary Rose* 1545.

sleeve/gaiter. The Museum also holds a child's white mitten. It is knitted from the top of the finger pouch towards the wrist and has a very simple black and white pattern around the top of the wrist.

Edward VI (1547–53)

Sporadic references to knitting remain from the reigns of Edward VI and Mary. Most interesting are those found in the Middleton manuscripts, printed in the *Report of the Historical Manuscripts*

62 Sleeve or stocking-leg from the *Mary Rose* 1545.

Commission (1911), which contain the account books of George Medley of Tilty, near Dunmow in Essex.

On 21 April 1550 a little boy, four or five years old, arrived with his baby sister at Medley's home. Their father had been killed at Norwich eight months earlier in Robert Ket's rebellion about land rights, and George Medley was now their guardian. The little boy was Francis Willoughby, who, 30 years later, was to be the builder of Wollaton Hall, the great Elizabethan mansion at Nottingham.

Hardly had the children arrived at Tilty before, in July 1550, the account books show twelve pence being paid 'for my nephew Francis for a pair of knit hosen' (400). In September another pair was bought for fourpence (401), and four pounds of wool were bought for 3s.4d. for knitting hose for Francis (402). We learn the name of the knitter, Elizabeth Ennyver, who was paid fourpence for knitting a pair of sleeves (405).

In 1554, when he was probably 9 years old, Francis went to school in London. The last piece of knitting for him is recorded in 1558, when tenpence was paid for the 12-year-old's cap (414).

The account books are incomplete. There are more remains from 4 February 1572, 'to a poor woman for knitting two pairs of hose for the children, sixpence' (425); and tenpence 'for a pair of knit hose for the kitchen boy' (435). These later entries belong to the days when, as we shall see, all

England was knitting. The entries for Francis Willoughby's boyhood reflect the time when it appears that woollen footwear and sleeves were knitted chiefly for children and working folk.

Examples of sixteenth-century woollen stockings for children can be seen in several English museums. Those in the Museum of London and the Strangers' Hall, Norwich, have the heels turned in garter stitch. For some reason the knitter avoided purling – perhaps he did not know how to purl.

In June 1552 the royal printer Richard Grafton produced his customary collection of acts of parliament. One of them (*anno 5 + 6 Ed VI cap 7*) was an 'act limiting the times for buying and selling of wools' and mentions 'camlets, worsted, says (a type of serge), stamine (a light woollen cloth), knit hose, knit petticoats (i.e. shirts or vests), knit gloves, knit sleeves', and various other items made of wool. This was one of three acts aimed chiefly at preventing wool merchants from hoarding wool to make unreasonable profits. It was not printed in *Statutes at Large* 1735 because it had been annulled. That it was drafted and printed at all indicates that the trade in knitted goods was considerable in 1552, already noteworthy enough to attract legislation. Sleeves (probably simple tubes for working folk, like the piece from the Mary Rose, though they may have been dressier items), undershifts and gloves are added to the caps and hose which are the expected mainstays of the knitwear trade.

If woollen knitted goods were made in England

during this reign, silk ones are certainly imported. Howes (see page 68) says that King Edward VI had a pair of long Spanish silk stockings sent him for a luxurious present. Sir Thomas Gresham gave them (*Annals* 867). We shall find Gresham continuing to import Spanish stockings in Elizabeth's reign.

Linthicum notes that the Earl of Northumberland had silk knit stockings in 1553. Yet stockings cut from cloth continued to be worn, not least by the upper classes. Edwin Sandys 1516–88 was vice-chancellor of Cambridge University. He was imprisoned for supporting Lady Jane Grey, and Holinshed tells an elaborate story about the hose tailored for him when he escaped in 1558 (iii 1148). After Elizabeth's accession Sandys became archbishop of York.

Mary Queen of Scots

Is it likely that Mary Queen of Scots, as a little girl living at the court of Henry II of France, learned to knit stockings? John Loudon, writing in *Scotland's Magazine* in 1957, described a Latin reader that was owned during the 1930s by Sir Alexander Seton, a descendant of the Mary Seton who was one of the Queen's famous 'four Maries'. In the book there was a manuscript note in bad French:

> Quand vous voudrez commance la chausse, faite douze vi poinct, et en faite un doit sans estreicy, et puis fait cinq estrouy de dio en dis et neuf estrouy de set a set et cinq autre estrouy de cinq en cinq. (39)

Loudon assumed it had belonged to the Scottish queen and that she wrote the knitting notes in it. He may have been right, but he offered no proof. He went on to claim that the notes mention purl stitches. They do not. They refer to decreasing in the leg of a stocking.

Alphonse de Ruble has dubious evidence about Mary knitting. In *La Première Jeunesse de Marie Stuart* (1891), he quotes her household accounts for 1551 as recording an order for 'laine torse pour apprendre a la reine d'ecosse a faire ouvrage' (40). Mary was then 9 years old. *Ouvrage* means 'needlework'. The following year there were

orders for *estamet* (which probably means worsted), both red and white, to make stockings for Mary. It is not clear that she made her own.

Knitting can hardly by that time have become a pastime for noble ladies. If it had, the lack of other evidence is remarkable.

There can, however, be little doubt that Mary wore knitted stockings at her execution in Fotheringhay Castle on 8 February 1586. The manuscript endorsed *Executio reginae Scotorum* and printed by Mary Monica Constable Maxwell Scott in *The Tragedy of Fotheringhay* (1895) says 'her nether stocks of worsted, coloured watchett, clocked with silver and edged at the tops with silver, and next her legs a pair of Jersey hose white' (242). Mary wore white stockings, under a pair of sea-blue socks decorated with silver. Both pairs were knitted; but by 1586 knitted socks for ladies were common.

Mary I (1553–8)

Knitted silk gloves were certainly among the New Year gifts given to Queen Mary. S.W. Beck in his classic work, *Gloves, their Annals and Association* (1883) claimed that Lady Grey had given 'two pairs of working gloves of silk, knit' to Princess Mary at the new year of 1536, but John Nichols the Georgian antiquary includes the same phrase in his *Manners and Expenses* (1797) as referring to 1556 when several pairs of gloves 'wrought with silk' and others which appear not to have been knitted were given to the queen by gentlemen and gentlewomen. The rank of the donors suggests that the gifts were expensive but not extravagantly so. In the same year Sir Leonard Chamberlain gave the queen four pairs of hose 'of Garnsey making'.

A tantalizing reference of the 1550s comes in Nicholas Udall's play *Ralph Roister Doister*. Udall was a schoolmaster and this play, based on ideas taken from Terence, was written originally for schoolboy performance about 1553, though not printed until 1566. In the third scene three girls sing as they sit at their work:

Work, Tibbet; work, Annot; work, Margery.

Sew Tibbet; knit, Annot; spin, Margery.
Let us see who will win the victory.

We can only guess at what and how Annot knitted.

Queen Elizabeth (1558–1603)

Elizabeth ascended the throne in 1558. During her reign knitting became an established feature of the English scene, and spread rapidly throughout the country. The story of her own first silk stockings is usually, but wrongly, attributed to John Stow, as though it appeared in *The annals or general chronicles of England*, published by Stow in 1580. Although he revised the *Annals* four times before he died in 1605, he never mentioned the Queen's stockings. Their story first appeared in the much expanded edition of the *Annals* published by Edmund Howes in 1615. This was 55 years after the event, when it was hardly within living memory.

In the second year of Queen Elizabeth, 1560, her silk woman, Mistress Montague, presented Her Majesty with a pair of black knit silk stockings for a new year's gift; the which, after a few days of wearing, pleased Her Highness so well that she sent for Mistress Montague and asked her where she had them, and if she could help her to any more; who answered, saying:

'I made them very carefully of purpose only for Your Majesty; and seeing these please you so well, I will presently get more in hand.'

'Do so,' quoth the Queen, 'for indeed I like silk stockings so well, because they are so pleasant, fine and delicate, that henceforth I will wear no more cloth stockings.'

And from that time unto her death the Queen never wore any more cloth hose, only silk stockings. (867)

This account has been much romanticized, especially by the printer and framework-knitter, John Alexander, in *Ye historie of ye first paire of silke stockings, made in this country and worn by Elizabeth* (1884). The story has also been wrongly interpreted. It does not, for instance, claim that these were the first stockings, or even the first silk stockings that were known in England. It suggests that silk stockings were not made in England by 1560 and says clearly that Queen Elizabeth was not accustomed to them. The incident refers to a date very early in her reign when she was only 26. Before coming to the throne she had lived virtually under house arrest in the country at Woodstock and elsewhere, under a regime which would not have allowed her opportunity to enjoy rare and costly Spanish imports. Cloth hose were still the usual wear for the nobility.

Mrs Montague's gift is not connected with the yellow silk stockings now kept at Hatfield House that are said to have belonged to Queen Elizabeth. The stockings in the story were black. Unfortunately the lacy pattern of the Hatfield House stockings has been called 'Mrs Montague's Pattern'. The dating of these stockings is in some doubt. They are certainly women's stockings, of knee length with cloth tops.

Beckman pointed out that a similar story was recorded by Johann Joachim von Rusdorff (1589–1640) in *Consilia et Negotia Politica*, published at Frankfurt-am-Main 1725. Rusdorff travelled in England in 1613–16 and was here on embassies in 1619 and again from 1622–27. He therefore knew a good deal about the English court 10-20 years after Elizabeth's death. His book is in Latin. The silk stockings story can be translated as follows:

In England that most happy and illustrious queen, Elizabeth, wielded the sceptre and wore the crown about eighteen years before her feet were clad in silk stockings. It happened then that the Countess of Derby, a lady of the bedchamber and superintendent of the Queen's women, presented the queen with a new year's gift of a little present of knitted (*ex reticulatis nexibus colligatorum*) silk stockings made in Milan. The Queen tried them and was pleased with their comfort and softness. Thereafter she began to wear silk stockings. Hitherto she had used only stockings of wool made in England. (283-4)

Eighteen years after Elizabeth's accession would have been 1576. Von Rusdorff's story can be made to harmonize chronologically with Edmund Howes's only if von Rusdorff made an error of 'eighteen years' for 'eighteen months'. If that detail could be amended, there would still be the difficulty of Mrs Montague (who could have worked under the Countess of Derby) making the stockings in Howes's version, while in Rusdorff's they came from Milan. Rusdorff is, however, quite clear that the stockings were a new experience for Elizabeth personally, because they were of silk. John Nichols (1823) records that at New Year 1561 Elizabeth received at least three pairs of silk knit hose as gifts from commoners. Her partiality was quickly known. Howes's version of the story of her first pair fits the date of this and other evidence.

The port books of 1560–80 show expensive silk stockings being imported from Spain, and a letter quoted by Dean Burgon in his *Life of Sir Thomas Gresham* (1839) adds a further instance. Sir Thomas was Queen Elizabeth's leading financier and had agents in several continental cities, among them one Edward Hogan in Seville. In a letter of 30 April 1560 Gresham wrote to Sir William Cecil (later Lord Burghley, but already Secretary of State): 'I have written to Spain for silk hose for you and my lady, your wife'. On 7 May he wrote again: 'I have sent you herewith two pair of black silk hose and . . . pair for my lady your wife'. The dean also notes that the 'note of goods lacking' from a plundered Spanish ship, dated 24 May 1563, includes 'diverse pairs of hose'.

It is clear that in the early 1560s Spanish silk stockings were still costly luxuries in England. As late as 1578 Robert Dudley, Earl of Leicester, the land's greatest dandy and nearest to the Queen, was getting his silk hose from Granada. A letter from his agent, John Barker, written at Sanlucar on 10 June that year, promises to send two pairs of silk stockings on the ship *Mathew* of London, saying he will get more from Granada that summer, but complaining that the Spaniards 'make things substantially but not handsomely'. (Thomas Wright, *Queen Elizabeth and her times* [1838; II, 84]).

Howes's other stocking story concerns worsted stockings:

> In the year 1564 William Rider, being an apprentice with Master Thomas Burdett at the bridge foot over against St Magnus church, chanced to see a pair of knit worsted stockings, in the lodging of an Italian merchant that came

from Mantua. He borrowed these stockings and caused other stockings to be made by them; and these were the first worsted stockings made in England. (867)

A marginal note says: 'The Earl of Pembroke the first nobleman that wore worsted stockings.' A few pages later Howes adds:

> Within a few years began the plenteous making both of jersey and woollen stockings, so in a short space they waxed common. (869)

He distinguished between jersey, woollen, and worsted stockings, but it is not clear exactly what the words meant to him. Most likely the clue to what he declares was first made by Rider is not in the material but in the word 'stockings'. He clearly means long stockings for men. So far as we know, earlier woollen stockings were nether-stocks (what would now be called 'socks'). Men had worn long stockings, in the form of cloth hose, for centuries. The new Elizabethan fashion for extremely short trunks required sheer stockings, hitherto made of cloth or knit silk; but by 1564 it had become possible to knit long stockings of fine worsted – a technical achievement very different from making the coarse socks now in the Museum of London. Not the least of reasons for this development was the increasing availability of fine steel knitting-needles.

Knitting needles

Draw-plates for making wire were known in Germany some three or four centuries earlier, and in Coventry, at least by 1430; the first mechanization of wireworks, by waterpower, however, was begun near Tintern Abbey in 1566–7 by William Humfrey, assay master of the Royal Mint. With Lord Burghley's support, Humfrey got Christopher Schütz of Annaberg in Germany to come and help. The work was slow in developing, but 30 years later it was supplying 5000 workers in England who made wool-cards, pack-needles, knitting needles and birdcages among other things. The factory was owned by the Society of the Mineral and Battery Works, which built a second wire-mill in 1607, higher up the Wye at Whitebrook. John Zouch, a member of the society, started a wire-mill at Makeney, near Duffield, Derbyshire in 1581, and Thomas Steere did the same at Chilworth, Surrey in 1602; but the monopoly managed to suppress both projects (see H.R. Schubert, *History of the British Iron and Steel Industry*, 1957, 292-303).

The first fine wires caught the imagination of poets. Even before Elizabeth's day beautiful hair had been compared to wire. Shakespeare poked fun at the simile in Sonnet CXXX:

If hairs be wires, black wires grow on her head.

But Spenser revelled in it. In *The Faerie Queen* (about 1587) he wrote:

'Her long loose yellow locks like golden wire
Sprinkled with pearl, and pearling flowers a-tween.'

Later on, cruel Furor

'Shaked his long locks, coloured like copper wire.'

It is hard now to recapture the fascination of metal wire when it was a fresh modern invention. Steel knitting needles were part of the new age's wonders. The word for them, however, was not fixed. John Florio's Italian dictionary of 1598 mentions 'knitting needles'; the inventory of John Farbeck, a Durham mercer, dated 20 November 1597, mentions 'knitting pricks'. They were often called 'wires'. 'Pins' as we shall see, was used in Essex in 1580.

The Sture glove

From Sweden we have information of a different kind. Sten Svantesson Sture, a young man of 25, was captain of the warship *Svansen* when he was killed in a sea-battle against Danes and Lübeckers off Rügen in 1565. Relics of his clothing were laid up in the family chapel in Uppsala cathedral. In 1660 the town physician, Stalhof, described among these garments a black felt hat with a label attached to it identifying it as Sten Svantesson's. Fastened to it was a small knitted glove.

The glove still exists. It is 17cm long and 7 cm

across the palm (6¾ x 2¾ in.), stockinet in stranded knitting of gold thread and coloured silks, at about 9 stitches to 1 centimetre (⅜ in.). The thumb is built up from an interruption of one round of knitting at the side of the palm, and has neither gore nor gusset. The thumb and all the fingers are tapered by decreases set all round and up the whole length of the digit.

Finger rings are simulated by three rounds of gold thread. The main part of the hand is patterned with a fretted design over narrow bands of colour. The ground is now beige. The other colours used are light orange-red, pale green, white, yellow and maroon. Across the palm are the words FREVCHEN SOFIA in capital letters. Sten Svantesson is said to have been betrothed to a German girl. This tiny glove clearly belonged to a girl and was doubtless being worn as her favour in battle. Perhaps it was made in Germany. (Colour plate 3.)

Stockings

English stockings

In England knitted fabrics soon attracted the wrath of moralists. George Gascoigne (1525?–77) was a Bedfordshire man, educated at Trinity College, Cambridge, who became a senior barrister of Gray's Inn in his late twenties. He wrote poetry, plays, masques, and criticism and was much at court. Not long after attending Elizabeth and the Earl of Leicester at the famous revel at Kenilworth Castle in 1575, he published his poem 'The steel glass' in which he took a puritan view of dress, including knitting:

Our bombast hose, our treble double ruffs,
Our suits of silk, our comely garded capes
Our knit silk stocks and Spanish leather shoes
(Your velvet serves oft times to trample in),
Our plumes, our spangs and all our quaint array
Are pricking spurs, provoking filthy pride,
And snares unseen which lead a man to Hell.

('Garded' means trimmed, and 'spangs' means spangles.)

Knitting had made entry into high fashion. The puritan pamphleteer and ballad-maker, Philip

Stubbes, in *The Anatomie of Abuses in England* (1583) was even more virulent, specifically about stockings:

> Then they have nether stocks to these gay hosen, not of cloth (though never so fine), for that is thought too base; but of jarnsey, worsted, crewel, silk thread and such like, or else at least of the finest yarn that can be got; and so curiously knit with open seam down the leg, with quirks and clocks about the ankles, and sometimes, haply, interlaced with gold or silver threads, as is wonderful to behold. And to such impudent insolence and shameful outrage is it now grown that every one almost, though otherwise very poor, having scarce forty shillings of wages by the year, will not stick to have two or three pairs of these silk netherstocks, or else of the finest yarn that can be got, though the price of them be a royal or twenty shillings or more, as commonly it is, for how can they be less when as the very knitting of them is worth a noble (six shillings and eightpence) or a royal (eleven shillings and threepence), and some much more?

As for women's stockings, they were 'green, red, white, russet, tawny and else what; which wanton light colours any sober chaste christian . . . can hardly . . . at any time wear'.

William Harrison (1534-93), rector of Radwinter, and later canon of Windsor, published his *Description of England* in 1577. In the section of trees he mentioned 'the alder, whose bark is not unprofitable to dye black withal, and therefore much used by our country wives in colouring their knit hosen'. In the chapter on 'Apparel and attire', however, he was far from thinking of the black stockings of farmer's wives when he castigated the lewd fashions of women, especially their 'coloured nether stocks'. When he reissued the book in 1586 he expanded this to 'diversely coloured netherstocks of silk jersey'.

A further reference to dyeing is well known. *Exchequer King's Remembrancer Memorial Rolls: Easter Term 26 Elizabethae* 108 tells how two Londoners from near Paul's Wharf, James Austen of St Benet's and Richard Rogers of St Peter's, were charged in 1584 with having dyed a thousand dozen of knit hose with logwood at the Surrey town of Kingston. James and Richard, probably itinerant dyers, were handling vast quantities of stockings. Logwood was a Central American tree, imported in log form because the heartwood yielded a dye that was good for black, blue and violet. It was immediately popular, but soon prohibited by law because the colour quickly faded.

We know something of the colours that were fashionable for men's stockings in France in the first half of the seventeenth century. There were at least fifty shades, some with straightforward colour names, some with metaphorical names surprisingly like those used for women's stockings in the twentieth century. Hippolyte Roy in *La vie, la Mode et le Costume au Dix-Septième Siècle* (1924) published a facsimile of a dyer's advertisement from Neufchâteau in Lorraine printed in 1607, and the Huguenot scholar Theodore Agrippa d'Aubigné in his anti-catholic satire *Les Aventures du Baron Faeneste* (1630) quotes a similar list. The names include Dying Monkey, Merry Widow, Lost Time, Resuscitated Corpse, Amorous Desires, Monkey's Smile, Sad Friend, Mortal Sin, Sick Spaniard, Colour of Hell, Doe's Belly, Kiss-me-Darling (Baise-moi-Mignonne) and Brown Bread, as well as several betraying a scatological sense of humour. Perhaps some of the latter were invented by d'Aubigné for the sake of satire, but most of the others occur in the Lorraine dyer's list. The range is chiefly in the pinks, beiges and flesh tints.

A scrap of evidence for English colours comes from Ben Jonson's play *Every Man out of His Humour* (1599), where the comic fop Fastidious Brisk tells of 'two pair of silk stockings that I put on, being somewhat of a raw morning, a peach colour and another' (IV iv). For elaborate patterning we can refer to portraits such as that of Queen Elizabeth's devoted Lord Chancellor, Sir Christopher Hatton (colour plate 4), owned by the Earl of Winchilsea, and another of the Earl of Leicester, shown in Herbert Norris *Costume and Fashion* (1938). Their stockings are white and have large diamond patterns, apparently in purl stitches, at the top of the leg. The stockings worn by the elegant young man in Nicholas Hilliard's famous miniature of 'An unknown youth leaning against a tree among roses' painted about 1588 (and now in the Victoria and Albert Museum) look plain enough, but they are worn with extremely small trunk hose and were hand knitted to a point of perfection, to serve an extravagant fashion.

Indeed, the chief service knitting rendered to fashion was the flattery of the male calf, from the reign of Elizabeth I till the invention of trousers two and a half centuries later. The dramatists, especially in the reign of James I, did not miss opportunities for poking fun at young men's vanity. In 1598 Jonson's *Every Man in His Humour* has the silly country boy Stephen flattered by Brainworm the servant, who says silk stockings would show off his legs better. Stephen's rejoinder is: 'The stockings be good enough now summer is coming in – for the dust. I'll have a pair of silk against winter, that I go to swell in the town. I think my leg would show well in a silk hose.' (I.iii.43). Young Loveless, the prodigal in Beaumont and Fletcher's *The Scornful Lady* (1610) is a figure of fun because he is satisfied with 'carnation jersey stockings' (I.i); while the young gallant, Haddit, in Robert Tailor's play of 1614 *The Hog Hath Lost his Pearl* is quite clear that no woman will fall for a young man in woollen stockings (I.i); and Mistress Openwork in Middleton and Dekker's *The Roaring Girl* (1611)

regrets that many handsome legs in silk stockings have villainous splay feet, for all the great roses of ribbon on their shoes (IV ii. 8).

This elegant legwear brought a strange new embarrassment: laddering. The word 'ladder' did not appear until after the 1914-18 war (when women's artificial silk stockings became visible below short skirts), but in 1614 Ben Jonson began *Bartholomew Fair* by having the stagekeeper come out on the stage and pretend: 'He that should begin the play, Mr Littlewit the proctor, has a stitch new fallen in his black silk stocking. 'Twill be drawn up ere you can tell twenty'. Middleton and Rowley in *The Spanish Gipsy* (1623) refer to 'a stitch in a man's stocking, not taken up in time' that 'ravels out all the rest' (II i).

Italian stockings

The story of knitting outside England is at present much mistier. Of Spain and Italy we know almost nothing beyond what we have already gleaned, save for a pair of stockings found in Florence in 1857. They are now in the Palazzo Pitti, but they were taken from the tomb of Eleanora of Toledo, wife of Cosimo I de'Medici, Grand Duke of Tuscany. She died of malaria in 1562, aged 40. Her silk stockings, now discoloured, were probably originally crimson.

63 The crimson silk stockings of Eleanora of Toledo, 1562. Palazzo Pitti, Florence.

64 Detail of the stockings in fig. 63.

They would reach to the knee only. The silk garters were apparently tied below a top that turned over like a little English boy's stocking. The pattern of these turnover tops (seen in reverse in the photograph) consists of a narrow band of plain knitting with two zigzag lines of purl running round the stocking, divided by two purled rounds from the broad central band of the turnover. The broad band has a trellis of purls, two purls wide, with plain lozenges between the trellis purls. Each lozenge contains four eyelets. The turnover is completed by a second narrow band with zigzags.

The legs and feet have broad vertical stripes, alternately an 8-stitch stripe of double moss-stitch and a 9-stitch stripe of 'double garter stitch' (2 rounds purl, 2 rounds plain). These broad stripes are divided by narrow stripes each consisting of reversed stockinet, edged with a single wale of plain stitches and with a central wale which alternates 1 plain, 1 purl, vertically.

These are elegant and elaborate stockings.

French and German stockings

The classic quotation about French stockings comes from François Eudes de Mezeray *Abrégé Chronologique* published in Amsterdam 1688, where he says that Henry II was the first to wear silk stockings in France, which he did at his sister's wedding to the Duke of Savoy in 1559 (vi 289). John Nichols, referring to this story in *Progresses and Public Processions of Queen Elizabeth* (1823), drily notes that Henry was on his deathbed when this marriage was solemnized (1 xliii); de Mezeray, however, adds that silk stockings only really began to be worn at the French court during the troubled times of Charles IX (1560–74) and Henry III (1575–89), after which the bourgeoisie quickly followed suit.

Beckmann adds a detail: the wife of Geoffrey Camus de Pontcarré at the court of Henry III was given silk stockings as a Christmas present by her nurse, but she refused to wear them because they were too gay. Yet even Beckmann cannot tell us much about Germany. He has a story in the same vein about Barthold von Mandelsloh, privy counsellor to the margrave John of Custrin. He procured silk stockings from Italy and wore them on weekdays. The margrave reproached him: 'Barthold, I have silk stockings also; but I wear them only on Sundays and holidays'. Beckmann adds that by the end of the century Leonard Thurneisser was wearing silk stockings every day at the court of Brandenburg.

Irena Turnau has published a little information about sixteenth century stockings in eastern Germany, based on preserved examples. In 1946 three stockings were found in the badly decayed coffins of the Pomeranian princes under the castle at Szczecin. They are now kept in the National Museum of the city. Two of them form a pair, found in the coffin of Duke Barnim XII, who was buried in 1603. They are 59 cm long with the foot 23 cm long (23¼ x 9⅛ in.), made of dark brown (perhaps originally black) silk in stockinet, plain and unadorned. They may well have been imported from England or western Europe, but they could have been made in Pomerania.

The third stocking is bigger, 69 cm (27⅛ in.) long, and made of brown silk, now much damaged and frayed. Its date is unclear, but it has small holes in the hem for tapes to tie the stocking above the knee, and could well be of late sixteenth-century date. It may be of Spanish origin, for Irena Turnau compares it to Spanish stockings found in the tombs of Adam Parzniewski, buried in Warsaw in 1614, and Tycho Brahe, buried in Prague in 1601.

Herbert Norris in *Costume and Fashion* (1938) quotes a letter from London to Duke Frederick of Württemberg in 1595, sending him 12 pairs of fine silk stockings at six French crowns a pair. We shall see that English woollen and worsted stockings were much exported by that time.

Knitters' guilds were not formed in Britain, but they flourished on the continent. Strasbourg had one in 1535, Prague in 1570. Extant statutes date only from the early seventeenth century (Neisse 1602, Strasbourg 1603, Vienna 1609). The 1605 Strasbourg statutes list the masterworks to be made in 13 weeks: a cap, a pair of gloves, a woollen 'waistcoat' and a flowered carpet. Some of these continental guilds survived until the eighteenth century, when they eventually gave way to

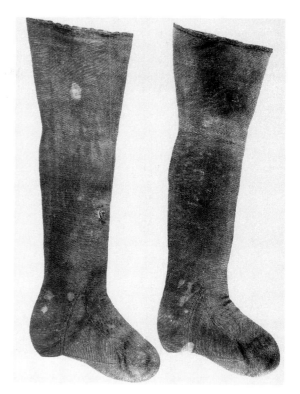

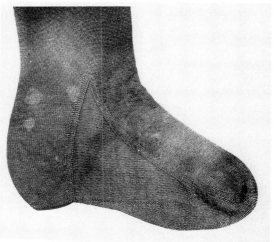

65 Stockings from the coffin of Duke Barnim XII of Pomerania (1549-1603), found in the crypt of Szczecin castle chapel in 1946.

framework knitters. Irena Turnau has summarized their story in her book in Polish.

Gudrun Ekstrand has published an account of hosiery in Sweden during the sixteenth and

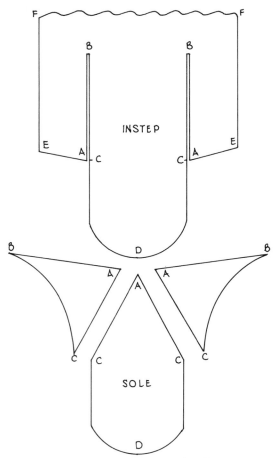

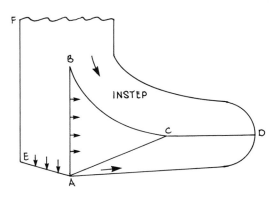

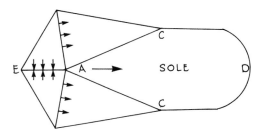

66 The structure of sixteenth-century knitted silk stockings. FE = leg seam; EA = heel seam bound off; AB = gusset stitches picked up; AC, BC = instep shapings. Cloth hose (left) were cut on bias. See A. Harmand *Jeanne d'Arc: ses costumes, son armure* (1929), p. 133.

seventeeth centuries: 'Some early silk stockings in Sweden' (*Textile History* 13(2), 1982 pp 165-82). She records that King Erik XIV in 1566 had 27 pairs including ten red, eight black, four violet, and others pink, yellow, brown and ash grey. Johan III, who died in 1592, was buried in Uppsala. When his tomb was opened in 1945-6, he was found wearing yellowed silk stockings in stockinet with a single wale of purls as a seam at the back of the leg. The legs were 55 cm (22 in.) long, the feet 24. The thigh was begun with 254 stitches cast on. The calf was fully fashioned. There is no way of knowing where they were made.

The article is accompanied by a valuable series of photographs showing stockings with the same construction of the heel as in the stockings of Duke Barnim XII of Pomerania, similar to the English pattern of 1655 described on page 83. The simulated seams in the feet imitate the structure of stockings cut from cloth.

Rural knitting

Although knitted hose were subject to satire, the activity of knitting quickly attracted an honest reputation as a craft of domestic tranquility. Shakespeare did not write of 'the knitters in the sun' in *Twelfth Night* until 1601, but Sir Philip Sidney began to compose *Arcadia* about 1577. The story begins with two very young men being shipwrecked, and one of them being rescued by two shepherds who take him home to Arcadia. Arcadia is described in Book 1, chapter 2:

There were hills which garnished their proud heights with stately trees; humble valleys whose base estate seemed comforted with refreshing silver rivers; meadows enamelled with all sorts of eye-pleasing flowers: thickets which, being lined with most pleasant shade, were witnessed so to be by the cheerful deposition of many well-tuned birds; each pasture stored with sheep feeding with sober security, while the pretty lambs with bleating oratory craved the dams' comfort; here a shepherd's boy piping as though he should never be old; there a young shepherdess knitting and withal singing, and it seemed that her voice comforted her hands to work and her hands kept time to her voice's music.

A less idyllic allusion to the countryside was discovered by C. Willett Cunnington in the Essex Record Office. In 1580 there was stolen from a hedge (the sixteenth-century clothes line) 'a pair of knit sleeves, being not full finished, with the knitting pins' (88). Records of theft contribute to our knowledge of domestic knitting, and indicate that knitting quickly became part of rustic economy, introducing a new labour, even a new drudgery, into working people's homes.

During the second half of the sixteenth century, knitting became an important source of income in many parts of England. Dr Joan Thirsk has summarized the situation in a series of essays and articles (listed in the bibliography). She shows that all the English districts that were important centres of industrial cottage knitting in the eighteenth century had already become knitting districts by the beginning of the seventeenth. Richmond and Doncaster; Norwich, and the north-east coast of Norfolk; Shepton Mallet, Wells and Glastonbury; Sherwood, Leicester and Northampton, (she estimates that by the end of the Tudor period knitting occupied nearly half the spare time of Midland cottage farmers); Garsdale, Dentdale and Kendal. In this last area cottage knitting was encouraged by the division of property on inheritance into small parcels. The octogenarian Edward Lande, giving evidence before the justices in 1634, submitted that the tenements had become 'so small in quantity that many of them was not above three or four acres apiece, and generally not above eight or nine acres, so that they could not maintain their families were it not by this industry in knitting coarse stockings'.

This rapid and successful diffusion of knitting skills throughout working-class England in the time of Elizabeth has scarcely been noticed by historians. It should rightly be counted as a significant element in the flowering of sixteenth century commerce and culture. We have at present no clear evidence that hand knitting had similar development in Wales or Scotland before the seventeenth century.

Elizabethan exports

In an essay called 'The fantastical folly of fashion' (1973) (the title is another quotation from William Harrison, the canon of Windsor), Dr Thirsk has drawn a detailed picture of sixteenth and seventeenth century English stocking knitting. She bases her conclusions on a variety of documents, including contemporary records of seaport trade kept in the Port Books. Thus she shows instances in the 1560s and early 1580s of silk stockings being imported from Spain at very high prices. By the end of Elizabeth's reign, however, worsted stockings from England were being exported to Germany, France, Italy, Holland and Spain. There was then a tremendous variety of qualities and styles, partly dependent on the great variety of wools from local breeds of English sheep, partly a response to the enormous demand from all social classes in so many European countries.

Queen Elizabeth had to take a personal interest in such a growing and important export industry. The description of her visit to Norwich in 1578 has often been reprinted from Raphael Holinshed's *Chronicles of England*. A pageant was put on for her in the parish of St Stephen:

Upon the stage there stood at the one end eight small women children spinning worsted yarn, and at the other end as many knitting of worsted yarn hose; and in the midst of the stage stood a pretty boy richly apparelled, which represented the commonwealth of the city who said:

... We bought before the things we now do sell:
These slender imps, their works do pass the waves;
God's peace on thine we hold and prosper well;

Of every mouth, the hands the charges save.
Then through thy help and aid of power
    divine
Does Norwich live, whose hearts and goods
    are thine. . .

This pleased her Majesty so greatly, as she particularly viewed the knitting and spinning of the children, perused the looms and noted the several works and commodities which were made by these means.

Twenty years later Sir Thomas Wilson, keeper of the state records at Whitehall, wrote *The State of England 1600.* He said of Norwich 'the accounts having been made yearly what children from six to ten years have earned towards their keeping on a year . . , it hath been accounted that it hath risen to £12,000 sterling which they have gained, besides other keeping, and that chiefly by knitting of fine jersey stockings, every child being able at or soon after seven years to earn four shillings a week at that trade' (1936 ed. 20).

More and more English knitted goods were 'passing the waves'. Richard Hakluyt, the great geographer, in his *Principal Navigations* records the advice he gave in 1580 to Arthur Pet and Charles Jackman, who were setting out on behalf of the Muscovy Company to discover the north-east passage to China. The explorers were to take 'knit stocks of silk and orient [brilliant] colours, knit stocks of Jersey yarn of orient colours', knit gloves, purses and nightcaps, as well as 'deep caps for mariners coloured in stammel, whereof if ample vent may be found, it would turn to an infinite commodity of the common people by knitting' (1903 ed: 269). These red stocking-caps were to remain in wear for three centuries, and for most of that time were to remain on the English export lists. Yet the striking point in Hakluyt's advice is his concern for developing hand knitting as an industry for the poor people of England.

It is small wonder that William Lee's invention of the knitting-frame, some time between 1589 and 1600, aroused no enthusiasm in England. The story that he demonstrated his 'ingenious engine' before the Queen in person is probably fictitious, but it is clear that he was unsuccessful in promoting his frame because it threatened the livelihood of the poor handknitters. We know almost nothing of Lee. In spite of the legend, he was almost certainly not a priest. He was born at Calverton, a village in Sherwood Forest, where hand knitting already flourished; and he died in France some time after 1614. He was a remarkable man, the first to take a scientific interest in the structure of knitted fabric.

Knitting schools

This rapid growth of stocking knitting during Elizabeth's reign led to the first schools for teaching knitting. Surviving records are patchy, but enough to show that both urban and rural communities found it necessary and useful to organize knitting schools in the second half of Elizabeth's reign. Knitting was often seen as a way of keeping people out of mischief and of relieving their poverty.

At Winchester in 1578 the House of Correction articles provided that women should spin and knit. In October 1591 the city of Lincoln entered into an agreement with John Cheseman the knitter to start a knitting school, Cheseman undertaking 'in consideration of six pounds being given to him to discharge his debts, to set to work in his science all such as are willing to come to him, or are sent by the aldermen; and to hide nothing from them that belongeth to the knowledge of the said science . . . .' Knitting instruction at Lincoln continued at least until 1718.

Leicester's school is described in the *Records of the Borough.* On 21 January 1597 the minutes of Common Halls contain a memorandum on a poor relief scheme: 'It was agreed to lend unto the wife of Thomas Clerk, shoemaker, in respect she doth keep enough poor children in work in knitting of jersey, xx*li* for a year'. In fact the financial arrangements fell through and Clerk's wife received only half the sum promised. This Leicester school seems to have survived until the reign of Charles I.

At York the records are fuller. On 3 April 1588 the House Books of the city record a loan of 20 shillings to Awtherson (?) for one year 'in consideration that she teaches poor children to knit.' In 1593 the knitting school had overseers, and a review of its operations and premises was carried out. Francis Newbie was 'governor and teacher'. In September some of the poor children of the school were provided with coats 'of the cheapest grey that can be gotten.' On 5 October it is clear that John Cheseman was also on the staff. He must have come over from Lincoln. During the following summer (1594) John Addison's house was taken over and adapted for use by the school, with a new door made into Common Hall Lane. Cheseman was still teaching in 1595, when Thomas Smythson left in his will an annual grant of £5 to help the school and its poor scholars. The York school flourished for some years. Peter Metcalf was the teacher in 1614, when the school was in St Antony Hall.

In 1622 the justices for Aylesham, Reepham, Eynesford, and South Erpingham in northern Norfolk ordered that poor children be put to school to knitting and spinning dames, under the supervision of the churchwardens and 'overseers for the poor' who would pay dames when the parents were not able. Some years earlier, not far away, the Assembly Books of Great Yarmouth reflected the complex of poor relief and public order that inspired local authorities to take an interest in knitting schools. On 22 May 1605 it was agreed that 'all knitters which do wander knitting in the street shall be taken by the aldermen, constables, or any other freemen and immediately shall be carried to Bridewell (jail), being found (away) from their master's or dame's door.'

In another rural area, William Borlase in 1624 founded a free bluecoat school at Great Marlow, Buckinghamshire, for 24 boys and 24 girls. The girls were to learn knitting, spinning and the local lace-making – but the girls' school did not continue long.

By 1623 also the Lilley and Stone School at Newark, Nottinghamshire, was in existence as a jersey school. According to B.M. Dibb in an undated pamphlet *Notes on the Lilley and Stone Charities*, stockings were still being knitted and stored at the school as late as 1860.

The new draperies

The early years of Elizabeth's reign, about 1567-68, had seen the arrival of the 'new draperies', with various opportunities for enterprising management. In theory the term covered cloths lighter and finer than the old English cloths, made by more highly skilled and better-paid workmen, though in practice the term was very widely applied. Stockings were counted as 'new draperies'.

Many of the craftsmen were refugees from the Continent. With them came entrepreneurs and financiers. Licences were issued. Among others, a document in the Domestic State Papers called 'My Brother Peck's Certificate of New Draperies in the County of York' 1595 deals with the knitted stockings which were being made in large quantities at Doncaster and Richmond, and throughout the North Riding.

Details of the stockings, their construction and patterns, are almost completely lost; but Dr Thirsk has mapped out the story of the trade, especially in export from England during the last third of the sixteenth century. She reckons that by the end of the century England and Wales had about 200,000 knitters producing about 20 million pairs of stockings a year for the home market. During the seventeenth century the export trade, which began before 1580, built up to about one and a half million pairs a year. In 1576-7 stockings were being sent from Chester to Dublin; at the same time they were going to Calais, and by 1599 there were regular shipments of English stockings to Dieppe and Calais from Dover. Some Dover stockings went to Ostend. By that year London too was sending stockings, largely made in Norwich, to La Rochelle, Rouen and Bayonne in France; by Amsterdam and Hamburg to Holland and Germany. Cornish-knit stockings went to Flushing and La Rochelle. East Anglian stockings went through Yarmouth to Rouen, La Rochelle, Flushing, Rotterdam and Civitavecchia.

It is evident that England was the leading producer of stockings by 1600. This pre-eminence was based on England's old superiority in wool production and the growing improvement in the quality of worsted stockings. Even Spain, which had first sent knitted silk stockings to England,

67 The sky blue waistcoat believed to have been worn by Charles I at his execution 30 January 1649.

became England's customer once wool had established itself as the ideal yarn for knitting. A pamphlet was published in London in 1615 under the initials C.T., with the clumsy title, *An advice how to plant tobacco in England with the danger of the Spanish tobacco.* On the second page C.T. says that up to seven or eight years earlier the Spaniards had traded tobacco for fish, wine, spirits, and other goods including woollen stockings; but they were now sated with such goods and demanded money in purchase. Thereafter France and Flanders became the principal markets for stockings. The knitting-frame was soon to develop in France, but British hand-knit stockings contined to be exported until the latter part of the eighteenth century.

Irish hose

The place of Ireland in this trade is obscure. Dr Thirsk suggests that in the seventeenth century Ireland did not buy fine jersey stockings but purchased the more durable woollen or worsted stockings made in northern England. Yet Irish stockings are themselves mentioned as being purchased in England. Lincoln Cathedral Library preserves a copy of a broadsheet headed 'Proportion of provisions needful for such as intend to plant themselves in New England for one whole year', printed in London by Fulke Clifton in 1630. The apparel section of the list includes four pairs of Irish stockings, costing 4s. 6d. This looks to be a very cheap price. The explanation may be that the Irish stockings were not knitted, for Alice Morse Earle in *Costume of Colonial Times* (1894) finds a seventeenth-century reference to Irish stockings being 'much more serviceable than knit ones' (140). The Massachusetts Bay Company list of 1628 gave the price of knit stockings as 2s. 4d. a pair, while Irish stockings were only 11d. or 13d. a pair. They were possibly made of cut cloth or felt (139).

'Waistcoats'

Stockings were not the only garments knit in Elizabethan and Jacobean times. Some body garments were knitted too. The Burrell Collection

68 Pale blue silk 'waistcoat' in damask knitting.

in Glasgow has a jacket, most likely intended for a woman, knitted in stockinet with yellow silk and gold thread. A bold and florid motif is repeated all over it in purl stitches with beige thread and gold. It is described as Elizabethan but is more probably seventeenth-century and may have been remade in the eighteenth century.

Similar in technique is the elegant pale blue shirt or vest now in the Museum of London. There is little doubt that this was the shirt worn by King Charles I at his execution on 31 January 1649. William Sanderson in his life of Charles printed in 1658 records that the King on the scaffold in Whitehall was attended by William Juxon, Bishop of London. 'The bishop put on his (the King's) nightcap and unclothed him to his sky-coloured satin waistcoat'. Waistcoat then meant shirt or vest. This garment passed into the hands of Dr Hobbs,

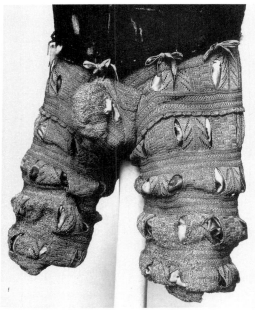

69 A rare example of sixteenth-century man's knitted trunk-hose, now in Dresden. Made in gold-coloured silk.

the King's physician, who was also present on the scaffold. Dr Hobbs's daughter Susanna inherited it. She married Temple Stanger of Rawlings, Oxfordshire, and the Stanger family authenticated the relic in 1767.

The garment is in excellent condition, though

heavily stained. Whether the stains are from the blood of the decapitation has not been proved. The craftsmanship is excellent. The tension is 8½ stitches to the centimetre. The knitting begins at the lower edge and is done in the round. The shoulders are grafted. The sleeves are also knitted in the round, from the wrist upward, and neatly seamed into the scyes.

A similar sky blue 'waistcoat' is in the costume collection of Drummond Castle, Perthshire, and a red one in Copenhagen. They are all made of silk, finely knitted, with the damask pattern in moss-stitch. Nothing is known of the provenance of these beautiful garments (see fig. 68).

The silk knitted trunkhose at the Historical Museum in Dresden probably date from the middle of the sixteenth century. Their colour is old gold. They are liberally slashed with carefully constructed slits (made in the knitting, not cut in the fabric after making). The fabric is patterned with narrow bands of moss stitch and faggot stitches as well as simulated strappings. We do not know how frequently such trunkhose were knitted nor where they were made. English sixteenth-century records do not mention them.

Wensleydale

At the other end of the social scale in the reign of Charles I we have one quaint note of peasant knitting in the northern dales, not from Dentdale, but from Askrigg. Richard Braithwaite (1588–1673) was born near Kendal and educated at Oxford. He is believed to have served in the King's army during the Civil War. He wrote much, but is best known for *Barnabae Itinerarium* (1638), a long travelogue of England in rhymed Latin verse. He translated it himself as *Drunken Barnaby's Four Journeys*, published in diglot editions. Of Askrigg in Wensleydale he wrote:

Veni Askrig, notum forum,	Then to Askrigg, market noted,
valde tamen indecorum.	but no handsomeness about it.
Nullum habet magistratum	Neither magistrate nor mayor
oppidanum ferre statum.	ever were elected there.
Hic pauperrimi textores	Here poor people live by knitting
peragrestes tenent mores.	to their trading breeding fitting.

The Latin says that they 'weave' whilst walking around, and that they are very poor. Again we notice the lack of a Latin word for 'knitting'. The picture of incessant knitting at daily tasks became familiar in all areas of rural stocking-making.

'Brocade'

Another group of patterned garments may belong to the seventeenth century: the so-called 'Florentine jackets' of which there are several in the Victoria & Albert Museum. They are very small – only 72.5 cm (29 in.) round the chest and 55 cm (22 in.) long. Similar garments exist at Whitworth

Art Gallery, Manchester, and in various European and American collections. They are knitted of silk in two colours, and sometimes have purl stitches to enhance the brocade effect. Some are lined with woven cloth, and all have been sewn from quadrangular pieces of knitting.

Though they are called Italian, there is no evidence to connect them with Italy. They were worn until well into the eighteenth century, for a London paper of 1712 reported the theft of a 'green silk knit waistcoat with gold and silver flowers all over it' and Alice Morse Earle quotes American colonial newspapers referring to 'Saxon green knit waistcoats', 'silk-knit waistcoats', and a 'white silk knit waistcoat piece' in the middle of the eighteenth century.

70 A jacket of brocaded knitting in green and yellow silk with silver-gilt thread, seventeenth or eighteenth-century, origin unknown. Length 57.5 cm, width 37 cm; sleeve 40 cm (23 x 14 + 16 in.). Gauge: 60 stitches to 10 cm (4 in.).

71 Detail of the green silk jacket in illustration 70, showing the long floats on the reverse, suggestive of framework knitting.

Gravenor Henson declared that the Spaniards invented a method of working flowered waistcoats on the frame by making inlays of gold, silver and coloured silks, and says that the method was imitated successfully in England. Josias Crane, a framework knitter of Edmonton, devised the method. He and J.P. Porter patented it in 1768. It required a man and a boy to work the machine together, and the quality of the work was not as good as could be produced by hand, though the price was high.

A century later both machine and fabric had been lost, but Henson knew those who spoke of these 'brocades' 'in raptures of their superlative beauty' (326 ff).

Although Henson seems to imply that some brocaded waistcoats were hand-knitted, we have no clear evidence. More probably the framework knitters were imitating woven brocades and possibly the so-called 'Florentine jackets' we have in England now were made of 'knit silk waistcoat pieces' produced in or near London. The square pieces of which they are made and some long loose floats on the poorly-finished reverse side of the fabric suggest the products of Crane's machine. Similar jackets now in Scandinavia are believed to have come from England.

Of course it is not impossible that the brocades were made in Italy by machine knitters. In a voluminous collection of letters on agriculture, industry and commerce entitled *Dell'agricoltura, dell'arti, e di commercio in quanto uniti contribuiscono alla felicità degli stati* published in 1763–7 by the Venetian Antonio Zanon, there is an obscure account of the introduction of the knitting frame to Italy. Having given a curiously muddled story about the craft having been invented by the French, who forgot it and relearned it from the English, Zanon tells of the first knitting machines being taken to Venice in 1614 by Antonio Correr on his return from a spell as ambassador to England.

The most interesting part of Zanon's story is that the workers – presumably hand knitters – of Venice were so distressed by the advent of the frames that

72 A jacket of brocaded knitting in coral pink silk and silver-gilt thread, of unknown origin. 1600-1800.

the latter had to be moved from their first home at Udine further away to Gradisca. It seems that stockings were made there for the Austrian market. Zanon shows that commercial knitting was done in Northern Italy in the mid-seventeenth century, both by hand and frame. He does not show that brocade knitting was done there. It would be wise to drop the names 'Florentine' and 'Italian' until their correctness is proved.

The Commonwealth (1648-60)

The most important knitting event of the Commonwealth period was the granting of a charter of incorporation to the Framework Knitters' Guild on 13 June 1657. Hand knitting was not to feel the full impact of this for a decade or so. The craft went on much as before.

The earliest known and datable written recipe for a knitted garment was printed in 1655. It occurs in an anonymous medical compendium called *Natura Exenterata:* or *Nature unbowelled by the most exquisite anatomizers of her,* published in London by H. Twiford, G. Bedell and N. Ekins. It is a small volume, a household handbook. Pages 407-16 deal with 'knitting network', which is really netting. Pages 417-19 give 'The order how to knit a hose'. The 'order' is written in a single sentence, three pages long. It is hard to follow, unclearly expressed and incomplete. The leg shapings are vague, and the foot and toe are not described. Most of the instructions describe the clock (a long slender triangle made with purl stitches) and the turning of the heel. The hose is made on four needles. (See below, p 239 for an edited version of the recipe.)

The export of stockings continued during the Commonwealth. It is mentioned in Volume II of the *Reports on Various Collections* of the Historical Manuscripts Commission 1903, in a pleasant essay called 'An English traveller's first curiosity' – an account of England's pride and products, written by Henry Belasyse (or Bellows) of a famous family of Yorkshire landowners. The essay is dated April 1657 and includes this sentence: '. . . our stockings are in great request all Europe over, especially in

73 A reconstruction of the heel of the stocking for which the recipe is given in the earliest extant English knitting pattern, *Natura Exenterata* 1655.

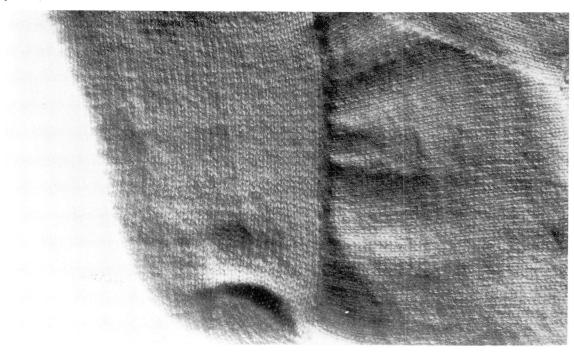

France and Flanders, so that almost, the whole man is not only covered and thatched, but is even fine and neat in our cloth, stockings and shoes' (200).

A trivial point of vocabulary is illustrated in a play published in 1659, *The Amorous War* by Jasper Mayne (1604–72). This play was probably written in 1648, before the execution of Charles I, and so reflected the manner of that time. Towards the end of the drama two women who have been masquerading as soldiers doff their disguises and reveal their true sex. This is described as:

> Amazon fighters turn to our own court women,
> And my two troiluses transformed to knitsters.

'Knitsters' is a feminine form of 'knitter'. By 1648 it had probably lost its exclusive gender-link, but the association of knitting with domestic femininity (at least by London playgoers) is clear.

The Amorous War was published after the death of Oliver Cromwell when the country was in sad disarray. In the same year the date 23 June 1659 was written by hand on the British Library copy of a tract dated 1660 entitled *A seasonable exhortation of sundry ministers in London to the people of their respective congregations*. It was certainly issued before Charles II returned in May 1660, for its preface wonders if there is to be an opening of 'a door of hope'. The message addressed by 63 incumbents of London's city churches to their congregations, refers to the 'distracted state of religion' and attacks papists and protestants alike. Sabbath profanation is a matter of great concern. The priest-signatories complain of 'some working the works of their ordinary callings in knitting and sewing of garments in our public assemblies, yea, even in the very pulpit in the time of God's public worship, to the great affront and contempt thereof'.

There are unattested tales of knitting in church. This is the only one of which I have found real evidence.

From the Commonwealth period, too, comes evidence of the social significance of the colour of stockings. Cromwell's short-lived parliament of 1653, usually nick-named the Barebones Parliament, after its fanatical member Praise-God Barbon, was also called the Blue-Stocking Parliament. Sir John Bramston, a royalist judge, records this in his autobiography written in 1683. Blue or grey was a cheap and unfashionable colour, and blue stockings meant mean and puritanical wear. They continued to have similar significance a hundred years later when eighteenth-century literary ladies' clubs were called blue-stocking clubs because the botanist and author Benjamin Stillingfleet attended Mrs Montagu's house wearing homely grey or 'blue' worsted stockings instead of formal black silk.

4 The Restoration to 1835

The Restoration and framework knitting

The Worshipful Company of Framework Knitters had its charter enrolled in the city archives in July 1657, and Charles II renewed it in 1664. Yet the development of machine knitting was slow; its influence on hand knitting was not fully effective for nearly 200 years.

Dr Stanley Chapman of Nottingham University has listed the complex reasons for which hand knitting flourished as a domestic industry so long after framework knitting became technically successful. Hand knitters could respond to changes in fashion more readily than the early framework knitters. Men's stockings were particularly liable to the vagaries of fashion until the 1670s, when men began to wear sober-coloured stockings to match their suits. Partly because the market was fickle, entrepreneurs were loath to invest heavily in setting up frames. Hand knitting was cheap because it was a sideline. Women, children and old people could be fully active on the farm and still each knit a pair of stockings a week, which they did the more willingly during the winter months, when outside work largely ceased. For such work, small cash returns were acceptable.

Moreover, it is a mistake to think that the early knitting-frame quickly speeded up the bulk production of stockings. A framework knitter working hard might produce ten pairs a week, while a good hand knitter could make six. In practice most framework knitters worked a part of the week only and so probably produced no more than about two-thirds of their capacity. The hand knitter could work almost anywhere at almost any time, and combine knitting with a large number of other jobs; the framework knitter could work only by daylight, confined to his machine. Up to 1750 the speed advantage of frame-knitting was not enough to cause the northern hand knitters of wool stockings any serious competition; and for nearly two centuries after 1750 – at least until the advent of high quality man-made fibres – the quality of hand-made hosiery was recognized as superior. Frames, however, were used for expensive items, such as waistcoats.

There is no hint of a threat from machinery when *The Life of Marmaduke Rawdon of York* was written in 1668, shortly after his death. Doncaster is there said to be 'famous for knitting stockings, waistcoats and women's petticoats' (1863 ed. 115-6). Leicester, however, was soon to feel the effect of the new technology. According to James Thompson's *The History of Leicester in the Eighteenth Century* (1871), the woolcombers in 1674 were producing 800 tons of wool annually for the spinners and stocking-knitters, keeping 2000 poor folk at such work in Leicester and district – an extensive hand knitting industry.

Nicholas Allsop is said to have set up the first knitting-frame in the town about 1680. He was not immediately successful, perhaps because the poor hand knitters were so militantly opposed to him. According to John Throsby's *The History and Antiquities of the Ancient Town of Leicester* (1791):

The family of Pougher in Leicester was one of the first that made any great progress in the stocking business. It was the practice of the hosiers, on the first establishment of the business in this place, to send their hose for sale on a horse in panniers. So great was the dislike, or rather prejudice, of the lower orders to the hose wrought in a frame, on account of the knitters, that when the business was about to be established, we are told that the frames were set up in cellars, from the street, and other secret places, where they worked by night as well as day. (403)

In many other parts of the country hand knitting would be seen as a way to improve the lot of the poor for at least another hundred years. At this period Thomas Firmin in *Some Proposals for the Employing of the Poor* (1678) urged that workhouse-schools should be set up in parishes where the poor would learn spinning, knitting, lace-making and plain work. He claimed this had been done

in other countries with so great advantage that there are few poor children who have attained the age of seven or eight years that are any charge to the parish or burden to their poor parents; and Mr Chamberlain, in the book entitled *The present state of England* page 37, has observed that in the city of Norwich it hath been of late years computed and found that, yearly, children from six to ten years of age have gained £12,000 more than what they spend, and that chiefly by knitting fine jersey stockings. (6) (see above p. 76)

Knitting had soon ceased to be the work of master craftsmen. It was a drudgery of the masses before the horrors of the Industrial Revolution made their lives even harder. In 1699 the children at Bishopsgate workhouse in London were set to sew and knit (E. Lipson *The Economic History of England*, 1931, p. 476). Firmin's idea was being taken up.

East Anglia was still a centre of the industry. Celia Fiennes, that doughty traveller, daughter of a Parliamentarian colonel, remarked on her way through Beccles in 1689 that 'the ordinary people both in Suffolk and Norfolk knit much'. At Wymondham she

'went through lanes, where you meet the ordinary people knitting four or five in a company under the hedges; to Attleborough . . . still finding the country full of spinners and knitters . . .' (1947 ed. 150)

Daniel Defoe's accounts

The Norwich hand knitters were not to survive long. The machine knitters moved in on them, not in Norwich, but by creating a new industry in London. Daniel Defoe (1660-1731), novelist and pamphleteer, is specific about this. He was interested in the subject because when he was a young man in his twenties (certainly by 1683 and perhaps as late as 1692) he had been a hose-factor (that is, a wholesaler, superior to a retailer or 'hosier') in London. In 1704 he wrote *Giving Alms No Charity* in which he noted the decline of Sudbury in Suffolk and Farnham in Surrey as hosiery markets and told the sad story of Norwich:

The city of Norwich and parts adjoining were for some ages employed in manufacturing stuffs and stockings. The latter trade, which was once considerable, is in a manner wholly transported to London by the vast quantity of hose woven by the frame, which is a trade within these twenty years almost wholly new. Men on the knitting frame perform that in a day which could otherwise employ a poor woman eight or ten days . . . so many stockings as were made in London, so many the fewer demanded of Norwich; and whereas the hose trade from Norwich once returned at least 5000 shillings per week and, as some say, twice that sum, 'tis not now worth naming. (18)

Defoe seems to have exaggerated the relative speed of framework knitting. There must have been other factors at work to explain why the Norwich handknitting industry collapsed so completely and so soon. Proximity to London was only one reason. Defoe's other writings show how the regions varied in the effect they received from the expanding framework installations.

Later, in *A Brief Deduction of the Origins, Progress and Immense Greatness of the British Woollen Manufacture* (1727), he was more specific about the date of the change:

About the time of the French refugee immigration the stocking manufacture took a new turn all over England from knitting to weaving or frame-making, to the great loss of the poor, who were quite struck out of work by them being wrought on the frame. (41)

He was referring to the influx of Huguenot refugees from France after the revocation of the Edict of Nantes in 1685, though he dated their arrival as 1682-4 and described them as settling in Spitalfields.

In the same pamphlet he declared that only a small quantity of yarn stockings was still made at Richmond and Barnard Castle and that Wales produced very few coarse yarn stockings (5). We shall see, however, that in these and other areas the hand knitting industry was to flourish long after Defoe's day. His remark about Farnham market in *Giving Alms No Charity*, for instance, needs to be read with a remark from *The Natural History and Antiquities of Surrey* – written in 1673 by John Aubrey, the author of *Brief Lives*:

From Michaelmas to Christmas the market here is good for oats and a great market for Welsh stockings.

(1719 edition iii 347)

The Welsh knitters were still able to earn money two hundred years later (see page 162).

Defoe's record of English knitting, however, recognizes that the London, Leicester and Nottingham framework knitters did not ruin the hand knitters in all districts as they did in East Anglia. *A Tour through the Whole Island of Great Britain*, published 1724-6, tells of Gloucestershire knitting of stockings at Tewkesbury, Worcestershire at Pershore and Evesham (letter 6); Somerset knitting at Wells, Shepton Mallet and Glastonbury – chiefly for the Spanish trade (letter 4); and Dorset knitting at Wimborne where 'the inhabitants, who are many and poor, are chiefly maintained by the manufacture of knitting stockings, which employs great part indeed of the county'. Defoe records that Stourbridge (Stourminster) and the country round, 'was once famous for making the finest, best and highest prized knit stockings in England; but that trade now is much decayed by the increase of the knitting-stocking engine or frame' (letter 3).

At Richmond, Yorkshire, he said:

You see all the people, great and small, a-knitting; and at Richmond you have a market for woollen or yarn stockings, which they make very coarse and ordinary, and they are sold accordingly; for the smallest sized stockings for children are here sold for 18 pence per dozen or three-halfpence a pair, sometimes less.

This trade extends itself also into Westmorland or rather, comes from Westmorland, extending itself hither, for at Kendal, Kirkby Stephen and such other places in this country as border upon Yorkshire, the chief manufacture of yarn stockings is carried on. It is indeed a very considerable manufacture in itself and of late mightily increased too, as all the manufactures of England indeed are. (Letter 8)

About the same time Defoe was writing *The Complete English Tradesman* (1726). There he listed the clothes of the poorest countryman as including 'stockings being of yarn from Westmorland', while the middling tradesman, a market-town grocer, might have stockings made of 'worsted, not of yarn'. These came from Nottingham and were machine-made; the Westmorland yarn stockings were hand knitted. The distinction is important and illuminates one reason why hand knitting as a cottage industry survived so long in competition with the knitting frame: it produced different types and qualities of hosiery.

Defoe mentions knitting in his picaresque novel *The Life and Adventures of Captain Robert Singleton* (1720). Towards the end of the book a certain Robert Knox tells how he was shipwrecked in Ceylon in 1661, where he stayed for nearly 20 years. At one point, when he was bored because he had only two books, he bartered 'a knit cap' for a bible. Later, in 1679, he and his friend Stephen Rutland, hiding from the local police while they were trying to escape to a Dutch fort, 'sat down to knitting' while they hid. When they went onwards with their journey, 'having got a good parcel of cotton yarn to knit caps with', they used the caps to barter for dried meat.

Defoe's story is founded on fact. The real Robert Knox (1640-1720) published his *Historical Relation of the Island Ceylon* in 1681. He was 19 years old in 1659 when his father's ship put into Cottiar Bay for repairs after a storm. Sixteen men went ashore and were held by Rajasingha II, the King of Kandy, who was constantly struggling with the Dutch and the Portuguese, and detained all peaceable Europeans to stop them carrying away intelligence for his enemies. The detainees were kept apart from one another, fed and housed, but given no money. Most of them went native and married Sinhalese women. Only Robert Knox and Stephen Rutland stayed single and found their way, wearing nothing but sarongs, through the jungle to a Dutch fort in 1679.

During their captivity they learned to knit cotton caps as a means of earning cash. 'The ordinary price we sold these caps for was nine pence apiece, in value English money; the thread standing us in about threepence. But at length, we plying hard our new-learned trade, caps began to abound and trading grew dead, so that we could not sell them at their former price', wrote Knox. He and Rutland traded caps for dried meat as a cover-story on their dangerous escape journey in 1679. None of them knew how to knit when they landed in Ceylon, but had learned knitting from a Tamil boy Knox's father had brought from Porto Novo, in Madras province.

This is the earliest English reference to knitting in the Indian subcontinent, but it is likely that Defoe knew of cotton knitting in India from other sources than Knox. Thirty years after Defoe wrote *Captain Singleton*, Malachy Postlethwayt in his *Dictionary of Trades* included under the heading 'Hindostan' a brief note on 'great quantities of cotton stockings knit' at Pulicat, near Madras. Pulicat was the chief depot and port of the Dutch East India Company on the eastern coast of India. The Dutch had been there since 1509. Hindu traders (called banyans) and Jews were the chief traders, and the stockings were exported to all the European factories in India. It is generally assumed that the European traders taught Indians to knit. Certainly stockings knitted in southern India during the nineteenth century and now kept in the Victoria & Albert Museum are constructed in the European fashion. None of the seventeenth-century Pulicat stockings has survived. Knox's Tamil servant almost certainly knew of knitting from this industry on the Coromandel coast.

Other eighteenth-century writers

Although it was the work of the poor, educated people knew how knitting was done. Joseph Addison (1672-1719) has a whimsical portrait in *The Spectator* of Wednesday 4 July 1711 of Sir Roger de Coverley's friend, William Wimble. Will is the younger brother of a baronet, between 40 and 50 years old, but insufficiently occupied because he does not inherit the estate, and has no profession.

> He is extremely well versed in all the little handicrafts of an idle man: he makes a mayfly to a miracle . . . . Will is a particular favourite of the young heirs . . . . He now and then presents a pair of garters of his own knitting to their mothers or sisters; and raises a great deal of mirth among them by enquiring as often as he meets them, *how they wear?*

Addison could make a joke about a man knitting. It was no joke for Elizabeth Elstob (1683-1756). Daughter of a Newcastle merchant, she published notable works on Anglo-Saxon but depended upon patronage. In 1734/5 she was in straitened circumstances and in replying to George Ballard, who had returned one of her manuscripts, on 7 March that year, she explained that she could not teach the necessary feminine arts of spinning and knitting. 'I wear no stockings but what I knit myself', she wrote, but pleaded that she was not proficient enough to teach knitting.

Samuel Johnson (1709-84) was younger than Elizabeth Elstob. When he visited Aberdeen in August 1773, as he noted in *A Journey to the Western Islands of Scotland*, he was impressed by the fact that 'the manufacture which forces itself upon a stranger's eye is that of knit stockings, on which the women of the lower class are visibly employed . . .' While in Aberdeen he was given the freedom of the city, to which he referred five years later, when he was 69 years old:

> 'A man would never undertake great things, could he be amused with small. I once tried knitting. Dempster's sister undertook to teach me; but I could not learn it.' *Boswell*: 'So, Sir, it will be related in pompous narrative, "Once for

his amusement he tried knitting; nor did this Hercules disdain the distaff."' *Johnson*: 'Knitting of stockings is good amusement. As a freeman of Aberdeen I should be a knitter of stockings.' (Boswell's *The Life of Dr Johnson*, 7 April 1778)

Eighteenth-century encyclopaedists refer often to the stockings of Aberdeen, and usually repeat much the same list as Defoe gives of English towns where stockings are made. Malachy Postlethwayt's *Universal Dictionary of Trades and Commerce* (1751) adds to Defoe's list Chipping Camden; Christchurch in Hampshire, where gloves were made as well as stockings; Bruton in Somerset; Bridgnorth in Shropshire; Northampton; and Peterborough for the making of stockings 'in which the poor are constantly employed'. The appendix to Adam Anderson *A Historical and Chronological Deduction of the Origin of Commerce* (1764) mentions the Channel Islands for coarse woollen stockings; Berwick for worsted stockings; Wells, Norfolk, Tewkesbury, Bridgnorth, and Kendal for stockings of unspecified type.

Adam Smith in the fifth edition of *The Wealth of Nations* (1789) asserted that:

Stockings in many parts of Scotland are knit much cheaper than they can anywhere be wrought upon the loom. They are the work of servants and labourers, who derive the principal part of their subsistence from some other employment. More than a thousand pairs of Shetland stockings are annually imported into Leith, of which the price is from five pence to seven pence a pair. At Lerwick, the small capital of the Shetland Islands, ten pence a day, I have been assured, is a common price of common labour. In the same island they knit worsted stockings to the value of a guinea a pair and upwards. (x.1)

The economic value of handknitting was of varying importance to the knitters. In some places it made a vital difference to the income of the household; in others the income from knitting was a dispensable extra. This point among others is made clear by Professor T.S. Willan in *An Eighteenth-Century Shopkeeper: Abraham Dent of Kirkby Stephen* (1970).

Abraham Dent kept a general store. Professor Willan's book is based on the accountbooks of the business for 1756-77 and some further letters. Dent's first business at market on a Monday morning was the buying of stockings. Knitting was clearly a part-time occupation for daughters at home and for women servants in farmers' households, but in labourers' households wives and sons could be knitters, while in widows' houses everyone might knit. Dent wrote to his London customers in June 1784 that the knitting of stockings was 'chiefly done from September to February (that is, between haymaking and lambing times), when the people have no other employ, or else they could not be done for that price.' In small hamlets and isolated fell farms knitting may have developed, or continued, as a winter pastime.

Dent was able to give orders for stockings and gave worsted to the knitters for the best merchandise. His wool came from County Durham or Newcastle, though Arthur Young said that Kendal knitting wool came also from Leicestershire and Warwickshire. Most of it was woollen 'yarn', not worsted. Much of the output was designed for army use, especially during the Seven Years War, 1756-63. Among the kinds of hose mentioned in Dent's documents are: 'marching regiments, guards, sergeants, mariners, invalid'; grey, fine ribbed worsted, fine ribbed yarn, blue women's, sergeant's stoved (i.e. shrunk), men's white stoved, white worsted, ribbed loop, loop worsted, loop yarn. But the knitters would not always do what the merchants wanted. After a very severe winter and a hard spring with snow on the ground for 15 weeks, Dent wrote on 9 April 1785:

Never since I sold hose have I experienced the difficulty in getting hose. Wool as high price as ever I knew it; knitters saucy and not to be had to our wish . . .

Hosiers were always complaining about prices. R. Campbell in *The London Tradesman* (1747) again helps to explain the persistence of handknit stockings; but he whined about the price:

Knit stockings are much preferable in durableness and strength to those made on the loom, but the time employed in knitting stockings of any fineness raises their price too much for common wear. The Scotch make the best knit stockings of any people in Europe and sell them – at exorbitant rates: thirty shillings for a pair of white knit stockings from Aberdeen is a common price, and some amount to four pounds. (*215*)

Richard Rolt plagiarized this passage in his *New Dictionary of Trade* in 1756.

John Dyer (1700-58) the poet, rector of Catthorpe, Leicestershire, from 1741–51, and then incumbent of Coningsby, Lincolnshire until his death, wrote a learned and didactic poem called 'The Fleece', published in 1757. It was admired by Gray and Wordsworth, more grudgingly by Dr Johnson. Although it describes in historic detail the story of wool from lambing to weaving, handknitting is not once mentioned. England and especially Leicestershire are praised; also the knitting-frame,

> Whose numerous needles, glittering bright,
> Weave the warm hose to cover tender limbs:
> Modern invention; modern is the need.
>
> (III 158-60)

Dyer ignored handknitters chiefly because they had disappeared from Leicestershire, where the knitting-frame was now well established.

Knitted carpets

In various European museums and collections and one American museum there are large rectangular pieces of multicoloured knitted fabric that are often called 'masterpieces'. Some of them are thought to have been knitted as examination pieces qualifying for admission to craft guilds, but because others were clearly made to order for customers, it is better to stick to the old term 'carpets'. 'Carpet' does not imply floor-covering. For Shakespeare a carpet was a table-cloth, and oriental carpets are often used as wall-hangings. Knitted carpets have been used in both these ways, and possibly also as bedcovers.

All the known carpets were described by Irena Turnau and Kenneth Ponting in an essay published in 1976. They listed 29 carpets or fragments, of which ten were not traceable but were known by photographs and published descriptions. Some of them were lost during the Second World War. Of the remaining 19, four are in the Musée de l'Oeuvre Notre Dame, Strasbourg; three (the finest collection) in the Musée des Unterlinden, Colmar; three in the German National Museum, Nuremburg; two in the National Museum at Wroclaw (Breslau); one each in the Pasold Foundation and the Victoria & Albert Museum, London; Schloss Pommerfelden, Bamberg; the Metropolitan Museum, New York; the Moritzburg State Gallery, Halle; and the State Art Collections of Görlitz and Augsburg.

The earliest records of carpet-knitting refer to Prague about 1600, the latest to Alsace about 1780. During the seventeenth century Alsace and Silesia became the chief centres of the craft, though carpets were also knitted in south German cities of other regions, such as Frankfurt-on-Main and Vienna. They are essentially a south German product.

In size they vary from 3.10 x 2.15 m (10 ft 2 in. x 7 ft) down to 1.20 m (4 ft) square. Some are oblong, but most are approximately square. Their structure is that of stranded knitting for the most part, though some have the floats woven in across the back. It is not impossible that they were made on a series of double-ended pins, but more likely that they were looped on a frame fitted with pegs. Surprisingly, the method of knitting has been neither remembered nor recorded.

Most are coarse and heavy work, but one carpet at least is worked at a tension of 28 stitches to 10 cm (4 in.). All are worked in stockinet throughout, using from six to twenty different colours. The background colour, whether light or dark, is usually unchanged throughout the work. The Silesian carpets in particular are often fulled,

74 Silesian knitted carpet from the city hall at Breslau (Wroclaw) 1674. 3.10 x 2.15 m (3⅓ x 2⅓ yd.). The colours include three blues, two reds, three greens, three fawns, two browns, black and grey. Restored in 1760.

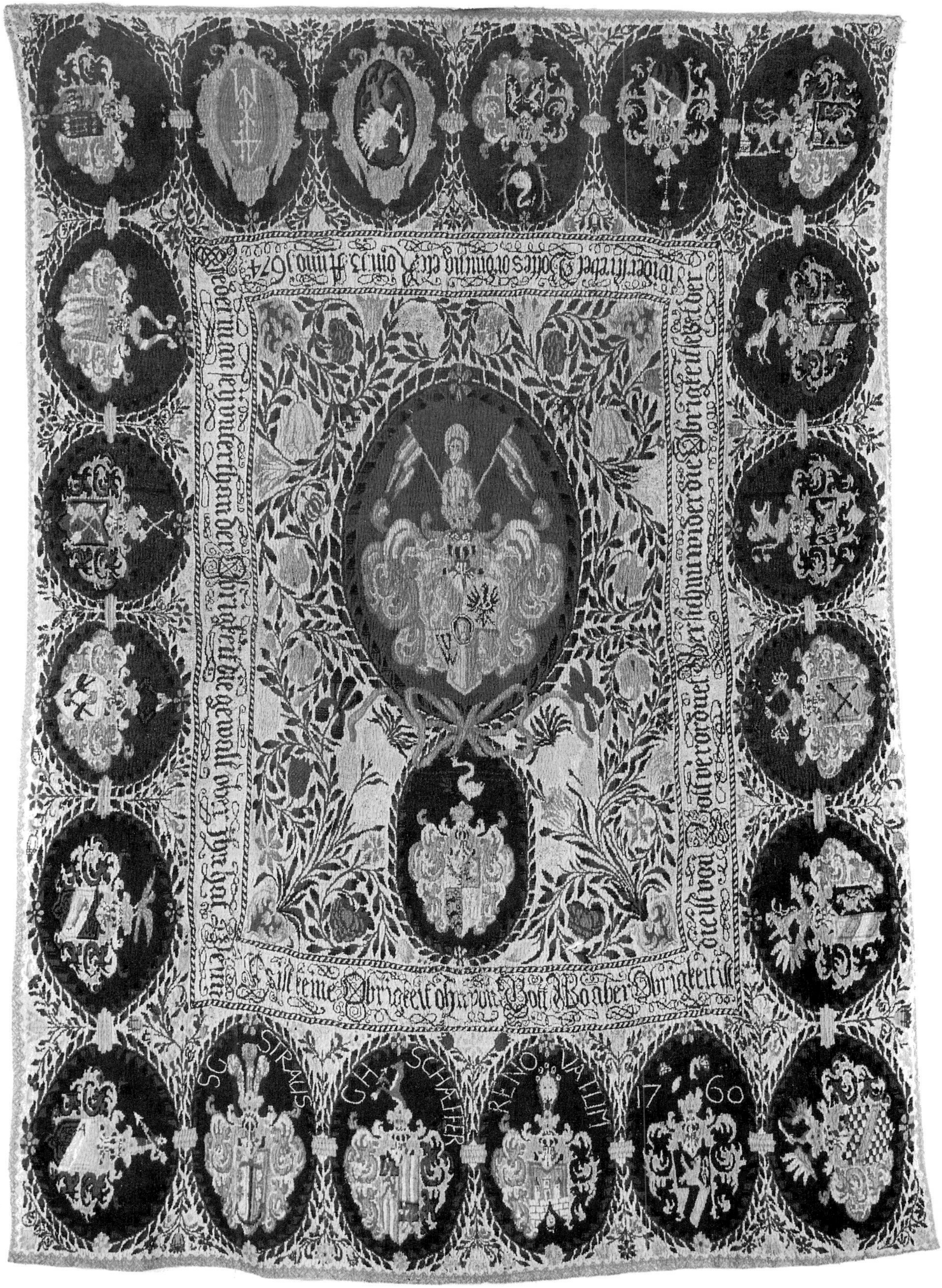
SG STRAUS
1760

sometimes so much so that the face of the carpet shows a felted nap and the structure of the knitted stitches cannot be discerned.

The finest of the Silesian carpets is also the biggest. It is kept in the National Museum at Wroclaw, and is a tablecloth 3.10 x 2.15 m (10 ft 2 in. x 7 ft), made for the city hall. In the centre is a cartouche with a half-length figure of the risen Christ surmounting the arms of the city. Twenty-one oval cartouches represent eight councillors, eleven aldermen, and two town clerks, and are spaced around the carpet to indicate the place of each man at the table. The background is closely covered with foliage and flowers. On a narrow inner border, making a rectangular frame for the two central cartouches, is an inscription quoting the thirteenth chapter of the Epistle to the Romans in German: *Let every soul be subject unto the higher powers, for there is no power but of God. The powers that be are ordained of God. Whosoever therefore resisteth the power, resisteth the ordinance of God. Rom 13. Anno 1674.* Eighteen different colours of wool are worked on a dark background.

Another Silesian carpet, now lost, was the only one known to us which had no pictorial design. It was made in 1667 by Baltazar Böhme at Neisse, and was 2.20 x 1.80 m (7 ft 2 in. x 5 ft 11 in.). It appears also to have been a table-carpet. The groundwork was Renaissance-style floral designs and wyverns (two-legged dragons). The centrepiece was the coat-of-arms of Neisse with its six white lilies.

Later Silesian carpets (at least, those known to us) abandon heraldry for pictures. Naive pictures of Christ in the Garden of Gethsemane (1688), the Holy Trinity (of doubtful orthodoxy, 1734) and the Last Supper (c1750) suggest that bible themes were staple, but there is a particular charm in the naivety of a portrait of Frederick the Great on horseback dated 15 February 1763. Sadly it is now lost.

The Alsatian carpets that survive are dated 1705–81. They are typically light in colour, entirely overlaid with multicoloured flowers and a sprinkling of birds (peacocks and parrots) and animals (lions, unicorns, leopards and deer). Adam and Eve sometimes appear among the foliage. There is usually a floral border, and a central motif: a coat of arms, the Paschal Lamb, or a Bible picture. The resurrection of Christ, his crucifixion, and Jacob's dream are the favourites.

The German carpets resemble the Alsatian ones closely, save that the imperial double-headed eagle and lion rampant figure significantly. They are dated 1690–1768. One of 1735 has a picture of the spies sent into the Promised Land by Moses, who came back with a huge cluster of grapes borne between them on a staff (Numbers 13.23). Another of 1754 shows Abraham being restrained by God from sacrificing Isaac.

It is hard to say whether the knitted carpets were made by catholics or protestants. The evidence is biassed towards a protestant origin, more because of the lack of favourite catholic symbols of the period than because the motifs are typically protestant.

Some of the carpets are fine works of art; most of them are more curious than beautiful. We have no way of guessing how many were made and have not survived. One of them could take up to six months to make, and the process must have been cumbersome. They may have been cheaper than tapestries, but in the end tapestry weaving had all the technical and artistic advantages. Carpet-knitting could not hope to survive the Industrial Revolution.

Dutch white knitting

The Victoria & Albert Museum possesses a petticoat knitted in cream two-ply worsted, 312 cm (10 ft 5 in.) in circumference and 77.5 cm (30¼ in.) deep. It is covered with a rich damask of birds, animals and foliage worked in varied patterns of purl stitches. The gauge of the knitting is 88 stitches to 10 cm (4 in.). Some of the animals – rhinoceros, lion, leopard, cranes, peacocks, storks and others – are strikingly naturalistic designs, beautifully worked in well adapted patterns of stitch. It is a huge and heavy piece of work, and the method of knitting is far from clear; it would be hard to work on needles (there are 2,650 stitches to a round), whilst pegframe technique would be complex. This work has always been dated

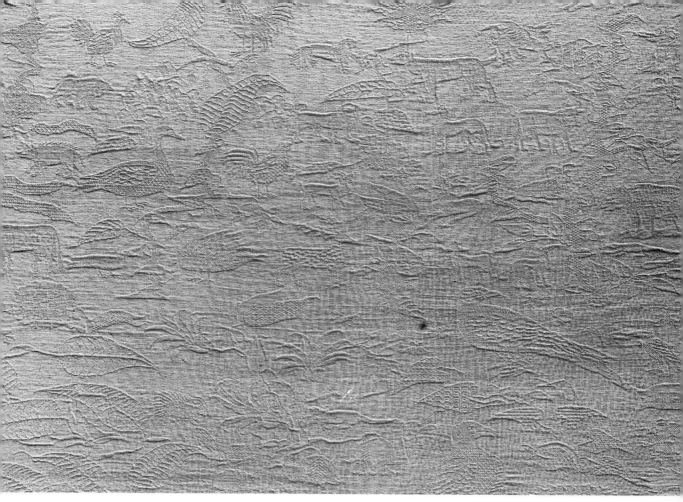

75 White worsted damask knitting of the eighteenth-century, probably Dutch. Knitted in the round with a circumference of 312 cm (125 in.).

between 1600–1800 and described as Dutch, but there has been no evidence to support this account of its origin.

Some circumstantial evidence has recently come from a petticoat of similar knitted fabric that was sold at Christie's in South Kensington on 14 July 1981. This one was covered with a diaper design in which each lozenge bore a different pattern. (In the published photograph, at least, they were all different. If every diaper in the whole petticoat was different, the work was a tremendous *tour de force*.) One diaper bore the crowned initials G.R. The petticoat was dated 1722 and discovered in America. Christie's believed that it was made for the de Rasière family of Middelburg in Zeeland. The arms showed the owner to be a descendant of Laurent de Rasière, whose son Isaac worked in the New Netherlands (New York State) in the 1620s. This does not prove that either petticoat is Dutch, but it tends to that conclusion.

Cotton

Mary Thomas, relying on the fact that cotton became more popular in western Europe during the eighteenth century, called the early 1700s a 'grand epoch of white knitting'. As the 'Dutch petticoats' show, white knitting was also done in worsted. Cotton yarn was scarcely available – if at all – to European knitters before 1740.

Wool could be produced locally, and the clinging effect of the microscropic scales on its fibres made it easy to spin, even in people's homes. Cotton had to be imported from hot countries and was difficult to spin into yarn because its fibres are like smooth scraps of tape. In India cotton was spun to make muslins and calicoes, but it lacked tensile strength and so was generally unsuitable for knitting. Indian cotton was used in Elizabethan England, unspun, as bombast for stuffing in shaped doublets and the like. About 1580 cotton yarn was introduced with the 'new draperies', but, because it was weak, was chiefly woven on a linen warp to make fustian. In 1698 Celia Fiennes found cotton being handspun at Gloucester and being knitted into stockings, gloves, waistcoats and petticoats.

According to Henson the first use of cotton in hosiery was when stockings were machine-made with Indian-spun yarn at Nottingham in 1730. The quality was not good. Although hand-spun cotton from Tewkesbury improved during the next thirty years and much effort was put into inventing machinery for spinning cotton, good knitting cotton could not be machine-spun before James Hargreave invented his 'spinning jenny' about 1764. Subsequent improvements came swiftly, especially through the work of Samuel Crompton and Richard Arkwright. The latter moved from Lancashire (already the home of cotton-weaving) to the East Midlands and met Jedediah Strutt, who established cotton-spinning mills in Derbyshire during the 1770s. By the 1780s machine-knit cotton goods were becoming commonplace.

Strutt's mills produced cotton yarns suitable for hand knitting for something like two hundred years. It was by no means always white: Strutt's strong brown cotton was famous at an early date. Lace, hosiery (some of it possibly, though not certainly, intended for dressing corpses) and bedspreads were hand-knit in cotton. Most surviving work must date from after 1780, and earlier attributions need to be treated with caution. A splendid bedspread at St Fagan's Folk Museum, Cardiff, is dated 1818.

Cotton by no means ousted knitting wool. Woollen socks and stockings continued to be the most important hand-knitted product until half way through the twentieth century.

Russia

Fragments of material said to have a knitted structure and dating from 1100–1600 have been found in various places in the USSR and are kept in Russian museums. Irena Turnau says that the first mention of knitted woollen stockings in Russia dates from the late sixteenth century. She is more certain about some of the seventeenth century pieces, especially the veils called *klobuk*. Several of these knitted veils are kept in the Palace of Armour in the Kremlin. In form they are soft domed hoods which extend at the sides to the shoulders and at the back to the nape, and have a broad lappet falling to the breast on either side of the face. Two examples have an embroidered motif over the forehead: a six-winged seraph. Such headdresses are worn by priests who are monks and by bishops, over their brimless hats. The lappets are not chinstraps. The embroidery and the pale colour suggest that these were made for the Patriarch or Metropolitan of Moscow. The knitted ones in the Kremlin are said to be knitted in silk on five needles, but they have never been carefully described.

In the same museum is a pair of raspberry-coloured knitted silk gloves, attributed to the first half of the seventeenth century. They are heavily embroidered, especially on the very large cuffs, which are of yellow satin heavily ornamented with gold lace, and thread, spangles and pearls. Gloves do not, however, form part of the vestments of the Russian Orthodox Church; these were probably made by Roman Catholics outside Russia.

In the 1630s knitted stockings were required for the army regiments that were organized on western lines. Knitters were engaged in the Moscow, Vladimir and Galitch districts, but almost nothing is known of them. It was a period when western fashions were painstakingly imitated. Framework knitting was introduced into Moscow in 1704, and to other Russian towns some 50 years later. In the late eighteenth century knitted stockings, socks, gloves and mittens were widely sold in Russia, but detailed information is scarce, and we know nothing of hand knitting.

Even the extensive wardrobe of Peter I (1672–1725) tells us little. The Hermitage Museum in

Leningrad has three of his hats, thought to have been brought back from Holland when he had been observing industry there in 1696–7. They are made of coarse undyed wool in stockinet, worked in the round on five needles, with a wide brim and a high crown. One is brown, the others each in different shades of grey. Peter's nightcap is knitted in stockinet in grey-fawn wool. His stockings are said all to be machine-knitted, as are other royal Russian stockings. Knitted bedcovers exist in the Suvorov Museum in Leningrad and some other north Russian towns.

Officers' dress in the eighteenth century required sumptuous sashes. The knitted silk military sashes in some Russian museums may have been knitted by hand.

Leo Tolstoy (1828–1910) gives interesting indications of the social status of Russian knitting in *War and Peace*. This novel was written in 1863–9, but describes the period 1805–20, before the author was born. It is probably best understood as describing knitting in Tolstoy's own early lifetime. In this period it was the servants who knitted stockings. The nurse, Anna Makarovna, will be described later (see p 106). Another old nurse knits stockings while Prince Andrei Bolkonsky's son is being born (IV 8); and an old manservant sits knitting stockings in the vestibule at the time of Count Kyril Bezukhov's death (I 22). Countess Natasha Rostova was no servant, but she sat knitting a stocking by the deathbed of Prince Andrei. 'She had learned to knit since Prince Andrei had once said to her that no one made such a good sick-nurse as an old nurse who knitted stockings, and that there was something soothing about knitting'. (XII 16 Constance Garnett's translation.) In retirement the widow Maria Akhrosimova, that 'terrible dragon', knitted while newspapers and new books were read to her (VIII 6). Earlier, it was a sign of Princess Hélène Kuragina's changed attitude to Pierre that she began knitting a striped scarf for him (III 1).

The true history of Russian knitting may never be known, for there appears to be a dearth of written evidence. It seems on the whole unlikely that it really flourished before the eighteenth century, when machine knitting rapidly became important. The immigration of Germans (the 'Volga Deutsch') under Catherine the Great probably stimulated the craft. Certainly today in Moscow tourist shops one can buy shawls made in the Orenburg region, which was established in the eighteenth century. These shawls are lacy, with uncomplicated patterns, and made of silky animal fibre, possibly goathair.

The French Revolution

The French Revolution occupied every English mind from 1789 onwards. At the time there was no suggestion of connecting it with knitting, though eventually the story of the *tricoteuses*, the knitting women by the guillotine, took on mythic value. This was especially true in England after Charles Dickens had exploited the idea in *A Tale of Two Cities* (1859). In that novel, Thérèse Defarge, leader of the female rabble in the Faubourg St Antoine during the Terror, knits constantly, even knitting symbols that form a register of the names of the condemned aristocrats.

'All the women knitted. They knitted worthless things; but the mechanical work was a mechanical substitute for eating and drinking: the hands moved for the jaws and the digestive apparatus: if the busy fingers had been still, the stomachs would have been more famine-pinched . . . on the women sat, knitting, knitting. Darkness encompassed them . . . . where they were to sit, knitting, knitting, counting dropping heads.' (II xvi)

This is sensational writing, but historical nonsense.

Dickens relied for his detail on Thomas Carlyle *The French Revolution* (1837). Carlyle mentions the *tricoteuses* very briefly as shouting from the gallery of the National Convention in November 1792, supporting the Jacobins in the debate before the trial of the King (III i 5). He mentions them again as being finally dispersed when the *jeunesse dorée*, in the reaction against the bloodshed of the Terror, closed the Jacobin club on 12 November 1794 (III vii 4). Dickens was probably also inspired by the rhetoric in the English translation of Alphonse de

Lamartine *History of the Girondists* published in London in 1848. Lamartine tells how Hébert and Chaumette egged on the sadism of the women of Paris in October 1793 by getting the Commune of Paris to organize them. An *arrêté* was issued on 6 Nivose of Year II (26 December 1793):

> 'They shall assist in the national fêtes,' said the decree of the Commune, 'with their husbands and their children, and they shall knit there.' From thence originated the name of *tricoteuses* (knitters) of Robespierre, a name which defamed that sign of handiwork and of the domestic hearth. Every day detachments of these mercenaries, paid by the Commune, distributed themselves about the entrances of the tribunal, upon the route of the tumbrils, and upon the steps of the guillotine – to greet death, to insult the victims, and to glut their eyes with blood.

Such pictures of the *tricoteuses* as exist show them knitting stockings. They began to be noticed when they took their knitting with them to sit in the public gallery of the National Convention, just as they might have taken it to any show or gathering. Stanley Loomis in *Paris in the Terror* (1965) describes them, with the street-vendors of violets and brandy who harried passers-by, as the only group that enjoyed the Terror (340-1).

Ironically, it is the same year, 1793, that gives us one true story of a knitting saint: Jean-Baptiste-Marie Vianney, the famous curé of Ars (1786–1859). He was born at Dardilly, 8 km (5 miles) north-west of Lyons, and was 7 years old when the Terror raged in that city. According to the classic life by Francis Trochu, *The Curé d'Ars* (1927), he and his little sister Marguerite went out every day to graze the family donkey, cows and sheep. They took their knitting with them, since it was the custom for shepherds of both sexes to make stockings while looking after their beasts. Jean-Marie carried a statuette of the Madonna in his blouse. He made a shrine for it with leaves and flowers in a hollow tree-trunk and used to say to Marguerite: 'Knit my stocking. I must go and pray down there by the brook.' (5,8). The pretty story indicates how the children of a French peasant family were kept clothed. Even as late as 25 January

1839 *The Nottingham Journal* reported that four-fifths of the hosiery made in France was still knitted by hand.

Aberdeen

Ishbel Barnes has described the Aberdeen stocking trade in *Textile history* 8. It can be traced to an entrepreneur of the Cromwellian period, named George Pyper, who organized the people of the district in an industry of knitting fine stockings. They were soon being exported, but the trade had difficulties in maintaining a consistent standard of product and in competing with stockings made elsewhere.

Thomas Pennant (1726-98), to whom half the letters in Gilbert White's *Natural History of Selborne* are addressed, gave figures for the Aberdeen trade in *A Tour in Scotland* (1769): 69,333 dozen pairs of stockings a year, averaging £1.10.0 per dozen, of which 14 shillings was paid to the knitters (112-3).

The stocking machine arrived in the city late in the eighteenth century, after the mechanization of the carding and spinning of wool. The hand knitted stocking trade peaked in the 1790s, when Aberdeen hose were sent to London, Holland, France and Italy. Then came the Napoleonic wars and the full impact of machine knitting. By the time of the *New Statistical Account* of 1845, the hand-knit stocking industry was on its last legs, though Aberdeen was producing coarse knitted vests for seamen, and blue bonnets.

Comparable in many ways with similar cottage knitting elsewhere in Britain, it had one interesting social distinction, recorded by William Kennedy in *Annals of Aberdeen* (1818).

> The spinning of wool and knitting of stockings were regarded more as a species of amusement by the females than as a laborious employment, and gave little interruption to their ordinary avocations. The ladies did not think it derogatory to their rank and situation in life to exhibit the productions of their own labour and to receive remuneration for it.

And a footnote records that Lady Mary Drummond,

daughter of the Duke of Perth, made and sold three pairs about 1733 (II.iii.199). Scottish society was evidently less pretentious than fashionable London.

Late eighteenth-century writers

At the same time another gentle and devout person was recording domestic knitting in a different social stratum: the poet William Cowper (1731-1800). He lived with the widowed Mary Unwin, of whom his cousin Lady Hesketh wrote from his house at Olney in 1786:

Her constant employment is knitting stockings . . . . Our cousin has not for many years worn any other than those of her manufacture. She sits knitting on one side of the table, in her spectacles, and he on the other, reading to her, in his.

Cowper's turbulent inner life was solaced by the village life of Olney, and later of Weston Underwood. From Weston he wrote to Mrs King, wife of the rector of neighbouring Pertenhall in Bedfordshire, in December 1788: 'Mrs Unwin, who, because the days are too short for the important concerns of knitting stockings and mending them, rises generally by candlelight . . . .' Shortly afterwards Mary fell on the gravel walk when it was covered with ice during a severe frost. While she was getting better at the end of January, Cowper was writing to Lady Hesketh:

Yesterday an old man came hither on foot from Kimbolton. He brought a basket addressed to me from my yet unseen friend Mrs King. It contained two pair of bottle-stands, her own manufacture; a knitting-bag; and a piece of plum cake.

(This is the first recorded use of the word 'knitting-bag'.)

Knitting was done by those without social pretensions. Jane Austen was born in 1775 and began writing her major novels in 1797. Her last books were published in 1818, a year after her death. In all her six great novels only two characters knit, and they are both ladies in straitened circumstances. One is the widow of a priest, living in genteel poverty: Mrs Bates in *Emma* (1815). She is very old, almost past everything but tea and quadrille (an undemanding card game). She sits cosily knitting, and when she cannot knit she falls asleep. Jane Austen's other knitter is in *Persuasion* (1815–16); the poor 31-year-old widow Mrs Smith. Her nurse, Mrs Rooke, taught her to knit 'little thread-cases, pincushions, and cardracks' which she declared was 'a great amusement'. Mrs Rooke sold them for her in Bath. The 'ladies' of Jane Austen's novels do not knit.

Distinctly further down the social scale were the yeoman farmers and village tradesmen. Mary Russell Mitford in *Our Village*, published between 1819 and 1832, and therefore spanning the 1820s, has little to say about knitting in Berkshire. She only tells us that the conservative Mrs Sally Mearing, managing her own farm still at 65, regarded cotton stockings as modern iniquities and wore stockings of black worsted.

George Eliot's *Adam Bede* is more informative. Although not published till 1859, it is based on the author's memories of rural life during her childhood in the 1820s near Nuneaton. The story is set in 1799–1807. Knitting in this book is practically synonymous with stockings. Adam Bede, a young village carpenter, wears dark-blue worsted stockings with his leather breeches; Joshua Ram, cobbler and village clerk, wears ribbed worsted; Martin Poyser the farmer wears 'excellent grey ribbed stockings' knitted by his wife; and Hetty Sorrel, a teenage girl, wears brown stockings. When the old man Taft goes on to the village green in the evening to hear a Methodist preacher, he wears a brown worsted nightcap.

George Eliot used knitting both to set the scene and to illuminate her characters. Mrs Poyser always kept her knitting ready at hand, and always knitted those grey worsted stockings. It was the work she liked best, and she did it 'with fierce rapidity, as if that movement were a necessary function, like the twittering of a crab's antennae.' She knitted standing as well as sitting. This is a scene of autumnal afternoon sunshine in 1801:

The milking of the cows was a sight Mrs Poyser loved, and at this hour on mild days she was usually standing at the house door with her knitting in her hands, in quiet contemplation.

Knitting readily fits into a scene of symbolic tranquillity, but George Eliot keeps it in the appropriate social class. Mrs Irwine, the bachelor rector's mother, a close parallel to Jane Austen's Mrs Bates, has her knitting by her while playing chess with her son. When the parish clerk comes in, she picks it up to disguise the curiosity that makes her stay to hear what he has to say.

In describing Adam's widowed mother Lisbeth, George Eliot exploits the emotional expressiveness of knitting. Lisbeth, waiting for her son to come home in the evening, 'stands knitting rapidly and unconsciously with her work-hardened hands' at the door of her house. When moved emotionally she throws the knitting down. Later, left alone, after feeding the dog, 'Lisbeth sat down to cry over her knitting'; and when Adam reproached her for sitting in the dark on a Sunday evening, she said: 'What am I do to wi' burnin' candle of a Sunday, when there's on'y me, an' its sin to do a bit o' knittin'?' (The forbidding of Sunday knitting survived in some families well into the 1930s.)

Lisbeth's anxiety about Adam's engagement to Hetty Sorrel is expressed in terms of knitting:

> She'll ne'er knit the lad's stockins, nor foot 'em nayther, while I live; an' when I'm gone, he'll bethink him as nobody 'ull ne'er fit's leg an' foot as his old mother did. She'll know nothin' o' narrowin' an heelin', I warrand, an' she'll make a long toe as he canna get's boot on . . .

Pride in making stockings that fit is part of the experience of many old ladies still living.

At the end of the eighteenth century knitting was a recognized part of frugal living in areas where it had never been an important source of earnings. In other areas it was still a real industry. David Macpherson in the appendix to his *Annals of Commerce* (1805) inserted 'A commercial gazetteer' in which he listed as knitting towns: Aberdeen (producing goods to the value of £100,000 annually, made by men and boys as well as women, whereof two thirds go to Holland and Germany, one third to England, Portugal and America), Christchurch (now making gloves and silk stockings), Dent, Kirkby Stephen, Kendal,

Richmond, Shetland, Sanquhar in Dumfriesshire (formerly noted for a special sort of worsted stockings, the demand for which had fallen off since the American War of Independence, 1776–83), and Peterborough, which still had some hosiery trade.

Knitting and the morals of the poor

Macpherson does not mention Rutland in his *Annals of Commerce*. Rutland, however, figures in Sir Frederick Morton Eden's book *The State of the Poor* 1797. Sir Frederick makes an interesting general comment, expressed by other eighteenth-century writers, that southerners buy clothes while northerners make them. Some northerners had never bought stockings. Rutland gets special mention by Eden because of the Rutland Society for Promoting Industry among the Infant Poor of the County. It was founded by some of the clergy and gentry of the smallest county in 1785, to give financial encouragement, chiefly for spinning but also for knitting. Sir Frederick notes that premiums were given in three age groups: children under 10, 8 and 7 respectively. In 1786, 22 premiums were given; in 1793, 89. According to the record book of the Society, now in the County Archives at Leicester, David Tomlin of Ayston was in 1795 given a premium of five shillings for knitting at the age of 3.

Children started knitting at a very early age. Redhead, Laing and Marshall in *Observations on the Different Breeds of Sheep* (1792) include among Kendal manufactures: 'Stockings of skin wool from Leicestershire, Derbyshire, etc., knitted of three threads by men, women and children, who are put to this work as early as at four years old.'

The imperious work ethic was to remain dominant in views on the education of children for another century. Poor children were taught knitting as though it were a Christian virtue. One indefatigable educator was Catherine Cappe (1744–1821), daughter of a Yorkshire vicar. Catherine lived in York, where she became a Unitarian and, in 1788, second wife of Newcome Cappe, minister at a dissenting chapel in St

Saviour-gate. She published two books about her educational work: *Observations on Charity Schools* (1805), in which she said knitting was to be taught to all pupils, including the least able ones; and *An Account of Two Charity Schools* (1800) in which she described her practice. She gave rewards for knitting, 1½d for three stockings a week or for four mittens (115). In 1786-7 the Grey Coat School supplied a knitting sheath and a new set of knitting needles to every girl at Easter (58). In 1786 a knitting school for children too young to spin worsted was added to the spinning school. Entrants became eligible for the spinning school by knitting a stocking in the course of a week.

Catherine Cappe's *Memoirs* were published posthumously in 1822. She was obsessed by her doctrine of profitable labour. Even when she was nursing her 72-year-old sister-in-law, Mary Cappe, during the latter's last illness in the winter of 1805-6, Catherine notes that Mary 'would extend her weak emaciated arms as if knitting, sewing or spinning and still endeavouring to occupy herself with the greatest assiduity.'

A greater woman educator of the period was Hannah More (1745-1833), who is credited with having started Sunday Schools in the Church of England. She and her sister Martha began their 'school of industry' in Cheddar on 25 October 1789. Although they did not teach knitting, they taught spinning. When they assessed progress five weeks later, the spinning proved to be unprofitable. Martha wrote in her journal, *Mendip Annals* (1859): 'We were then driven to the necessity of spinning worsted for the stockingmakers of Axbridge.' (24). This gives evidence of an Axbridge industry of which little is known.

Hannah More also connected knitting with virtue and frugality in her famous tract *The Shepherd of Salisbury Plain*, originally published in *The Cheap Repository* (1795), a collection of edifying pieces for Sunday reading. The shepherd is nauseatingly pious and tells how industrious his children are. 'Our little maids, before they are six years old, can first get a halfpenny, and then a penny, a day by knitting.' (12). All the children gathered dropped wool from the plain. The little girls prepared and spun it. Both boys and girls knitted stockings, using undyed wool 'for poor people must not stand for the colour of their stockings . . . Our little boys knit it for themselves while they are employed keeping crows in the fields and after they get home at night. As for the knitting the girls and their mothers do, that is chiefly for sale, which helps to pay our rent.' (15).

The rural industry

By the end of the eighteenth century the rural hand knitting industry was in irreversible decline. It remained strongest in the dales of Yorkshire and Westmorland, and there are scattered indications of its persistence elsewhere. *The Hampshire Repository* (1799), reporting on the parish of Christchurch, said:

> The poorer sort of women in the town and its vicinity are chiefly employed in knitting stockings, by which means they earn on average about 4s. a week. Not less than 10,000 people are engaged in this manufactory. It is an observation that young women brought up in this employment rarely make good servants. (II 165)

J. Claridge in *General View of Agriculture in the County of Dorset* (1793), a survey for the Board of Agriculture, wrote:

> At Wimborne there is a manufactory of worsted stockings in which upwards of 1,000 women and children are employed in knitting, who earn 1s. to 1s. 8d. for labour, the cost of the worsted being about 2d. or 2½d. per ounce, and 8 ounces to each pair of stockings, which when manufactured are worth from 3s. 6d. to 4s. per pair; and from the time necessarily occupied in the manufacturing of the article, these seem but very low wages accruing to the labourer. (40)

John Byng, fifth Viscount Torrington, staying in Askrigg on 18 June 1792, noted: 'The business of the poor is knitting of worsted hose, a very idle employ: and that I might *encourage* the manufactory, I purchased a pair for 8½d. to put on if well wetted.' (1936 ed. III 86). In the same year Joseph Budworth in *A Fortnight's Ramble to the*

Lakes was still writing that 'both men and women were knitting stockings as they drove their peat carts into town' at Kendal (1795 ed. 37-8); and in 1801 2400 pairs of stockings was the average weekly quantity sent to Kendal market.

We have two detailed sources of information about the knitters of Westmorland in the late eighteenth century. One is *A Memorial to the Trustees of Cowgill Chapel*, a booklet not published until 1868, when its author was 83. He was Adam Sedgwick, by that time professor of geology at Cambridge. He was born in Dent vicarage in 1785, and lived there till he was 19. His reminiscences were chiefly of the 1790s. He tells of the picturesque galleries which jutted out of the first floors of the houses, overhanging the street, where spinning and carding were done in the daytime for the coarse yarn called 'bump'.

With nostalgic pleasure he recalls the 'sittings' for knitting in the evening, when groups of family parties foregathered.

From one side of the fireplace ran a bench, with a strong and sometimes ornamentally carved back, called a 'lang settle'. On the other side of the fireplace was the patriarch's wooden and well carved arm-chair; and near the chair was the 'sconce' adorned with crockery. Not far off was commonly seen a well-carved cupboard or cabinet, marked with some date that fell within a period of fifty years after the restoration of Charles the Second; and fixed to the beams of the upper floor was a row of cupboards called the cat-malison, the 'cat's curse', because from its position it was secure from poor grimalkin's paw. One or two small tables, together with chairs or benches, gave seats to all the party there assembled. Rude though the room appeared, there was no sign of want. It had many signs of rural comfort: for under the rafters were suspended bunches of herbs for cookery, hams (sometimes for export), flitches of bacon, legs of beef, and other articles salted for domestic use.

They took their seats, and then began the work of the evening, and with a speed that cheated the eye they went on with their respective tasks. Beautiful gloves were thrown

off complete, and worsted stockings made good progress . . . . No one could foretell the current of the evening's talk. They had their ghost tales, and their love tales, and their battles of jests and riddles, and their ancient songs of enormous length . . . . Or by way of change, some lassie who was bright and renable was asked to read . . . and, apparently without interrupting her work by more than a single stitch, would begin to read, for example, a chapter of *Robinson Crusoe* . . . no sound was heard but the reader's voice and the click of the knitting needles, while she herself went on knitting; and she would turn over the leaves . . . hardly losing a second at each successive leaf, till the chapter was done. Or at another and graver party someone perhaps would read a chapter from the *Pilgrim's Progress*.' (70-3)

The picture is one of modest competence and pleasurable knitting, rather than of poverty. 'Dent was then,' says Sedgwick, 'a land of opulence and glee.' Yet he insists that the industry was already in its decline. The people of Dent looked back to greater days for knitters when Abraham Dent had his shop in Kirby Stephen before the American War.

The other account of Dentdale in the eighteenth century tells a different story. It refers to a date at least 30 years before Adam Sedgwick's boyhood and is the most famous literary record of Dentdale knitting: the little story 'They er terrible knitters e' Dent' published by Robert Southey in *The Doctor* (1834–7). The story came from Betty Yewdale of Rydal, who was known also to William Wordsworth. It tells of her childhood about 1760. The Yewdales lived in Langdale and sent Betty and her sister Sally, then aged about eight and six, to Dentdale to learn to knit. The children hated the constant knitting, both at home and at school. At last, one snowy evening they ran away. After spending a night at an alehouse near Sedbergh, they reached Kendal the next day, before trudging home to Langdale – a journey of 48 km (30 miles) all told.

'Terrible knitters' meant 'obsessive knitters'. The story includes some interesting details. Three or four yarns would be wound together in one ball, each to be knitted off by a different child. This encouraged speed, because a slow knitter would tangle the others' yarns. Both boys and girls were taught together. They sang knitting songs, one stanza to each needle's knitting. One song had to have the name changed every time, and they went through all the villagers:

> Sally an' I, Sally an' I,
> For a good pudding pie,
> Taa hoaf wheat, an' tudder hoaf rye.
> Sally an' I for a good pudding pie.

Betty recalled knitting coarse worsted stockings, gloves, nightcaps, waistcoat 'breasts' and petticoats. 'We strave on allt' day through neet and day. Ther was nought but this knitting!'

The early nineteenth century

Thirty years into the nineteenth century, cottage hosiery-making had declined even more. The *Victoria County History* for Somerset shows that at Glastonbury Richard Chapman of Benedict Street was the only remaining hosier in 1830, though stocking-making continued in Shepton Mallett, Bruton and Wells. The Parliamentary Commission for the *Reports on the Administration and Practical Operation of the Poor Laws* (1834) found some knitting still being done in Rutland at Ayston (for the Leicester trade) and Whissendine.

These reports also told of knitting in cottages south of the Thames. William Sleeth of Albany Road, Southwark, worked from 1819 to 1831 in a firm that dealt chiefly in home-knitted goods. The business was constant, abundant, but not excessive. By the end of the period, however, no young people were being trained as knitters. Only the older workers continued, 'but they got the reward of their struggle in the monopoly of the supply, when all the most supine had ceased to contend with the progress of the factories.'

In the early 1820s a family in Sussex might earn from £12–20 a year by knitting. This was additional to the labourer's earnings. Sleeth claimed that such earnings had been common. The general shop of the village was the place where the wool was dispensed, the hosiery returned, and the cost of the labour promptly paid – more often in 'tea, soap, tapes, needles, etc.' than in cash. Sometimes earnings were allowed to mount up with the hosier before being drawn. One family, consisting of a man past 50, his elder sister, three orphan nieces and one nephew, received three years' accumulated earnings in cash, more than £43. The sister was 'a bit of a shrew'. The girls slackened during her last illness and when she died they gave up knitting altogether.

Mr Sleeth partly blamed the parish relief allowances for the decrease of cottage knitting, and claimed to know of 500 families that gave up knitting during the 1820s. By 1828 so little knitting was being done south of London that his firm ceased arranging to collect the work and relied instead 'solely on the West of England, in parts where the parish allowance had not extended'. Yet prices were more than double what could have been earned when more knitting was done. 'But the labour was continuous and irksome; even the cleanliness which was indispensable to putting the work out of hand in a proper state, the confinement to the house, perhaps the control of the old people' were uncongenial. 'Pauper women are all gossips, the men all go to the alehouse; the knitters had little time for either . . . .'

Mr Sleeth would not have it that hand knitting disappeared simply because of the knitting machine. He wished 'to be understood as speaking of the disappearance of these people all through, not as the result of competition with manufacturers, but as the consequence of the diminished industry of parties who had virtually a monopoly in their own hands, but who wanted motives to continue the industry necessary to its preservation.' He thought parish relief encouraged idleness (xxvii 51-2).

In the same parliamentary report of 1834 a similar story is told of Weyhill near Andover in Hampshire, where paying relief had been avoided by setting up a parish knitting scheme:

> There are no girls at parish work at this time as their parents will not send them to knit stockings, which is a very unpopular sort of work with the poor, nothing being to be got at it but by constant work. This sort of employment has done much good in the parish, preventing many

labourers from applying for relief, who would have done so if the parish had nothing to set their children to do . . . . (xxviii 301A)

The knitting of the Dales declined less sharply. In June 1826 Henry Brougham, the later law-reformer and Lord Chancellor, was campaigning for election to parliament in Ravenstonedale. A local antiquary, W. Nicholls, recorded the story much later in *The History and Traditions of Ravenstonedale* (?1895). Brougham addressed the inhabitants 'from the gallery of the Black Swan Inn; and in the course of his speech, seeing several women and lads knitting whilst listening to him, said, 'This parish ought to be called "the knitting dale".' While the women laboured in the field, the men sat knitting stockings under the hedges, basking in the sun. (II 179)

The continued importance of knitting in this area was underlined by Sir Francis Hastings Doyle, commissioner for Yorkshire and Northumberland, in compiling the Parliamentary *Report on the Employment of Women and Children in Agriculture* (1843) who visited the area in January. His comment on their income is particularly interesting:

There is a district of the northwest of Yorkshire called the dales, where there is no tillage: the whole country is one large grazing and breeding farm. With the exception of a few men employed in draining, there are no labourers properly so called, the house servants of each farm being sufficient to accomplish all that is requisite. This state of things has driven the people to seek subsistence by indoor occupation, *viz.* by knitting stockings, jackets, sailor's caps, etc. There is a manufactory of that nature at the small town of Hawes, the master of which delivers the wool to the villagers as far as ten miles around. They work it up at home and bring back the articles, when finished, to the mill. A clever knitter might perhaps earn 3s. in any given week by incessant toil, but on average it would require industry and skill to realize 2s. 6d. in that period. A child, according to its age and proficiency, earns 6d, 9d, up to 1s. 3d. in the same time. The people, I need not say, are poor and live hard, but the small amount of their

earnings is in some degree compensated by the cheapness of provisions and the low rent of their cottages. (xii 295)

Mr Balderton of Sedbusk, near Hawes, wrote of the chapelry of Lunds, where there were less than 100 souls. He said the poorer class subsisted chiefly on oatbread and milk, bought from local farms. A woman knitting for 10 to 12 hours could scarcely earn 6d a day, a boy or girl 3d or 4d. Knitting was scarcely enough to earn a livelihood for the young women. Yet many places throughout Yorkshire (Acaster, Strensall, Dunnington, North Grimston, Pocklington, Patrington, Marrick, Beverley) mentioned rural knitting, it being specially noted at Beverley that children learned to knit before they were 10 (348-53). Sir Hastings Doyle was right to notice the special situation in the western dales. We shall find abundant evidence of a continued cottage knitting industry there for at least another half century. (See pages 119–24.)

For the rest of England, apart from a remarkable persistence in part of Hampshire, near Ringwood, knitting ceased to be profitable for gain, though it remained an important element in cottage economy. Esther Benzeville (1768–1851) was the daughter of a French protestant emigré silk-weaver of Hackney. She married the Reverend J.P. Hewlett in 1809, and the Reverend W. Copley after Hewlett's death in 1819. She wrote improving works for the young, published *The Sunday Scholar's Magazine* and *The Christian Gleaner*, as well as being much involved in the Religious Tract Society and publishing *The Comprehensive Knitting Book* (1849) – all of which earned her an obituary in *The Family Friend* (1858) (165). In 1825 she published *Cottage Comforts*, which includes a paragraph on knitting:

It is work that may be taken up and laid down in a moment. A set of needles may be bought for a penny, and a ball of worsted for another. It may be done at any light or with a child in the arms; and when you are tired of stirring work, knitting serves very well for a rest. In summer time you can take a walk in your garden and knit as you go – and a pair of knit stockings, when they are done (at little odds and ends of time), are worth at least three pairs of the best wove ones that you can buy. A thrifty cottager's wife has no stockings for her husband or herself but what she knits, at least until she has children old enough to do them for her. A good knitter, too, has generally got employment if she chooses to take it in; and if the scraps of time so employed add but sixpence to her weekly income, it is not to be despised. She may sit and blow the fire long enough before she finds sixpence in the ashes, or loll over her hatch long enough before she sees one roll down the street. (45)

Educational books

The Church of England, too, encouraged knitting as part of the general imposition of a heavy work ethic on the poor. The first extant knitting book of the nineteenth century came from the National Society for Promoting the Education of the Poor in the Principles of the Established Church throughout England and Wales, which eventually established the many 'National Schools' throughout the land. This National Society was founded by Andrew Bell (1753–1832), a Scottish priest who ran the Male Orphan Asylum in Madras from 1789 to 1796. There he evolved a system of monitors by which the older children taught the younger ones. When he returned to Britain he applied his 'Madras System' here. In 1832 his principles were employed in *Instructions on Needlework*, a handbook for use in the National Society's schools. The last four pages of the 25 deal with knitting. A thumb method of casting on is taught in it; yarn is called 'worsted'; plain and turned (i.e. purl) stitches, recovery of dropped stitches, narrowing and widening (i.e. decreasing and increasing), turning a heel, and casting off a flat toe are all described. The whole book has samples of sewing and knitting glued in throughout, including a miniature white sock.

Another publication from the National Society, *The Knitting Teacher's Assistant: designed for the use of National Girls' Schools*, appeared before March 1838, possibly six or seven years earlier. This remained a standard educational work for half a century. The last known edition was edited by

76 A rosewood table believed to have been used for knitting, made about 1820 in the Cotswolds. There was originally a gallery around the top. Height 74.5 cm, diameter 41 cm. (30 x 16½ in.).

Elvina Mary Corbould in 1877, when the publication number reached 43,000. The contents are restricted to stocking-making and presented largely in question-and-answer form, like the Church Catechism.

Equally practical was *The Workwoman's Guide* (1838), in which the writer set out to help educated women teach the working classes to sew better. It is a compendious book, economical rather than ornamental. For the impoverished curate's wife there are even patterns of clerical robes. The knitting section consists of 40 pages, with a strong emphasis on footwear, but allowance for pretty shawls and some simple elegances. Acknowledgements are duly made to *The Knitting Teacher's Assistant*.

German and French books

Between 1748 and 1787 at Augsburg Albrecht Schmid published *Allerhand Mödel zum Stricken und Nähren* ('assorted patterns for knitting and needlework') in five parts. The first part alone is in the British National Art Library. It consists entirely of plates showing designs on graph paper, equally suitable for stranded colour-knitting, plain-and-purl embossed knitting, or cross stitch. There is a strong presumption that some of the patterns were originally cross-stitch motifs.

The largest group of designs is of stocking clocks, and there are a number of borders. Some are all-over patterns. Only a few are successful as designs for knitting in two or more colours.

The same failure to discriminate between designs for embroidery and for knitting is to be seen in another publication. Published in Nuremberg by Susanna Dorothea Rieglin, it appeared in at least four parts, for the National Art Library holds Part IV only, dated 1760. It consists of 18 plates, very like those of Schmid's *Allerhand Mödel*, but it has an elaborate title page consisting of an involved sentence beginning *Neues und zum Stricken dienliches Mödelbuch* ('book of new and useful knitting patterns'). The patterns are explicitly for ladies to use in making bonnets, gloves and stockings. There are some admirable all-over patterns for knitted fabric, including the ubiquitous eight-pointed cross or 'star' that appears wherever coloured patterns are knitted. The smaller motifs were adapted for knitted bijouterie.

A third book is large, an oblong folio. Called *Die Kunst zu Stricken in ihrem ganzen Umfange* by Netto and Lehmann, it was published in Leipzig in 1800. A French version, *L'art de tricoter developpé dans toute son étendue* was produced in 1802. More plates of graphed designs form the bulk of the work, but there is also a lengthy introduction. I have not discovered an earlier book which describes handknitting. (Schmid and Rieglin published charts, but no text.)

The opening sentence shows the authors' sense of occasion: 'Knitting is ordinarily the pastime of country women.' They clearly intend to change the craft's image. Herr Netto is explicit. He tells how

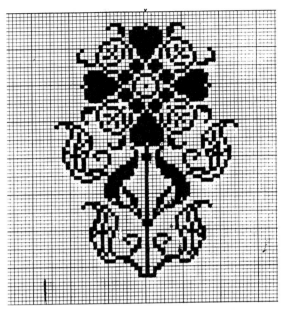

77 Floral design from Reiglin, *Mödelbuch* 1760.

78 Floral design from Reiglin, *Mödelbuch* 1760.

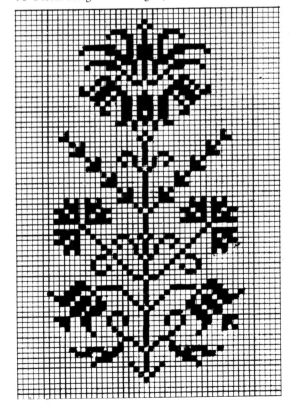

79 All-over pattern from Schmid, *Allerhand Mödel* 1748.

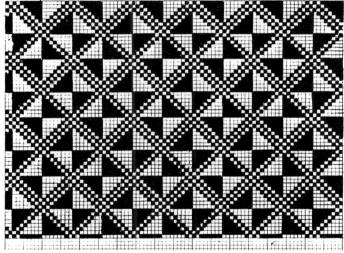

80 All-over pattern from Reiglin, *Mödelbuch* 1760.

when he was young he met a formidable Swiss male knitter called Dubois, who stayed in Leipzig in 1779-80, giving knitting lessons to ladies at a rate of one thaler for an hour's session. In 1778 M. Dubois was in Hanover, and he went on later to Dresden and Breslau. His clientele was small because his fee was high, but 20 years later there were still a few ladies in Leipzig who could pass on what they had learned from him. Herr Netto

learned from them. Herr Lehmann, who enjoyed knitting stockings, joined in producing the book, although Netto admitted it was unusual for men to be interested in the craft.

Dubois worked with hooked needles, so fast that the eye could not follow the movement. Using heavy yarn, he could finish a man's stocking within an hour. He kept his ball of yarn in one pocket, held the yarn in light tension under his arm, passing it through a horn ring hooked on his left breast. He ensured the absolute similiarity of two stockings in a pair by knitting both at once, one inside the other, using one set of needles and two yarns at the same time. (The two stockings were kept separate by working alternately purl with the outside yarn and plain with the inner. The outer stocking was made inside out.) This method is also mentioned by Leo Tolstoy in the epilogue to *War and Peace*, written in 1869, but referring to 1820. There Anna Makarovna, the nurse, always made a solemn ceremony of pulling one stocking out of the other in the presence of the children when the pair was finished (ch. 13).

Netto's book refers to the knitting of 'jugs' in Newgate Jail; but the description is of a sock rather than of the purse called a pence jug. In fact the whole text abounds with obscurities, and is by no means a teach-yourself manual, though it attempts to describe knitting movements. Casting on is done with one needle in the right hand.

There are 25 plates, each duplicated, one set in black and white, and the other hand-coloured. All the designs are delicately decorative and feminine, clearly based on drawing and embroidery, and showing no understanding of design derived from the nature of knitted fabric. They include clocks, borders, friezes, and pictures of fruit, flowers, birds, emblems, urns and neo-classical fragments of architecture. They are intended for multicoloured stockinet. Subtle shading by knitting two differently coloured yarns into one stitch is suggested.

Die Kunst zu Stricken is not a book to enthuse a knitter of today, but it marks an early step towards the increased popularity of knitting as an accomplishment for the drawing room. This development is underlined in a French book that followed it: Augustin Legrand *Traité du Tricot* (1817).

Legrand is eloquent. He has written a book on embroidery already, and has now learned enough about knitting to write on that subject too. Knitting, he says, is less esteemed than embroidery, being the universal occupation of peasant women, but if well done is fully suitable for *personnes distinguées*, and should not be considered the realm of industrious and indigent mothers only.

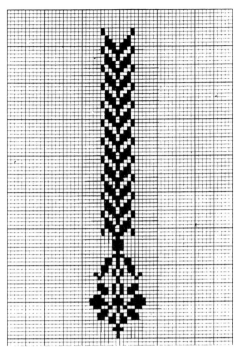

81 Clock from Netto and Lehmann *Die Kunst zu Stricken* 1800.

82 An urn from Netto and Lehmann 1800.

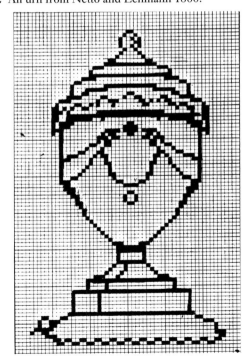

He knows a little of the history of sixteenth-century knitting, and quotes freely from Netto and Lehmann, on whom he depends heavily. He goes further than they did, by providing chapters on making a number of children's garments, mittens, and card-cases. Like Netto and Lehmann, he often gives very obscure descriptions. At the back of the *Traité* he advertises a collection of hand-coloured designs for cross-stitch or knitting *en grains*, representing garlands, vases, landscapes, with an assortment of bags and purses to be made *en perles*. Such references to knitting with beads are rare.

Lord Howick's gloves

Newarke Houses Museum, Leicester, possesses a remarkable pair of gloves. They are knitted in fine white worsted with fancy patterns worked in stranded colour-knitting of red, green and blue. Around the wrist of each Leicester glove is the inscription 'Lord Howick MP 1833'. Each glove is 22.5 cm (9 in.) long and 9 cm (3½ in.) wide. There has been some shrinkage, but the gloves were never large for a man's hand. The tension is six stitches to the centimetre in plain stockinet and seven stitches in the coloured patterns. The short wrist is made of six rows of 2-plain 2-purl ribbing. There are no gussets, quirks or fourchettes and no gore at the thumb-base. The thumb is built on a horizontal slit in the palm. The cast-on is double-ended. The finger tips are decreased regularly at three points.

The motifs resemble nineteenth-century sampler motifs. The horizontal bands each consist

83 Lord Howick's gloves 1833. Knitted in white, red, blue and green worsted.

of one motif repeated. Starting from the wrist, they are: 1 a small red crown; 2 a large blue bowl with green leaves and red carnation flowers; 3 small blue heart outline; 4 a red peacock with returned head, and blue crest 'eyed' with red; 5 open red diamond. Between the larger motifs there are irregular 'raindrop' spots of the same colour as the motif. The fingers and thumbs have, from base to tip, 1 a double row of counterchanged red and white squares; 2 red diamond outlines spaced; 3 continuous red diamond outlines; 4 tiny blue diamond outlines; 5 tiny counterchanged red and white squares.

Lord Howick was born Henry George Grey (1802–94), later the third Earl Grey. In 1833 he was Member of Parliament for Northumberland North. Were these gloves a gift? Were they ever worn? Who made them? At least they are dated.

English drawing-room knitting

We have little enough knowledge of knitting by ladies of leisure in eighteenth-century England.

Knitted items never betray much about their makers, and the dated items in the museum collections may have come from any sector of a wide social range, but their small size and prettiness put them in a category far removed from the stockings of hard-working cottagers. They may have been made for the maker's use or as gifts to friends; or they may have been the kind of thing that ladies in reduced circumstances, like Jane Austen's Mrs Smith, made for more or less surreptitious sale.

The Victoria & Albert Museum has a collection of the sort of pincushions Mrs Smith might have made. The oldest and largest, dated 1733 and measuring 18 cm x 11.5 cm (7 in. x 4½ in.), is worked in cream silk and silver-gilt thread at a tension of 9.5 stitches to the centimetre: two oblongs of stockinet, decorated with peacocks, fruit-sprays, carnations, and the initials 'EW'. In the centre of each piece is an octagonal motif. One of them can be found in Rieglin's *Mödelbuch*. The pieces have been joined by seaming, and the seams covered with silver-gilt cord.

The other three are pinballs, all round, roughly 4 cms (1⅝ in.) in diameter. The best known, in cream and brown silk, with a design of carnations and leaves (made by leaving out two of the eight points of a 'star' and replacing them with a stalk), is inscribed 'C. Osboldeston'. The tension is 11 stitches to the centimetre.

84 Three eighteenth-century pinballs. L to R: (*a*) 'An emblem of love' made at the Retreat, near York, *c.* 1800; (*b*) 'SF 1784'; (*c*) unnamed, but dated 1705 on the reverse.

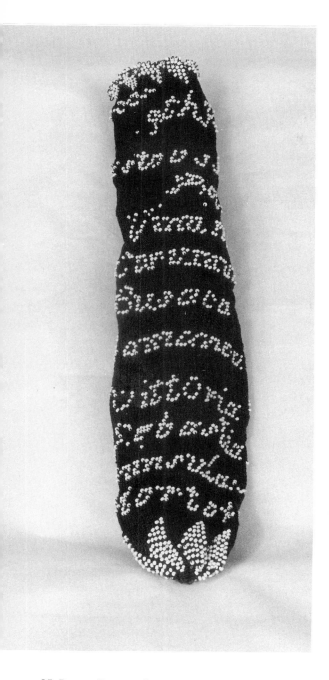

85 Purse of brown silk with white beads knitted in. The inscription, which is partly perished, lists major engagements of the Peninsular War 1808-13. Legible are: 9th Regt/ ? /Rolica/Vimiero/Corunna/ Busaco/Salamanca/Vittoria/St Sebastian/Nive Peninsula/Edwin Morton.

A red and pale grey pinball of similar size is inscribed 'SS loveth the giver 1782': and the third, in very dark brown, has a border and wreath with the inscription 'SL to RL 1805' worked in pale silk. Each is made of two octagonal pieces, sewn together and stuffed.

The Castle Museum at York has several similar pincushions and pinballs. Of these the oldest is dated 1709. It is a cream pinball, 4 cm (1⅝ in.) across, decorated with two brown birds and a green tree on one side, and a light brown eight-pointed star within a diamond on the other. It is knitted in silk at 11 stitches to the centimetre. More interesting is a slightly larger pincushion in the form of a navy blue silk disc, patterned with pale beige, knitted at a tension of 14 stitches to the centimetre. One side bears the inscription 'An emblem of love' with foliage and birds, the other a spray of flowers (including the familiar carnation) in a horn-shaped vase. A second inscription round the rim reads 'From the Retreat, near York'.

The Retreat was the first hospital in England for the cure of mental disorders, opened by William Tuke, a Quaker tea-merchant of York, in 1792 between York and Heslington. It is still in operation. The pincushion was probably made during the first 30 years of the hospital's existence. Tuke in his *Description* of the hospital (1813) mentions knitting as part of the therapy for female patients. His wife Esther, when opening the first local boarding school for girls, in Trinity Lane in 1795, had made a point of promising to teach knitting, along with needlework, English, handwriting and arithmetic, though she had set her face against teaching anything purely ornamental.

Literary evidence for drawing-room knitting is scarce. Thackeray's *Vanity Fair* gives rare references to knitting in polite society, but the characters mentioned are equivocal and the dating is suspect. Though *Vanity Fair* appeared in 1847, it told a story of events beginning in 1810, when Thackeray was only 1 year old. He studiously avoided anachronisms, but his modern editors, the Tillotsons, have discovered enough to warn us against the accuracy of his references to knitting. Thus, when in Chapter 4 we read of Becky Sharp, a young woman on the make, knitting a green silk purse for the clumsy Joseph Sedley as part of her campaign to persuade him to propose marriage, we have a clear picture of what such a woman might have done in 1847, but less certainly a true description of such a woman in 1810. By contrast, in Chapter 8 when we meet Lady Crawley in her country house, she is 'always knitting worsted' and in the drawing room after dinner 'took from her work-drawer an enormous interminable piece of knitting.' In the next chapter we learn that 'She worked that worsted day and night, or other pieces like it. She had counterpanes in the course of a few years to all the beds in Crawley.' The picture is carefully drawn: this was not drawing-room knitting. Lady Crawley was the daughter of an ironmonger, a misfit in society, whose ineptitude is typified by her knitting.

Thackeray does, however, give what must be a reliable reference to German knitting in Chapter 62. There he describes a journey through the cities of the Rhine, which he himself knew when he was 20 and visited Goethe at Weimar. 'They went to the opera often of evenings – to those snug, unassuming, dear old operas in the German towns, where the noblesse sits and cries and knits stockings on the one side, over against the bourgeoisie on the other . . . .'

So far as England goes, Thackeray's memory bridges the great change for knitting in England that happened about 1835. From that year onwards there was an explosion of knitting in the educated classes.

5 The Victorian age and the *belle époque*

Knitting and the gentry

About 1835 knitting became a fashionable pastime for English and Scottish ladies. The date is fixed by references in the first English knitting books, which appeared between 1835 and 1840. Their great popularity is proved by the huge numbers that were printed.

What were the factors that lay behind this development? Miss Lambert in her *Handbook of Needlework* 1842 noted the development of the fancy wool trade from Germany. After the defeat of Napoleon in 1815, trade with the continent was

86 Two reticules of knitted straw, with straw bobbin-lace trim and dyed straw embroidery. 1820.

thrown open and the wool dealers of Saxony (the region now in the German Democratic Republic, with its capital at Dresden and its wool industry centred on Gotha) established a regular trade with England. The Saxony wool was from merino flocks. Because of their fine soft wool, merinos had been introduced into most other European countries from Spain during the eighteenth century, but the Elector of Saxony had the greatest success with them. From 1765 to 1814 the number of merinos in Saxony increased, and the climate and soil fostered the production of silky, high-quality fleeces. Miss Lambert draws attention to this story as related in *Histoire de l'Introduction des Moutons à Laine Fine* (1802) by Count Charles Philibert de Lasteyrie du Saillant (English translation by B. Thompson, 1810).

These fine wools took dyes well. Wool 'tapestry work' often called gros-point, became popular in Germany before the fall of Napoleon. Patterns were imported into England from the early 1830s under the general name of 'Berlin work', and 'Berlin wool' became a familiar commodity. Not least because of its colour range, which was rich in both hues and tones, this attractive yarn stimulated the rise of knitting as an artistic pursuit.

Royal patronage played its discreet part. The young queen's bridegroom, Albert of Saxe-Coburg-Gotha, came from the centre of the German wool country. Victoria noted in her journal on 9 April 1841: 'Albert read to me out of "Oberon", whilst I knitted'. Her governess, Baroness Lehzen, did fine knitting and may have encouraged her.

A writer in the *Magazine of Domestic Economy*, early in 1838, remarked that fashion had 'of late years . . . . . allowed their [the knitting needles'] introduction into the drawing-room in furtherance of those schemes miscalled charitable, which require a constant supply of pretty articles, useless for every purpose except to get rid of those hours which, but for their aid, might not be so innocently disposed of.'

Jane Gaugain

Knitting recipes were called for. The earliest recorded publication, though no copy is known to survive, was the private printing for friends in 1836 of three recipes by Jane Gaugain of George Street, Edinburgh. In 1837 she published her first 'small work on fancy knitting'. In 1840 her collected recipes were issued in *The Lady's Assistant*, a book of 200 pages, containing netting and crochet as well as knitting, and expensively priced at 5s. 6d. An appendix was published before the year was out; Volume II, costing 10s. 6d, appeared in 1842, with an *Accompaniment* for half-a-crown in 1842; then in 1846 came Volume III, again 10s. 6d, or 12s. 6d. with plates. In 1843 there had been a *Miniature Knitting, Netting and Crochet Book* for one shilling, that ran to 23,000 copies by 1846, when a cheap selection of 'the more useful and saleable articles' appeared for 'that numerous and useful

class of females, whose pecuniary means are limited, but whose minds and products are well regulated and directed.' The title page calls it *The Knitter's Friend*, but the golden dye stamp on the cover says *The People's Book* and gives the price as 2s. 6d.

We know little of Mrs Gaugain. The Edinburgh Post Office directories list J.J. Gaugain as a fancy warehouse selling 'French bland (or blond, a lace of hexagonal mesh, originally of écru colour), flowers, cambrics, fans, materials for ladies' fancy work, braids and stationery' at 63 North Bridge in 1824. The following year the Gaugains were at an address in George Street. In 1827 they had moved along the street. Between 1830 and 1832 they occupied two premises successively in Frederick Street. In 1836 they were established at 63 George Street, where they were still at the time of their last entry in the directory in 1852-3, and whence all the knitting books were published. The changes of address suggest a developing business. The list of patronesses of the books is headed by the Queen Dowager, Adelaide, and continues with the royal duchesses and about 700 ladies, mostly Scottish.

The contents of Jane Gaugain's books are not frivolous. She gives recipes for caps, counterpanes, purses, baby clothes, shawls, bags, pin-cushions, doyleys, cuffs, muffs, spencers, blankets, scarfs, mittens, stockings, re-footing stockings, and a variety of fabric-patterns. Most of the fabrics are based on eyelets or faggots. Some of the patterns, such as the elaborate lace stocking in Volume III, copied from a Maltese original, are very difficult. On the whole the technique is good, but like many nineteenth-century writers she is liable to fail to prescribe the use of 'knit two together' and 'knit one, slip one, pass the slip stitch over' to produce symmetrically inclined decreases.

Jane Gaugain was proud of the abbreviations she used in her receipts and of which she was the inventor. They were partly initial letters for the words signified (B for back stitch or purl; T for take in, or decrease; P for plain stitch) and partly pictograms of the stitches (A for working three stitches into one). Inverted letters were used for some actions: inverted A for purling three together and inverted T for purling two together. Abbreviations were not adopted by other writers and they fell out of fashionable use until 1906, when a completely different set, the original of the abbreviations now in use, was invented for *Weldon's Practical Needlework*.

Mrs Gaugain gave some of her recipes extra charm by giving them mildly exotic foreign names: Maltese spotting, Barège scarf, Turkish, Pyrenees and Russian shawls, Alpine scarf. These names must be regarded with suspicion. Some are real indications of the place of origin of the pattern, but most are probably not. Jane Gaugain published 16 books containing knitting patterns between 1837 and 1854. She had died by 1863 when *The Lady's Assistant* was reissued in 12 parts 're-arranged and improved by the Proprietor', and published by Harrison of Pall Mall. In 1875 the 22nd edition was issued in a single volume.

Frances Lambert

Frances Lambert was an erudite woman. Her first publication was *The Handbook of Needlework* published by John Murray in 1842 at 9s 6d. A fifth edition appeared in 1847, (cheaper at 6s 6d) and there were at least two American printings. It is spangled with literary quotations, has informative footnotes, and one or two recipes in French. Knitting occupies 54 of her 360 pages, and she has an excellent essay on wools.

She is the first writer to give any attention to tension, though she does no more than warn her readers to knit at medium tension. She recommends making a selvedge stitch, usually by slipping the first in each row, calling it an 'edge stitch'; and she suggests that stitches to be held should be left, not on a needle, but a piece of coarse silk. She also says 'It is easiest to learn to knit by holding the wool over the fingers of the left hand; the position of the hands is more graceful when thus held.' This method was already known in England because *The Workwoman's Book* (1838) calls it 'Common Dutch Knitting'. It was not the traditional English method. Interestingly, Miss Lambert commends it for its elegance rather than its supposed speed.

In 1843 Miss Lambert issued *My Knitting Book*. It partly repeats the knitting section of her earlier

book and gives the first account of needle sizes. She had 'some time since' invented a 'standard filière' or disc-shaped gauge punched with holes sized 1–26 according to the British Standard Steel Wire Gauge. Although this scale was not constant in its minute measurements, and sizes below 16 (1.5 mm) hardly survived into the twentieth century, it remained the standard for British needle sizes until 1977. Size 26 was 0.4 mm.

In this book, too, the author explains the origin of the name 'brioche'. 'Brioche' is the stitch for making a doughnut-shaped cushion 'so called from its resemblance in shape to the well known French cake of that name.' Her colour-schemes are slightly subtler than Jane Gaugain's. The latter freely mixed brilliant colours in many shades. Miss Lambert tends to cerise and brown; claret and green ; 'four shades of sable'; claret and blue; lilac and white.

In 1845 she produced *My Knitting Book: Second Series* in the same style and format. It contains a cabled pattern and a variety of fabric stitches. By 1847, 23,000 copies had been printed, and 42,000 of the first volume, which had also been translated on the continent of Europe, and reprinted in America. Each volume cost 1s 6d.

In 1838 Kelly's Post Office directory of London gave Miss Lambert's address as 7 Conduit Street. She was then embroideress to the Queen and had a repository for fancy needlework and drawing. By 1842 her address was 3 New Burlington Street. We know no more.

Miss Watts

The Ladies' Knitting and Netting Book, published anonymously in 1837, says that 'At a period when all fancy works are so justly appreciated and highly patronized, it is presumed that this little volume, the only one hitherto published on this subject, may be valuable'. The book sold out in nine months, so a second edition was issued in 1838. In 1839 there was a 'second series' and in 1843 a 'third series'. By 1844 the author's name, Miss Watts of Islington, had appeared on *The Illustrated Knitting, Netting and Crochet Book*. Yet it seems that

87 An 'Octagon Cover for an Easy Chair' designed by Mrs Warren. The design was published in five instalments of *The Family Friend* 1850. Knitted by Edna Treen, 1985.

there were at least two authors, for in the 1843 book they refer to themselves as 'the authoresses'. Perhaps their punctuation of *Miss Watts'* was intended to imply a plural name.

Cornelia Mee

On another writer of the same period, Cornelia Mee, we are better informed. Her great-grandson Sir Patrick Reilly had a memoir of her privately printed for the family in 1983. She was born Cornelia Austin in Bath on 23 April 1815. Her father, Thomas Austin, was a haberdasher and undertaker who had recently moved to Bath from Hackney, where he had been a bookseller. Her maternal grandparents were German refugees. Cornelia was baptized by the famous William Jay of Argyle Street chapel, the leading non-conformist minister in the town. Her mother died in childbirth in 1829, and her father, at the age of 45, in 1830. Cornelia at 14 was one of seven orphans.

In 1837 she married Charles Mee. They had a Berlin warehouse, or needlework shop, at 41 Milsom Street. There she prepared the *Manual of Knitting, Netting and Crochet*, first published in 1842, which was to be her most important work. Her first baby died in 1840, but she had three more daughters by 1844. While she was bringing up these tiny children she published 19 items on needlework in the six years 1842–47, most of them on crochet, which she claimed to have invented 'nothing being known till she published her first book on crochet but the common shepherd's-crook crochet'. (The words appear on the cover of *Bijou Receipts for Baby's Wardrobe* published about the time of her death.)

In 1847, together with her sister, Mary Battle Austin, who was then 18, she started a monthly magazine *The Worktable Magazine*. It appeared for six months, then ceased. In 1848 Cornelia alone published a tiny book of *Polka Jackets in Knitting and Crochet*. The *Manual of Needlework* followed in 1854 and *The Alliance Book of Knitting, Netting and Crochet* in 1856. *The Manual of Needlework* was her last long book. Thereafter she produced nothing bigger than 32 pages, usually priced at one shilling or sixpence.

Early in 1858 the Mees moved to London and conducted their business from 229 Regent Street, though Cornelia sometimes visited Bath and met clients and pupils at No 3 Vineyards. In the spring of 1860 she moved her London house and business to Brook Street, by Grosvenor Square. It was a select and fashionable district, where only the most discreet of businesses could have been conducted. Mary Austin lived with them.

Cornelia continued to publish crochet manuals, and in 1861 the first of four 'series' or volumes of *The Knitter's Companion*, of which the third book confusingly had a second title: *The Queen's Winter Knitting Book* (1862). It cost 6d and its origin was explained:

> So many applications have been made for rules for making warm things for the poor of Lancashire, this little book has been hastily arranged in an inexpensive form to meet the wishes of many benevolent ladies who are occupying their time in working for the distressed operatives.

The distress in Lancashire was caused by the loss of the textile industry's main source of cotton because of the American Civil War.

About 1874 Cornelia moved to 1 Langham Place. It is possible that her husband parted from her. It seems that both Cornelia and her sister were ill. They continued to prepare knitting and crochet recipes for publication, but now in the form of 'bijou cards'. Secondhand copies of their books were very expensive and hard to find – there was a change coming in the publishing climate. Mary Austin died early in 1875. Cornelia Mee died a few months later, in the home of her married daughter in Stoke Newington. Her husband died in Bath in 1888. Her business was carried on by her unmarried daughter, Agnes Cordelia, till it petered out about 1890.

Cornelia Mee dominated the polite English knitting and crochet world for 30 years. She saw herself as an innovator and constantly drew attention to the new ideas in her books. Her books were mostly small, but they sold prodigiously – certainly more than 300,000 copies in all.

The first series of *The Knitter's Companion* alone was issued in 55,000 copies (11 editions) between

1861 and 1875. All her patterns were essentially useful. Though she made a point of prettiness, she did not encourage frivolity.

Mlle Riego de la Branchardière

Mlle Eleanore Riego de la Branchardière was in many ways a rival to Cornelia Mee. Her publications began in 1846 and the last appeared in 1888. Like Mrs Mee, she was acclaimed as the inventor of crochet. When Mrs Rivers Turnbull of the *Queen* newspaper edited a posthumous selection of Mlle Riego's work in 1904, she confidently declared that Mademoiselle had been the best writer of her day on crochet, knitting, lace-work and tatting. She won the only gold medal awarded for crochet at the Great Exhibition of 1851, and in fact wrote far more about crochet than knitting.

According to Mrs Turnbull, Mlle Riego was born in England, the daughter of a French nobleman driven from France by the Revolution, and an Irish lady. She took an interest in the Irish all her life and encouraged the development of Irish crochet lace. At her death she left most of her fortune for the benefit of Irish industries. She claimed that her first professional knitting was for the Duchess of Kent, Queen Victoria's mother, and was proud to work for the women of the royal family.

Her *Knitting Book* of 1847 was unusual in that it began with illustrated instructions on how to knit. Most other books of the day assumed a knowledge of fundamentals. Her pictures show the needles being held under the palms of the hands in the traditional manner, not in the new elegant fashion promoted by such as Frances Lambert. (See fig. 16.)

In 1867 her address was 2 Old Quebec Street; in 1886 it was 43 Southampton Row. She won needlework medals in 1851, 1855, 1862, and 1872, and worked 'by appointment' for the Princess of Wales. Throughout her career she noted anxiously that her work was being plagiarized and pirated. It seems that she did not marry.

The drawing-room books

What Jane Gaugain, Miss Watts, Frances Lambert and Cornelia Mee began about 1840 turned into an avalanche of books in 1846 and 1847. Little books of knitting patterns appeared all over England, generally from ladies who had an interest in teaching needlework or selling needlework materials and tools. Nearly all the books were very small and some were slender volumes. A few were downright shabby, especially the penny numbers on cheap paper, sold uncut, at the time of the Great Exhibition of 1851. Yet others had illustrations of great charm.

Many are very poorly edited. Recipes are impossible to follow or contain alarming mistakes, though all claim to be edited with care and precision. The authors expected knitters to be skilled in using the sometimes very sketchy outlines provided in the recipes; there is hardly ever a word about tension, and sometimes not even a suggestion about needle size.

Noble and gentle patronage is often claimed. It was good business practice to do so. So perhaps, too, was the high moral and even religious tone of the editorial comment. It must be admitted that this moral tone is least obvious in the better known writers, and that the most solemn and pious effusion is from an anonymous work: Clarke and Company's *The Ladies' Handbook of Knitting, Netting and Crochet*, which sold well in 1842 and 1843. It drew liberally on the work of Frances Lambert and others. But it was original in urging 'the youthful female, as she plies her needle or exercises her judgment or ingenuity in the choice of colours or materials, or in the invention of new developments of creative genius, ever to remember to exercise those powers as a Christian . . . and let her be careful to make all she does a sacrifice acceptable to her God . . . .' In 1843 the 'young votaress of the needle' was further adjured that she should 'ever bear in mind that the time employed in those pursuits will be accounted lost or improved, by the impartial judge of all, just in proportion as they have been made to serve the purposes of selfish gratification or to minister to the development of an elevated moral character, generous and warm affections, and the cultivation of these virtues which, as essentials to the Christian character, shall outlive the ravages of time, and qualify the soul for all the beatitudes of a coming eternity.'

This is the very antithesis of that frivolity with which twentieth-century writers like to tax Victorian lady knitters. Because of an occasional recipe for a knitted napkin for a Stilton cheese and a delight in miniature creations, Victorian knitting is quite unfairly dismissed as trivial. I can allow that *The Floral Knitting Book* (1847), with its instructions for knitting artificial fuchsias, geraniums, narcissus, snowdrops, and yellow jessamine is not to the taste of the 1980s; but I doubt if Victorian products were more horrid than the plastic flowers and knitted toilet-roll covers in vogue today.

Miniature knitting, in a strict sense, is rare. Abbot Hall Art Gallery, Kendal, possesses a notable piece: a pence jug 1 cm (³⁄₈ in.) high, coral pink in colour, with two cream bands. It consists of 24 rounds of ribbing, 36 stitches in circumference at the widest point. It has survived because it

88 Pence jugs knitted from Victorian recipes. L to R: (*1*) Hope *The Knitter's Friend* 1847; (*2*) & (*3*) E.M.C (Corbould) *The Lady's Knitting Book* 1st series, 1874; (*4*). Miss Lambert *My Knitting Book* 1847. (*1*) and (*4*) were reprinted in other books as late as 1891 and 1892. E.M.C. called (*4*) 'Etruscan'.

belongs to a pedlar doll or 'notion nanny', kept under a glass bell-case. Pedlar dolls were made in the late eighteenth and early nineteenth centuries. The Abbot Hall example has a vendor's stall stuffed with a magpie collection of miniature bric-a-brac – books, toys, stuffed birds, jewellery, and much else besides – among them the tiny pence jug. It is dated about 1820.

Mrs Banks

Mrs George Linnaeus Banks was in several ways a typical knitting writer of her time. She was born Isabella Varley, daughter of a Manchester haberdasher, in 1821. As a little girl she knitted doll's clothes with sewing cotton on dressmaker's pins. She became a schoolteacher and in 1846 married a liberal journalist from Birmingham. In the following year, aged 26, she published *The Lace Knitter's Intelligible Guide* at the height of the knitting book boom.

Her husband's career took her to live in Harrogate, Birmingham, Dublin, Durham, Sussex and Windsor, before they settled at Islington in 1861. Shortly before George died in 1881, Isabella began her most important novel, *The Manchester Man* (published 1896). They both wrote prolifically. For some years she issued quarterly needlework patterns, including at least 96 numbers

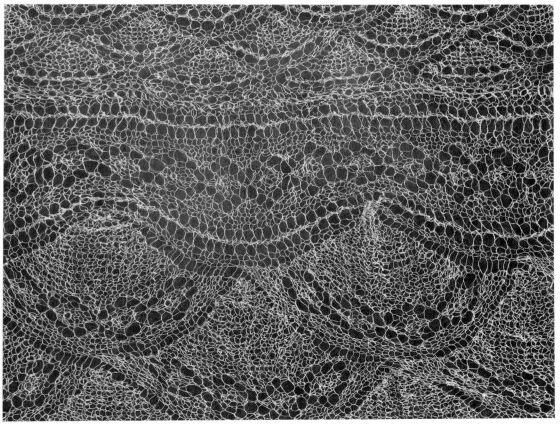

of *Light Work for Leisure Hours*. Mrs Banks died in 1897. Her biography was written by E.L.Burney (1969).

Azores Lace

Very delicate lace is knitted on the Azores, those nine Portuguese islands in the warmer part of the north Atlantic. Frances Dabeney wrote about the islands in *Harper's Bazaar* 2 December 1893:

'In 1841 or 42 an impulse was given to the knitting of fine open-work hose, which is done by the peasant women on five very fine, slightly curved, barbed needles . . . The knitting of aloe lace has reached perfection, both in variety of patterns, which, like those of the open-work hose, are generally original, and invented by the knitters themselves; and in the delicacy of the fibre, which is split many times. Shawls, dresses, fichus, in fact anything for which lace may be properly used, are made in aloe.' (996).

The aloe fibre, derived from the century plant, *Agave americana*, is known as *pita* in Portuguese. Hence Azores lace is also called pita lace. The plant was introduced to the islands during the second quarter of the nineteenth century in a deliberate attempt to produce a textile-fibre crop. The knitted lace, which is centred on the town of Ponta Delgada on the island of Sao Miguel, has close similarities to the knitted lace of Spain and Portugal.

The Dales knitters

By the beginning of Queen Victoria's reign the hand-knitting industry of the Dales had dwindled. From Richmond it had virtually disappeared, but further west it continued to be important, as the parliamentary commission had discovered in 1831. The whole subject has been admirably treated by Marie Hartley and Joan Ingilby in *The Old Handknitters of the Dales* (1951). What I have written here is inevitably much indebted to their work. (See pages 100-2.)

The classic account of the Dales knitting in mid-Victorian times was written by William Howitt (1792–1879). He was a Nottingham chemist, an industrious author and a keen tourist. His description of Dentdale in *The Rural Life of England* (1844) (307-10) is comprehensive and typical of the whole region.

Men, women and children all knit. Formerly you might have met the wagoners knitting as they went along with their teams; but this is now rare, for the greater influx of visitors and their wonder expressed at this and other practices has made them rather ashamed of some of them and shy of strangers observing them. But the men still knit a great deal in the houses; and the women knit incessantly.

They have knitting schools, where the children are taught, and where they sing in chorus knitting songs, some of which appear as childish as the nursery stories of the last generation. Yet all of them bear some reference to their employment and mode of life; and the chorus, which maintains regularity of action and keeps up the attention, is of more importance than the words. Here is a specimen:

Bell-wether o' Barking cries 'Baa, baa',
How many sheep have we lost today?
Nineteen have we lost, one have we fun';
Run Rockie, run Rockie, run, run, run.

This is sung while they knit one round of the stocking; when the second round commences, they begin again:

Bell-wether o' Barking . . .
Eighteen have we lost, two have we fun'; . . .

And so on till they have knit twenty rounds, decreasing the numbers on the one hand and increasing them on the other.

These songs are sung not only in the schools,

89 *(facing page, above)* Azores shawl. Nineteenth century. Made of pita, the fibre of an agave. 222 cm by 105 cm (88 x 42 in.).

90 *(facing page, below)* Detail of the shawl in 89.

91 Azores lace mat. These mats, unlike German lace in similar style, usually have the border knitted as a strip and sewn on, as in this example. Twentieth century.

but also by the people at their 'sittings', which are social assemblies of the neighbourhood, not for eating or drinking, but merely for society. As soon as it becomes dark and the usual business of the day is over and the young children are put to bed, they rake or put out the fire, take their cloaks and lanterns, and set out with their knitting to the house of the neighbour where the sitting falls in rotation, for it is a regularly circulating assembly from house to house through the particular neighbourhood. The whole troop of neighbours being collected, they sit and knit, sing knitting songs and tell knitting stories. Here all the old stories and traditions of the dale come up; and they often get so excited that they say, 'Neighbours, we'll not part tonight,' – that is, till after twelve o'clock. All this time their knitting goes on with unremitting speed. They sit rocking to and fro like so many weird wizards. They burn no candle, but knit by the light of the peat fire.

And this rocking motion is connected with a mode of knitting peculiar to the place, called 'swaving', which is difficult to describe. Ordinary knitting is performed by a variety of little motions, but this is a single uniform tossing motion of both the hands at once and the body often accompanying it with a sort of sympathetic action. The knitting produced is just the same as by the ordinary method.

They knit with crooked pins called 'pricks', and use a knitting-sheath consisting commonly of a hollow piece of wood, as large as the sheath of a dagger, curved to the side and fixed in a belt called the cowband. The women of the north, in fact, often sport very curious knitting-sheaths.

1 The Chur relic purse. Fourteenth century, possibly made at Regensburg. *(Museum der Kathedrale, Chur)*

2 The Sens purse, probably originally used for relics. Thirteenth century. *(Musée de Sens)*

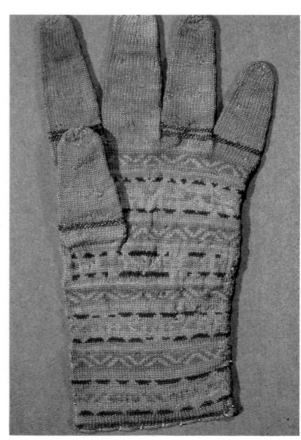

3 The Sture glove, 1565. *(Riksantikarieämbetet, Stockholm)*

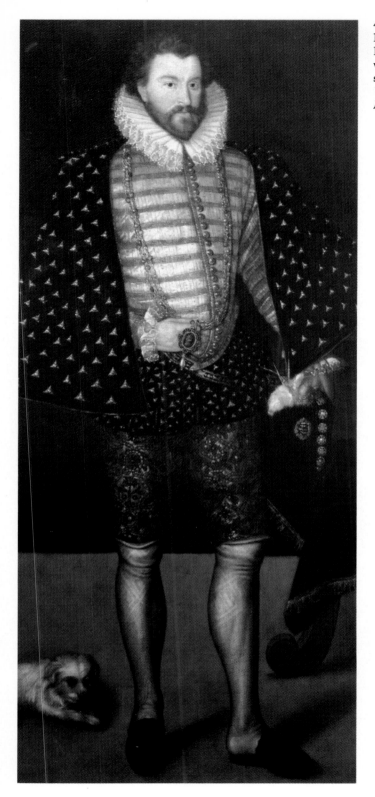

4 Sir Christopher Hatton (1540-91), Queen Elizabeth's chancellor, wearing knitted damask stockings. *(The Earl of Winchilsea and Nottingham)*

5 An Armenian cap from Isfahan. Nineteenth century. *(Victoria & Albert Museum)*

6 Socks of unknown provenance, probably Kashmiri. *(York Castle Museum)*

7 Early Aran cardigan, 1937. *(National Museum of Ireland)*

8 Aran style in outré fashion. A suit by Jean-Paul Gaultier (b. 1952), 1985. *(Niall McInerney)*

9 *Woolcraft*, second edition, c. 1916. *(Patons and Baldwins Ltd)*

10 Knitting changes its image with the minidress, c. 1970. A pattern leaflet cover. *(Sirdar plc)*

11 Keishō-in's jacket, made and worn by Hashimoto Osamu (b. 1948), 1984. Keishō-in (1624-1705) was the mother of the fifth Tokugawa Shogun. *(Kawade Shobo Shinsha, Tokyo)*

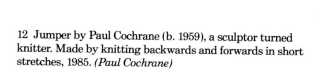

12 Jumper by Paul Cochrane (b. 1959), a sculptor turned knitter. Made by knitting backwards and forwards in short stretches, 1985. *(Paul Cochrane)*

13 Jumper by Kaffe Fassett, 1985. *(Steve Lovi)*

14 Designs by Patricia Roberts (b. 1945), 1986. *(Patricia Roberts)*

We have seen a wisp of straw tied up pretty tightly into which they stick their needles; and sometimes a bunch of quills of at least half-a-hundred in number. These sheaths and cowbands are often presents from their lovers to the young women. Upon the band there is a hook, upon which the long end of the knitting is suspended, that it may not dangle. In this manner they knit for the Kendal market, stockings, jackets, nightcaps, and a kind of cap worn by the negroes, called "bump-caps". These are made of very coarse worsted, and knit a yard in length, one half of which is turned into the other before it has the appearance of a cap.

The smallness of their earnings may be inferred from the price for the knitting of one of these caps being threepence. But all knit, and knitting is not so much their sole labour as an auxiliary gain. The woman knits when her household work is done; the man when his out-of-door work is done; as they walk about their garden or go from one village to another, the process is going on.

The songs seem to be special to the Dales. Like another, quoted by Mrs T. Hesketts Hodgson of Newby Grange in a lecture 'On some surviving fairies' to the Cumberland and Westmorland Antiquarian Society in 1900 –

Bulls at bay, kings at fay,
Over the hills and far away –

they seem not to have meant much. Barking is said to have been a hill above Dent, and Rockie the name of a sheep dog. The tune called 'Dentdale' in some hymnbooks (beginning with *The English Hymnal* 1906) may have been used for a knitting song. It was collected by Ralph Vaughan Williams in Dentdate in 1904. John Mason, the man who sang it to him, used the words of 'Tarry woo'', a wool-carding song recorded, and probably written, by the Scottish poet Allan Ramsay in the 1740 edition of his *Tea Table Miscellany* (378-9). Tarry wool was the bane of the carders, for Stockholm tar was used as a rough medicament by the shepherds. (Hence the proverb about not spoiling the sheep for a ha'porth of tar, which townspeople later changed to a proverb about a ship.)

Another knitting chant was the Cumbrian sheep-counting by scores: *yan, tan, tethera, methera, pimp* and so on – a much corrupted Celtic tradition (*Notes and Queries* 1863 iv. 205). Counting in scores was common for country knitters throughout Britain.

Howitt's description of 'swaving' is puzzling. In the 1940s Hartley and Ingilby saw 79-year-old Mrs Crabtree of Flintergill in Dent knitting in this way:

The secret of the method is the rhythmic up and down movements of the arms performed so that the right needle 'strikes the loop' without the least hesitation. The body sways up and down in sympathy with this action, which is something like the beating of a drum. It is impossible to do it in slow motion and the loops fly off quicker than the eye can see.

'Swaving' is a dialect word that means 'swinging' or 'waving'. It is not peculiarly restricted to knitting, and is probably no more than a description of the rocking motion of the knitter's

92 The Tarry Wool song.

Oh tar-ry wool, oh tar-ry wool, Tar-ry wool is ill to spin.
Card it well, oh card it well, Card it well 'ere you be-gin

body. Though soothing, it is unlikely that the rocking motion helped the knitting. Mrs Clara Sedgwick of Cowgill, who was 83 when I visited her at home in Settle in 1982, learned to knit as a child in Dentdale and was at a loss to understand how the swaying helped the knitting. She said a knitter could not achieve speed or sway pleasantly backwards and forwards in a rocking chair until she 'got going'.

There is difficulty in accepting Howitt's and other accounts as they stand. If the knitter's whole body moved forwards and backwards at each stitch, then in view of the fast rate of knitting described, the action would have been more like violent shivering than swaying. It would also have been extremely exhausting. Howitt says the body 'often' accompanied the tossing motion of the hands. I have little doubt that visiting observers, perplexed by the difference between the movement of the hands and the customary knitting habits of townsfolk from early nineteenth-century times onwards, failed to distinguish between the body action and the needle handling. Mrs Sedgwick in 1982 knitted like a Shetlander, keeping the right-hand needle still and putting the loop on to it by a movement of the left-hand needle, which was promptly and rhythmically moved again to 'knock off' the new loop. The action is quite unlike drawing-room knitting, and was probably normal throughout Britain and Europe among peasant and industrial knitters from the sixteenth century onwards.

Clara Sedgwick knitted with needles parallel to the floor, even pointing slightly down and away from the body. This is clearly much more efficient than the common habit of pointing the needles upwards. She also maintained a very tight tension, aided by winding the yarn twice round the index finger of her right hand. She said she was taught always to leave her work in the middle of a row, not at the end. This was possibly intended to be a rule for knitting in rounds.

Dales knitters used knitting sheaths, often of the shape called 'goose-wing', though more elaborate forms and much simpler forms were also made. The simplest of all was a spindle, hollowed at one end to take the needle but decorated with the lightest of grooves turned on the spindle. The belt

was worn high on the waist, the sheath tucked into it near the right armpit at an angle that would bring the needle in front of the chest for knitting. The right-hand needle was thus held almost immovable, and the fingers of the right hand had little to do but throw the yarn over the needle-tip for each stitch. 'Working with short needles', meaning working as near the tips as possible, was taught from an early age as the only sure way of attaining speed and regular tension.

The needles were bought straight but soon assumed a natural arc or curve, which has led to them being called, somewhat misleadingly, 'crooked needles' by Howitt. The points were not sharpened, merely blunted. The bullet-shaped points were perfectly efficient, given the style of knitting used, in which the loop was placed on the right hand needle, rather than the right-hand needle inserted into the loop.

A variety of hooks was used to support the weight of the work as it grew. The best recorded

93 Two-colour pattern of an Aberdeen glove, early to mid-nineteenth century. Originally wool, black on red.

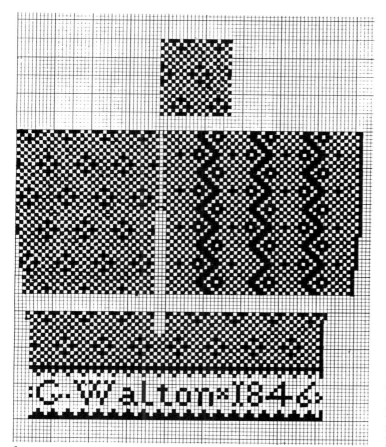

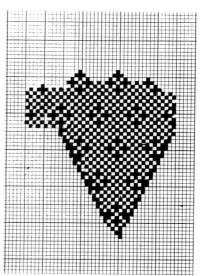

b

94 (*a*) The pattern of G. Walton's glove of 1846. Dark brown and natural creamy white. (*b*) The thumb gore. The eight additional stitches above the wrist are made by: firstly, increasing one on either side of the outer seam stitch; secondly, increasing one on either side of the central stitch in each of the zigzag lines on the back of the hand. The rectangular section is the part of the hand above the thumb opening.

a

are called top-crook and top-string. A tape was fastened to the knitter's belt by the knitting sheath and brought behind the back to the knitter's front left-hand side, where it was tied to the top-crook, which was hooked into the knitting. As the stocking grew, the knitter pulled at the tape on the right side and brought the knitting round her waist at the back. This method was supposed to assist the production of even tension. The top-string was an S-shaped hook used like a top-crook. A similar effect could be obtained by pinning work in progress to the right hip with a safety pin, once safety pins became generally available.

Stockings were the principal garments made in the Dales, as they were everywhere else. Next in importance were the gloves. The patterns of the extant gloves in various collections and museums show marked similarities to the gloves of Sanquhar. Most of them are in two-colour stranded knitting. The 'midge-and-fly' pattern was very commonly used for the fingers, and palms were made in the 'shepherd's plaid' pattern. The wrists were often decorated with the owner's name and the year-date.

They were by no means always knitted in dark and light natural wool – though a fine pair in the Wordsworth Museum at Grasmere is in écru and brown. It bears the name G. Walton and the date 1846, and came from Deepdale in Cumberland. The design is complex and has a rich effect, clearly the result of a design tradition. The cuff has a fringe of knitted loops.

Hartley and Ingilby describe a pair dated 1841 with the name 'Mary Moor's'. This is done in mauve and scarlet wool, with green and white stitches in the centre of the pattern on the back, and a green fringe. Black and red was a common combination of colours, as it was elsewhere; but by the first quarter of the twentieth century, especially when silk was used, white gloves with patterning in black, fawn, light green or pale blue were made. Some early-twentieth-century examples from Dentdale are kept in the museum at Hawes, and at Gawthorpe Hall, Padiham.

The most important of the other garments made were the frocks, or 'jackets', which today we should probably call jerseys or jumpers. Hartley and Ingilby quote letters of 1830 and 1831 which mention the frocks, especially 'spotted frocks'. Apparently none have survived but it is clear that the patterns were of the 'midge-and-fly' variety that would have approximated to the tradition of Cumberland weaving with black and white to produce an optical grey (John Brown's hunting colour). The necklines varied: some had roll collars, some had crew necks.

C. Nicholson *Annals of Kendal* (1861) also refers to 'single and double scarlet caps, Kilmarnock and plaid caps, made principally for exportation to America and the West Indies'. Account books refer to Dutch caps (said to be like sunbonnets) and charity caps (dyed blue, black and green, with ribbons to tie under the chin, for children in charity schools). A letter from Hebblethwaite Hall Mill near Sedbergh, dated 23 November 1826, suggests that the Kilmarnock caps were blue with a chequered red and white band and required nine pairs of needles in the making. The caps, like all the knitted goods, were dressed at the mill before going to retail. Caps were also fulled and given a pile.

'Bump' is frequently mentioned. It was very coarse undyed yarn, worked on thick needles. 'Open as bump knitting' was a proverbial simile derived from the looseness of bump fabric. Such knitting was shrunk and dressed at the mill before it went to the retail market.

William Howitt's wife, Mary, was also an author. In 1840 she published a novel: *Hope On, Hope Ever*, a story of Dentdale with several references to local knitting. Everyone said the trade was better in their father's time (6); the wool was sorted into fine for stocking legs, coarse for the feet (96); an old woman getting up to go from a knitting session 'rolled up her knitting without even getting to the middle of the seam needle' (96); and a great red

95 Replica of a glove owned by G. Walton of Deepdale, 1846. Original in the Grasmere and Wordsworth Museum.

comforter was knit of 'a new sort of wool, called German wool, very soft' (196). This marks the contact between the Dales tradition and the new approach to knitting in the drawing rooms of London, Bath, Edinburgh and the seaside towns.

The disappearance of the knitting sheath

A knitter whose experience, unless she was borrowing other people's memories, spanned parts of two centuries, wrote 'From a dame to her scholars', which was prefaced to Rachel Jane Cattlow's *Practical Knitting for the Working Classes*, by R.J.C., published at Cheadle in 1846.

'Tis seventy years or thereabouts
  since I was taught to knit,
and on a cricket I was placed
  by our good dame to sit.

My needles were of wire that bent,
  not like your steel so polished;
and to my frock a sheath was pinned,
  which now is quite abolished.

A bit of worsted served my turn,
  which twirled and twisted sadly;
Strutt's good brown cotton in those days
  would have been hailed most gladly.

Now your old dame gives this advice
  to the rising generation :
that whilst children are young they learn to knit,
  whatever may be their station.

96 British knitting sheaths from West Yorkshire. The second from the left is a turned spindle; the third a goose wing; and the fourth fashioned of tin to be sewn to a belt. The horse-hair-stuffed pad on a belt is from Shetland.

I think if you will give good heed
  to the following explanations,
you'll find that your stockings and socks and gloves
  will answer your expectations.

Rachel's book was printed again in 1847. It contains little more than a collection of patterns for stockings, gloves, knee-caps and a sleeve. The second part is 'for the working classes' and contains hosiery in coarse wool, worsted and brown cotton. Attention is paid to the 'mirroring' of paired shapings.

The story of Victorian knitting was not simply the tale of the drawing room. Working class knitting had changed too: needles and yarn had improved, and the knitting sheath was passing out of favour. There were two reasons for the disappearance of the knitting sheath. One was the simplicity of doing without it. When speed was less essential, the sheath was an encumbrance. (It survived longer in the Yorkshire Dales, where speed remained important.) In other places the principle of the sheath survived after the sheath itself fell out of fashion. Winifred Paynter in *Old St Ives* (1928) writes of a Cornish school-dame who was using a wooden fish-shaped sheath in the 1850s (29). Mabel Kathleen Ashby in her biography of her father *Joseph Ashby of Tysoe 1859–1919* (1961) describes her maternal grandmother Harriet Ashby in the late 1880s, when Harriet was 60, always wearing 'a linen apron with her knitting-pin holder twisted into its waist-tapes' (171). That was in Warwickshire. As late as 1902 Mrs Rivers Turnbull in Volume II of Chapman and Hall's *The*

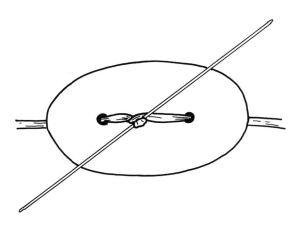

97 A Cornish tack, or cardboard substitute for a knitting sheath.

Woman's Library describes the Cornish tack as 'a flattened piece of cardboard or leather with a tape run across and through it. This tack is tied round the waist and brought into position at the left side (she seems to mean the observer's left side); and one knitting needle is twisted firmly into the cross tape, and thus held securely while the stitches are being knitted off. When cardboard and leather are not obtainable, a small pad of rag or straw is often used' (288-9).

The other reason for dispensing with the knitting sheath was noted by Mrs Willans in *The proceedings of the Society of Antiquarians of Newcastle-upon-Tyne* (1920). She said the sheath was not favoured by the educational authorities, 'it being considered liable to produce weak chests and round shoulders'. She went on to suggest that knitting without the sheath was more typical of the south of England. This was true by Mrs Willan's time, but had not been true earlier. The tendency of the sheath to encourage poor posture was, to say the least of it, debatable.

The Great Exhibition 1851

The first international exhibition of the products of industry, opened in the marvellous Crystal Palace in Hyde Park in 1851, has probably attracted more attention in knitting history than it merits. The reason for this lies in the presence of items from the exhibition in the Victoria & Albert Museum.

One virtuoso piece is a little lace dress, made with 6564 m (6000 yards) of fine sewing cotton in 1,464,859 stitches. Sarah Ann Cunliffe of Saffron Walden took five months to make it, working seven hours a day. As an example of industriousness and patience, it is remarkable, and perhaps this moral value led to its inclusion in the exhibition. The real purpose of the exhibition was better served by the more abundant examples of machine-knitting from Leicester and elsewhere.

Another well-known piece is a panel, 80 x 38 cm (32 x 15 in.), knitted in stockinet with the text of a prayer in purl stitches. A knitted lace border has been attached. The prayer is that 'for the High Court of Parliament' from the Book of Common Prayer, with the motto 'God Save The Queen' appended. This may be the piece exhibited in the Great Exhibition as knitting by a blind person (Class XIX No 214). It is a typical Victorian curiosity with its elaborate craftsmanship and display of heavy piety.

The catalogues are of some interest. The Jury Reports of the exhibition add little to our knowledge, save for a note by D. McDougall of Inverness to the effect that 'The peasants of Argyllshire, Ross-shire, etc., are afforded employment in knitting while attending flocks and doing other desultory employments. Cotters, once half starved . . . now possess money, placed in savings banks' (1050).

There were other similar ventures by enlightened landlords trying to help their tenants to earn by knitting, especially in Ireland during the middle of the century.

Victorian Scotland

Gairloch, a parish on the west coast of Scotland, was one of the places where the peasants earned money by knitting. They concentrated on fancy stockings for men, at first under the direction of Lady Mackenzie. She was quoted by J.H. Dixon in

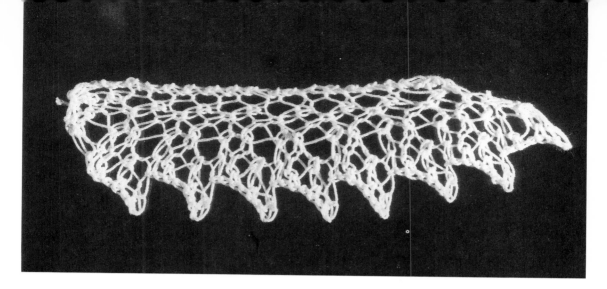

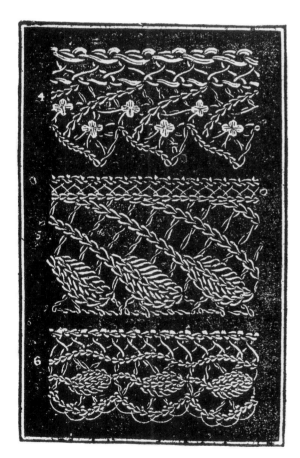

98 Illustration of three lace edgings from *The Royal Exhibition Knitting, Netting and Crochet Book* by W. Carter, ?1851. Original size 8 x 12.5 cm (3 x 5 in.) (see figure 99).

99 Lace edging No 4 from *The Royal Exhibition Knitting, Netting and Crochet Book*, knitted by Edna Treen, and revealing artistic liberties taken by illustrators of some Victorian books. No 40 mercerized cotton on 2 mm needles. Size 10 x 3 cm (4 x 1⅙ in.). (see figure 98).

Gairloch and Guide to Loch Maree (1886) as saying:

> At my first visit to Gairloch, in 1837, I employed a lady from Skye, who was staying at Kerrysdale, to instruct twelve young women in knitting nice stockings with dice and other fancy patterns. When I came to act as trustee, and to live constantly at Flowerdale, I started the manufacture of the Gairloch stockings in earnest, having spinners, dyers and knitters all taught and superintended during the ten years I resided there. On my leaving and going abroad, Sir Kenneth gave the concern into the hands of the head gamekeeper, Mr George Ross.

It is possible that these were the first 'tartan' or 'Argyll' stockings, for, as Dixon notes, tartan stockings were earlier made of tartan cloth, cut on the bias. Tartan patterns were not the only ones favoured at Gairloch. By the end of the nineteenth century a Gairloch stocking might be diapered with a pattern of stags' heads.

Stockings from Scotland inspired stocking-knitters in England. John Leng of Dundee at the end of the Victorian age published a number of recipes for Scottish knitters, including fancy stockings and caps, by Helen Grieg Souter, who wrote under the pseudonym of Aunt Kate. Some of these recipes were collected with other Scottish recipes by Lady Veronica Gainford and published as *Designs for Knitting Kilt Hose and Knickerbocker Stockings* (1978).

Scottish caps

Helen Bennett has written a comprehensive account of Scottish knitting. It is generally parallel to the English story, beginning with the bonnet-makers of Dundee forming a trade guild in 1496. Similar groups existed in Edinburgh, Aberdeen, Perth, Stirling and Glasgow by the end of the fifteenth century. The bonnet-makers of Kilmarnock are recorded from 1656.

The flat blue bonnet was mentioned by Fynes Moryson in his *Itinerary*, as having been the wear of husbandmen and servants in 1598. During the seventeenth century it became, in its various forms, the typical male headdress of Scotland. For centuries after the knitted bonnet or cap had disappeared from England it remained popular in Scotland.

The bonnet-makers also produced boot-hose and other coarse knitting. Bonnets and stockings were the staple Scottish mainland knitting. By the eighteenth century the black or blue cap was beginning to be ornamented with a red-and-white dicing (chequers), or regimental colours, on the headband. At Kilmarnock bonnet-making by hand continued till 1870, but then it declined and disappeared. Today Scottish bonnets are machine-made.

Mrs Gaskell

It is only to be expected that Elizabeth Gaskell's *Cranford* (1853), a chronicle of female society, should tell something of knitting. The genteel, but not affluent, ladies of Cranford knit a lot. They can knit in the dark, and do so to save candles, or when waiting to be taken out to see a conjurer's show. They read aloud to one another while knitting, and Miss Matty, at least, makes a point of sitting with her back to the light.

Miss Matty knitted quantities of garters, in various dainty stitch-patterns. She knitted garters of elaborate design while sitting at the counter of the sweetshop that reduced circumstances forced her to run, but 'the difficult stitch was of no weight upon her mind, for she was singing in a low voice to herself as her needles went in and out'.

The ladies bought Shetland wool by post from Edinburgh. Miss Pole and Miss Brown developed a special intimacy on the strength of being mail-order customers together and trying out new stitches. They were also ready to learn from cottage knitters, for one morning Lady Glenmore and Miss Pole were seen 'setting out on a long walk to find some old woman who was famous in the neighbourhood for her skill in knitting woollen stockings'.

In *Wives and Daughters*, written mostly in 1865, Mrs Gaskell says less about knitting than in *Cranford*, but one passage makes a comment on yarn and naming-customs. Lady Harriett says to Molly:

> 'People in the last century weren't afraid of homely names. Now we are all so smart and fine: no more 'Lady Bettys' now. I almost wonder they haven't re-christened all the worsted and knitting-cotton that bears her name'.
> 'I didn't know there was a Lady Betty's cotton', said Molly.
> 'That proves you don't do fancy-work . . .'

In truth it was Lady Betty's wool, rather than cotton. Very soft fine wool under that name was used from the 1830s to the 1920s. No one knows who Lady Betty was. Possibly it was Lady Betty Germain (1680–1769), friend of Jonathan Swift, and sometime lady-in-waiting to Queen Anne. In her widowhood she went to live with the Sackvilles at Knole in Kent, where she survived for 50 years as a guest of her friend, the Duchess of Dorset. Two of her spinning wheels, one for flax and one for wool, are still preserved at Knole.

Fisherman knitting

The jersey has long been thought of in Britain as the typical sailor's garment. Several researchers, beginning with Gladys Thompson, whose classic *Guernsey and Jersey Patterns* was published in 1955, have diligently collected old garments and patterns from the fishing communities of the Scottish and English coasts. In 1983 Henriette van der Klift-Tellegen did the same for Holland and published *Nederlandse Visserstruien*, published in English as *Knitting from the Netherlands* two years later.

Some of these books, notably Rae Compton's *The Complete Book of Traditional Guernsey and Jersey Knitting* (1985), have shown a sense of history, but only Mary Wright, in *Cornish Guernseys and Knitfrocks* (1979) has tackled the history of the subject seriously. Like Michael Pearson in various publications that culminated in his *Traditional Knitting* (1984), all these writers have concentrated on the technique of knitting the fisherman's jersey and on collecting patterns for the typical damask fabrics in which it was made. Museum collections of fisherman knitting are forming, notably at Cromer and on the Isle of Man.

Fishermen's wives did the knitting. Feminine feel for decoration in dress evolved the fine patterns that became the pride of their menfolk, who, on doffing their jackets, exposed the ornamental knitting of the shirt. So the underwear

100 Mrs Noel Gladys Thompson (1887-1974) author of the classic *Guernsey and Jersey Patterns* (1955), outside her home, Maiden Folley at Youlton, Yorkshire, in the 1960s. Her cardigan, probably machine-knitted, aptly illustrates the mid-twentieth century's tendency to regard knitwear as unsmart.

101 Handknitted gansey in typical Sheringham style, with the patterns known locally as 'coil-o'-rope' and 'herringbones'. Worn by John 'Sparrow' Hardingham, fisherman and coxswain of the Sheringham Lifeboat RNLB *Foresters Centenary* 1947-50, and thought to have been knitted in the 1920s.

102 Fishermen outside Cromer parish church. Enlarged detail from an engraving by John Buckler (1770–1851) dated 1847.

103 Three fisherlads of Fife in ganseys, probably of the 1930s.

became outerwear. Some writers have over-emphasized the water-turning quality of fisherman's knitting. Oilskins or tarred jackets covered the jersey in bad weather. The real values of the knitted shirt lay in its comfortable fit, its warmth, and its splendid appearance. Its appearance was so highly esteemed that by the end of Queen Victoria's reign, a young man might wear his jersey at his wedding or at a feast.

The earliest printed reference to a fisherman's jersey has been found by Mary Wright in a newspaper report of the Cornwall Lammas Assizes of 1858 when William Walsh, aged 20, was sentenced for the theft of clothing, including a guernsey-frock, from James Carter of Illogan. Mrs Wright also shows that Richard Poppleton of Wakefield was spinning '0½ worsted', such as was used for jerseys, as early as 1846. Cromer Museum possesses a fine print of Cromer church by John Buckler, dated 1847, which shows three fishermen wearing what may well be knitted jerseys. They are tiny figures, 15 mm (½ in.) high, that clearly show the baggy trousers called slops, and stocking-caps. Their upper garments are not definitively clear, but they cling to the chest and back like jerseys, and are certainly not jackets. Charles Dickens in *Dombey and Son* (Chapter ix) describes the slopsellers' shops of 1848 near the India Docks, with 'guernsey shirts, sou'wester hats and canvas pantaloons . . . hanging up outside'. Fishermen had probably adopted the sailors' fashion.

Garments for the upper body had been knitted since Elizabethan times. We are woefully lacking in detailed information about the 'waistcoats' of those days and the provenance of the beautiful seventeenth-century shirts that have survived. (See above, p 79.) They were knitted in the round, with a damask pattern of plain and purl stitches, and in these points resemble the fisherman's jersey. They were underclothes, knitted shirts like the *nattrøjer* of Denmark, a similar type of garment that dates from at least the late seventeenth century. In such garments, surely, we must look for the ancestry of the fisherman's jersey.

The development of machine-knitted garments early in the nineteenth century was also doubtless a factor in the emergence of the sailor's jersey. References to jackets, shirts and frocks are not always clearly to knitted garments, but 'guernsey' and 'jersey' were words of long standing as synonyms for 'knitted'. Many of the early references, though they often have a nautical or sporting context, suggest machine-knitted garments. (John Jamieson's dictionary had carefully defined 'frock' as 'a sort of worsted netting worn by sailors, often in lieu of a shirt', as early as 1825.) *Chambers' Edinburgh Journal* mentions a guernsey frock aboard ship in 1832. In 1835 Charles Dickens, telling the story of 'The loving couple' in *Sketches by Boz*, described a crew of eight oarsmen at a picnic, wearing blue striped guernsey shirts. In 1839 Etonian teams were playing in white guernseys with pale blue facings, according to a report in *Bell's Life in London and Sporting Chronicle* of 16 June. In 1845 an amateur boatman wore 'a fez cap and a striped guernsey', as he ogled the girls on an Irish beach, according to *Ainsworth's Magazine* (499). *Tom Brown's Schooldays* tells how each house at Rugby School had its own jersey (about 1837). *Felix on the Bat* (1845) recommended a thin jersey 'not too tight in fit' for wearing under the shirt by boys playing cricket.

Football and rowing shirts have rarely, if ever, been hand knitted. It is possible that the relatively expensive machine-knitted jerseys or guernseys of the well-to-do were bought by sailors in port with cash to spend. Henry Mayhew in *London Labour and the London Poor* (1861) described 'sailors in striped guernseys'; and sailors on the high seas were notorious dandies. The coastal fishermen were never flush with cash, but sailor's dress may have stimulated them to persuade their womenfolk to knit guernsey shirts. While this sequence is purely conjectural, it is clear that knitted shirts appeared in Britain as sportswear and sea-wear before 1850, and began a trend in costume that eventually produced late twentieth-century knitted leisure wear.

The fishermen never took to striped ganseys. They wore either dark blue, or, in north Devon for example, dark grey. 'Navy blue' is a colour description dating from about 1840, although naval officers had changed the colour of their uniforms from 'French navy' to dark blue before 1800. Plain dark colours may have appealed to the fishermen because they were cheaper or considered more dignified. Blue has often been an honourable colour for the poor, from China to proletarian France.

The Royal Navy was slow to adopt the jersey. G. Rawson's edition of Nelson's letters (1960) shows Nelson writing to the Commissioners of the Navy on 20 November 1804 about 'guernsey jackets of a new manufacture' that he had issued to his men. He approved of the jackets but said they were 'considerably too narrow and short to be tucked into the men's trousers'. When the seamen were on the yards, reefing or furling sails, the jackets rubbed out of their trousers, exposing them to 'great danger of taking cold in their loins' (434).

Concern about the sailors' midriffs was also shown by Captain Charles A. Baker, commanding HMS *Drake*, in a letter to the Navy Board of 28 May 1822, preserved in the National Maritime Museum, Greenwich. He had tried 'double worsted knitted drawers', which he considered as good as 'double knitted jackets for usefulness, warmth, and protection to the loins', noting that they gave general satisfaction to the seamen, while 'the small flannel drawer' was invariably refused.

Yet the knitted jersey did not become part of dress for naval ratings until 1881, and was not mentioned in the uniform regulations until 1892. There had been various requests on the subject before Commander-in-Chief Portsmouth tried again in October 1879. The Lords of the Admiralty refused permission for the jersey, and recommended an extra flannel vest under the frock in very cold weather. Their reluctance is not explained. In February 1881 permission was given for boys in training ships to wear white jerseys and men on Home Station to wear blue ones. The blue ones had to be of 'worsted, closely knitted, without pattern, with a collar one inch deep and long sleeves; front and back alike.' (Dress regulations 1892.16). The negative reference to the elaborate jerseys of fishermen is striking.

The 'fisher gansey' evolved after the Industrial Revolution, during the Romantic period. It quickly attracted its own romanticism. Some modern writers have developed this romanticism, listing the local names of the stitch motifs as though they had more significance than they have, and creating a mythology of family patterns with the value of working-class 'coats-of-arms' – a fancy similar to what has been foisted on the patterns of Aran. Rae Compton has shown more sense of history in her book on guernseys and jerseys in which she points

out that fishermen travelled all round the coast of Britain – as their girls also did, to gut and pack herrings in ports far from their homes. From the Hebrides, clockwise round Scotland, past Northumbria and East Anglia to Cornwall, British seamen's jerseys are essentially the same.

Audrey M. Journeaux published the oldest dated pattern in *Jerseys Old and New* for the Jersey Federation of Women's Institutes about 1970. The date of the pattern was 1889. It is possible that some of the details of the technique reflect the practice of Channel Island knitters in the eighteenth century and earlier. The Islands'

104 The fashion for women to wear fishermen's jerseys, drawn by George du Maurier in *Punch*, 28 August 1880.

SIC TRANSIT!
ALAS, FOR THE PRETTY JERSEY COSTUME! 'ANDSOME 'ARRIET, THE 'OUSEMAID, HAS GOT IT AT LAST, AND IT FITS HER JUST AS WELL AS HER MISSUS.

tradition of knitting was much weakened by the slump of the early nineteenth century, but home knitters may have retained old techniques such as the 'Channel Island cast-on', and employed them when the fashion for fishermen's jerseys reached the islands in the middle of the nineteenth century. This cast-on may have originally been used on stockings. (See page 191.)

Only Gaelic and Norwegian have adopted 'guernsey', in the forms *geansaidh* and *genser*, into the vocabulary of dress. The Dutch, however, have given the garment a distinctive addition of their own. Many Dutch jerseys have a drawstring with pompoms threaded into the neck of the jersey.

In Britain jerseys have been knitted in 3-ply, 4-ply and 5-ply worsted, which was not oiled. The tension of the finest may be 48 stitches to 10 cm (4 in.), and the damask patterns are sometimes of great beauty. Most garments were knitted in the family, but some work was contracted out. Mary Wright has given some account of this outwork in her work on Cornish knitting.

Machine-made guernseys were being worn by the fishermen in the later nineteenth century. Wilkinsons are a noted Cornish firm. Corah of Leicester was advertising fishermen's wear in 1862, including 'Cornish handknitted franklins'. Corah played a part, too, in the curious fashion of the 'jersey dress' for ladies in 1879–80. The Princess of Wales and her children were photographed aboard the Royal Yacht in 1878 wearing jerseys; *Punch* published two cartoons showing how servant-girls copied their mistresses, who had copied the fishermen. The jersey flattered the female bosom for a season or so, and has become curiously connected with Lillie Langtry, the Jerseywoman who was then at the height of her notorious affair with the Prince of Wales. It is more likely that the Princess of Wales started the fashion.

After the First World War jersey-knitting declined in fishermen's homes. The jersey became the uniform of the typical boatman on ferries and pleasure boats all over the world, and fishermen never completely gave it up, but it was usually machine-knitted. Though Gladys Thompson and others already mentioned, who began recording the old hand-knitted patterns in the 1950s, have

stimulated a limited revival of handknitted jerseys, one rarely sees a garment of the quality worn 50 or 60 years ago by John 'Sparrow' Hardingham of Sheringham. Few handknitters have time or courage for such a project. The best jerseys were knitted in a woman's spare time and social hours over many months.

Jerseys were not the only things knitted by fishermen's wives and daughters for their menfolk. They knitted underwear, especially drawers or underpants, and long seaboot stockings. The underwear had no known special features, but the thigh-length off-white stockings made of heavy wool were distinctive. The heavy ribbing at the thigh can be seen showing above the sea-boots in some pictures of fishermen at work. No one has yet studied these stockings, whose coarseness and heaviness contrast strikingly with the fine knitting of the best jerseys.

The Crimean War

The Crimean War of 1854-6, a confused attempt to stem the spread of Imperial Russian power, was the first war in which people knitted at home for their armies overseas. The amount of knitting done during the war has been exaggerated. The magazines of the day do not mention the subject. Mlle Riego added a title page to her *Winter Book* for 1854, calling it 'Comforts for the Crimea'; and there was a letter in *The Times* on 5 December 1854 addressed by 'A Yorkshire woman' to 'the women of England' asking for brown-drab worsted socks and stockings, as well as crochet mitts, to be made and donated for the soldiers. The writer suggested that the best division of labour would be for the mitts to be made by ladies, while the poorer women of the town or village should be provided with yarn and given 4d a pair for knitting socks. Alas, the despatch and delivery of these goods was as inefficiently organized as everything else in the campaign.

Three words connected with knitting are commonly said to have originated during the war. All three stories are suspect. Since the 1880s 'balaclava helmet' has meant a knitted helmet, covering the head, ears, and neck, with an opening for the face. Such a garment existed before the Crimean war, for it was patented by James Martin of Walworth in 1848 as 'The Protector'. Mlle Riego gave a crochet receipt for it in her 1854 booklet, but did not call it 'balaclava' and gave no directions for knitting it. It was also called Uhlan cap and Templar cap. Not until 1881, 17 years after the battle of Balaclava on 25 October 1864, do we find the balaclava helmet mentioned by that name in print. How the name came to be applied is unknown.

'Cardigan', meaning an informal woollen jacket, is derived from the title of the Earl of Cardigan (1797–1868), who led the charge of the Light Brigade at Balaclava. There is no evidence that he wore such a garment during the three short months he spent in the Crimea, from 12 September to 8 December 1854. The autumn weather was oppressively hot by day when he arrived, increasingly chilly by night, and as winter approached the earl lived on his yacht *Dryad*, moored in Balaclava harbour, going ashore for battles and other daytime activities.

A 'cardigan body warmer' might have suited his needs, but, if he had one in the Crimea, nobody recorded it. The word first occurs in print in 1868, the year of his death. It is more likely that he used the garment during his last years at Deene Park, Northamptonshire. English country houses were notoriously cold.

'Raglan', meaning a garment shoulder-seamed back and front from under the armpit to the side of the neck, is named after Lord Raglan (1788–1855), the unfortunate commander-in-chief who was made scapegoat for the many mistakes of the war. It is first recorded in 1864, in Webster's *American Dictionary*, and has no special connexion with the war. Raglan sleeves in knitted garments, such as cardigans, were first made about 1912 or 1913, just before World War I.

Teacosies

Teacosies were invented by the Victorians, but, though some connoisseurs of tea believe cosies spoil tea by stewing it, they are not decorative trivia. They are still made, and even sold commercially. The first recorded use dates from 1867, and the cosy quickly found a place on the teatables (and kitchen tables) of all social classes.

Knitted fabric, with its excellent insulating properties, was ideally suited for making teacosies. At first the designs were various forms of inverted bag to cover the whole pot, handle, spout and all. In 1893 *Weldon's Ladies' Journal* (1 February) recorded a new fashion, the bachelor teacosy, and gave a recipe for it. The bachelor cosy has two holes in the sides, one for the handle and one for the spout, 'so there is no occasion to remove the cosy when pouring out tea'. Bachelors may be naturally lazy about removing teacosies, but married people prove equally willing to use the bachelor cosy.

The knitted cosy, always available at sales of work and parish bazaars, gives opportunity for fancy designs. Crinoline dolls, thatched cottages, beehives, brooding hens, pineapples, even television sets and electric toasters have been the models for knitted teacosies that hover uncertainly between trivial novelty and serious pop art. New patterns still appear, especially in autumn magazines.

The 1870 Education Act

There was a change in English publications on knitting about 1870. Some of the older books remained in print, and were even reprinted for ladies' use, but the books of Elvina Mary Corbould had a new simplicity. Magazine items on knitting were beginning to appear, though outside needlework magazines they did not become regular features until after the First World War. There was a new public for the printed word. The work of the National Society and other educational enterprises had enlarged the number of knitters who could follow a printed recipe.

A further great fillip to their development was provided by the Elementary Education Act, 1870. This act was a natural follower of the 1867 Reform Act, extending political democracy through the education of the working classes, and helping Britain meet the industrial and commercial threats coming from the newly united American States after the Civil War of 1861–5 and from flourishing Germany after the Peace of Prague in 1866. Germany's technical and elementary education was much superior to Britain's.

One of the prime movers in getting the act passed was Anthony John Mundella 1825–97. He was born in Leicester, the son of an Italian immigrant, but in his early twenties became a partner in a Nottingham knitting firm, and was subsequently member of parliament for Sheffield for 30 years. He travelled in Germany to study education, and after the 1870 act was passed, he was involved in drawing up the annual codes or syllabuses that introduced manual skills into public education. References to knitting according to 'Mundella's code' are relatively common.

The codes were severely practical: boys were to learn to knit as well as girls, though only for the earliest part of the curriculum. (According to Winifred Paynter (see p 125) at St Ives the boys knitted while the girls sewed.) In 1879 the code included much practice in stockinet on two needles, and proceeded to wristlets or muffatees made on four needles. At the point where the girls began to be taught separately (about seven or eight years) stocking-knitting was taught. 'A long full-sized stocking' was the peak of elementary school knitting. A severely practical *Standard Guide to Knitting* appeared, to help the teacher.

The old church schools had earlier had their own books. *The Industrial Handbook* of 1856 had been published by the Society for Promoting Christian Knowledge, aimed at a wider public than schoolteachers. Ironically, it was a better and more imaginative book than what was produced as a result of the 1870 act.

The Society continued to publish knitting books, and especially the work of Miss Henrietta Warleigh. Her father, after 12 years as rector of Ashchurch near Tewkesbury (an old stockinger district), became vicar of Castleton near Sheffield,

until he died about 1891. Henrietta published five very practical knitting books between the mid-1870s and the early 1890s. Finally, from retirement at Copthorne in Surrey she edited *Ladies' Work for Sailors*, a delightful booklet for the Mission to Seamen, in 1902 (fig. 114). All the books had repeated reprints. They covered gloves, lace edgings, doyleys, and other useful items, as well as hosiery.

Fancy knitting was now becoming a possibility for the working classes as well as the middle classes. Samuel Beeton published *Beeton's Book of Needlework* in 1870, after his wife's death; and the associated firm of Myra and Son issued knitting lessons in a volume of 'The Silkworm Series' (charmingly illustrated with silkmoths and mulberry sprays on the cover). But this was in the late 1880s, by which time Weldons and Mrs Leach were well under way with their large publishing programmes.

Weldon's Practical Needlework began to be published in 1886. It was a monthly publication, with 12 numbers to each annual volume. Each number consisted of 16 large pages and was devoted to a single branch of needlework, such as knitting, stocking-knitting, crochet, tatting, smocking, macramé and various kinds of lace and embroidery. The issues relating to each branch were treated as distinct series, with their own sequences of numbers. This complicated system results in such complexities as: *Weldon's Practical Needlework* No 400, Vol 34. *Practical Knitter*, 111th series, published 4/19 (that is April 1919). The series continued at least until 1929 when the 165th series of the *Practical Knitter* was published. The month and date in numeral code, as just quoted, first appeared in July 1915. (See appendix on page 242.)

The price in 1886 was 2d. In 1916 it was raised to 3d. The publishers proudly kept all back numbers in print – with the result that the advertisements in reprints of early editions may have been changed. Nevertheless *Weldon's* is a mine of information about home knitting and the development of fashion, from the high Victorian taste of 1886 to the brink of the 1930s.

Leach's Penny Knitter started in January 1892. It was less well produced, printed on newsprint and sometimes naively illustrated. The recipes in *Weldon's* often appeared also in the *Penny Knitter*, whose cheapness made it available to a poorer class of reader. Accurate dating of issues is sometimes very difficult, but publication appears to have continued in the first decade of the twentieth century.

Thérèse de Dillmont (1846–90)

The *Encyclopaedia of Needlework* published by the Dollfuss-Mieg Company (DMC) contains a notable knitting section of some historical value. The *Encyclopaedia* was written by Thérèse de Dillmont, who was born in 1846, the daughter of a professor of architecture at the Imperial Military Academy in Vienna. When Thérèse was eighteen, she obtained an imperial bursary to train as a teacher, but before long she and her sister Franziska had opened an embroidery studio in Vienna.

In October 1884 she moved, without Franziska, to Dornach, a village near Mulhouse. Almost at once she contracted with the important local haberdashery manufacturing firm of Dollfuss-Mieg to edit needlework albums. In 1886 her *Encyclopaedia* appeared in both German and French versions. English, Italian and Spanish translations soon followed. In 1890, aged 45, Thérèse married Joseph Scheuermann of Vienna. Four months later she died at Baden-Baden.

Subsequent editions of the encyclopaedia, some as late as the 1930s, are difficult to date. Those giving 'Editions de Dillmont' as publisher date from after 1927, when DMC formed a publishing auxiliary under that name. Those giving Dornach as the place of publication date from before 1923, when Dornach was absorbed into Mulhouse. There was a 'new and enlarged' English edition in octavo in 1930. Thérèse also produced four excellent booklets for DMC on knitting. They are undated.

Queen Victoria

Knitting is an unlikely occupation for a monarch, whose life is rarely private. Like painting and carpentry for princes, knitting and needlework are for princesses: pastimes that are likely to fade from life after accession to the throne. It is hard to find mention of knitting in the accounts of Queen Victoria's life and reign until the very end. Elizabeth Rosevear, in the 1902 edition of *A Textbook of Needlework, Knitting and Cutting Out*, quotes a Daily Telegraph report of the colonial tour made by the Duke of Cornwall, later King George V, in 1901. At one point the young duke went up to a man in the crowd because he recognized the man's scarf as one that had been made by his grandmother, Queen Victoria. The Duchess, later Queen Mary, with tears in her eyes, told the man how she had often taken up the stitches again when the tired old queen had dropped them; and said: 'Your scarf must be one of the six scarves (there were but six of them) which the dear Queen was knitting before she died. They were her last pieces of work'.

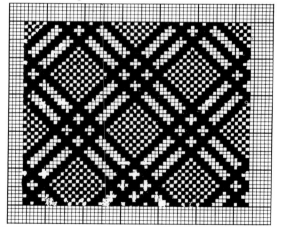

105 A successful 'Highland check' in two colours, 1896.

The Boer War

The Boer War (1899–1902) aroused an interest in knitting for the troops that revived the atmosphere of the Crimean War. It is difficult to find printed evidence and patterns that were certainly inspired by the war, but Flora Thompson has a vivid passage in *Heatherley*, which describes her life at Grayshott in Surrey from 1897 to 1901.

> Women of all ages knitted comforts for the soldiers. Many had first to learn to knit . . . cargoes of khaki socks, scarves, kneecaps and balaclava helmets were soon being despatched to the front. Later on, soldiers invalided home reported that in some places the veldt was strewn with these votive offerings which, though kindly meant, were less in demand in the South African climate than they had been in the frozen trenches before Sebastopol.

Flora did 'her first piece of knitting since she had left off wearing home-knit wool stockings in the winter', and she grew very tired of it before it was finished. Had anyone then told her how many miles of knitting she would do in her lifetime and what a great solace it would become to her, she would not have believed them'.

106 A cardigan of the *belle époque* that has never gone out of fashion. Designed by Marjory Tillotson *c.* 1909-10.

The belle époque

Edwardian publications have more recipes for knitted adult clothes than early and mid-Victorian issues had. Motoring and golf were new elements in the life of the leisured classes, to which others aspired. House parties included tennis as well as shooting. Knitted clothes, warm and comfortable, were suitable for such amusements. Women's coats, short and long, were knitted. Men's jerseys and cardigans, always with sleeves as yet, began to be less unusual. Knitting silk ties for gentlemen was a popular pastime.

But among the working classes, fishermen alone wore knitted jerseys. Agricultural and factory workers never took to them. Agricultural workers had scarcely done so before their numbers were drastically reduced by the revolution in agricultural methods after the 1950s. Even the knitted jerseys of the Women's Land Army in the Second World War were rarely worn at work. They were kept for occasions when uniform was required. Today's industrial workers have knitwear, but almost entirely machine-knitted.

6 The First World War and after

The First World War

The First World War stimulated British knitting to the point where it was regarded as a national mania. Dorothy Peel described it well in *How We Lived Then* (1929). She wrote of how women knitted socks, mitts, body belts, helmets and other comforts for the soldiers in France. They knitted at the theatre, in trains and trams, in restaurants and canteens as well as at home. 'It was soothing to our nerves to knit, and comforting to think that the results of our labours might save some man something of hardship and misery, for always the knowledge of what our men suffered haunted us' (60-1).

Wartime knitting peaked in 1915. Jessie Pope wrote sentimental verses that epitomized the emotion. They appeared in the *Daily Mail* and in *Punch*, and were reprinted in her books of war poems, contrasting the comfort of fireside knitting with the hardships of soldiering in France or sailing on the high seas. Every piece of knitting that came from home brought 'a smile and a hope and a prayer'. *The Family Journal* in December 1916 published Queen Mary's Appeal for woollies, together with both words and music of a song entitled 'The knack of knitting'. This was deliberately light-hearted, not to say facetious, and made a joke that remained popular for many years, describing knitting as 'lumps of air with wool around'.

Women who had difficulties with their knitting were teased mercilessly. As early as 18 November 1914 *Punch* published a full-page cartoon with four pictures: a desperately anxious woman knitter in two successive stages of distress; a pair of mittens of unequal size arriving in France; and the soldier recipient using one of them as a foot-muff. Dorothy Peel wrote that so many knitted goods went to France that men cleaned their rifles and wiped their cups and plates with surplus socks and comforters. Knitting was a war activity for the lonely and worried women, and at the same time an expression of love, perhaps never more emotional

THE HISTORY OF A PAIR OF MITTENS.

107 The knitting mania of the First World War as treated by E.H. Shephard in *Punch*, 18 November 1914.

108 A trompe-l'oeil jumper designed by Elsa Schiaparelli and knitted for her by Armenians in Paris 1927. Two yarns are used throughout. The yarn not appearing at the front is woven in behind at every fourth stitch, with placing of the woven loop staggered in alternate courses.

than when it relieved British women in the terrible days of carnage in the Flanders trenches.

School children were encouraged to knit, as many school logbooks show. All ages of women in Britain were knitting for dear life in something like a national addiction. Not surprisingly, they continued knitting when the war was over. That is part of the explanation of the jumper craze of the 1920s.

The jumper craze

That jumper knitting was a craze is amply proved by a popular song of 1920 called 'All the girls are busy knitting jumpers' by R.P. Weston and Bert Lee. A song of unparalleled inanity, it started with the first line of 'Baa, baa, black sheep' and achieved no higher wit than a pun on a girl knitting 'two plain' being 'too plain', and the joke about holes with wool round them.

Numerous patterns for long straight jumpers were issued throughout the decade. Of special interest is a Weldon's leaflet of jazz jumpers, published in 1922. This was the precursor of the Fair Isle fashion, and is chiefly concerned with floral designs in bands on the borders of garments. The instructions show that the differently coloured yarns were to be twisted at every stitch, in the method now usually called 'weaving'. The stranding of colours, already used in Shetland and elsewhere, did not come into popular British knitting until the Fair Isle fashion arrived a couple of years later. (See the section on Fair Isle knitting, p 181.)

Chanel, Schiaparelli and Diaghilev

Gabrielle Chanel (1833–1971) and Elsa Schiaparelli (1896–1973) dominated high fashion in the 1920s, and both made significant use of knitted fabric. Schiaparelli's famous *trompe-l'oeil* jumper of 1927, black with a simulated white collar and floppy bow, was a witty refinement of a trend that had been established since shortly after the 1914–18 war. The French magazine *Madame* published recipes for jumpers (called *casaque*) at least as early as 1920. Chanel's story that she had invented the jersey dress in the summer of 1914 at Deauville by whipping an Englishman's sweater off a wicker chair and tying it round her waist with a handkerchief has all the marks of a trivial incident invested, intentionally or not, with an historic importance that it did not possess.

Yet Chanel certainly gave knitwear a boost, typified by her designs for the costumes of Diaghilev's ballet *Le train bleu* in 1924. The idea came from Jean Cocteau: to build a ballet round the athletic games of young men showing off on the beach at Deauville – to which a chic new express, dubbed 'the Blue Train' after the long-established service to Nice, had begun taking Parisians in 1923. Most of the dancers, as flappers and their boyfriends, wore hand-knitted bathing suits, of a unisex design. Ninette de Valois, as one of the flappers, recalled Chanel changing the original beige to the royal blue she eventually wore. Lydia Sokolova, in *Dancing for Diaghilev* (1960) recalled how daring her costume seemed: cyclamen pink shorts and vest, with black and white stripes round the skirt. Anton Dolin, in *Last Words* (1985), recalled how Chanel had designed his black and white costume. Leon Woizikovski, as a golfer, wore a knitted jersey which was meant to resemble the Prince of Wales's famous Fair Isles, but was in fact of a much simpler design, typical of Chanel.

109 Anton Dolin and Leon Woidzikovsky dancing in the Diaghilev ballet, *Le Train Bleu*, London, November 1924. Hand-knitted bathing costume and imitation Fair Isle jersey by Chanel.

Le train bleu was the peak of fashion, hugely successful both in Paris and in London, but it was never danced again after 1925. The immediate reason was that Dolin left Diaghilev; but the chic bathing costumes were soon no longer chic. Male swimsuits were moving inexorably towards topless trunks, and women's costumes were becoming smaller and sleeker.

Bathing costumes

Knitted fabrics are much used for swimwear, because their elasticity makes them both comfortable and attractive. Machine knitting has provided the bulk of knitted swimming and bathing costumes, but hand knitting was used from about 1890 to 1950, especially in the 1930s and 1940s.

In the 1890s both men and women when bathing wore skirted tops with short sleeves, teamed with knee-length drawers. It was unusual at this period for hand knitters to tackle anything so large, and hand-knitted bathing suits are not recorded.

For serious swimming, however, men had a topless style. *Caleçons* (thigh-length drawers) or briefs ('triangles') were worn when men swam for sport. The 'regulation university suit', a black or navy, rarely red, one-piece covering the person from throat to thigh, was required when there were spectators; but in swimming baths and when ladies were not present, *caleçons* and triangles were worn. Matthew Webb wore 'small trunks' for his famous Channel swim on 24 August 1875.

At the end of the century some of these garments were hand-knitted. *Weldon's Practical Knitter* (34th series, 1897) gives a 'triangle' pattern, suggesting the colour should be plain navy blue or coloured horizontal stripes. (Blue-and-white or red-and-white were favoured.) The 51st series in 1900 has a pattern for a *caleçon* with a very high, slightly frilly waist, in elegant wasplike stripes of white and colour. Both garments are designed the same back and front. The *caleçon* would certainly not have stayed up on a serious swimmer; the triangle has a drawstring at the waist.

During the *belle époque* men's topless styles seem to have been less used. Both men's and women's bathing wear slowly became simpler. The sleeves were removed, the neckline deepened, the legs got shorter. Although the skirt began to disappear from men's costumes, a tight short skirt remained popular throughout the 1930s, and some men's costumes (including handknitted ones) had a front skirt even after the Second World War.

By 1925 however, the young and fashionable were accelerating the diminution of the bathing suit and turning it from a severely practical to an unabashedly glamorous garb. Coloured and patterned suits for both sexes were recorded in California by the American journal *Men's Wear* in June 1926.

Already in 1925 *Punch* had depicted men wearing topless trunks at continental watering places. Laurence Olivier wore them in the film *Perfect Understanding* released in 1933, and the Duke of Kent was photographed wearing them in

110 Man's bathing suit hand-knitted in maroon-red wool. Stockinet with garter-stitch straps and borders, *c.* 1936.

that year. Trunks required a belt, usually of white webbing.

The one-piece suit was only slowly ousted by trunks. In the name of sunbathing and its good effects, the one-piece in 1930 was contrived to leave the back bare, and open panes were inserted in the flanks. The shoulders were reduced to straps, and necklines plunged. Hand-knit patterns were published for such garments, suggesting Art Deco colours – orange, beige, cream, brown and grey – especially for the part above the belt. The belt was adopted for the one-piece as well as for trunks.

During the same decade hand-knitted bathing suits for women went from the arch prettiness of a suit in orange and royal blue which had a skirt of six orange petals falling round the waist (published in *Fancy Needlework Illustrated* No 103: 1931), to superb sleek designs of real beauty.

By the end of the 1930s trunks were gaining in popularity for men. The women's much abbreviated bikini, started in France in 1946, had

2763 PATONS & BALDWINS' HELPS TO KNITTERS PRICE **2**ᴰ

111 A bathing costume recipe *c.* 1935.

lasting success. Most women took to the two-piece suit, leaving the midriff bare as well as the back. By 1955 men were wearing bikini briefs.

Hand-knitting patterns continued to appear, standard trunks for men and excellently designed two-piece costumes for women. They were published in leaflets and magazines until 1951. By then nylon fabrics had been developed and soon the male bikini was being made so narrow at the hips that in 1956 the Army's official magazine, *Soldier*, was advertising men's swimming briefs with 1½ in. (4 cm) sides. The belt had gone. The hand-knitwear designs could not produce an exiguous garment that would fit and stay on without a belt. When Lycra was produced in 1960, a filmy woven fabric appeared, lighter in weight than anything knit and many times more elastic,

and even machine-knit fabric retreated from the swimwear field.

Hand-knitted bathing suits looked and felt thick, were not streamlined and sagged when wet. Designers strove to improve them by using carefully chosen stitch-structures, especially after World War II. Spinners marketed non-shrink, non-stretch yarns, such as Paton's 'Crocus' bathing-costume wool, as early as the 1930s. Hand-knit suits were unsatisfactory because they were usually made too large; but the sales of the special yarns and the pattern leaflets show that swimwear has a real, if brief, place in the history of hand-knitting.

Marjory Tillotson

Marjory Tillotson (1886–1965), the first English designer of hand-knit clothing on a grand scale, exercised a dominant influence on British handknitting from 1910 until after World War II. The Tillotsons had been in the textile business since Robert Tillotson moved from Lancashire to Sowerby in Yorkshire and became a cloth master early in the seventeenth century. A descendant, John Tillotson, married Alice Langton of Melton Mowbray and in the 1880s was owner of Atlas Carpets of Halifax.

They had ten children. Marjory, the third child, was considered the family dunce, yet at school she won a national drawing competition three years running and went on to Leicester School of Art to study carpet design. She began to work for Atlas Carpets, but the Edwardian era was hard on the smaller carpet firms: Atlas Carpets was absorbed by the great John Crossley and Co., in 1906. The Tillotson girls had to find other ways of earning their living.

Marjory's younger sister, Muriel, became secretary to Frank Mills, managing director of the spinning firm, J. and J. Baldwin, Halifax. In 1908 Mills visited Germany on business and there saw for the first time knitting pattern leaflets. He asked Muriel Tillotson to undertake a demonstration department for the firm and produce leaflet material. Muriel was not attracted by the idea, and

112 Marjory Tillotson, the leading designer of hand-knitwear in England before the Second World War. The photograph was taken in 1912.

suggested her sister take over the organization. Marjory established the new department with a group of girls recruited from the mill, and soon issued her first leaflet. Although called a 'Beehive Knitting Booklet', it was a pattern for a crochet jacket and cap. The second leaflet was for a knitted jacket.

Marjory lectured in Canada and America in 1912. Her output of patterns continued. She produced 10 'Busy Bee' books and 25 'Beehive Booklets'. Some time before 1913 she wrote the first edition of *Woolcraft*. Her name never appeared on that brochure, but through it her influence was enormous.

When J. and J. Baldwin amalgamated with John Paton's in 1920, they also absorbed Whitmore's of Leicester, on whose staff was Edward Richardson, a buyer and seller of raw wool. He married Marjory Tillotson in the same year. After 1924, when her second daughter was born, Marjory worked only as a free-lance designer and writer. In 1929 she was asked to prepare the knitting and crochet chapters for Blackie's *Modern Needlecraft* (1932), edited by Davide C. Minter. This led to Pitman publishing

her *The School Knitting Book* (1931) and in 1934 *The Complete Knitting Book*. The latter was revised four times, appearing last in the fifth edition of 1948. It was still in print in 1967, having held its place as the standard English book on the subject for over 30 years. Yet it was 50 years before its time in urging the presentation of recipes in diagram form.

Her daughter Selina went to Halifax School of Art in 1938 to study dress design, and mother and daughter were soon co-operating in making made-to-measure knitted suits for women. When war broke out a year later they were called upon at very short notice to produce patterns for comforts for soldiers and sailors.

After the war mother and daughter separated

113 The first English pattern leaflet, 1908. It is labelled as a knitting booklet, though the recipe is for crochet. By Marjory Tillotson.

BEEHIVE KNITTING BOOKLETS No. 1.

RAGLAN COAT CAP & SCARF

Made in an easy Crochet Stitch from

TRADE B·B MARK

BEEHIVE DOUBLE KNITTING WOOL

J. & J. BALDWIN & PARTNERS LTD.
HALIFAX
· ENGLAND ·
ESTABLISHED 1785

PRICE ONE PENNY (or by post 1½d.)

their interests for administrative reasons – Selina's work attracted purchase tax, her mother's did not. They continued, nevertheless, to work closely together, until Selina moved to Louth, in Lincolnshire, where she developed exclusive suits, knitted in pure wool bouclé on 2³⁄₄ mm needles by 150 outworkers.

Marjory was working almost full-time again. Many of her patterns were printed by Watmough's of Bradford, who had become leaders in this field of printing. She designed for Marshall and Snelgrove, Lee Target, Copley-Smith, Golden Eagle and Emu Wools among others, fulfilling her aim of working as a designer for 50 years. Her last order was completed after her 75th birthday in 1961. When her husband retired in 1954, they moved to Harrogate. Marjory died in 1965, at Rishworth, near Halifax, after several years of distressing heart trouble.

Woolcraft

Hardly a home in England was without the booklet *Woolcraft* between the wars. It contained excellent succinct instructions for the basic techniques of knitting and crochet, together with a good repertory of basic garment recipes. The garments were always designed for women knitting practical and warm clothes for their families, and the price of the booklet was comparable to that of a weekly magazine.

The first edition was made for J. and J. Baldwin of Halifax, just before the outbreak of war in 1914, by Marjory Tillotson. The cover showed a beautiful young woman in a spotted foulard tie, white blouse and black skirt, knitting a sock. The price was twopence. A revised edition was soon called for.

Before the war ended a third edition appeared. A rather plainer lady in a white dress graced the cover, on an orange background. The price rose to threepence; but before 1920 yet another edition, with a green background to the lady on the cover, came out at fourpence halfpenny. In 1920 Baldwins amalgamated with Patons of Alloa. The cover of *Woolcraft* became first blue and then (for the sixth edition) yellow, and the price was sixpence. The contents were revised and re-arranged, but without major change, save that accurate tension measurements first appeared in the sixth edition.

Sometime in the mid-twenties the style of the typography was changed again and some features of Paton's equivalent booklet, *The Universal Knitting Book*, were brought in. The orange and black cover showed a highly sophisticated Art Deco lady, rather like a witch. Fair Isle was referred to in the advertisements, but not in the text.

The eighth edition had a blue, orange and black cover in slightly less formal Art Deco, showing a more domesticated knitter; but it is the ninth edition, of 1933, that seems to have gone through most impressions. The fluffily soft lady on the orange and brown cover was fully domesticated. This was the edition that introduced the 'auto' heel for stockings, copied from machine-knit hosiery.

The contents changed little when the edition of 1937 appeared with a skein of red wool on the cover. The price remained sixpence: but within a year or two the red skein had gone up to sevenpence. About 1939 the twelfth edition had a green skein on it and cost eightpence. The contents had been abridged and reset; yet the sole reflection of changing fashions was the inclusion of the pixie hood. This edition was soon re-issued at ninepence.

Wartime Economy Standards for Book Production were promulgated in 1942. The only edition of *Woolcraft* produced under them was the thirteenth, a slim booklet of only 48 pages, deprived of recipes for adult outerwear. The skein of wool on the cover was blue and the price ninepence. From the thirteenth onwards all the editions were numbered on the cover, and every edition had a new cover design.

Britain cheered up in 1950 and the fourteenth *Woolcraft* had a cartoon on the cover. The influence of James Norbury began to show in some new designs included, and the price went up to one shilling.

Norbury's touch is unmistakable in the fifteenth edition, 1952. Fair Isle patterns appear at last. The price is one shilling and sixpence. Further editions appeared in 1956 and 1962. The price stayed at one shilling and sixpence, but in 1962 (seventeenth edition) the garments were photographed on living models for the first time.

In 1967 the eighteenth edition cost two shillings and sixpence, man-made fibres got belated acknowledgment, and the recipes were like the plainer pattern leaflets of the time. In 1973 the price went up to 30 new pence, in 1977 to 50p and in 1981 to 85p. The 1985 edition had a colourful and nostalgic cover to celebrate Patons' bicentenary, but the contents had changed little in the two decades since 1967. The price was now letter-coded so that it could change with inflation.

One feature is common to all editions from the first to the last: every one contains a recipe for knee-cap warmers. They are a symbol of the neatness, the conservatism, the practical purpose of the most influential knitting publication ever.

Woolcraft even made its mark in the literature of the Bloomsbury set. David Garnett poked fun at an imaginary booklet called 'Advanced woolcraft for all occasions' in his macabre story about obsessive knitters, 'Purl and plain', published in 1973 but probably written in the 1930s. The Bloomsbury women certainly knitted. Edith Sitwell confessed in a letter that she thought nothing of Virginia Woolf's writing, though she considered her 'a beautiful little knitter'. Mrs Ramsay's heather-mixture stockings, made in the *Woolcraft* tradition, feature in Virginia Woolf's *To the Lighthouse* (1927).

Charity knitting

Charity knitting is an offspring of drawing-room knitting: ladies knitted warm comforts for their coachmen. There was some ambivalence about knitting for the poor, because Victorian gentlefolk thought the poor should be encouraged to be industrious, and knitting had for centuries been a cottage occupation. Knitting for soldiers was more appropriate.

Knitting for the unemployed was occasionally encouraged, as at the time of industrial distress in the Lancashire cotton towns in 1862. The

114 Henrietta Warleigh's last booklet, 1902. Size 11.7 x 8.6 cm (4²⁄₃ x 3³⁄₈ in.). The contents are almost solely knitting recipes, including gloves, shields (chest protectors), seaboot stockings and Uhlan caps.

economic depression of the early 1930s stimulated another burst of philanthropic knitting. Early in 1932 the Personal Service League was founded, with Lady Londonderry as chairman. Queen Mary became patron of the League, which worked from headquarters at 38 Grosvenor Place, lent by the Duke of Westminister.

The Duchess of York (the present Queen Mother) joined the knitters – and placed a room in her house at 145 Piccadilly at the disposal of the league. Men's and boys' pullovers and cardigans were specially asked for. On 2 November 1934 *The Times* asked every woman in Britain to knit one garment for the unemployed during the winter. It was hoped that 100,000 garments would be received from the National Knitting Appeal.

The league continued to exist for at least ten

years. A letter from the chairman in *The Times* of 31 January 1940 indicates that the Personal Service League was handling all supplies of wool for the Royal Naval Comforts Fund and for knitting for the Royal Air Force. The League was acting as a distributing agent under the Wool Control Board and between 1 October 1939 and 1 January 1940 had distributed over 100 tons of knitting wools to more than 50 regimental comforts funds. Throughout the war the work continued. Aid was given to refugees, often using American gifts. The Personal Service League was last mentioned in *The Times* on 1 November 1945.

Since the Second World War British women have knitted for the poor in other countries. Aid organizations took up what the missionary societies had long been doing. Countless patchwork blankets, using up huge quantities of yarn oddments, have been sent to such places as Korea during and after the Korean war of 1950-3. They continue to be sent, together with children's clothes, to many Third World countries. Oxfam, in particular, has taken trouble to commission and distribute suitable recipes.

Charitable work in a different sense, but still a lively section of knitting in Britain, is the making of small objects and garments for bazaars. Most of the major spinners publish patterns for such work. Unhappily, because of the low prices for which bazaar articles are sold, the quality of design is very poor. Teacosies, toilet-roll covers and toys comprise the bulk of the output, which is usually much inferior to similar small objects made in the nineteenth century.

Scandinavia and the Baltic

The National Museum in Copenhagen possesses a silver knitting-needle holder, dated to the 1570s. The oldest fragment of Danish knitting is a piece of wool dyed with indigo, damask-knitted with eight-pointed stars in diamonds. Denmark is thought to have knitted before Sweden and Norway. Iceland claims a woollen mitten excavated at Storaborg dated to the first half of the sixteenth century. Certainly the tenants of the Bishop of Holar in northern Iceland were knitting stockings in 1581.

Each country has special traditions. The soft *lopi* wool of Iceland was originally one stage in the preparation of spun wool. It was used experimentally in machine knitting by a home knitter in 1920 and became popular for handknitting during the 1930s. Colour-dyed *lopi* has appeared in the 1980s. Characteristic national patterns in colour-knitting can be seen in the Faeroes. The mittens of Latvia are distinctive in their highly ornamental designs. Knitting is known in Lapland, and has a strong tradition in Finland, but historical studies are not yet available.

Norway was possibly later than her neighbours in taking to knitting. Widespread use of knitwear dates only from the mid-nineteenth century. In all three countries stranded-colour knitting became popular from 1830 or so; body garments such as we might call jerseys, however, seem to have been in use in Sweden since the middle of the eighteenth

115 The 'poor man's brocade' – a Swedish version of the universal 'carnation' motif.

century. Elsa Gudjonsson quotes an Icelandic manuscript pattern book dated 1776, which seems to resemble German pattern books of the same century.

During the twentieth century Sweden has seen two notable experiments in cooperative knitting. Binge, or the Halland Knitting Cooperative, was begun in 1907 by Berta Borgstrom at Laholm. The workers produce 'traditional' patterns, which have by now become standardized and are done almost entirely in red, white and blue stranded knitting. Many of the garments – striking when first seen, because of the stark colours – look like uninspired Shetland patterns without the good colour-sense that typifies Shetland work. Yet Binge knitting is done according to charts issued by the central management, which also supplies the wool.

Bohus knitting was differently conceived. It was founded by Emma Jacobsson (1883–1977), née Stidsny, wife of the governor of Bohuslan province, and organized from her official residence in Göteborg, to help counteract the effects of unemployment among the stonecutters of the province. Wool was distributed to outworkers, whose number reached a maximum of 870 in 1947. In 1956 production was at its height, but no replacement could be found for Mrs Jacobsson when she retired, and Bohus Strickning ceased to operate in 1969.

The patterns were not inspired solely by traditional Swedish folk knitting. The founder, who had once set out on an artistic career in Vienna, sought inspiration for Bohus patterns from many sources, and gathered a team of gifted designers around her. Their fabrics were not restricted to stockinet. Their use of purl stitches on the right side of stranded knitting was famous, and they were highly inventive in combining colour with fabric texture.

Mary Thomas

Mary Thomas's two books are not unfairly nicknamed 'the knitter's bible'. They have stayed in print for nearly half a century and are standard professional references for technique.

She was born Mary Hedger in 1889 at Wantage, Berkshire. Educated in music and art, she was drawn to fashion journalism and in her twenties went to America to work as a fashion artist for the *New York Pictorial Review*. In June 1913 she returned to Europe and, after war broke out, went to France as an army nurse. There she married Arthur Thomas, an officer of the Bedfordshire Regiment. By 1916 she was living in St Mark's, Cheltenham, doing fashion drawings for Harrods and active in the Cheltenham Women's Suffrage Society.

She never lost her interest in women's rights, but fashion was her world and journalism her work. She lived in the West End of London, enjoyed the then new luxury of air travel, and flew regularly from Croydon to the Paris dress shows, where she claimed acquaintance with Elsa Schiaparelli. She became fashion editor of *The Gentlewoman*, and her

116 Mary Thomas (right) at Ascot 14 June 1921.

two children, Gavrelle and Richard, were dragooned into service as juvenile models for fashion photography.

In 1930 she became editor of *The Needlewoman*; but in 1933 she and her husband separated; and in 1935, much to her indignation, *The Needlewoman* was bought by George Newnes. From then on she worked as a free-lance writer.

She turned to writing books and began with two successful titles on embroidery: *Mary Thomas's Dictionary of Embroidery Stitches* (1934) and *Mary Thomas's Embroidery Book* (1936). The second established the style and character she later applied to her knitting books. In 1938 she produced *Teach Yourself Embroidery* in the English Universities Press series.

By 1936 she was hard at work on what she intended to be an exhaustive compendium of knitting history and technique. It soon became clear that she must do the work in two stages. *Mary Thomas's Knitting Book* appeared in 1938, and *Mary Thomas's Book of Knitting Patterns* in 1943.

The clarity of her descriptions of knitting technique and methods is remarkable. She analysed and classified hand knitting in a way that has become normative. Her treatment of knitting history was less certain, but this was only to be expected at that stage of the study. She first drew attention to Asian and East European knitting and travelled Europe to find knitted garments in museums.

She died in 1948, whilst her book on crochet was still in the planning stage. In the last ten years of her life she had been a member of the London Buddhist Society.

World War II

Knitting for the armed forces in the Second World War could be done in three colours, for 'Air Force blue' had been added to navy blue and army khaki. Such knitting was more highly organized than it had been during the First World War. It was also less obsessive, because the slaughter and hardship of men in the second war, grievous though it was,

never ran at the concentrated pitch of horror that was so protracted during the 1914-18 war.

In the second war the British government was much concerned about morale at home. Rationing was successfully managed, not least for clothing. A system of coupons for cloth and clothing included knitting wool. Designs were published with notes about the economical use of clothing coupons. Unravelling garments in order to knit the yarn again became a normal skill for any knitter. Ingenuity developed spontaneously, and the improvement in British designs after the war was partly prompted by the stimulus derived from wartime problems.

117 Probably the last leaflet for a man's bathing costume, *c.* 1946. An austerity format 14 x 23 cm (5½ x 9 in.), of the war and post-war years.

3ᴅ—BATHING TRUNKS—2 SIZES—485·

Patons Purple Heather Fingering 4-ply

P&B
WOOLS

Koster and Murray

118 Post-war knitting 1946. An illustration from Koster and Murray *The Weekend Knitting Book* 1946.

Jane Koster (1900–) and Margaret Murray (1906–74) were leaders in hand-knitting design from 1940 until the 1950s. Jane married Margaret's brother Rowland Koster. Another brother, Douglas, had a design studio in Lincoln's Inn. From that address the sisters-in-law launched a child model agency that developed into a notable partnership in knitwear design.

In 1940 Odhams Press published their first book of knitting patterns, *Practical Knitting Illustrated*, which was reprinted seven times and remained in print for a decade. It was followed by almost annual Koster and Murray titles: *Knitting for All* (1941); *Complete Home Knitting* (1942); *Knitted Garments for All* (1944); *Modern Knitting* (1945); *Practical Family Knitting* (1946); *Knitting Illustrated* (1948); and *Complete Family Knitting* (1949). After their association with Odhams ended, the firm published other knitting books in the same format, but lacking the distinction of the Koster-Murray

partnership. All their books were reprinted, some several times.

In 1944 they published the first technical account of Yugoslav knitting. In 1950 they wrote *The Minerva Knitting Annual* (see page 210), named after their office at Minerva House in Wellington Street, near Aldwych. The annual contains their most discriminating collection and showed a pioneer interest in the history of British knitting. They published booklets and wrote for the daily and monthly press, as well as designing for Sirdar, Lee Target, Lister, Templeton, Wendy, Hayfield, Twilley and other spinners. Jane Koster was in charge of the firm's public relations, while Margaret Murray took care of the technical side, including the recipe-writing. In 1958 their partnership ended. Jane Koster continued with her daughter Jan, who had been working with Koster and Murray for some years; Margaret Murray began working with her daughter-in-law. Jane Koster made a notable collection of knitted items, especially British jerseys and ganseys. She was also a successful lecturer and television speaker.

James Norbury

James Norbury was the strongest single influence in British knitting during the 25 years after the Second World War, through his writings and his designs. Norbury was born at Knutsford in Cheshire on 24 February 1904, son of a village blacksmith and a village dressmaker. He was brought up largely by his grandmother, who encouraged him to knit. He later claimed that he could turn a sock heel before he was five and was knitting garments for others by the time he was nine. During the First World War he went from door to door selling knitted kettle-holders from a borrowed baker's-basket to raise money for the Red Cross.

At the age of 19 he sold a design for an artificial silk jumper to a firm of spinners. He worked as a designer for the spinning firm Copley Smith, and in 1946 became chief designer for Patons and Baldwins. From the early 1950s he became the BBC's television knitter – a fat, bearded fellow with chubby fingers, roundly admonishing viewers about bad knitting habits. He retired in March 1969 and died peacefully on 26 July 1972 at Isle Abbotts near Ilminster in Somerset.

During his professional career with Patons he travelled widely, especially in Europe, searching for traces of knitting history. He liked nothing better than going to provincial towns to present knitwear fashion shows. There was more than a little of the showman in him.

His first book was *The Knitter's Craft* (1950), in which he was already dictating that the needles should be at least 13 inches long (33 cm), the righthand one tucked under the arm, the lefthand needle doing all the work. His next book, *Let's Learn to Knit* (1951), sold on his television reputation.

In *Knit with Norbury* (1952) the pedagogic tone was well-established. Marjorie Proops of the *Daily Herald* wrote in the foreword that he 'will dictate his patterns as a writer dictates a manuscript; and from the quick-fire dictation emerges a sweater or a suit that women rave about'. He had already done a booklet of attractive patterns for her: *The Daily Herald Family Knitting Book* (1951).

In autumn 1952 *Wool Knowledge*, organ of the International Wool Secretariat, began to publish 'Knitting Yesterday and Today', three articles on the history of knitting. His lecture to the Royal Society of Arts on 'The Knitter's Craft' had been printed in 1951. In October 1952 he lectured to the Wool Education Society on 'Design in Knitting'.

His name was good for sales. *James Norbury's Crochet Book* (1952) and *Let's Learn to Sew* (1953) and *Counted Thread Embroidery* (1955) were off his main subject. Meanwhile he was writing advice to knitters in his firm's annual booklets, hammering away at tension control and the proper laundering of wool.

The year 1957 saw three Norbury titles published: *The Structure of Knitted Fabrics*, an unsigned book for the International Wool Secretariat which does not live up to the theory suggested by its title; *Odhams Encyclopaedia of Knitting*, the bulkiest of his books, republished in 1968 without his name; and *The Penguin Knitting Book*, a compendious collection of recipes, some of them distinguished. In the same year Oxford University Press published Volume III of *A History of Technology*, to which Norbury contributed 'A note on knitting and knitted fabrics'. Much of the article is about sprang; the part on the history of knitting is mostly wrong. He says, for instance, that hand knitting virtually disappeared from southern England from the end of the reign of Elizabeth I to mid-Victorian times. Yet at that time there was no textile historian in Britain doing better than Norbury.

Knitting is an Adventure (1958), dedicated to journalist and writer Ursula Bloom, is an attractive book of 'fashion knitting' with a deliberate aura of glamour. The dust-jacket declares that Norbury was a leader of the brighter-wear-for-men school, a gourmet, an opera fan, an animal-lover (he published *Your Pets and Mine* in 1955), a character. There is journalistic flair in his presentation of the romantic legends of Aran and Shetland, the

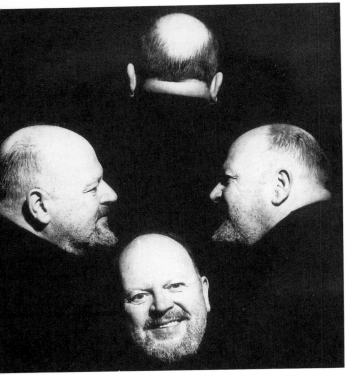

119 James Norbury, 1904-72.

romantic appeal of Italy and Scandinavia. And the last chapter is about home knitting machines.

In 1959 Norbury edited the excellent knitting section of the English translation of Ruth Zechlin's *The Girl's Book of Crafts*; and his lecture to the Wool Education Society, 'News about knitting', was published. *Knitting for the New Arrival* (1960) was dedicated to the tiny babe who adorned the frontispiece. It is possibly the most stylish baby-knitting book ever published.

Traditional Knitting Patterns (1962) has probably retained more influence than any of his other books. It consists of stitch and fabric patterns attributed to different countries, but undated and otherwise unidentified. Some of those labelled as British certainly come from Victorian publications; a 'Spanish' Adam and Eve is from Danish cross-stitch.

There was now a lapse in Norbury's book production before BBC Woman's Hour published *Knit! with James Norbury* (1968). This is a simple, almost severe book, entirely about technique, with no recipes, no history, no romance and no guesswork.

His last book was *The Family Knitting Book* (1969). The introduction 'In praise of knitting' is a mish-mash of historical bits and pieces. Norbury now claims 50 years' experience of knitting: 'I was a foolhardy lover who has always been prepared to throw his loyalty and devotion at the feet of Mistress Knitting'. The designs in the book are among his best.

Colourful, gifted, self-centred, for all his faults Norbury was a notable designer and the only person of his day who tried to learn about the history of knitting. Because he lacked training as a historian he made many mistakes but he did open up the subject as a whole.

Viennese lace

In the eighteenth century, 'Vienna lace' was a bobbin lace, usually in earth colours of green and brown. It was revived after 1890 at the Imperial Central School of Lacemaking in Vienna, which also produced 'Vienna lace' in needlepoint. Knitted lace in Germany and Austria goes back at least as far as *Anweisung zur Kunst-Strickerei* by Charlotte Leander, published in its third edition at Erfurt in 1843. When Aurelie Obermayer-Wallner published *Die Technik der Kunst-Strickerei* at Osnabruck in 1893, and republished it at Vienna in 1896, she proudly announced on the title page her high Viennese patronage. The book is full of lace patterns, but like Leander's they are little if at all different from Victorian English designs, though they include some edgings for fans. Even today the museum authorities in Vienna know nothing of the 'Viennese lace' described by James Norbury and other English writers.

The delicate designs that are now called Viennese lace may owe their origin to Herbert Niebling, who in the 1920s began to revive and develop the designs of the Biedermeier period (1820–48). He wrote no books, but his designs were published in periodicals by Burda. He died in the 1960s. Other designers between the two world wars were Christine Duchrow, who published in

Berlin and some of whose designs strongly resemble Azores lace; and Erich Engeln, whose patterns were published in Augsburg. Many of their designs were round or oval lace mats. All their designs were much more delicate than nineteenth-century lace from Britain and Germany.

Viennese lace has become well-known in Britain and America through the work of Marianne Kinzel (born 1908), an Austrian educated in Prague, where she had extended training in the Needlework College. She married Walter Kinzel, a teacher of mathematics, and they lived in Prague. After Hitler's invasion of Czechoslovakia in autumn 1938 they came to work as teachers in Newcastle-upon-Tyne. In 1948 Mrs Kinzel published the first of her lace patterns, calling them 'Viennese' simply because she had learned her skills from a Viennese lecturer, not because there was any recognized school or tradition of knitted lace bearing that name. Her designs have a personal style that is notably different from the work of other designers, and are of great beauty. In her later books she abandoned the epithet 'Viennese' and called her work simply 'modern lace knitting'.

So it appears that 'Viennese lace' is an accidental name for a tradition that developed relatively recently in Germany and Austria. It has, however, considerably increased the scope of decorative knitting.

Tyrolean and Bavarian knitting

James Norbury seems to have invented the name 'Tyrolean knitting' in his *Encyclopaedia of knitting* (1956). He used it to describe cable and bobble patterns, particularly those that were ornamented with embroidery. The name was probably an example of his flair for giving a good name on the basis of mental association rather than historical investigation.

Rae Compton in *The Complete Book of Traditional Knitting* (1983) has a section on Central Europe which points to Norbury's source. There is a tradition from that region, including Austria and Bavaria, of knitting stockings with intricate ribbing,

cabling and interlacing of ribs. Rae Compton believes it goes back to the eighteenth century. It certainly flourished during the nineteenth century.

There is no evidence that body-garments were knitted in this style before the twentieth century. The strong similarity of the technique to modern Aran knitting rouses a suspicion that Central European technique, particularly the decorative use of ribs of twisted stitches, may have reached the Irish knitters through Central European immigrants to the United States of America.

The renaissance of the 1970s and 1980s

Two books appeared in the autumn of 1977 which signalled, if not created, a renaissance in British knitting: *The Art of Knitting* edited by Eve Harlow and *Knitting Patterns* by Patricia Roberts. *The Art of Knitting* typified growing interest in the history of the craft and a widespread desire to seek inspiration in the past. It was a colourful book, containing pictures of historical knitted pieces from museum collections with suggestions for adapting fabric patterns from them. The new designs were generally not skilful, and the historical blurb, though industriously worked up from most of the available sources in English, was clearly not written by a historian. Not really a good or reliable work, it was yet important, for colour and curiosity about history are essential to the knitting renaissance.

Patricia Roberts's book was even more important. Born in 1945 at Barnard Castle, she was trained at Leicester College of Art and Design. From 1967 to 1971 she worked on *Woman's Weekly* and *Woman and Home*, editing their comparatively staid knitting receipts. In 1969 the Shetland education authority invited her to teach knitwear design to Shetlanders, but Patricia now prefers to emphasize how much she learned about Shetland knitting skills.

Her own first published patterns appeared in magazines for teenagers, such as *19* and *Honey*. In 1972 she turned freelance. Very soon her creations were being sold in expensive shops in London and

120 Lace dress, knitted in one piece from fine black-dyed Shetland wool and mounted on pink rayon net. *c.* 1960.

New York. In 1974 increasing difficulties in buying natural fibre yarns and the limited colour ranges available led her to start selling knitting kits by mail order. The kits consisted of a recipe with the yarns required for making it up, and have been widely imitated.

20 Patricia Roberts Knitting Patterns appeared in 1975. It was a high-quality fashion publication, like a superior magazine, that put hand knitting into a new perspective, determinedly shedding the dowdy domesticated image. Almost annual softback pattern books of similar type have followed that trail-blazer. The 1977 hardcover book was a compilation of the first three softbacks. Further hardbacks, based on the softcover volumes, appeared in 1981, 1984 and 1985.

Meanwhile, in 1976 the first Patricia Roberts Knitting Shop had opened in Kinnerton Street,

Knightsbridge; Patricia Roberts yarns were marketed; and Patricia Roberts garments began to be exported to Europe, East Asia and Australia as well as America. Eventually there were four shops in London, others in Hong Kong, Melbourne and Nicosia.

Patricia is married to John Heffernan, an industrial designer. Her success lay in her feeling for the craft as well as for the clothes. She designed clothes that were both technically outstanding and visually pleasing. Her early designs were often inventive reinterpretations of older patterns, especially Shetland patterns, but she has developed complex techniques of fabric construction (colour plate 14).

Her patterns continue to appear, and her third collection of them in hardback was produced in 1986. She remains the greatest success in 'designer knitting'. 'Designer' has become an item of marketing jargon, essentially silly (because every garment ever knitted has to be designed), but now commercially elevated to a kind of snobbish superiority. Knitwear 'designer' businesses have proliferated all over the land, and advertise their products as exclusive, and therefore expensive. If they are handmade, the products have to be expensive, because they cannot be produced fast, nor in great quantity. Unhappily, much of the 'designer' output is not of Patricia Roberts quality.

The reason for the burgeoning of this industry lies in the establishment of many schools of fashion and garment design throughout Britain during the 1960s. Knitwear attracts designers, most of whom are young, because it suits the needs of the period. Knitwear is comfortable, and casual clothes are increasingly worn by all classes and age-groups; knitwear is versatile, and can be both stylish and colourful; and it is easier and cheaper for a designer to amass a wide variety of knitting yarns than to collect a wide variety of fabrics.

The weakness of this design explosion has lain in ignorance of the techniques and resources of handknitting. Designers have taken or made coloured graphic designs on paper and forced them into knitted form. Some have taken inferior designs and sold them by a witty gimmick. The famous sweater that gained great popularity because the Princess of Wales wore it was scarlet, with solid rows of white sheep all over it, but was a success because a single black sheep was introduced to the flock.

Poor design sells well, if it is cheap, in most fields; but good design comes to the top. There are signs of improvement in knitwear design, not least under the influence of Kaffe Fassett, a gifted colourist (colour plate 13).

Kaffe's first design to be published was called a 'Moroccan waistcoat', which appeared in *Vogue Knitting*, Spring 1969. Born in San Francisco in 1937, he gave himself the name of Kaffe (rhyming with 'safe') when he went to boarding school aged 14. He then won a scholarship to study painting at the Museum of Fine Arts in Boston. By 1964 he had moved to London, where he began to establish a reputation as a painter of still life and portraits, especially children's portraits. He delighted in still life with intricately patterned fabrics, and when he and his friend, the dress designer Bill Gibb, were visiting Holm Mills in Inverness, he discovered the coloured wools produced for Shetland knitting. He bought a range of 20 colours.

Fired with delight at the colours, as he later related, he learned to knit in the train returning from Inverness to London. All 20 colours went into the first cardigan he made. Then came the *Vogue Knitting* waistcoat, and the Italian designing firm, Missoni, commissioned work from him. Since then, though he continues to paint and to design cross-stitch patterns (commonly called 'tapestry') and furnishing fabrics, he has become most famous for his knitwear designs. He has worked with a number of firms, but his best known collaboration is with Rowan Yarns of Huddersfield, which has spun ranges of knitting wool to his colour specification.

A typical Fassett garment is designed for one size and is asexual. It is made in stockinet with, perhaps, ribbed welts and cuffs. The colour is what makes his work outstanding. No other designer has such a sure touch with colour schemes. Part of his secret is to use a large number of hues and shades in one garment, sometimes several score. Kaffe has not influenced knitting technique or garment shape – his garments are of long-lasting styles – but his influence is great. His book *Glorious Knitting* (1985) was a runaway success, far more rapidly sold out than any of the other successful knitting titles of the mid-1980s. It is also the most artistically literate of knitting books.

Tessa Lorant

Tessa Lorant is one of the small number of women in England who bring a mathematically trained mind to their knitting. She has also a flair for reviving nineteenth-century patterns and re-editing them. Born in Berlin in 1929, she had a Hungarian father and an American mother. Almost at once the family moved to Vienna, where Tessa learned to knit in the German fashion, though she never became adept at it. In 1938 the family came to England, and when she went to university in 1947 she read mathematics. Her tutor was both a keen geometer and a keen hand knitter, who interested her pupil in the topological characteristics of knitted loops. At the same time Tessa learned to knit in the British way, carrying the yarn on the right hand. In 1951 she was given United States citizenship, moved to New York and became a computer programmer. Interest in computers led her to machine knitting.

She married an Englishman, took his citizenship, and returned to England in 1954, where she improved her knitting and crochet while bringing up her children. Her husband encouraged her to produce *The Batsford Book of Hand and Machine Knitting* (1980), in preparing which she became interested in nineteenth-century patterns. She republished some of these in *The Batsford Book of Hand and Machine Knitted Laces* (1982), which was quickly followed by six books on machine knitting, crochet and yarns, and four books of re-edited nineteenth-century patterns, issued from her husband's Thorn Press at Godney, near Glastonbury: *Knitted Lace Edgings* (1981), *Knitted Lace Collars* (1983), *Knitted Quilts and Flounces* (1982), *Knitted Shawls and Wraps* (1984), and *Knitted Lace Doilies* (1986).

Tessa Lorant has a distinctive intellectual approach. She is concerned to preserve old fabric patterns by re-editing the recipes. She has devised a symbolic method of recording the patterns which makes possible the transfer of many to knitting machines. She also researches methods of dressing knitted fabric, experiments with the properties of modern yarns, and has produced several gauges and other mathematical aids for knitters.

Audrie Stratford

Audrie Stratford is another woman who takes an intellectual pleasure in knitting. Miss Stratford lives in King's Lynn and earns her living as the proprietor of a string of menswear shops in East Anglia. She was born in Johannesburg in 1907, learnt to knit at the age of four, and claims to have knitted continually ever since. She was educated at King's Lynn High School and took a degree in physiology at Bedford College, London. From 1932 to 1948 she taught physiology at Chelsea Polytechnic.

The turning point in her life, so far as knitting was concerned, came in 1948, when she spent a year as a guest of the Western Australian Association of Women Graduates. The Association had the laudable and imaginative idea of inviting a war-weary Englishwoman from the International Federation of University Women to spend a year in Australia, simply resting, or otherwise enjoying a fallow period, while contributing to the restoration of international communications for Australian university women, who had been isolated during the war. Miss Stratford admits to some unease about accepting the invitation literally and taking a year's rest. While resting, she naturally knitted. Noticing the importance of the cardigan in Perth, where the cool of the evening is never cool enough for an overcoat, but the cardigan is ubiquitous, she decided to knit cardigans as tokens of gratitude for her stay. As she planned her gifts she began to realize how bad her knitting habits were. She started to criticize her work fundamentally before she returned to England, and is still learning. In 1958 and 1967 she visited Shetland, where she learnt much from what she heard and saw.

In 1972 her book *Introducing Knitting* was published. It was the first book to tackle fundamental questions of hand-knitting technique in terms of time-and-motion efficiency. In it, Miss Stratford proposed definitions for parts of the loop, introduced a variety of ways of casting on, (some of her own invention, such as silk-linked cast-on, which has been widely adopted) and generally encouraged a questioning approach. In 1978 she published privately for use by the Townswomen's Guild in King's Lynn the 32-page *Nowadays Knitting for New Knitters*, which condensed her message. Then in 1980 came a more ambitious but still privately published brochure *Better Knitting Made Easier for Blind People*, accompanying an audio-cassette. The written text contains lucid descriptions of knitting action.

Audrie Stratford's rigorous mind cannot disguise the sheer pleasure that she takes in life and her sense of fun. Without a sense of fun no knitter could have begged dough from a baker, rolled it into 'yarn', knitted it up, and persuaded the baker to bake knitted croutons. She has also knitted with spaghetti for yarn, sharpened two broom handles to knit a poncho, and with 20 yarns together, made an inch-thick mat.

Hashimoto Osamu

Hashimoto Osamu was born in Tokyo in 1948 and educated in the Arts School of Tokyo National University, where he became well versed in the culture of the Edo period (1605–1867) and Kabuki drama. He is a popular essayist and writer of historical tales, as well as a television personality and an inventive knitter, who has held several exhibitions of his work.

In 1982 Nihon Vogue, the leading publisher of knitting books in Japan, published *Chiyarenji Nitto: Otokoga Amu* ('Knitting challenge: men too can knit'), a beginner's book for four sweaters, all conservative in style. The most difficult was a simple Aran jumper. In 1983 Book 2 of the same title appeared. It contained three basic designs: a sleeveless pullover, crew-neck sweater, and cardigan, each with three variations. This book also contained pictures of Hashimoto's knitted *happi* coats, in multi-coloured designs derived from Edo period fabrics and pictures. A green coat was thickly splattered with pink cherry blossom, a red one with the same flowers in white. A sweater called 'Spring mist on distant mountains', in typically Japanese colours of navy blue, white, ochre and turquoise, had a scarlet border; a black coat carried huge waves of the sea and a sickle moon, recalling the nineteenth-century Japanese masters of the coloured woodblock print. These were picture-knits of remarkable quality.

His third and largest book came in 1984: *Otoko no nitto: Hashimoto Osamu no teitori ashitori* (subtitled in English *Osamu's Knit-Book*) published by Kawade Shobo Shinsha. As well as being a beginner's manual, *Osamu's Knit-Book* contains pictures of a rich collection of his work, modelled by young writers and pop singers. Some of the designs are posters knitted into sweaters bearing pictures from popular cartoons, or photographic renderings of singers such as the young man Sawada Kenji, nicknamed 'Julie'; or a portrait of David Bowie, called 'Arajin Sen', (*Arajin Sen* is the Japanization of 'Aladdin Sane', a Bowie record of 1973). Others are inspired by designs from *kabuki* costumes and kimono fabrics.

He has made some experiments in texture and style. 'Capulets' ball' is a zany interpretation of a slashed Elizabethan doublet; 'Stripper', named after Sawada's song 'Love is a stripper', has deliberately dropped stitches in the sleeves. His rendering of the simple shapes of traditional Japanese garments as knitted clothes is less striking than one might expect, but is notably successful.

Hashimoto designs unrepeatable garments, not planned for retail. His colour schemes and motifs owe much to his study of the Edo period. The frivolously 'pop' presentation of his work should not distract the historian from its craftsmanship.

Men knitters

There is nothing sex-linked about hand knitting. Yet in twentieth-century Britain it became unusual for men to knit. John Cathcart Wason (1848– 1921) an Old Rugbeian barrister and Ayrshire farmer, when he was MP for Shetland and Orkney made a sturdy defence of knitting as his hobby in *The Sun*, 22 February 1902, that showed he was eccentric in his social class.

Certain groups of men, however, still knitted. In the upper classes most little boys were taught the simplicities of plain and purl, especially if they had nannies to teach them. Knitting was taught to boys in kindergartens, and by many mothers and aunts. The purpose was usually either to keep hyperactive boys quiet or to respond to their insistent demands to be shown how knitting was done. Mechanical toys, school sports and other hobbies usually forced knitting out of a boy's interests before he was 10. By that time some had learned the mystery of turning a stocking heel, and not a few teenage boys were proud to use that skill to assist sisters, school matrons, aunts and other approved women who were less sure of the technique.

Geoffrey Fisher, Archbishop of Canterbury 1945–61, bringing up his sons in the 1930s and 1940s, had them all taught to knit. He said,

> 'Knitting is a distinct virtue. It's reflective and repetitive. Whenever you are engaged in doing a purely repetitive thing, your mind can reflect upon life.'

In 1985, 4 per cent of the priests in the diocese of Leicester were competent knitters – some of them because as poor curates they had learned to help their wives make clothes for their growing children. Bishop Denis Victor (1882–1949) used to knit on tedious boat journeys in his huge diocese of Lebombo (Mozambique).

Significantly the one of Archbishop Fisher's sons who continued to knit in later life was a doctor. Surgeons, with fingers accustomed to fine work with thread, often like knitting baby clothes. Charles Montague Fletcher (born in 1911), the distinguished epidemiologist, twice cured himself of smoking by knitting, and the equally distinguished gastro-enterologist Sir Francis Avery Jones (born in 1910) was a knitter.

Some famous, and many less famous, soldiers knitted. General Sir Charles Gardner (1898– 1983), governor-general of Tasmania, was one. Colonel Michael Ansell (born in 1905), who was blinded in 1941 at the age of 36, reckoned that knitting saved his reason during his first few months of blindness, when he was a prisoner-of-war at Rouen, undergoing four unsuccessful operations. At that time he was forced to lie flat with his head between sandbags. Many a soldier learned to knit during prolonged spells in the sick bay.

Other soldiers were taught to knit as part of their training. For those who were sent to Finland during 1938-9 for training with ski-troops, knitting was part of survival training. Others learned during the tedious waiting of Middle Eastern campaigns, or as prisoners-of-war. I know of an Italian prisoner-of-war who knitted coloured gloves for a little Yorkshire girl.

Sailors were the group most famous as knitting men. The story that Nelson knitted is probably apocryphal, but Mary Thomas, in an interesting article 'Our knitting forces' in *The Queen's Book of the Red Cross* (1939), talks of sailors' knitting. She noted that they liked beaded knitting, often held the needles 'flat in both hands' (i.e. under the palms) and formed their stitches in what she called the 'uncrossed eastern' or 'combined eastern-and-western' methods (see p 209). She said men prefer round knitting to flat knitting; are strongly drawn to stranded-colour knitting; dislike following written directions; prefer making things for their womenfolk, children and homes; produce firm even fabrics; and enjoy creating fabrics more than styling garments. She is less convincing when she claims that most men like to carry the working yarn over the left hand.

The most amusing publication encouraging men to knit is Dave Fougner's *The Manly Art of Knitting*, a 64-page booklet published by Scribners of New York in 1972. The cover shows a cowboy knitting on horseback. The recipes include a dog blanket, a saddle cloth, and a hammock knitted on shovel handles or billiard cues. The author breeds the spotted Appaloosa horses on his ranch in California, and claims that knitting strengthens his hands and improves his tennis.

It is now less surprising for a man to knit, and, although they are few in number, some of the most successful knitwear designers are men (colour plate 12).

The Knitting Craft Group

In 1975 a dozen or so major British hand-knitting wool-spinners founded the Knitting Craft Group of the British Hand Knitting Association, directed by Alec Dalglish. The group's activities are concerned with the teaching of hand knitting as a craft. It produces resources for teaching (booklets, packs, project leaflets, wall-charts, audio-visual material) and conducts in-service training programmes for teachers, including talks, displays, workshops and weekend courses.

In the mid-seventies there were signs that hand knitting was not being taken up by the young, and it was not being taught in schools. Partly, no doubt, owing to the activities of the Knitting Craft Group, by 1986 the average age of knitters had come down. Hand knitting is counted as the most popular indoor leisure activity for women, and half the women in the country, some 13 million, are believed to be knitters, with a growing proportion between the ages of 17 and 24. The introduction in 1988 of the General Certificate of Secondary Education will further favour this trend. Yarn crafts will have a new place in the textile syllabus, encouraging an exploratory and 'creative' approach.

The Knitting Craft Group has developed knitting as an artistic expression, promoting knitted pictures and knitted 'sculpture', dolls, toys, and small objects. Jan Messent has been the Group's principal designer, exploiting the possibilities of yarn texture, stitch structure and colour in ways that parallel the 'knit art' movement, which is chiefly American, and the more playful aspects of fashion knitting.

The Knitting and Crochet Guild

Miss Lily Wood of Lancaster and Miss Laura Richardson of Ambleside took up a suggestion from the Federation of British Craft Societies and convened a meeting at Preston on 27 April 1978. At that meeting the Knitting and Crochet Guild was founded, with Miss Richardson as chairman and Miss Wood as treasurer. Pauline Turner, a

121 Knitted sculpture of fungi and lichens by Jan Messent.

crochet expert, undertook, with the craft machine-knitter Kathleen Kinder, to issue a newsletter. Knitting and crochet were late in being sponsored by a British guild to promote, encourage and improve them.

The guild caters for members practising the three crafts of hand knitting, machine knitting and crochet. A quarterly magazine, *Slipknot*, tackles these subjects at a technical level higher than what appears in commercial knitting magazines, encouraging critical approaches to technique and historical study, and also recording contemporary developments. Exhibitions, competitions and excursions are organized, and a score of local branches have been established.

Outwork

Home knitting as a source of extra income has never entirely died out. In Shetland it has the strongest tradition, but even in England it is still done.

In 1926 Helen Elizabeth Fitzrandolph and Mavis Doriel Hay published three volumes on *The Rural Industries of England and Wales*, based chiefly on field work done three or four years earlier. Most of their comments on knitting are, curiously, in the second volume, *Osier-growing and Basketry*. They attributed the cessation of stocking knitting in the Yorkshire Dales to the very low income (3s. or 4s. a week) that it produced (138), but asserted that, only several years before, some had been done, especially in the villages of Ravenstonedale and Dent. At that late date the orders were unusual:

> 'stockings 34 inches long and 13 inches in the foot were ordered by the London County Council for sewer men, and somewhat similar ones were required by submarine men, for whom they were ordered by the Admiralty'.
>
> (122)

Fitzrandolph and Hay also recorded that a considerable quantity of stockings was made in Leicestershire as outwork for shops. This was unknown to the organized part of the hosiery trade and was commoner before the First World War (122). The woman who received the wool from the shop might, in her turn, be responsible for giving it out to other workers (134). Outwork knitting was thought to be a good occupation for elderly women whose eyesight was failing (137). The story of Ringwood and Blandford gloves is told elsewhere (see pp 191-4).

Today the chief product of outwork knitting is sweaters and cardigans. The rates of pay for such work are deplorable. A woman in Lincolnshire who in 1985 knitted excellent Aran-style garments for a shop in Newark could not earn more than 10 pence an hour, at a time and in a place where a charwoman might earn up to £2 an hour.

That was in the provinces. Things are no better in the capital. In 1984 an upmarket firm of outfitters in the West End of London was paying the knitter £6 for a sweater that retailed at £200, claiming that it could not afford to pay more. In spite of such low rates, knitting magazines constantly carry advertisements seeking more home knitters, and the knitters prefer to receive a pittance rather than nothing at all.

The homeknitter who sells direct to the wearer fares better. Work is done to order and there is no middleman; but not many knitters have the necessary business sense to organize a bespoke garment business. The total quantity of home knitting for profit has now dwindled to something barely significant.

Spinning firms

The major spinning firms have been important in the development of hand knitting, for they have not only produced the yarn for knitting, they have increasingly provided most of the recipes for garments since the First World War.

James Baldwin (1746–1811) established a wool-washing and cloth-fulling business in Halifax in 1785. He took his son John into partnership, trading as J. and J. Baldwin. They developed a spinning mill and spun both woollen and worsted yarns. The firm's 'Beehive' trademark became world-famous. (Another Halifax spinner, Baldwin and Walker, used the 'Ladyship' brand-name.)

John Paton (1768–1848) founded his firm at Alloa, Clackmannanshire, in 1813. Paton's ran in competition with J. and J. Baldwins' until April 1920, when they combined as Patons and Baldwins. The firm became part of the Coats Paton group in 1961. From 1932 to the communist take-over of 1952 Patons operated a spinning mill in Shanghai. They also had a mill in Launceston, Tasmania and in 1949 they published *Woolcraft* in Bengali (see pp 145-6).

Sirdar was begun at Ossett, Yorkshire in 1880 by the brothers Tom and Henry Harrap, and called Harrap Brothers. Ten years later they moved to Bective Mills in the village of Alvethorpe, near Wakefield. The name of the mill was probably borrowed from the title of the Countess of Bective, who had given her name to a movement to encourage the wearing of British materials made from British wool. In 1908 Tom Harrap's son Fred, 27 years old, was left in sole control of the firm, which was then spinning wool for weaving and machine knitting. In the early 1920s he switched to making hand-knitting yarns and rug wools; and in 1924 he concentrated on selling direct to retailers, under the brand name Sirdar. Sirdar, 'commander-in-chief', was the title of the British commander of the Egyptian army, to which Lord Kitchener, a national hero, was appointed in 1892. Fred Harrap used it in admiration of Kitchener.

Another old firm that still survives is Richard Poppleton. The original Richard Poppleton set up a worsted spinning mill in partnership with Robert Henry Barker at Wakefield in 1833. The partnership was dissolved in 1847 when Poppleton moved to Victoria Mills, Horbury. The following year a disastrous fire caused the firm to move to nearby Albert Mills, where it now operates. Poppletons exported knitting wool and supplied much of the navy blue yarn required by the Royal Navy in the 1890s. As far back as 1846 they were spinning and selling the wool preferred for fishermen's guernseys.

The history of all the spinning firms is a subject for a separate book, which would throw much light on nineteenth- and twentieth-century knitting in Britain. It would include the history of synthetic yarns, the search for satisfactory treatment of wool against shrinkage, and the growth of the recent fashion for undyed, untreated wool from specific breeds: Jacob's, Wensleydale, Herdwick, Black Welsh, Suffolk, Swaledale and others. It would also examine the interest in mixed fibres that began in the 1970s, and the fashion for cotton knitting that took off in the early 1980s.

Leading spinners are actively involved in the publishing of garment recipes in women's magazines. Patterns are published in order to sell wool. Most of the magazines have knitting editors, and spinners use this means to promote their products in a hugely expensive operation (colour plate 10).

The end of hand-knitted stockings

Socks and stockings were the most frequently hand-knitted garments from the beginning of popular knitting until the 1950s. Today they can hardly be seen, and only the old can remember how to turn a heel without referring to a book. The cheapness of machine-knit stockings, especially when produced in low-wage regions such as East Asia, has finally banished the home-made stocking. Home-made stockings, partly because of knitters' habits, partly because men liked them, survived in dwindling numbers until about 1970. A few patterns only remain in print; and hosiery wool, though still spun, is not readily available. Stockings were always dull work. Today's knitter expects more pleasure from the craft.

That pleasure comes in high degree from the variety of yarns available for hand knitting. Man-made fibres, usually marketed under brand names, but essentially polyamides (such as nylon), polyesters and acrylics, proliferated after 1950 and were for a time cheaper than wool, until world oil prices increased in the 1970s. Wool never surrendered its pre-eminence for the craftsman knitter, and remains his most esteemed yarn, though yarns of blended wool and man-made fibre are economical and popular. Fancy yarns such as bouclé and chenille have periodic fashion peaks, and since 1983 summer knitting in cotton and other vegetable fibres has become important. Mohair has become increasingly popular. Knitting with a mixture of yarns has become something of a craft fad, nourishing an ill-defined obsession with 'texture'.

Western Europe shares its yarns and patterns internationally as never before, but cheap machine-knitted goods from Taiwan, Hong Kong and Korea ensure that no one needs to knit in order to keep clothed. Hand knitting has moved up-market.

7 Some local traditions of the British Isles

Wales

Tradition has it that Welsh cattle-drovers brought Welsh hand-knit stockings to sell at English fairs. The drovers certainly went to Farnham, which is the source of the earliest mention of Welsh stockings. John Aubrey, author of *Brief Lives*, noted in his *Perambulation of Half the County of Surrey* (1673): 'From Michaelmas to Christmas the market here is good for oats, and a great market for Welsh stockings'. (1719 ed. iii 347). This suggests that the trade was well established by the reign of Charles II. The Welsh drovers had been coming into England since the sixteenth century – the days of the legendary outlaw drover Twm Shon Catti, the Welsh Robin Hood – and Welsh cottage knitting may, like the cottage industry of the English Dales, have begun in the sixteenth century. The mention of *knyrk-hosan* (clocks) in William Salisbury's Welsh dictionary of 1547 is suggestive, but because he defines *gwau* (the later word for 'knitting') only as 'web', he gives no clear indication of knitting in Wales.

The eighteenth century

Thomas Pennant, to whom half the letters that compose Gilbert White's *Natural History of Selborne* were addressed, published in 1778–81 *A Tour of Wales in 1773*. He wrote of Bala:

> noted for its vast trade in woollen stockings and its great markets every Saturday morning when from two to five hundred poundsworth are sold

each day . . . . Round the place women and children are in full employ, knitting along the roads; and mixing with them Herculean figures appear, assisting their Omphales in this effeminate employ. During the winter the females, through love of society, often assemble at one another's houses to knit, sit round a fire and listen to some old tale or some ancient song or the sound of a harp, and this is called *cymmorth gweu* or the knitting assembly. Much of the wool is bought at the great fairs at Llanwrst in Denbighshire. Close to the southeast end of the town is a great artificial mound called Tommen y Bala, in the summer time usually covered in a picturesque manner with knitters of both sexes and all ages (II 67-8).

The Ladies of Llangollen, Sarah Ponsonby and Lady Eleanor Butler, were not tourists. They were Anglo-Irish women who eloped together and set up a literary ménage in Llangollen which became something of a tourist attraction. Sarah knitted a stocking pattern she had learnt in Ireland (see Elizabeth Mavor *The Ladies of Llangollen* (1971), p 209). Lady Eleanor recorded the local knitters in her journal on 22 November 1781:

> White glittering frost. Country magnificently beautiful. A fair in the village. What a picture might be drawn from our parlour window of the crowds descending the opposite mountain and passing through the field before our cottage: some on horseback, some on foot, all comfortably clad, each bringing their different commodity to the fair, as cattle, pigs, poultry, eggs, cheese, woollen cloths, baskets, woollen wear, spinning wheels; the women knitting as

they went along, the young people in their best apparel.

A less romantic view was taken by Walter Davies in his *General View of the Agriculture and Domestic Economy of South Wales* (1799). He noted that stockings were the only things manufactured in Brecon. They could be bought in the markets for 8d a pair, and he reckoned that the raw materials cost 5d. A woman could card, spin and knit four pairs in a week, if she worked hard. This would earn her a profit of a shilling a week, and a shilling would buy only a gallon of wheat at some seasons.

In 1795 David Davies, rector of Barkham, Berkshire, published *The Case of Labourers in Husbandry*, and showed proper concern for his motherland.

> The knitting of coarse woollen stockings chiefly employs boys, girls, and grown persons of both sexes in the inland part of Merioneth. That it is an unprofitable manufacture is evident as they knit walking, talking, begging, without hardly ever looking at their work; and though they exhibit an instance of unexampled industry, yet they are obliged to beg to make up the deficiencies of their earnings. (191)

Arthur Aikin, chemist and geologist, was an observant tourist, and he wrote a *Journal of a Tour through North Wales* (1797). He described the Bala market much as Pennant had done, but noticed that the people knitted gloves and 'wigs' as well as footwear, and that Welsh hosiers purchased them in Bala market to take them to the shops and warehouses of the adjoining English counties. He particularly noticed the colours of the stockings, 'greys of a thousand shades, white, blue, red, etc, from six to nine shillings per dozen' (23-4, 82).

Walter Davies, in *Agricultural Survey of North Wales* (1810), described in some detail the price of stockings made in the Bala and Corwen district ('a most mountainous tract') showing that it had risen considerably since 1747. By 1810 the annual trade in stockings at Bala was reckoned to be worth about £18,000.

122 Women knitting at Barmouth. Drawing by Sarah G. Carr/Lushington. 1815.

The nineteenth century

John Evans, of Jesus College, Oxford, printed his *Letters from a Tour through North Wales* in 1804 and included an elegant page on Bala knitting, plagiarized from Pennant and Aikin. Richard Aikin, a dilettante litterateur, published *A Voyage round Great Britain* 1814, with fine plates by William Daniell, in which he described the women knitting as they walked with loads on their heads. Richard Fenton, a Welsh lawyer in London, appended some notes of the antiquary William Williams of Llandegei, dated 1814, to his *Tours in Wales 1804–13*, published in 1814. Williams said that at Llanrwst £300 worth of stockings was sold in the morning before the market began, by the knitters themselves (311).

The last of the literary tourists was that self-centred show-off, George Borrow. In 1854 he deposited his wife and daughter in an inn at Llangollen while he went off walking all over North Wales from August till late October. He published his account of his doings in 1862 as *Wild Wales*. He described knitting as 'the general occupation of Welsh females'; noticed a woman seated by the roadside at Pentre Foelas knitting; and three times added character to his narrative by remarking on a woman sitting knitting in a cottage or doorway. Once when he was unsure of his whereabouts in Anglesey, a woman who passed by knitting told him it was Llanbedrgoch.

Cwm Eithin

The classic account of Welsh knitting, however, was written by Hugh Evans. He was born at Llangwm near Bala in 1854 and as a youth was an agricultural labourer in the district around Cerrigydrudion. It was a depressed time and place for farming, so at 19 he went to seek his fortune in Liverpool. He became a carpenter and joiner and about 1885 began to sell Welsh books. Eventually he opened a bookshop, and in 1896 a printing business. Ten years after that he founded the newspaper *Y Brython*, in which he wrote articles about the people and place of his boyhood, 'the gorse glen'. As an old man he published the articles in book form, entitled *Cwm Eithin* ('gorse glen') (1931). He died in 1937. An English version of his book came from the Brython Press, Liverpool in 1948.

Although the book is a heartfelt record of real poverty, it has abundant touches of gentle wit, and it says much of knitting. First is the tale told by Richard Jones of Ty Cerrig about his childhood in the 1790s. In a desperately bad autumn when the corn crop failed, Richard's mother suggested to her husband he should take on the churning, bedmaking, washing-up and cleaning, in addition to his outside work, so that she could knit stockings. She also spun the wool, which her husband carded. She set herself the target of three stockings a day; and all through the winter she rode

fortnightly to Ruthin to sell her stockings to the hosier and buy grain to feed her family (13-15). Knitting-money alleviated the hardships. Hugh Evans tells of another family in about 1818 living in a bracken-thatched house where in the evening father sat at one end of the hearthstone and mother at the other, while the children sat in a semi-circle in front of the fire. They all knitted stockings, and the mother expected to take six pairs to market every Saturday.

Evans's second classic description is of *noswaith weu*, the knitting party, remarkably like the Dales and Channel Island evening parties for knitters. Evans thought the custom had been at its height in the later eighteenth century:

The guests were usually young people, both male and female. The girls arrived first, and it was considered to be the proper thing for the young men to linger a little before putting in an appearance. When all had come, the womenfolk would begin to knit and one or two lads, inveterate jokers, would also produce needles and yarn and begin to knit garters. To tell the truth, there was not very much solid work done at a *noswaith weu*, as so much time was spent laughing at the stories and in picking up stitches after the lads had plucked out the needles.

Another revealing section of *Cwm Eithin* is the description of wool-gathering. Poor women would set out in late June or early July under the leadership of a woman well on in years who was a good gossip and negotiator. They would follow a set course in a territory recognized as theirs, and call at every farm where sheep were kept. There they would beg handfuls of fleece-wool from the farmer's wives, and in some places, space to sleep the night, for the whole journey lasted several days. They also collected scraps of wool from bushes, hedges and walls, stuffing all into sacks or pillowcases that they carried. The strongest gatherer had three bags, one on the back and one under each arm, each containing up to four pounds of wool. The whole outing was hugely pleasurable as well as an alleviation of poverty.

Evans adds some stray remarks about the colours used in knitting.

123 Edward Llwyd of Bala, photographed about 1875 and believed to be one of the last of the local stocking-knitters.

The men folk wore grey stockings that did not show the dirt, stockings knitted from a mixture of white and black wool dyed in what was called 'pot blue'. This was the cheapest and least decorative dye, but the women folk, who did all the dyeing, took care to have gayer colours for their own stockings and other garments ... Very smart-looking stockings were made by dyeing one half of the hank while leaving the other half white; the resulting stockings were the colour of a grey horse. Other stockings were knitted in two colours in alternate stripes.

He also mentions gathering lichen for dye, and says his old Uncle William was one of the last to cling to the mixture of black and white wool.

Within living memory

In a notable article 'Stockings in Wales', S. Minwel Tibbott described the whole industry, making it clear that Welsh cottage knitting flourished still in the 1850s and survived in the Edwardian years. No peculiarly Welsh patterns have survived. *Weldon's Practical Needlework* published a 'Welsh heel' for a stocking in 1886, which may or may not have been truly Welsh or popular in Wales.

Welsh technique was essentially the same as that of the rest of Britain. Knitting sheaths were used, the hands were held over the needles (they are in old Welsh photographs), the right forefinger, in Minwel Tibbott's words, 'acting as a shuttle, making the least possible movement and attaining a speed of two hundred stitches a minute' (see fig. 15). An S-shaped yarn-hook was used to suspend the ball of yarn from the waistband. Even the windpipe or 'thropple' of a goose, with small stones inside it, and the ends joined to make a tubular ring, was used as the centre of a ball of yarn, just as it was in the northern Dales of England. When the ball ran across the floor in a firelit room the rattle of the stones helped in its discovery. Competitions in which knitters sat together working equal lengths of yarn were similar to Northern English devices to encourage speedier work.

Minwel Tibbott, using much material from taped informants, also records the Cardiganshire practice of knitting blue-grey stockings with tops and toes in natural white yarn. This was explained as a way of benefiting from the lanolin in undyed yarn, making the fabric warm and waterproof. Stockings produced for market were made in plain stockinet but stockings for the family were ribbed or cabled. Clocks, also called quirks, were worked with purl stitches or cables.

The coming of the railways and the development of machine-knitting technology disrupted the trade of the hose factors. The lot of Welsh rural folk improved a little, and by the 1920s cottage knitting as an industry had virtually disappeared.

Shetland – centre of the seaways

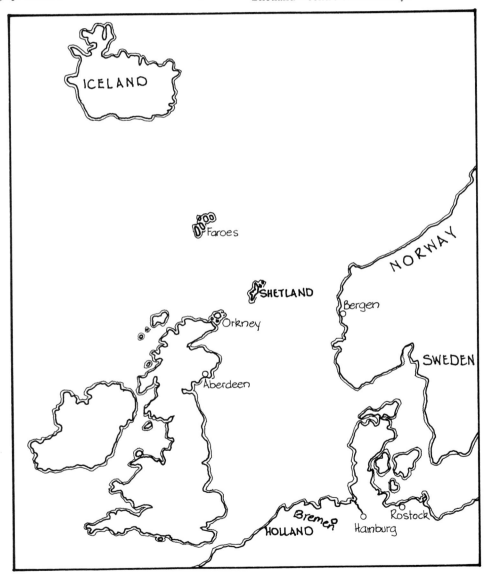

Shetland

Hjaltland is a group of windswept islands set in the ocean west of Norway, where the North Sea becomes the Atlantic Ocean. It is a stark dark country, made mostly of black peat and rock, with no trees. There is little night in summer and little daylight in winter. Most of the people live in scattered hamlets, as crofters and fishermen. Life has always been rugged in such a remote place, poised halfway between Britain and Scandinavia.

The land is remote and the landscape bare, but its position has ensured that the people are not backward. Hjaltland is set where the north European seaways cross between Germany, Britain, Scandinavia and the North Atlantic routes. For centuries it was part of the Norwegian realm, until, politically, it was ceded to the king of Scotland in the thirteenth century. Scottish rule brought Scottish immigrants, especially landlords and clergy, who blended with the Scandinavian islanders to form the modern Shetland stock. Shetland or Zetland (both originally pronounced the same) became the British version of Hjaltland. The old Norn language gave way to English, but Norn words persisted as elements in the local dialect, and Scandinavian culture has left discernible marks on the life of Shetland to this day.

This cultural mingling contributed to the distinctive tradition of Shetland knitting, which has flourished since the seventeenth century. The fine wool of the native breed of sheep, the long dark winters that necessitated indoor activity, and the trading opportunities provided by the regular visits of foreign seafarers encouraged the development of the craft.

The seventeenth century

There is no evidence of where the Shetlanders first learned their knitting. The craft must have come by sea, and probably from Britain, because no Norn words are recorded as knitting terms. Shetland dialect uses English dialect words for knitting. As knitting spread through western Europe in the sixteenth century, it was probably not slow in getting to Shetland. Gordon Donaldson in *Shetland Life under Earl Patrick* (1958) suggests that

> local wool and local work no doubt went into the socks which are mentioned from time to time (in documents of the first quarter of the seventeenth century). There were two thefts of socks in Bressay . . . and one in Unst.

A court book for October 1615 records the theft of a black ewe, from whose wool a pair of socks was made (*Orkney and Shetland court books 1614–1615*, edited by R.S. Barclay (1967), 109); and the earliest account in English of the northern isles, by Richard James, printed in *Orkney Miscellany* i (1953), originally written early in the seventeenth century, even says that the women of Shetland were 'given to knitting mittens and stockings which the Hollanders and English do buy for rarity' (50). (James was a learned Anglican priest, born in 1592, who travelled as chaplain to Sir Dudley Digges on an embassy to Russia in 1618. His manuscript account of Poland, Shetland, Scotland, Wales, Greenland and other countries is in the Bodleian Library. He died in 1638.)

A Description of the Western Islands of Scotland, written by Martin Martin about 1695, and published in 1703, says:

> The Hamburgers, Bremers and others come to this country about the middle of May, set up shops in several parts, and sell diverse commodities, as linen, muslin, and such things as are most proper for the inhabitants, but more especially beer, brandy and bread: all of which they barter for fish, stockings, muttons, hams etc. And when the inhabitants ask money for their goods, they receive it immediately.

At the same period John Brand published *A Description of Orkney, Zetland, Pightland-Firth and Caithness* (1701). He gives a little more information about the hand knitting industry and its place in the island economy:

> Hollanders . . . repair to these waters in June . . . for their herring fishing . . . . Stockings are . . . brought by the country people from all quarters to Lerwick and sold to these fishers,

for sometimes many thousands of them will be ashore at one time, and ordinary it is with them to buy stockings to themselves and some likewise do to their wives and children – which is very beneficial to the inhabitants, for so money is brought into the country, there is a vent for the wool, and the poor are employed. Stockings are also brought from Orkney and sold there.

The Gunnister grave finds

The earliest datable pieces of knitting to be found in Shetland date from this time. They were found on 12 May 1951 in a shallow grave on the uninhabited moor at Gunnister, in Northmavine parish. The body was that of a young man, who had been buried in all his clothes, which were warm enough to suggest winter dress and had all been remarkably preserved in the peat. The coins in his purse were Dutch and Swedish currency of 1680–90 – reflecting the trade at Lerwick with continental fishermen. The quality of cut of his jacket and breeches was good, but his stockings were patched and his shirt and outer jacket were ragged; we cannot judge his social standing. All the clothing can be seen in the Royal Museum of Scotland in Edinburgh, and a complete and accurate description was published in *The Proceedings of the Society of Antiquaries of Scotland* 86 (1951–2).

There were two caps in the grave. One that was found on the man's head was of heavily felted wool, 20 cm (8 in.) deep and 60 cm (24 in.) round the bottom edge, of simple hemispherical shape with a turned-back brim 3¾ cm (1½ in.) deep. The knitting is stocking stitch, worked on four needles at 9 stitches to the inch. The top is shaped by 8 lines of decreasing in the arms of a cross. The work was started at the brim edge. There is a row of small holes at the turning-back line, and a pattern on the brim that, so far as the felting makes analysis possible, seems to be made by knitting 3 rounds plain then one round of knit 2 together, knit 1, make 1, knit 1, repeated all round the cap. There are 5 repeats of the pattern all told.

The second cap was found wrapped round a horn spoon in the man's pocket. This cap is slightly bigger in circumference (61 cm (24 in.)) but a little shallower (19 cm (7½ in.)), knitted in stockinet at 8 stitches to the inch. The brim is not turned back, but turned under and hemmed down, with a tiny knitted loop on the crown. The inside still shows an interesting pile or nap made of tight loops of unspun fibre producing a bouclé effect. Both caps are brown.

The gloves are mid-brown in colour, made of soft, long-staple wool, worked in the round with no seam, at 17 stitches to the inch. The cuffs are 35 cm (14 in.) round at the edge and have a horizontal pattern of 6 rows garter stitch, 5 stockinet, 5 garter stitch, 6 stockinet, 3 purl rows separated by 2 plain, 8 rows of stockinet, and 5 rows of garter stitch. The cuff has decreases along the outer side only. The thumb gore is shaped by increasing from the top of the cuff pattern, and the rest of the glove is in stockinet, decorated with three arrows on the back, pointing from between the fingers towards the cuff. Each arrowhead is made of 1 purl stitch on the first round, 2 purls divided by a plain in the second round, and 3 purls divided by 2 plains in the third round. The shaft of the arrow is worked by 2 purl stitches divided by a plain stitch in each alternate round, the purl stitches always in the same two wales.

The fingers and thumb are made by casting-on and picking-up stitches in the fashion still customary. Each glove is 34 cm (13½ in.) long, and 25 cm (10 in.) round the palm.

The stockings are 58 cm (23 in.) long from top to heel, and 27½ cm (11 in.) in the foot. The wool is heavy 2-ply of mixed dark brown and black fibres, knitted in the round at 7½ stitches to the inch. The top is cast on with 114 stitches and begins with 7 rows of garter stitch. The rest is in stockinet, except for the clocks and a panel at the back.

The panel is alternating rows of (a) K1, P1, K3, P1, K2; and (b) K2, P1, K3, P1, K1. This produces two moss stitch ribs, divided by two wales of plain stitches, and bordered by single wales of plain stitches. The thigh is knitted straight for 5 cm (2 in.); 14 decreases (two away from the back panel) are made in the next 12 cm (4¾ in.). The calf takes 13 increases in 10 cm (4 in.); then 2 cm

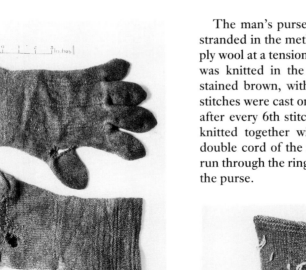

124 Gloves from the Gunnister burial.

The man's purse is multi-coloured, with yarns stranded in the method now called Fair Isle, in 2-ply wool at a tension of 11½ stitches to the inch. It was knitted in the round in undyed wool, now stained brown, with a red and white pattern; 86 stitches were cast on, with a chain of 7 loops made after every 6th stitch, the last loop of the 7 being knitted together with the 6th cast on stitch. A double cord of the main colour knitting yarn was run through the rings thus made, and used to close the purse.

(¾ in.) without increasing, and 13 decreases in the following 19 cm (7½ in.).

The heel is begun 51 cm (20½ in.) from the top. Twenty-four stitches, centred on the back panel, are worked for the back of the heel. The whole structure of the heel cannot be seen because the stockings are worn and patched.

The clocks, on both sides of the ankles, are made in a pattern of a diamond in moss stitch over an inverted pyramid in purling from which there is a vertical rib. The diamond begins with one purl stitch, increasing in each round to 2, 3, 4 and so on to 8 and back again to 1. The triangle begins with 17 purl stitches. The next round had 7 purl, 1 plain, 7 purl. There is one purl less each side in every round till the point is reached. The rib begins with 10 purl stitches, then alternate rows of (a) plain knitting and (b) P2, K2, P2, K2, P2 for 18 rows immediately before the heel shaping.

Then there is a fragment of knitting 11 x 7 cm (4½ x 2¾ in.), knitted in 2-ply yarn at 10½ stitches to the inch with a pattern of three concentric diamonds made by rows of increases and decreases. It has no worked edge and cannot be explained.

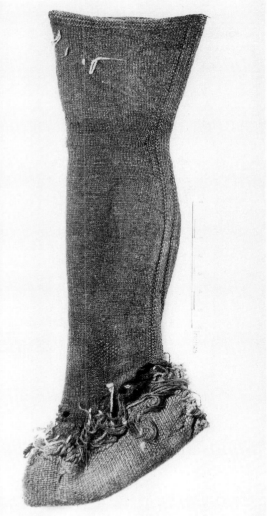

125 Stocking from the Gunnister burial.

126 Purse from the Gunnister burial.

After the casting on there are 5 cm (2 in.) of 2K 2P rib, then a row of purl; thereafter stockinet without shaping. After 12 rows there are 6 rows of red pattern; after 15 more rows, 5 rows of white pattern; after 5 more rows, 5 of red pattern. The bottom is closed by dividing the stitches into two equal groups and grafting them together. Three tassels, of a mixture of all three colours, are added: one at each corner and one in the middle of the bottom grafting (see fig. 133).

Were all these knitted items made in Shetland? It is likely that they represent the articles so much sought after by the Dutch sailors.

The eighteenth century

The eighteenth century is the peak period of those summer fairs at Lerwick, where the continental fishermen (all lumped together in Shetland speech as 'Dutch', though many of them were Deutsch from German ports) acquired local stockings. The

attraction of Shetland hosiery lay partly in the fine quality of the best work. There was also a large quantity of coarser knitting.

A 'gentleman who had resided five years on the island' of Shetland published in 1750 *An exact and authentic account of the greatest white herring fishery in Scotland* in which he described the common people of Shetland, 'man, wife and child', employed in knitting coarse stockings and making coarse woollen cloth in the winter, though in summer the men were 'obliged to go to sea a-fishing for cod and ling for the lord of the manor'. The coarse stockings

lay aside until the beginning of June, when their fair or mart with the Dutch begins, which they call Johnmas Fair. About this time the Dutch, to the number of ten or eleven hundred busses, have wet their nets upon the coast – which they are obliged to do against the 11th of June by an express act of the states-general of the United Provinces. Then they come to Bressay Sound to buy stockings.

The gentlewomen who work stockings for their amusement work them very fine, even so much so that one of the country who was here (in London) lately, and whom I knew there, told me he had sold a pair here of his wife's making for four guineas.

(25)

The modern writer, A.C. O'Dell, in *The Historical Geography of the Shetland Islands* (1939) quotes a manuscript record of a tour of Shetland in 1769 saying the wool 'is sometimes so fine as to be wrought into stockings which sell for a guinea or twenty five shillings a pair. The coarser part is formed into coverlets, and very cheap stockings.' (The coverlets were heavy woven rugs used as bed covers and pony blankets.) O'Dell also quotes a letter written by the chamberlain of the Dunden Estate at Sumburgh in 1784 about fine stockings:

at present there is such a prodigious demand for stockings of this kind in the town and through the country that I cannot possibly procure any of them but a few samples . . . .; I dare say there are many hundreds of pairs commissioned for, nay, I believe, even some hundred pounds value.

The trade with the Dutch herring boats had its ups and downs. Richard Gough in his 1806 edition of Camden's *Britannia* quotes Thomas Gifford writing in 1733:

These Dutchmen used formerly to buy a considerable quantity of coarse stockings from the country people for ready money at tolerable good prices, but for several years past that trade has failed.

Gifford was reporting the effect of a tax on foreign salt imposed in 1712. The purpose of the tax was to get the salt herring trade wholly into British hands, but it also removed the market for direct cash sales of hosiery.

Yet O'Dell quotes other manuscript sources showing how the stocking trade survived this setback by finding new export outlets. A note of 1735 says 'I did recommend to Polson's care 800 pairs of coarse stockings, which he was to sell at Lisbon for my account;' and an attempt to control the quality of the hose is recorded from the Garth estates at Dunrossness in 1733:

... for preventing the frauds formerly committed in making and selling of coarse stockings to the great hurt and prejudice of the country, that no person or persons within the said country make any single stockings or otherways insufficient of their kind for sale, or offer to sell the same, after the first day of November next to come until first showing them to one of the lawright men as mentioned, who is to put his mark of sale upon them of 1st, 2nd and 3rd socks, according to their goodness.

Another of the Garth papers records instructions of 1790 from the Commissioner of Supply to the stamper of woollen stockings in the parishes of South Unst. Stockings were to be checked for size and shape with wooden patterns provided by the Commissioner. The patterns were for men's, women's and children's stockings, and the stockings had to be 'knit of one sort of wool, worsted or equal size, free from left loops, hanging hairs, bunt cuts or mended holes.' Each stocking

was to be stamped 'near the brow' with a mark of four letters: U (for Unst), T A (the stamper's initials) and M W or C (according to the three pattern sizes). The stamping fee for a dozen pairs of single (that is ordinary quality) stockings was one penny. Double and fine stockings were stamped for two pence a dozen pairs. The stamper was to seize and hold stockings which were not of the prescribed quality. The workmanship of the knitters was not all beyond reproach.

George Low's account of *A Tour through the Islands of Orkney and Shetland* in 1774 tells of knitted goods other than hosiery.

The whole time the fleet (of continental fishing vessels) lay, the country people flocked to Lerwick with loads of coarse stockings, gloves, night caps, rugs and a very few articles of fresh provisions. Several thousand pounds are annually drawn for the first article, though a pair of stockings seldom sells for more than 6d or 8d. I don't say but they make finer stockings than these, having been informed of a pair of stockings made in Lerwick and sold at 36 shillings sterling; but the most valuable for the country in general, and the most profitable, the coarse ones, are of very thick thread, which consumes a great deal of wool, but requires not a great deal of labour.

Low also remarks that Fair Isle women knit stockings and gloves constantly.

The Old Statistical Account

At the end of the eighteenth century (1791–97), under the guidance of Sir John Sinclair, the 'Old Statistical Account' of Scotland was published. This was a detailed summary of the state of the country ('statistic' did not yet mean simply figures and tables) compiled from reports by presbyterian parish ministers. The ministers of Shetland had plenty to say about hand knitting.

James Sands of Lerwick wrote: 'The only manufacture carried on in the parish is the knitting of woollen stockings, and in this all the women are more or less engaged.' John Mill of Dunrossness reported that stockings, gloves and gaiters were again being sold to the Dutch fishers. Also on the mainland, James Sands writes of Tingwall:

> The women, when not busied about farm work, are employed in knitting coarse stockings. This has of late become an object worthy of their attention. Formerly the stockings of Shetland were sent to Holland and Hamburg, but the difference in their value since they found their way to other markets, particularly the English, is said to be nearly equal to the land rent of the country.

This was a markedly different judgement from that of John Morison of Delting, who said that the wives and children 'have not a probable chance of earning a penny, but the manufacture of single stockings, which is loss of time, to call it no more.'

Andrew Dishington, on the island of Yell, shared Morison's opinion:

> All the women, of every rank and distinction, are employed in spinning wool and knitting fine and coarse stockings, to their great loss and miserable misspending of their time; for if it were fairly calculated, they cannot earn by this species of industry three halfpence a day. The materials they consume in this gainful trade might be manufactured into good cloths of all sorts, which might serve all ranks for clothing and put a stop to that pernicious rage they have for foreign fopperies.

On the northernmost island of Unst Thomas Mouat and James Barclay reported: 'Almost every woman in the island manufactures fine woollen stockings. These are much valued for softness and warmth. The price which they bring is from 1s 4d to 2s 6d the pair.' Finally, the report of Fair Isle says that the inhabitants 'discover much dexterity in manufacturing their fine soft wool in stockings, gloves, night caps and other wearing apparel.'

Allowance must be made for the personalities of the ministers; yet the note about the fineness of the yarn on Unst, and the profitability of stocking knitting for those who lived near the export outlet at Lerwick, like the enthusiasm for knitting on Fair Isle, are points that fit well with the coming developments of the nineteenth century.

The Napoleonic Wars

In 1809 Arthur Edmondston of Unst published *A View of the Ancient and Present State of the Zetland Isles*. At the beginning of the second volume he discussed the hand-knitting industry and the effect of the Napoleonic wars upon it:

> Stockings have been made in Zetland which have sold as high as 30 shillings and as low as 5 pence a pair; and it is by no means uncommon to obtain the wool of which both kinds are manufactured from (different parts of) the same animal. Some years ago the coarse stockings were objects of general sale and great numbers were exported annually. Before the late and present wars interrupted the intercourse between the Dutch and Zetlanders, the quantity of stockings sold to these foreigners in the country by the manufacturers themselves was very great. Indeed the assemblage of busses in Bressa Sound about the 24th of June constituted an annual fair where every variety of this species of manufacture was exposed to sale.
>
> Besides the sale to shipping, stockings are bartered at Lerwick to the shopkeepers for such commodities as the people need, and, like the wadmal of Iceland, form a principal article of exchange in the country. As the stockings are all made on wires, the manufacture of them is very slow; so that, after deducting the expense of the wool, the reversion to the individual engaged in it is comparatively trifling.

The New Statistical Account

Half a century after Sir John Sinclair's Statistical Account was written, the New Statistical Account was compiled. It appeared in 1841. The section on Shetland says much less about knitting, and the paragraphs on Fair Isle do not mention knitting at all. Fair Isle, however, never had a resident minister to give detailed information, and nothing can be deduced from this silence. Thomas Barclay of Lerwick notes that the women of his parish knit stockings, mitts and hosiery of various kinds; but

James and John Ingram of Unst, whilst they give the only substantive entry on handknitting, also give a highly informative one:

> Articles of woollen hosiery, chiefly consisting of stockings and gloves, are the principal manufacture of this island. They are knit by the females and are highly prized for their softness and the beauty of their texture. The demand for Zetland hosiery is not nearly so great now as formerly; yet the quantity sold is still very considerable. Stockings vary in price from 1s to 10s per pair (a few pairs of extraordinary fineness are sold for £2 per pair), and gloves from 1s to 10s or even sometimes as high as 15s per pair.

Shetland lace

Steamer services with the mainland started in 1836; Scottish sheep breeds were brought to Shetland; and the postal service began in 1840. All these factors encouraged the knitters. Especially in the northernmost island of Unst, the spinning of very fine yarn was maintained. The articles knitted were still stockings and gloves, and Miss Lambert in *The Handbook of Needlework* (1842) states categorically that 'Knitting from the Shetland Isles is ... generally of one uniform colour.' Lace knitting, however, had begun in Shetland, especially on Unst. In 1843 Miss Lambert would herself publish a Shetland lace design in *My Knitting Book*. Jane Gaugain of Edinburgh had already published one in the second volume of *The Lady's Assistant* 1842.

Some writers have surmised that Mrs Gaugain got her lacy patterns from Shetland. In fact, Shetland got its lacy patterns from the mainland. The story is told in detail by Robert Cowie in his *Shetland and the Shetlanders* (also called *A Guide to Shetland*) published in 1871.

> The open lace knitting, for which the islands are now famed, was never heard of until a very recent period; and I have much pleasure in giving an account of its origin, kindly furnished by an accomplished lady of Lerwick, who is personally acquainted with all the circumstances.
>
> The late Samuel Laing, Esq., of Papdale, when a candidate for the representation of the county in 1833, was while in Lerwick the guest of the late Mrs Charles Ogilvy, to whose infant son Miss Laing afterwards sent a present of a beautiful christening cap, knitted by herself of thread such as is used in the manufacture of the celebrated Lille stockings. This cap was much admired, and a lady related to the family succeeded in making an exact copy of it. While doing so, it occurred to her that fine woollen mitts knitted in a similar style would look well; and she accordingly made a pair, and subsequently a very handsome invalid cap for a gentleman. This was in 1837, when the late Mr Frederick Dundas first became MP for the county. Having received the cap as a present, the honourable gentleman showed it to his landlady in Lerwick, requesting her to try to induce some of her young acquaintances to imitate it in shawls. This she did, but with little result.
>
> In 1839 Mr Edward Standen of Oxford, while travelling through the islands, saw a shawl which the above-mentioned lady was knitting,

127 A Shetland shawl.

and on his return to Lerwick he also mentioned the subject to the person with whom he lodged, urging her to advise young women to knit shawls of that description. Mr Standen, who was extensively engaged in the hosiery trade himself, now succeeded in giving fresh impetus to the fine knitting of Shetland, and, by introducing the goods into the London market, was the means of creating what had been for a few years previously followed as a pastime by a few amateurs into an important branch of industry, affording employment to a large proportion of the female population of the islands.

The articles first sent to market appear to have been somewhat rudely executed, having been knitted on wooden pins. However, steel wires were soon introduced and year by year the manufacture gradually improved, until it reached its present perfection. Many of the peasant girls display great artistic talent in the invention and arrangement of patterns, which are formed, as they express it, 'out of their own heads'.

The manufacture of fine Shetland shawls thus became common about 1840, but it was not till five years afterwards that the demand for them became very great. About 1850 the shawls were to some extent superseded in the markets by veils, in which a large trade was soon carried on. More recently neckties and various other fancy articles have been produced by the neat-fingered knitters of Zetland. The amount sold is said to yield £10,000 to £12,000 yearly. Wool from the native sheep has of late years become rather scarce, and therefore the importation of Pyrenean wool, mohair, etc., has been found necessary.

From 1840 onwards, shawls began to be exported to Scotland and England. In a few years they had become fashionable, and imitations of them were being knitted elsewhere.

It was the fine spun yarn of Shetland that stimulated this development, for the delicacy of the thread impressed people more than the beauty of the designs. In 1846 D. Sutherland, a free-church

minister of Inverness, published *Notes on a Tour of Shetland and Orkney*, September 1845, in which he wrote:

> Mrs I. showed us some beautiful specimens of shawls. The fibres were so slender and the texture so fine that one would mistake them for Brussels lace. Many young women in Unst and some in Lerwick employ themselves in the manufacture, and a proportion of the proceeds of the sale is intended for the cause of the Gospel. Knitting is the grand employment of all classes of females, high and low. The better classes display their taste in shawls and scarfs of every variety of pattern, shape and colour; and the humbler classes confine themselves to stockings, gloves and cravats. They are never idle. You see the lower orders busy knitting when footing their way through the marshes with creels on their backs.

An anonymous contributor to *Chambers's Miscellany of Useful and Entertaining Facts* described 'A visit to Shetland' in volume 8, issued in 1846:

> The wool is so fine that it may be spun into a thread as small as one of cambric, and this on a common lint-wheel ... a thousand yards are frequently spun from an ounce of wool, each thread being three-fold, or three thousand yards in all. Stockings knitted from thread of this quality are so light and fine as to be capable of being drawn through a finger ring; and for such so high a price as two guineas, and even more, has been paid. These used to be the most recherché articles of Shetland manufacture; but within these few years the cottage girls knit a variety of elegant shawls and scarfs in numerous ingenious patterns, mostly of their own invention, which are as beautiful as lace, and not above three or four ounces in weight.

Eliza Edmondston, a member of a landowning family in Unst, gives a slightly different account in *Sketches and Tales of Shetland* (1856).

> The spinning is all done by hand on a common lint-wheel. The staple of the wool is very short, and it is said cannot on that account be so well managed by machinery. The same

circumstance accounts also for the fact that Shetland hose, however pleasant in wear, are not very durable.

The finest wool is not carded, but combed out, and then teased by the fingers. It is mixed with grease, or a little fine oil, and a few persons who are very expert can spin from two ounces of raw wool *six thousand yards* of three-ply thread – a sufficient quantity to make a good-sized shawl. This process is very tedious and requires manipulations so nice, that very few persons ever attain the art in perfection. More usually a veil may be made of half an ounce, and a shawl of four or five ounces of wool. This will serve to explain that, unlike Berlin and other wools, which are sold by weight and spun by machinery, the finer the thread of Shetland, the more the labour. It is therefore disposed of by the cut or number of threads.

... the open-work knitting now so attractive to the poor artists, as well as to the public, is an invention for which the Shetland females themselves deserve all the credit. From the simplest beginnings, led on and encouraged by some ladies as a pastime, it has progressed from one thing to another till it has attained its present celebrity without the aid either of pattern-book or of other instruction than the diligence and taste of the natives themselves.

So the 'wedding-ring shawl' came into being. ('Ring-shawls' had been heard of before. The Venetian Niccolao Manucci, who described the Mughal court of India, 1653–1708, in *Storia do Mogor*, told there of fine woven Kashmir shawls that could be drawn through a thumb-ring.) The origins of the various lace patterns can hardly ever be known for sure. Mary Thomas was told by the Eunson family that only ten lace stitches were truly native to Shetland: Ears o'grain, Catspaw, Print o' the wave, Bird's Eye, Fern, Fir Cone, Spoutshell (or Razorshell), Old Shale, Acre (a furrow pattern) and Horseshoe. She published these stitches in *Mary Thomas's Knitting Book* 1938, noting that some knitters worked them on a garter stitch base, some on a stocking stitch base, and some on a base of stocking stitch with a purl row every third or seventh row. Different families have different names for the same pattern. The tradition grew

and expanded. There is no real value or meaning in the idea of 'truly native' patterns. The patterns that entered Shetland from the mainland in the 1830s were promptly naturalized, and a pattern invented by a Shetlander tomorrow will be just as 'truly native'.

Shetland lace articles have long been constructed so that they have neither cast-on edge nor cast-off edge. They begin and end with a single stitch and have edges knitted on the bias. This gives the shawls and veils a remarkable softness and elasticity. We do not know where or when this construction was evolved (see fig. 128).

It was only to be expected that there should be some evolution. This came about partly from aspirations to imitate the beautiful point-laces that were popular at various times. James Norbury in Odham's *Encyclopaedia of Knitting* (1957) writes:

'Mrs Jessie Saxby, who was a great collector of lace, visited Shetland in the nineteenth century, taking with her specimens from her collection; and I have it on good authority, from one of the Shetlanders whose grandmother met Mrs Saxby, that the lovely laces in the collection definitely helped to give renewed impetus to lace knitting in Shetland.' (Mrs Saxby was a member of the Edmonston family.)

In *Traditional Knitting Patterns* (1962) Norbury gave another story, telling how a Jessie Scanlon had taken examples of Brussels lace to Shetland, which inspired the Hunter family of Unst to invent lace patterns.

While the lace knitting was getting established, hosiery and gloves continued to be made. In October 1837 the *Shetland Journal* reported that Arthur Anderson had sent some fine stockings and gloves to the new queen and her mother, the Duchess of Kent. The Great Exhibition of 1851 included many hand-knitted items from Shetland: shawls, handkerchiefs, veils, gloves, mitts, stockings, knee-caps, leggings, night-caps, wigs, comforters and a shirt.

In 1883 John R. Tudor described the specialization of the knitters in various parishes: soft underclothing in Northmavine, stockings in Nesting, socks and haps (small shoulder shawls) in Walls and Sandsting; fancy gloves in Whiteness

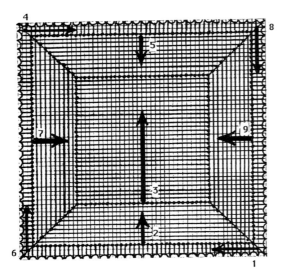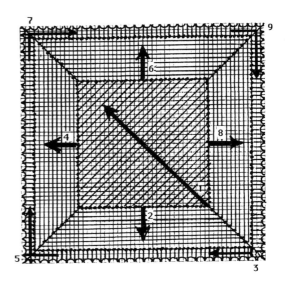

128 The structures of a Shetland lace shawl (left) and its English imitation (right) for less skilful knitters, called the Victorian 'Shetland' shawl. The Victorian Shetland shawl has an alternative order of 1, 2, 4, 6, 8, 3, 5, 7, 9. On both figs, plain lines indicate rows; dots indicate grafting or taking up of stitches.

and Weisdale; shawls and veils in Lerwick and Unst. (The fancy gloves of Whiteness were probably lace gloves.) (*The Orkneys and Shetland* 160)

Shawls

The lace shawls were not the only type of shawl that made Shetland famous. Plain knitted fabric shawls, often in garter stitch, with undulating borders made by alternating groups of increases and decreases (as it were a shale pattern without eyelets) were made in great numbers. They were probably the articles of uniform colour mentioned by Frances Lambert. Frank Barnard's pictures of 1890 suggest that these were used in daily wear by the islanders themselves. They usually had coloured stripes around the borders which Barnard calls zigzags, 'double or treble, the stripes a delicate pink, blue or dove grey on a field of

white; or coarser shawls with black zigzags divided by thin white lines, on a field of mouse colour, iron grey, or dark brown.' These were the Shetland shawls of the earlier Victorian knitting books, and the muted colours were the basis of the popular idea that Shetland colours are subtle and misty.

Fair Isle knitting

Shetland's other distinctive type of knitting is what is now called 'Fair Isle knitting', typified by coloured patterns using two colours in each row but sometimes a dozen or more colours in a garment. These patterns are first mentioned by Samuel Hibbert in his *A Description of the Shetland Islands* (1822) in relation to the caps worn by Shetland men. He sometimes calls this 'the red cap' and prints a drawing of it – a stocking cap with no discernible pattern in the sketch.

The boat dress of the fishermen is in many respects striking. A worsted covering for the head, similar in form to the common English or Scotch nightcap, is dyed with so many colours that its bold tints are recognized at a considerable distance, like the stripes of a signal flag. (96)

The knitted covering of the head, which the

master of a family wears, is an object of the Shetland manufacturers. Its shape has been described as resembling a common double nightcap, with this variation: that its extremity, to which is affixed a small tassel, hangs so low down the back as to resemble, in this respect, the cap of a German hussar. The variegated and fantastical colours which it displays are produced by native dyes, the collection of which was anciently an object of great importance. (441)

Hibbert was so explicit about the coloured caps that he would not have failed to mention coloured jumpers, had such things been worn. The Fair Isle technique began with the cap. The date is significant, because Hibbert wrote shortly after two-colour knitting came into vogue in Norway, and the stocking-cap is a typical Norwegian headcovering. Contact with Scandinavian fishermen was part of Shetland life, and who dare guess which side of the Norwegian Sea saw the first 'Fair Isle' knitting?

There is some doubt as to why the multi-coloured items came to be particularly associated with Fair Isle. The earliest mention of Fair Isle knitting comes from the correspondence of Sir Walter Scott. In 1814 he journeyed to the northern isles with a party of Commissioners for the Northern Light-House Services, inspecting the lighthouses. On 10 August he wrote, without a word of coloured patterns:

'The women [of Fair Isle] knit worsted stockings, nightcaps and similar trifles, which they exchange with any merchant vessels that approach their lonely isle. In this respect they greatly regret the American war; and mention with unction the happy days when they could get from an American trader a bottle of peach-brandy or rum in exchange for a pair of worsted stockings or a dozen of eggs.'

Three days later he wrote to his wife from Kirkwall:

'The women [of Fair Isle] knit stockings and a queer kind of nightcaps and mits. I have bought some, but they must be well scoured, for of all the dirt I ever saw, that of the Fair Isle is transcendent.'

The Armada story

There are still some who treasure the romance that Fair Isle knitting came from Spain with the Armada. This story is so tenacious that it demands careful attention.

Robert Sibbald in his *Description of the Islands of Orkney and Zetland* (1711) told of the wreck, but said nothing of the knitting. Hibbert, who in 1822 described the coloured caps, also described the Armada wreck, but made no connection between the two. In 1840 Catherine Sinclair, daughter of the originator of the Statistical Accounts, described Fair Isle and the Armada wreck in *Shetland and the Shetlanders*. She said nothing of coloured knitting, but, rather, commented on Shetland sheep that their 'colour is that peculiar brown and blue which the Shetland stockings usually exhibit.'

The legend first appeared in print in *A Voyage round the Coasts of Scotland* (1842), by James Wilson, a zoologist who visited the Scottish islands with Sir Thomas Dick Lauder in the previous year on an inspection of fisheries. He did not visit Fair Isle, but he wrote of it:

One of the most curious results connected with the temporary residence in Fair Isle of the foreign sailors is that the natives acquired, and their descendants have ever since preserved, a knowledge of the peculiar patterns of gloves and caps worn by the Spaniards, and to this day work them in various-coloured worsteds, exactly resembling the corresponding articles produced at Cadiz (II 411).

(Wilson bought his souvenir woollen goods in Lerwick and eagerly recorded the 'droves of women proceeding on their never-ceasing journey to the mosses in the hills for peats, with their cassies or straw bundles on their backs and knitting eagerly with both their hands' II 277.)

The legend next appeared in print in the *Official Description and Illustrative Catalogue* of the Great Exhibition of Works of Industry of All Nations in Hyde Park in 1851. One exhibit was 'Specimens of knitting from the Shetland Islands, showing 26 patterns used by the inhabitants. The art of dyeing wool is considered to have been taught them by

Spaniards wrecked there after the dispersion of the 'Invincible Armada'.'

It is noticeable that this attributes to the marooned Spaniards not the Fair Isle patterns, but the art of dyeing. The next connection of the patterns with the Armada was made by Eliza Edmondston in her 1856 sketch of knitters:

It is believed the Duke of Medina Sidonia, admiral of the Spanish Armada, and his followers, whose ship was wrecked on Fair Isle and who afterwards wintered in Shetland, were the first that taught these islanders the art of knitting. Certain it is that the painted-like manufacture of the Fair Isle people at this day is quite similar to what is made in the south of Spain.

Eliza Edmondston was a Shetland resident, but not an historian. It was not the Duke of Medina Sidonia who was wrecked on Fair Isle, but the Captain-General of supply-ships, Juan Gomez de Medina. The survivors did not winter in Shetland: they were on the Scottish mainland by early December. In justice to her it must be said, however, that she records only a 'belief' that the men of the Armada taught Shetlanders to knit, and drops only a hint, to be taken up by later writers, that Fair Isle coloured patterns may have come from Spain.

There is little or no reason to think that the Fair Isle patterns came from Spaniards. The connection of the patterns with Scandinavia is more convincing; and there is no evidence in Fair Isle of a tradition about their Spanish origin until later Victorians took up Mrs Edmondston's hint. The Shetlanders were then willing to believe it and to give names like 'Armada cross' to some of the designs, which were all too readily accepted by uncritical and romantic writers. The wool spinners and clothiers then encouraged the Armada legend in the promotion of Fair Isle garments – and who shall blame them for having an advertiser's eye for a good story?

A detailed account of the wreck is given in *Full Fathom Five* (1975) by Colin Martin, a professor of marine archaeology, who supervised the location and examination of the wreck site in 1970 and 1977.

The ship was *El Gran Grifón*, flagship of the squadron of *urcas* (supply hulks), under Captain-General Juan Gomez de Medina. She came from Rostock, one of the free-trading city states of the Hanseatic League on the Baltic coast of North Germany; and her name was probably taken from Rostock's civic emblem, a golden griffin. Little more than 20 years before the Armada came, a Swede, Sten Svantesson Sture, had been killed in a battle near Rostock wearing a multicoloured knitted glove from his betrothed Sofia pinned to his hat. When *El Gran Grifón* mustered at Lisbon on 7 January 1588, some of the 43 mariners aboard her probably spoke a Scandinavian language and came from a community where gloves and stockings were knitted, perhaps even in colour.

The ship got into trouble in the battle off the Isle of Wight on 3 August. She limped through the North Sea behind the rest of the fleet till she passed between Orkney and Fair Isle on 20 August. On 1 September she took aboard 250 men from another hulk, which was sinking. All contact with other ships was lost and *El Gran Grifón* was blown out into the Atlantic, west of Iceland, then back to Fair Isle, off which she anchored at sunset on 27 September. Probably some of the crewmen knew the waters around Shetland. At morning light they seem to have tried to beach the ship under the 150-foot-high cliffs of Stroms Hellier. There is an unexpectedly treacherous tide at the mouth of the inlet, and the ship went quickly to wreck, just giving her people time to escape.

Tradition quite plausibly says they climbed to safety up the masts and over the yards, which were leaning against the cliff. There were some 300 of them. They found only 17 families of islanders, living in mean hovels, keeping cows and sheep, and eating fish, barley-meal bannocks, butter and milk. The foreigners could not get away till 14 November. Fifty of them died of starvation during the seven weeks on Fair Isle. A tradition recorded by an Orkneyman in 1633 suggests that the islanders murdered some of them, but Spanish records and island tradition do not accept this. The tradition that the islanders were kind is stronger, and is confirmed by Spanish accounts.

The shipwrecked men were taken to Quendale, at the southern end of Shetland Mainland, where they stayed for about three weeks before they were taken to Anstruther on the Firth of Forth, where they arrived at daybreak on 6 December. Nearly two years after that they sailed home to Spain.

What sense does the legend of knitting make? In all, 250 men, most of them beardless youths, were stranded in Fair Isle for 48 days and on Shetland mainland for a further 3 weeks. They were not enemies, for Scotland was neutral in Spain and England's war. Their stay appears to have been peaceful. Some of them were probably men of the Baltic coast, not impossibly men skilled in knitting. There was yarn in Shetland, and knitting is just the sort of occupation that suits a sailor in enforced idleness – provided he has brought knitting needles with him or can improvise them. It is just possible that the story is true.

Or what about the story that the skill the survivors taught was dyeing? Were there not similar vegetable dyes on the Baltic coast? Sailors or soldiers wandering at a loose end on the little island might well light on dyestuff material and teach the locals about it.

There is nothing inherently impossible in this much contested story. The strongest point against it is that nothing is known of two-colour knitting on Fair Isle during the 300 years between the wreck of *El Gran Grifón* and the beginning of the nineteenth century.

Strong written evidence for the Armada legend being a piece of romantic imagining comes from John Russell's informative book *Three Years in Shetland* (1887). Russell was a presbyterian minister who went to the charge of Whalsay in 1873 and stayed in Shetland until 1876. His remarks on the connection between *El Gran Grifón* and knitting were intended by him to be conclusive:

Some have pretended to discover marks of Spanish blood in the dark complexion of the inhabitants of Fair Isle, and say that this arises from some of those who had been shipwrecked in one of the galleons comprising the great Armada marrying in the island; but the Fair Islanders repudiate the supposition with the greatest indignation. They say that the Spandiards during their stay lived entirely apart from the rest of the inhabitants and that the mutual attitude of the two parties was that of distrust and hostility rather than friendship and alliance. Nor do they believe that they learned anything in regards to dyeing and knitting from the Spaniards, though it has become the fashion to say so.

So the Armada story did not come from the islanders in the mid-nineteenth century. But how trustworthy was what they saw fit to tell tourists?

Shetland colours

The dyes are interesting in their own right. Writers on knitting too readily assume that multi-coloured knitting always begins with the use of different natural shades of wool. The Shetland sheep vary much in colour. Some of the colours have Norn names still: *moorit*, 'russet', an attractive medium brown, slightly lighter than milk chocolate; *shaela*, 'frosty', really blackish with whitish tips, giving a pleasant grey; *mooskit*, 'mousy' or 'dusty', a beige veering to grey or fawn (between which two colours Shetlanders do not readily distinguish); as well as off-white; and a sepia colour called 'black'. Modern taste may like the interplay of greys and browns, of dark and light, but this is a developed and sophisticated approach. In the post-Renaissance times, when knitting developed, men had stronger tastes in colour (though fewer names for hues than we have now). The whole point of colour was that it should be striking. Significantly our first description of Shetland coloured-knitting is Hibbert's tale of bright caps; and the Gunnister purse, one of the oldest pieces of multicoloured knitting in the British Isles, has dyed red yarn in it. 'Fair Isle' patterns were made with dyed wools from the start.

Hibbert listed four lichens used for dyeing. We now know them as *Ochrolechia tartarea*, dyeing reddish purple or 'korkelit'; *Parmelia saxatilis*, reddish brown or yellowish; *Xanthoria parietina*, orange; and *Parmelia omphaloides*, brownish or blackish purple. A further list was given by Thomas Edmondston, the brilliant Shetland botanist, in a letter to the Royal Botanical Society of Edinburgh, published in 1841 when he was 16 years old. He included only two lichen dyes but added other plants and imports.

Fair Isle stranded knitting was done for the sheer pleasure of the patterns and their colours. Extra density of fabric was not the reason for Fair Isle work. This can be stated with confidence for two reasons: the fact that it began with small garments and was done for many decades before it was used for body-garments; and the fact that the Shetlanders have never adopted stranded knitting using two yarns of the same shade – a technique that is used and perfected in Scandinavia and whose principal purpose is to provide a dense and insulating fabric.

The peculiar qualities of Shetland wool encouraged stranded knitting. The fibres are tacky and without gloss. The floats across the back stick lightly to the knitting and snag less readily than a lustrous worsted would do. The disadvantage of the yarn is that it requires careful laundering and dressing. A Shetland garment subject to careless washing will start to felt and go hard as a board. For this reason wet dressing under tension on a woolly-board or jumper-horse has been developed in the islands.

Fair Isle jumpers

Fair Isle jumpers seem to have been a later invention. William Peace of Kirkwall, who published many editions of his *Handbook to the Shetland Islands*, makes special reference to Fair Isle hosiery in 1867. He says it 'is of a very peculiar appearance, the patterns and colours being of all descriptions and shades'. He mentions hosiery only. The implication is that outerwear was not being produced in Fair Isle. Even in 1885, though he includes 'gloves, caps, stockings and vests' as multicoloured products, jumpers are not clearly mentioned.

I have found no picture of one dated before 1890, when Frank Barnard shows what just might be a Fair Isle sweater in one of the plates of his delightful picture book *Picturesque Life in Shetland*. The drawing is not clear, and interestingly the jumper is worn by a little boy. In another place in the same book Barnard quotes Robert Cowrie on

the 'variegated and fantastic hues which characterize such articles in the Fair Isle hosiery . . . obtained from natural dyes, chiefly lichens', red-purple, blackish purple, yellow brown and orange. (Incidentally Barnard also gives the false etymology of *moorit* from 'moor-red'. *Moorit* is a purely Scandinavian word meaning reddish.)

Victorian photographs never show Shetlanders wearing patterned jumpers. Plain ganseys can be found in photographs, as in Barnard's drawings, but not Fair-Isle-type designs. Although an engraving by Gustave Doré of Billingsgate fishmarket early in the morning, published in Blanchard Jerrold *London: a Pilgrimage* (1872), has been claimed to show a Fair Isle jersey, the magnifying glass proves that the black-and-white picture shows merely an English fisher-gansey in plain-and-purl patterns.

Fair Isle garments are said to have been supplied

Diehard (stroking his beard). " MY DEAR GIRL, IT'S OUR ONLY CHANCE LEFT. SOON AS YOU CAN IMITATE THIS WE'RE DONE."

129 The rage for Fair Isle jerseys illustrated by J.H. Thorpe in *Punch*, 11 February 1925.

130 Detail of a Shetland jersey with a pattern of anchors. About 1918. Yellow on 'black', and white on red.

for the members of the Scottish National Antarctic Expedition on the *Scotia*, planned by William Spiers Bruce and sponsored partly by the spinning firm Coats of Paisley in 1902–4. It is not clear that they included anything more than caps and mitts. The real popularity of Fair Isle jumpers and other articles came only after the First World War. The older garments in Scottish museums seem to be caps, scarfs, and socks. No museum jersey is certainly dated before about 1914.

The fashion explosion of Fair Isle sweaters in the 1920s is usually dated from 27 September 1922, when the Prince of Wales, then 27 years old, teed off at the Royal and Ancient Golf Club of St Andrews. His words in his *A Family Album* (1960), while they may over-emphasize the occasion, are responsible for the story:

> I suppose the most showy of all my garments was the multicoloured Fair Isle sweater, with its jigsaw patterns, which I wore for the first time while playing myself in as Captain of the Royal & Ancient Golf Club at St Andrews in 1922.

Fair Isle was not a shock to the fashion world in the 1920s. The vogue for 'jazz' decoration was already taking hold, and the many cartoons depicting Fair Isle in *Punch*, which were at their peak in 1925 and 1926, set Fair Isle in the context of the Jazz age. Since then Fair Isle has never completely gone out of fashion. Today almost any multicoloured knitting is called Fair Isle, whether made in Leicester or Tokyo; but the craft of hand-knitted Fair Isle is still at its best in Shetland.

Colour patterns and motifs

An outline history of Fair Isle style and colours can be discerned. The oldest examples appear to have been knitted in those natural-dye colours that Thomas Edmondston in 1841 told the Royal Botanical Society of Edinburgh were the only current native dyes of Shetland: rusty brown, red, black, and yellow. Together with three imported dyestuffs (madder, indigo and logwood) and undyed creamy-white wool, these provided the typical colour schemes of early Fair Isle knitting. Yellow and white motifs on a ground of banded

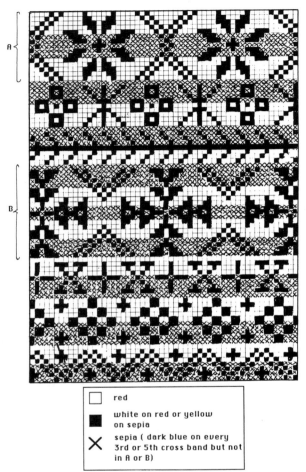

	red
■	white on red or yellow on sepia
×	sepia (dark blue on every 3rd or 5th cross band but not in A or B)

131 A typical Shetland jumper fabric pattern of 1910-20, with yellow-on-'black' and white-on-red, and OXO motifs.

red, indigo and black; or red and brown/black motifs on a ground banded in white and yellow give rich effects, more satisfying than the variations made with purple, blue, green and orange dyes after the coming of the cheap synthetic dyes to Shetland during the Victorian period.

These early simple but sumptuous colour schemes, made garish by the aniline dyes, gave way after the First World War to the British passion for beige which dominated even the jazz period.

Beige came with sophistication and the towns-man's nostalgia for the simple life. The Fair Isle of the 1930s had a background of beige or fawn or grey or 'game-fleck' like a partridge's back. Brown, green, yellow, blue and rust were typical contrast colours till the Second World War.

When did the gradation of tone in the background begin to appear? Probably not much until after 1945, since when it has been a mark of quality in Shetland work. About that time too came the vogue for 'peaked' or 'waved' patterns, in which rows of lozenges in graduated bands of shades of similar hues tend to obviate the monotonously horizontal character of Fair Isle patterns. During the early 1970s the earlier colour schemes of red, black, yellow and white had a certain revival as the museum services became more popular and designers grew more aware of the older work in museum collections. At the same time designers explored new sensitivity to colour, and Kaffe Fassett's conglomerations of crimson, rose, purple and black (for example) brought new life to the Fair Isle tradition, while Patricia Roberts and others knitted old Shetland patterns in dramatic new colour schemes such as emerald, amaranth and electric blue on a ground of midnight black, or with rapid random changes of colour for both ground and motif. By that time the patterns were no longer distinctive of the Shetland Islands.

The history of the motifs used in Fair Isle and Shetland knitting is difficult to unravel because there is no reliable way of dating the pieces that survive, and detailed pictorial records are rare before the 1920s. A plausible outline of the story suggests that the early patterns were all strictly horizontal bands of motifs, rarely each more than 15 rows deep. Bands of large motifs were divided by bands of smaller motifs, half or less the depth of the larger ones. The separation of approximately circular motifs by four diagonal corners produced the familiar so-called OXO designs. (The X mostly had a vertical line through its centre.) A second early style of small geometrical patches covering the whole fabric has been called 'diced'.

It is difficult to deny the common elements in the stranded knitting of Shetland and Norway. The early nineteenth century seems to be the time when both began, though the Norwegians made colour-pattern body-garments earlier than the Shetlanders. There was close contact between the two countries and they also spoke mutually

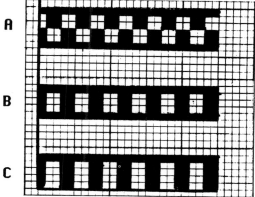

133 The colour pattern of the Gunnister purse.
A = red; B = white; C = red. (See pages 169-70.)

132 Undergraduates in fashionable Fair Isle jerseys, working the chief signal box at Bletchley during the General Strike. *Illustrated London News*, 15 May 1926.

understandable languages. There are, nevertheless, striking differences between the two traditions, both in the use of colour and in the placing of motifs. The Shetland OXO theme is typical of the islands, and so are both the bright colouring of Fair Isle and the softer shades of Shetland. The eight-pointed star (sometimes rather arbitrarily named 'the Selbu star' or miscalled a 'snowflake', in spite of the fact that a snowflake always has six points) is also called the 'Norwegian star'. Yet this motif is ancient and practically universal. It can be found in Romano-British mosaic pavements, in African textiles, in mediaeval Germany and many other times and places. It is typical of Norwegian patterns, but did not become a dominant design element in Shetland until perhaps the 1940s.

By that time fancy was ranging freely. Human and animal figures, such as enlivened Scandinavian designs, had long been used, though the Shetland pony has never vied with the Scandinavian deer as a knitted motif. Now novelties such as crowns and teapots, and naturalistic forms, usually from plants, multiplied. Shetland patterns had been recorded since the 1920s in children's exercise books, especially those made of graph paper. This method of recording stimulated the search for fresh ideas, and today many Shetland patterns have abandoned the horizontally banded structure for a development of the dicing tradition into an all-over pattern of large motifs, either geometrical or floral. One of the most interesting of these is said in Shetland to have been copied from linoleum flooring, though it appears in Annichen Sibbern Bøhn's 1947 book of Norwegian patterns.

The banded patterns continue to be made, and Shetland knitters have shown subtle skill in developing both motifs and colours. Shetland knitting is a highly personalized product of individual craftswomen. They are reluctant, as

135 The all-over pattern of a Shetland jersey that won a prize at a Lerwick Show in 1951, was used by Norbury as 'Autumn Leaves' in 1952, and given a new colour treatment by Patricia Roberts as 'Nutcracker' in 1981. (See page 154.)

most craftsmen are, to repeat a piece. The individuality of the hand knitter is what sets the Shetland or Fair Isle garment apart from the products of factory knitting by machines.

Home knitting

Though the luxury trades of lace and coloured work continued, Shetlanders still knitted for the family throughout the nineteenth and twentieth centuries. Jessie M.E. Saxby in *Auld Lerwick: a Personal Reminiscence* (1894) recalled how during the Crimean War, 40 years earlier, 'fishermen and others gave money and wool which were rapidly converted into mufflers, gloves, caps, etc.; old wives and little boys plied the knitting needles as well as women and girls . . . .'

Granny Mouat, born in 1873, lived on Noss, where Ursula Venables, who wrote *Life in Shetland* (1956), knew her in the 1940s and 1950s. The old lady recalled how her mother used to knit shawls and received three shillingsworth of goods at the local shop, according to the unjust truck system, or occasionally took shawls to sell in Lerwick.

In August I mind her knitting two shawls to buy

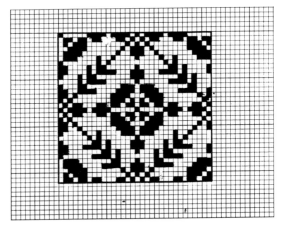

134 The Shetland all-over pattern said to have been taken from linoleum, but published by A.S. Bøhn in *Norske Strikkemønstre*, Oslo 1947.

me a pair of winter boots for school – we'd go barefoot, of course, all summer. She used to stretch her shawls on pegs on the green to dress them, but that autumn came so wet, the ground was ay too miry. (136–7)

In spite of the wet, Granny got her boots. She knitted her own first hap at the age of 5, and at 77 the only shawl she ever made of dyed wool.

Let an entertaining tale round off the account of Shetland knitting. James Wilson, in *A Voyage round the Coasts of Scotland* (1842) tells of a ruined building on the summit of Frau-Stack on Papa Stour.

> The laird of Papa, to preserve his daughter from the addresses of her lover, a certain udaller of Islesburgh, built the keep in question; but as the lady sat knitting one fine evening at the window of this her sea-girt prison, by some accident or other she let fall her clew of worsted, and on drawing it up she found a stronger cord attached to it. Continuing to draw the latter, she next discovered a stout rope, which she still continued to upheave, probably from mere curiosity, till to her astonishment she at last found her lover adhering tenaciously to its other end. (II 353)

She must have been a stout lass, and if the laird believed her story . . .

The Channel Islands

The history of knitting in the Channel Islands is in broad outline parallel to the story of cottage knitting in other parts of the British realm. It has, however, given to the vocabulary of knitting two terms that are now in worldwide use. Channel Islanders would probably wish to distinguish the history of Jersey from that of Guernsey (they took opposite sides in the Civil War), but there are many indications that their knitting was treated as indistinguishable, and there is no real distinction between 'guernsey' and 'jersey' as names for stockinet fabric. Indeed Philip Stubbes used 'jarnsey' as early as 1583.

Sir Edgar MacCulloch, lieutenant-bailiff of Guernsey, speaking to the Association Bretonne at Vitré in 1876 about Channel Islands trade with Brittany, summarized the earliest evidence for knitting in the islands. His talk was published in the Association's *Bulletin archéologique* (1877).

> On New Year's Day 1556, Queen Mary Tudor condescended to accept from the hands of Sir Leonard Chamberlain, Governor of Guernsey, four waistcoats (i.e. undergarments, what we should now call shirts or vests), four pairs of sleeves and four pairs of hose, all of the make of the island. In the inventories of the Royal Wardrobe of Scotland in the year 1578 we find three pairs of worsted hose and six pairs of gloves of the same material of Guernsey manufacture, and the unfortunate Mary Stuart wore at the time of her execution in 1587 a pair of white worsted stockings of the same fabric. Finally, in the wardrobe accounts of Queen Elizabeth of the preceding year, 1586, we find payment of 20 shillings for a pair of knit Guernsey stockings embroidered in silk: *por i par caligarum nexat de factura Garnesie operat in parte superiori et les clockes cum serico XXs.* (p 26)

MacCulloch's references need checking, especially because the quotation from Queen Elizabeth's account-book is an amalgamation of four languages. The gift to Queen Mary is recorded in John Nichols *Progresses and Public Processions of Queen Elizabeth* (1823) (I xxxiv), and there are variant records of Mary Stuart's stockings, but the drift of his argument is reliable: Channel Islands knitting was renowned in England when Queen Elizabeth came to the throne. MacCulloch might have added that William Camden, the great London antiquary, in *Britannia*, his survey of the British Isles (first published in 1586) said of Jersey: 'The women make great gain by knitting hose, which we call Jersey stocks'. Also, William Harrison in his *Description of England* (1587) spoke of 'women's diversely coloured stockings of silk jersey'.

At the same period cottage knitting was beginning in the rest of England, especially the northern Dales, while Shetland was probably not far behind. Speculation that the Channel Islands learned knitting directly from the continent is tempting but vain. They had local sheep, and islanders have few distractions. The new fashion for knitted hosiery stimulated an industry for export which the islanders must have welcomed.

The seventeenth century

There is firm evidence about knitting in the Channel Islands from the reign of James I. Jean de la Croix in *La Ville de St Hélier* (1845) quotes an act of Court of 19 July 1606 ordering that the people should not knit during the harvest or vraic-cutting season, under penalty of imprisonment in the castle on bread and water (130). (*Vraic* corresponds to 'wrack' and is a seaweed gathered for use as fuel or fertilizer.) The desertion of agriculture for the easier and more profitable work of making stockings was periodically the subject of legislation, especially in Jersey.

Philip Falle, who gave Jersey its first library and became a canon of Durham, in *An Account of the Island of Jersey* (1694) records another act of the court dated 21 April 1608, compelling all people above the age of 15 to relinquish knitting and assist the farmers at the vraic and corn harvests. A scarcity of corn had followed the difficulty of getting men to work out of doors 'because numbers of hale and strong persons occupied themselves with knitting stockings, disdaining labour.' (1837 edition, p 363)

Another writer, C. Le Lievre, in *A Brief Description and Historical Notice of the Island of Jersey* (1826) records an order promulgated by the court on 19 January 1608:

> Forasmuch as the traffic of knit worsted stockings brings great profit to the island, which is falling off and is greatly lost, little by little, because some are made with two threads when they used to be made with three for each pair; and for these reasons it is ordered that every one shall be bound to make each pair with three threads, under pain of forfeiture of the said stockings. (21–3)

Meanwhile the de Sausmarez family was organizing the export trade in Guernsey. Thomas de Sausmarez was supplying stockings and waistcoats to Thomas Greene, a clothier of London, at 2s. 3d.–5s. 0d. per pair of stockings and 14–20 shillings per waistcoat. One of de Sausmarez's memos of 1614 records how he sent Greene stockings to the value of £41.5s.0d. in part payment of an account for cloth bought of Greene.

On 22 June 1615 the Jersey court made an unusually personal order. It forbade one Philip Picot to knit in the company of young women, because of the scandal that had arisen. He might knit, but must knit alone and at home.

In 1624 a petition went to Westminster, asking parliament for increased wool supplies because 'more than a thousand souls have no other means to get their living' on the island of Jersey. Jersey stockings were being sold to England, France, America, and even to Italy. Jonathan Duncan in *The History of Guernsey* (1841) quotes the Oxford geographer Peter Heylin, saying that in 1629 St Peter Port on Guernsey was the beneficiary of a recent royal licence to import English wool. (230)

Heylin's book, *A Survey of the Estates of France and of some of her Adjoining Islands*, published in 1656, noted that 'The principal commodity which they use to send abroad are the works and labours of the poorer sort, as waistcoats, stockings, and other manufactures made of wool, wherein they are exceeding cunning'.

Elie Brevint of Sark in his journal of 1613–44, a manuscript preserved at the Seigneurie of Sark, describes the export business. He tells how merchants from the Channel Islands were given bills of exchange in Coutances in return for stockings, which were freely honoured because of the great value of this trade. The French even came to the islands to buy stockings for themselves at times when not enough were taken to France by the islanders. Brevint says stockings went also to other countries, especially Italy, because they wore better than silk stockings, which tended to be shrunk or spoiled by rain and damp.

The English Civil War of 1642 brought much trouble to the Islands, including disruption of this stocking trade. No wool could be got from England and the market there lapsed. George Reginald Balleine in *A History of the Island of Jersey* (1950) claimed that when the knitters began to use large needles to eke out their local resources, the French refused to buy.

After the Restoration

After 1647 and the end of the war, things returned to normal, indeed almost too much so, for with the renewed profits came the old anxieties. Jean Poingdestre, lieutenant-bailiff of Jersey, in *Caesarea, or a Discourse of the Island of Jersey* (1682) made the same point in more detail:

> The people who were wont to attend tillage, a painful occupation, and sowing hemp and flax for the making of cloth, finding now by experience more ease in knitting of stockings and waistcoats, have so generally – men, women and children – given themselves that way that none will assist husbandmen but with repugnancy and at such rates as cannot consist with that moderate price at which foreign corn is sold in the market. (4–5)

He then gives some details of the extent and nature of the trade:

> . . . the greatest part are knitters. For as there be many houses in which there are few or none, so there are a great many more where man, wife, children and all, beginning at the age of five or six years old, have no other employment and may be said to make (taking one with another) every one a pair of stockings every week – which must after my account come to more than ten thousand pairs weekly. All these stockings are bought by merchants of that profession every Saturday in few hours' time in the town of St Helery (not Hilary, as hath been by writers mistaken), where a plentiful market is kept that day all the year long, for all commodities in the manner of a fair; and having been washed and prepared by them, they are for the most part transported into France. Some few are also carried into Spain, of a different making from the rest, according to the use of that country. Few or none go to England, but knit waistcoats only. (5)

Three years later Philip Dumaresq, writing *A Survey of the Island of Jersey* (1658), gently commented on Poingdestre's account, calling knitting the 'lazy manufacture':

> Half at least [of the population] depend on the manufacture of stockings. Mr Poingdexter has very well observed that by many probable conjectures the island was heretofore more peopled than now, but passes by the chief reasons of it . . . the general neglect of husbandry, occasioned for want of hands that apply themselves to that lazy manufacture, is a primary cause . . .
>
> Neither, upon enquiry, do I find the number of stockings made there to come to ten thousand pairs a week . . . but believed by the most knowing to come to six thousand, one week with another; and allowing three pairs for one pound of wool, as the ordinary sort are, it will employ four score tods† weekly, double the number of what we are allowed to import.

The family de Sausmarez was one of the chief exporters of hosiery from Guernsey. Matthew de Sausmarez, related to Thomas who traded with Greene of London before the war, married his cousin Bertranne in 1672. Bertranne supplied the knitters with wool, told them what to knit, and bought the finished articles. Matthew managed the bookkeeping and despatching of the stockings. He had agents, Guernseymen and Frenchmen, at St Malo, Vannes, St Lô, Coutances, Laval, Lisieux, Rouen, and other places even as far away as Bordeaux. He also exported stockings made in Jersey.

His chief agent in Paris was Bertranne's brother Michael de Sausmarez, to whom he wrote frequent letters in French, addressed to Michael at the Bureau des Bonnetiers. A collection of these letters, written during the 1670s and 1680s, is kept at Sausmarez Manor.

The letters are tantalizingly allusive to the various kinds of stockings in which the family dealt. Most popular appear to have been *bas à canon*, long stockings with wide tops that were worn with the beribboned knee-length trousers then in fashion. The various patterns were indicated by code numbers, but we have no clue to what the numbers

†(The tod was 28 lbs weight).

meant. The prices in *livres tournois* went from £18 to £78 per dozen pair. In the English currency of the time this was from 2s.6d to 10s.10d a pair. Wages for workers and labourers ranged from a shilling to two shillings a day. The stockings exported to France were therefore luxury items.

Some of the stockings were white. Others were striped, either vertically or horizontally. A letter from a merchant in Paris to Michael while he was visiting Guernsey in May 1684 tells him that the vertical stripes have gone out of fashion, but the best selling kinds are light mottled stockings with horizontal stripes in black and white, blue and white, or green and white. The stripes must continue right up the thigh (not only half way up) and must be in bands of three: a black stripe between two narrow white ones; then a band of mottled yarn of a width equal to the three black and white stripes.

Some of the designs and colours mentioned are obscure. Often they are described as 'according to sample'. Grey-brown, iron grey, plum-colour, blue-and-white, white, white *rayiez de nouer et de blue* (striped black and blue), *rayé couleur de feu*, greyish white, bright reddish brown, marbled and *à l'écaille* (perhaps a shell pattern) are all mentioned. There is no mention of fashionable French colour-names such as those recorded for the period by Agrippa d'Aubigné. (See above p 70.)

Besides *bas à canon*, there were *bas à hommes* and *bas à enfants*. Women's stockings were rarely mentioned, but *rhingraves* were a kind of stocking for men that the de Sausmarez family vended. Rhinegraves were a form of short and very wide breeches, usually liberally decorated with ruffles and ribbons, more commonly called petticoat breeches, that were the height of fashion at the French and English courts during the early 1660s. The stockings worn with them had decorated tops that were usually allowed to fall over the garters in a deep ornamental flounce. These falling tops were also called canons, so the rhinegrave stockings may have been the same as the *bas à canon*. They were still being supplied to the French in 1680, for the French were not quick to follow the change to the severer form of coat introduced by Charles II in 1666, when rhinegraves suddenly ceased to be worn in England.

The eighteenth century

In 1678 relations between France and England worsened and trade suffered. Jean-Baptiste Colbert, the chief minister of France from 1661 onwards, penalized the Channel Islands by his policies to rectify France's desperate economic condition. Philip Falle in his revised work *Caesarea: or an Account of Jersey* (1734), speaks of the knitting industry in his own days, but refers back to the previous century:

> We have but one constant standing manufacture for exportation, namely that of knit hose or stockings, of which many thousand pairs are weekly made in the island and sold at St Helier every Saturday by the knitters to the merchants, who heretofore used to carry or send them to Paris and Rouen, and even so far as Lyons in France, and there had a good price for them. But when the famous Colbert set himself to advance the commerce and manufactures of that kingdom he caused so high a duty to be laid on this traffic as amounted to a prohibition. London is the present market for them, from whence they are with other English goods dispersed into various parts of the world. The wool they are wrought with comes to us from England, two thousand tods uncombed being a concession of Parliament allowed us yearly for supporting the said manufacture and employing our poor.

The trade continued during the eighteenth century. Under the article on Hampshire in Postlethwayt's dictionary of trades of 1751, we have an unacknowledged quotation from Philip Falle about Jersey knitting and a note about the stockings, gloves, caps and waistcoats knitted on Sark by men, women and children.

Thomas Dicey in *A Historical Account of Guernsey* (1751) also quoting, wrote of a development:

> They have but one constant standing manufacturing for exportation, namely that of knit hose or stockings (and, within these few years, breeches worked in the same manner) of which many thousand pieces are weekly made in this island – some have not scrupled to say ten

thousand, (32) . . . for wool received from England they return large quantities of worsted stockings, waistcoats and breeches. (33)

When Thomas Baker issued his *Southampton Guide* (1774) he still mentioned the wool imports:

The chief trade it (Southampton) has at present is with the Portuguese for wine and fruit and with the islands of Jersey and Guernsey, Alderney and Sark. There are several ships constantly sailing to and from these islands which, besides carrying most of the goods bought in England by the insular shopkeepers, carry away annually a quantity of unkembed wool, allowed by act of parliament as here specified: to Jersey 4000 tods; to Guernsey 2000 tods; to Alderney 400 tods; to Sark 200 tods. (20–1)

This information appears unreliable, for D.T. Anstead and F.R. Latham in *The Channel Islands* (1862) give the same figures for tod allowances granted by James II, a hundred years earlier (394). Southampton port records show that the whole quota was seldom drawn. Before 1739 only a third of what the islanders could have knitted with the full allowance entered England. When war with Spain closed the Spanish market that year, these imports increased, nearly doubling by 1745, when a peak of 26,000 dozen pairs of hose was reached. Twenty years later the count had fallen to 12,000 dozen, of which some 80 per cent came from Jersey. Guernsey had become an entrepôt.

The nineteenth century

After this, Channel Island knitting declined. England was more often than not at war; the French Revolution and Napoleon interrupted international trade; and framework knitting was taking over the markets. A tourist guide of 1802 by D.F.S., *The Channel Islands and Islanders*, tells details of folk life, but makes no mention of knitting. William Berry in *The History of the Island of Guernsey* (1815) included substantial chapters on commerce and products, but did not mention

knitting. In 1830 John Jacob, in *Annals of the British Norman Isles*, wrote

Guernsey was formerly famous for its worsted knit stockings, as well as undergarments called Guernsey frocks, but this handicraft is almost if not entirely lost. (I 463)

Yet the islanders were still knitting for themselves. *The Channel Islands* by H.D. Inglis, published in 1835, says of Jersey:

Many of the habiliments both of the men and women are of worsted which has been subjected to the knitting needle; and not only stockings and shawls, but petticoats and even small clothes are of this material and are the produce of domestic industry. (39)

In 1837 Edward Durrell annotated a new edition of Philip Falle's *An account of the island of Jersey*, originally published in 1694 and quoted above. Durrell's notes say:

While the stocking manufacture lasted . . . the distribution of the licences to import wool was a matter of some solicitation and even favour . . . .

The knitting of stockings was very considerable, even within the memory of man . . . now ceased altogether . . . the discouragement of the poor knitters began from the Jersey merchants, who were not only in the habit of allowing them the very smallest possible remuneration, but of paying them for the most part in goods. That and the superior cheapness at which stockings could be had from other places for the foreign market have ruined that branch of industry . . .

This may be called the land of knitters: there is scarcely a female but who can knit. Strangers may remark it as a peculiar feature of the character of the people, to see females of the humbler classes knitting as they move leisurely along the lanes in the country. Not many years ago they might have been seen in that attire going on a Saturday to St Helier's market. (384–5)

In his 1826 book on Jersey already quoted, C. Le Lievre wrote:

Though the manufacture (of stockings) in a certain degree still exists, yet it exists only by the industry of females. It is continued by them in the fields, and not infrequently on horseback; and it is the pursuit of all those whom age and infirmity have deprived of activity and vigour; but it no longer retards agriculture or withdraws the husbandman from the labour of the plough. (23)

Another mite of information about the post-Napoleonic period comes from *Caesarea* 'printed for T. Baker' in 1840. It says of Jersey:

Some [stockings] are still made, though to a very small extent; the use of machinery in the making of this article in England has caused the Jersey-made stockings to be confined to a limited home demand, the export not exceeding 1,000 pair annually, and these for the use of persons on the fishing stations in British North America. (72)

Many Channel Islanders eventually found their way to Newfoundland and took their knitting tradition with them.

The tradition was honoured at the Great Exhibition in London in 1851. Several items of silk knitting are mentioned in the *Official Descriptive and Illustrated Catalogue*, but Guernsey and Jersey frocks and shirts, both white and fancy, were shown by machine-knitting firms from Leicester. The life had gone out of Channel Islands knitting. *The Jersey Times* of 2 February 1851 bleakly recorded that twelve pairs of stockings were displayed in the exhibition hall in Hyde Park, 'showing the high perfection to which the article was formerly brought in Jersey'.

The veilles

Yet the folklorists and antiquarians never forgot. The knitting parties called *veilles* lingered on. Raoul Lempriere in *Customs, Ceremonies and Traditions of the Channel Islands* (1976) mentions that 23 December was called *la longue veille*. It was the end of knitting for the year and the knitted goods were got ready for market on the following day. The rest of the night was spent in merry-making. He quotes with relish Mrs L.L. Clarke's account, in *Redstone's Guernsey and Jersey Guide* (1843), of the *vin brûlé* (mulled claret or port with cloves, cinnamon and sugar) drunk at *la longue veille* (163).

The most charming description of the Island's communal knitting comes from J. Stead *A Picture of Jersey* (1809), but is a quotation from Richard Valpy (1754–1836) a native of Jersey, who became headmaster of Reading School. He was doubtless referring to his younger days in Jersey, before the French Revolution. He wrote Latin schoolbooks and was obviously the kind of classics master who strove to show that all Virgil's poems are pure.

Four thousand tods of wool are allowed to be yearly exported from England into Jersey, duty free and, having been finely combed and perfectly dressed, are knit into stockings, gloves, and various other articles of dress. This is the chief employment of the women. The dexterity and expedition with which they dispatch a pair of stockings are almost incredible. To them light and darkness are indifferent. A woman seen walking without a stocking in her hand is stigmatized with idleness. So attached are they to this employment that they have appropriated to knitting the name of work (i.e. *oeuvre*, from which is derived the verb *ouvrer*, which in this dialect signifies 'to knit'). In summer they assemble in large numbers and sit in a ring under the trees, which make of all the roads a continuous avenue; and the avocation must be urgent that can call them from the social party. In winter a number of houses send forth their fair ones *nocturna carpentes pensa puellae* ['girls carding wool at night' *Georgics* I], sitting on soft rushes carefully picked and dried for that purpose. There *seros hyberni ad luminis ignes pervigilant* ['they work through the winter nights by light of burning lamps'] and from the close of day till midnight an universal activity prevails. Nor let it be imagined that these hours are dull and tedious . . . . The young men, returned from their more hardy occupations of the day, repair to these cheerful meetings. There, seated in the middle of the ring, they pay their offerings at the shrine of Beauty and yield their souls to the impulse of love, which is here generally attended with an innocence and simplicity unknown in larger countries. (77–80)

In other words the knitting was in large part an excuse for boys and girls to meet and tease each other. Edmund Toulmin Nicolle in *The Town of St Helier* (1931) is franker:

As knitting was a purely mechanical work of the hands, the minds and tongues of the workers were free and unshackled. On dispersing from the gatherings some, disguised with masks, would go rollicking along from house to house and commit nocturnal depredations to the annoyance of the peaceful citizens. It would appear that at these parties dissolute songs were sung and stories of doubtful propriety retailed. (50–51)

John Louis Victor Cachemaille, a parish priest, describing the smaller community in *The Island of Sark* (published in 1928 from articles originally written in French in 1874–6), noted that *veilles* were held on Sundays, but then there was no knitting and only psalms and hymns were sung. This is probably true, and certainly more reliable than the scandalous stories in some modern books about the islands, that tell of surreptitious Sunday knitting and even of knitting being taken to church, where the clicking of the needles drowned the preacher's voice. Not only would no preacher worth his salt tolerate such behaviour, but a skilful knitter works silently.

Guernseys and jerseys

One final note is required. Most modern writers on the islands say that it is unlikely that the fishermen's garments now called guernseys and jerseys were ever made there before very recent years. In 1835 H.G. Inglis was explicit that the Channel Islands had no distinctive local costume, and F.R. Tupper printed in 1840 an account of Guernsey dress in 1780 which does not mention the Guernsey frock – nor does W. Plees in his 1817 chapter on Jersey dress. Seamen's guernseys and

jerseys were not so called because they came from the Channel Islands, but because their fabric had long been called guernsey or jersey before seamen took to wearing them. The 'traditional' jersey patterns published by the Women's Institute of Jersey are interesting, but scarcely go back earlier than the last years of Queen Victoria. When the islands took up sailors' jerseys, they seem to have preferred almost plain stockinet garments, with at most a discreet ornament on the shoulders and scye. Their particular contribution to knitting technique has been the knotted cast-on, which has become known to the rest of Britain since James Norbury introduced it in his *Encyclopedia* of 1956 (290). It is a variation of the older double-stranded cast-on with one needle, giving a knotted edge, strong and slightly decorative. We do not know how old it is (see page 133).

The other characteristic of the knit-frock now regarded as the traditional Channel Island garment is the bottom welt. This has vented sides, made by casting on the front and back separately and knitting the lower edge in two parts, taking both in to circular knitting when the welt is finished. The welt is worked in garter stitch or as a hemmed border in stockinet; rarely, if ever, ribbed.

Of recent years the Women's Institutes have fostered a knitting revival in the islands and the tourist trade is provided with 'authentic' knitted articles and patterns. In fact, Channel Island work was not distinguished for exclusive patterns. It provided for changing overseas fashions instead. Channel Island knitwear and hosiery were esteemed simply for their high quality and abundance.

Ringwood

Ringwood in Hampshire provides an example of hand knitting surviving as a local cottage industry half way through the twentieth century. The little market town is no more than 14½ km (9 miles) from Christchurch, a centre of stocking knitting where the trade lingered till the turn of the eighteenth century. Ringwood too was a centre for stockingers. In 1830 Pigot's *National Commercial*

136 Gloves knitted according to the Ringwood pattern by Beatrice Dennis of Ringwood 1985.

Directory spoke of the place as 'formerly a town of considerable note in the manufacture of stockings'. Henry Moody in his *Antiquarian and Topographical Sketches of Hampshire* (1846) looked back to the time when the trade had been extensive, 60 years earlier. In 1847 Pigot reported that the industry had almost, if not entirely, disappeared.

In 1855, however, the Cox family is recorded in the Post Office Directory as employing 250 women and children in knitting woollen and cotton gloves and worsted stockings. By 1859 William White's *Historical Gazetteer and Directory of Hampshire* was treating the firm as 'long celebrated' for the making of these articles, in which Charles Cox employed 500 people. The gloves were said to be 'of a peculiar kind'. The same was being reported by White in 1878, and in 1895 J.L. Green wrote in *The Rural Industries of England* that some amount of glove knitting persisted around Ringwood. He said the same for the villages about Blandford, 20 miles away across the Dorset border.

Cox and Hicks, founded in 1800, was the firm that chiefly controlled the trade, buying gloves in from the cottagers. Lillian Bursey remembers:

When I first went to school before the First World War, I used to pass a row of cottages where the women stood at their doorways with steel needles flashing. They were exceedingly fast knitters. The needles were rather thick and they used 4 ply wool, so the gloves were rather loose. The knitters were paid fourpence a pair for the knitting.

Cox and Hicks gave up their interest in gloves in 1913. In 1915 Herbert Horace Armstrong opened a wool shop at 21 High Street where he bought in Ringwood gloves and revived the industry. His daughter Alma (now Mrs Wilcox of Earls Barton) recalls women coming shyly to the shop, too embarassed to approach the counter, remaining on the door mat while they brought the gloves out of their bags. Mr Armstrong paid sixpence for each pair made. Paton's khaki 4ply wool was used.

After the war Ringwood glovemaking declined further until William Ayles, who had been a partner in Cox and Hicks, opened a new outfitter's business in the Market Square in 1927. Early in the 1930s his son Howard was buying American cotton in bulk in fourteen different colours, selling the gloves to London West End stores and eventually

employing 800 knitters, some as far away as Birmingham and London.

About 1941, when Churchill was appealing for aid to the people of Russia, 3000 pairs of navy blue Ringwood gloves were dispatched, but when Howard Ayles joined the Royal Air Force, the glovemaking lapsed. After the Second World War gloves continued to be knitted, mostly in Twilley's 'Lyscord' cotton yarn, yellow in colour and sold as 'riding gloves' but only in Ayles's own shops. They were made until Ayles finally gave up the trade in January 1958. By that time each knitter was receiving two shillings a pair, and imported gloves from the Far East could be sold retail for less.

Often one child knitted the wrists, and another the palms, while the mother worked the fingers. The fabric was so distinctive that in *Weldon's Practical Needlework* No 231 (1905) a recipe was given for it as 'Ringwood stitch'. (It was correctly photographed, but wrongly described.) The correct recipe consists of three rounds: one round of knit one, purl one; followed by two rounds plain. The purl stitches were referred to as 'knots'. The wrist was ribbed in two plain, two purl; the whole of the remainder of the gloves was in 'Ringwood stitch', including the thumb gore. There were no fourchettes between the fingers.

Twilleys eventually published the pattern, without the Ringwood name. Paton & Baldwin's *Woolcraft* from 1916 (perhaps earlier) until 1937 published a variant fabric as 'Man's Warm Glove'. Other variants of purl and plain, such as that with only one round of plain knitting between the plain-and-purl rows, are sometimes called 'Ringwood stitch', following Weldon's mistake. The principle of all the patterns is the same. The purl knots make the fabric trap enough air to provide extra insulation against the cold. It is remarkable that the pattern survived unchanged for about a century in commercial hand knitting.

Blandford gloves

J. L. Green also mentioned glove-knitting in the villages near Blandford in Dorset. It was still being done, he wrote, in 1895, but had been more

---

W. AYLES & SON,

Glove Manufacturers,

RINGWOOD.

═══════════

RINGWOOD HAND-KNIT GLOVES

Cast on ~~44~~ 40 stitches.

30 rows in cuff.

8 knots in gore.

6 knots in hand.

Fingers—1st, 10 knots.

          2nd, 11 knots.

          3rd, 10 knots.

          Little finger, 9 knots.

Thumb, 9 knots.

Use size 13 needles.

The instructions must be carried out exactly.

137 W. Ayles's instructions to home knitters of Ringwood gloves.

extensive 30 years earlier. Blandford is some 32 km (20 miles) west of Ringwood. The local tradition at Blandford is that before the Great Exhibition of 1851 the main cottage industry of the district was button-making, but this came to a swift end after the appearance at the Exhibition of a button-making machine. The cottagers then turned to glove-making, both in leather and in knitted yarn. Firms in Sherborne, Yeovil and Worcester employed the outworkers, whose produce was collected by local drapers acting as agents.

At the beginning of this century a knitter earned 4d a pair. By the time of the Second World War this had risen to 6d for women's gloves and 9d for men's. After the war the standard rate was 2s. 6d. From about 1920 to 1940 the principal agent was E.A. Harvey of the Market Place. Many of the knitters preferred to receive their remuneration in kind, especially men's clothing. From about 1946 to 1957 Ensor and Southcome of Eagle House, Blandford, made gloves by machine and by hand, and also employed outworkers.

Most of the knitted gloves seem to have been riding gloves of yellow cotton, though a newspaper report of 1936 told of Cheselbourne women who had been at the work for 40 years using green, red and blue yarn to make two-coloured gloves. The gloves were knitted on four needles, in two styles: 'Ringwood' and 'Shepton Mallet'. The latter pattern proves difficult to identify.

Aran

The three stormwashed Isles of Aran, Inishmore, Inishmaan and Inisheer, lie across the mouth of Galway Bay on the Irish Atlantic coast. They suddenly became famous in 1934, when the pioneer documentary film-maker, Robert Flaherty, released his film *Man of Aran*, a celluloid poem of hard life and high seas in his ancestral islands. He ran a vigorous publicity campaign, bringing Aran islanders to London and dressing cinema attendants in seamen's jerseys. Tam-o'-shanters called 'Man-of-Aran berets' had a brief vogue among the fashionable.

The jerseys worn by the cinema ushers were not what we now call Aran jumpers. It was not until the textile journalist, Heinz Edgar Kiewe, visited Dublin in the summer of 1936 that he discovered the first creamy-white 'Aran' jumper in a shop on Stephen's Green called Countryworkers Ltd. 'Countryworkers' was a cooperative movement which did much to preserve Irish country crafts, including basket-making, and helped develop the folklore collection at the Irish National Museum. Years later Heinz Kiewe described his find in *The Sacred History of Knitting* (1967): 'a peculiar whiskery-looking chunk of sweater in "Biblical white" . . . to us it looked too odd for words, being hard as a board'. He showed it to Mary Thomas, the fashion journalist, who eventually published a picture of it, with a partial description, in *Mary Thomas's Book of Knitting Patterns* (1943, 63).

A year after making this discovery, Heinz Kiewe saw Flaherty's *Man of Aran*. There are no white sweaters in the film, only a few dark ganseys of no particular distinction. The only shots of a woman knitting show a mother making a stocking and holding the needles in the ladylike manner, not the traditional way. Nevertheless, the stark beauty of the film moved Kiewe 'to revive a "Biblical white" fisherman's sweater'. During the 1939 war he explored sources for congenial wool of a whiskery type, and eventually found it in the Outer Hebrides. Slowly in the post-war years, as Britain emerged from austerity, 'Aran sweaters' began to become popular. The original one bought in Dublin was lost. New patterns were created, all with high-relief cabling and honeycombing. *Vogue Knitting* published an Aran pattern in 1956. By 1957 they were being worn in America. The fashion has wavered, but never yet disappeared. In the 1980s 'Aran' sweaters have maintained their popularity, not least because knitters enjoy creating the bold sculpted effects of the patterns. (Colour plate 8.)

Kiewe's romantic theory

Heinz Kiewe, who inspired the fashion, was born in Koenigsberg, East Prussia, in 1906. Five years earlier his father had opened a high-class clothing store in that city. In 1933 the family, like so many

138 A replica of the first Aran jumper to be noticed in England. The original was bought in Dublin in 1936 by Heinz Kiewe.

Jewish families, left Hitler's Germany and settled in England. They opened a shop in the Brompton Road where they made the acquaintance of the fashionable and the famous. When war came in 1939 there was a period of uncertainty for alien residents and the Kiewes moved to Oxford, because, Heinz said, his father liked coarse fishing. In 1940 he re-opened Art Needlework Industries Limited in Ship Street, a shop from which he exercised his influence over British fashion and needlework until he died in 1986.

Heinz Kiewe perceived a connection between Aran knitted designs and ancient Irish art. He never claimed that this was a scholarly theory: he accepted it as an intuitive perception. In a letter to me he wrote 'I never romanticized, yet never felt forced to believe in written documents during my 55 years of research in textile history.' So he began to describe Aran knitted patterns in terms of the 'white shirt of monotheistic cultures'. Before long publicists for wool spinners were crediting Aran knitting with thousands of years of history; amateurs and journalists were finding 'Aran-like' drawings in caves in far distant parts of Ireland; a whole code of mystic meanings was drawn up for the commonest Aran motifs; it was even claimed that the figures in the illuminated manuscript of the *Book of Kells* wore 'Aran' garments; and the Celtic monks were brought into the story. Aran knitwear was provided with its own mythology, and the garment-makers and wool-spinners made the most of this romantic appeal. The Aran islanders were not heard objecting: knitwear became a tourist sales item.

Academic historians were sceptical, though nonplussed. Knitting is not thousands of years old;

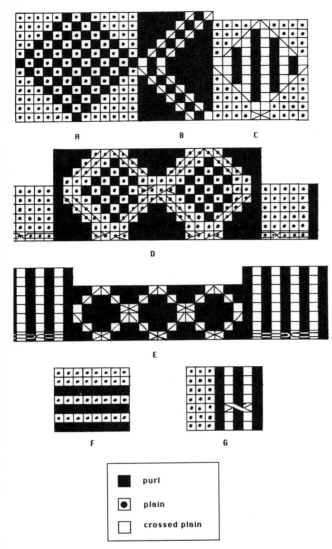

139 Pattern elements of the Kiewe-Thomas Aran jersey 1936. A–C = outside columns of the body; B–C = outside columns of the sleeve; D = centre panels of the body; E = central panels of the sleeves; F = band above welt; G = welt.

similarities between Aran design and early graffiti are the fundamental similarities of all simple geometric designs. Mystic meanings and evocative names for knitting patterns can grow up and catch on in a surprisingly short time; similarities between the decorations in the *Book of Kells* and those of Aran knitwear are superficial, while the differences between the two are fundamental (and those who

thought the human figures in the illuminations were wearing knitted cat-suits had to admit that the animals in the same pictures were similarly dressed, because both the men and the animals are decorated in the same way); and no one ever explained why the Celtic monks had been brought in. There was a recurrent story that the members of each family wore sweaters of distinctive patterns so that the corpses of those drowned at sea could be more readily identified. The same fiction had already been told of English seamen's gansies. When J.M. Synge's *Riders to the Sea* was quoted as evidence for this legend of Aran, it was disappointing to find that the identification of Michael's corpse in that play was based, not on the sweater design, but on a mistake in the knitting of his stockings.

The nineteenth century

In truth no early evidence of Aran knitting has been found. Roderic O'Flaherty (?1629–1717) wrote much of Aran and its saints in *A Chorographical Description of West or H-iar Connaught* (1684) but never mentioned knitting. Even the evidence of the nineteenth century is sparse. In 1888 Dorothea Roberts, writing in Oscar Wilde's *Woman's World*, mentions the low rate of wages for knitting in Aranmore (the largest island), though 50 years earlier Lord George Hill had encouraged the craft. She had for six years past been sending Alloa wools to Aran, encouraging the women to improve the standard of their jerseys, gloves and socks, mostly for children's wear (401).

In 1889 there was another potato crop failure in Ireland. There were at the same period disastrous slumps in the fishing industry. In 1891 the oddly named Congested Districts Board was established by the government to assist those districts where each family had insufficient land to maintain a minimum standard of living. Such districts were ecologically congested, but in such unproductive terrain were very sparsely populated. Major Robert Ruttledge-Fair, reporting on the Aran Islands, 31 March 1893, noted that it was said that more weaving and knitting were carried on formerly.

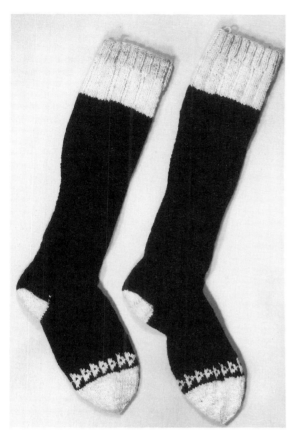

140 Dark blue stockings from the Aran Islands, made in 1937. Such stockings were mentioned in Emily Lawless's novel *Grania* in 1892, when they were typical of Aran life.

Knitting was particularly to be encouraged.

Emily Lawless (1845–1913) who was born and bred in western Ireland, published *Grania*, a novel about Aran, in 1892. She told a story of the apophatic courtship of two young islanders, Murdough Blake and Grania O'Malley. Emily Lawless emphasized that both sexes wore woven clothes of *bainin*, yellowish flannel, and says that the needlework of the islands was not neat. Although Grania knits from time to time, there is no suggestion that she makes anything other than the customary blue knitted stockings that all the women wear.

Four years after *Grania* appeared, the poet and critic Arthur William Symons (1865–1945) wrote a long article about a visit to the islands in *The Savoy* (No 6, pp 773–86) in which he refers several times to girls knitting. On Inishmaan, he said, 'a number of women . . . looked up at us out of the darkness of many interiors, from where they sat on the ground knitting or carding wool'. (83) But he did not mention the famous white sweater.

From Edwardian times, Aran, like other islands, attracted tourists. Oenone Somerville and Martin Ross, authors of the 'Irish Resident Magistrate' books, went there and published an account of their visit in *Some Irish Yesterdays* (1906). Though they commented on the islanders' dress, they never mentioned the high-relief Aran sweater.

The playwright, J.M. Synge, who based *Riders to the Sea* on his experience of Aran, went there every summer from 1898 to 1902. In *The Aran Islands* (1906) he describes the islanders' clothing, but never mentions knitting. He speaks of the women spinning wool and using it in natural white or indigo. He says many of the younger men have adopted 'the usual fisherman's jersey'; and that 'on these islands . . . all art is unknown'. It would be unbelievable that he saw ornately patterned cream sweaters and did not mention them in these contexts. This was not because the islanders kept them for winter wear, because on those windy rocks even in summer the young men wore jerseys.

Irish writers on the islands have been explicit that the cream sweaters are not ancient. Timothy O'Neill's *Life and Tradition in Rural Ireland* (1977) shows only simple fisher ganseys with cabled chests, and (like all other writers) uses the word *bainin*, 'whitish', (pronounced *bawneen* and appropriated by commercial spinners as a name for Aran-weight knitting-wool) for a lightweight woven white woollen jacket. Paul O'Sullivan in *A World of Stone* (1977), an exhaustive account of life on the islands, has much to say of Aran clothing, and again emphasizes the use of indigo dye. He adds that 'the knitting of the "Aran" sweater with its intricate patterns of stitching was introduced to the islands only after the famine, as a means of creating cash employment'.

Museum pieces

Most of the Aran knitwear in the National Museum in Dublin was collected in 1937, and acquired from Countryworkers Ltd. More was added in 1948. There are indigo or navy-blue stockings with white diamonds round the top and in bands round the white toecaps. There is a woman's red cardigan covered with a diamond trellis of travelling single rib, each diamond containing a bobble. There are blue sweaters covered with bobbles (colour plate 7). Among the 1948 sweaters is one decorated with simple broad welts of moss stitch, described on the card by Muriel Gahan of Countryworkers as 'a typical native design'. Its white colour alone differentiates it from the ganseys of England's eastern seaboard. The elaborate sweaters in creamy white are well represented in the collections for both number and fine workmanship, but they are clearly not the only 'traditional' form. All are knitted with mill-spun wool from Donegal, in flat pieces, carefully seamed. Cast-on is double-ended; cast-off is plain, even over rib. Back and front of a sweater are worked from bottom to top. All shoulders are unshaped, usually with a saddle. Stitches are picked up at the scye and the sleeve knitted from shoulder to wrist, producing inversion of the fancy rib at the wrist, as compared to the body welt. Side increases of the back and front pieces are made in body-long gussets of stockinet, with a central seam, which continues down under the sleeve. This is a structure quite unlike English and Scottish fishermen's ganseys.

There is in existence at least one other Aran sweater that claims to be an old original. It is in Paton's collection at Alloa and bears one of James Norbury's cards dating it to 1906. Unfortunately, the date cannot be regarded as reliable. Pictures of it were published in *Wool Knowledge* (Winter 1955) and with Norbury's lecture on 'Design in knitting' of 9 October 1952. It is made of rough, kempy, oatmeal-coloured wool of double-knitting calibre at 6 stitches to the inch in stockinet. The design contains many smooth bobbles, and it is knitted in the round with armholes cut and the inside of the seams covered with fine stockinet. The length from shoulder to waist is 63 cm (25 in.). The waist is 68 cm (27 in.) round, the chest 88 cm (35 in.). It is a small, closely knitted garment, with a rustic air despite its sophisticated design.

The true story

Rumours, mentioned with disbelief on one of the accession cards in the Dublin museum, suggest that 'Aran knitting' was brought to the islands from America. A Bavarian immigrant to the United States teaching Central European knitting to an Irish immigrant who brought the craft back to Ireland would explain the Aran designs. Yet there must be some connection with other British seamen's knitwear. The basic design is a gansey, and cable stitches are commonplace in the gansey tradition. Seamen met one another all round the coasts of Britain, married brides from distant ports and mingled their knitting traditions. Aran knitting must be understood in that context.

All the strands came together for the knitwear designer Rohana Darlington when she was in Aran on a Churchill Memorial Trust Travelling Fellowship in the summer of 1984. More persistent and less credulous than the usual tourist, after seeing the exhibits in the Aran folk museum at Kilronan she searched until she found herself in the home of Mary Dirrane on Inishmore. Mary was said by the islanders to know more of knitting than anyone else. Rohana wore a navy blue guernsey in flag and ladder pattern.

Seeing the sweater, Mary immediately declared that in the old days they had made similar ones on Inishmore, on 8 to 12 double-ended needles, but with patterns on the yokes only. Then she told how her mother, Margaret, with her friend Maggie O'Toole, had gone to Boston, Massachusetts, in 1906 with the intention of emigrating, and stayed on 'some islands off Boston'. There they learned to do cable, moss stitch, and trellis or lattice patterns in knitting from some 'foreign immigrant woman'. Before that the Aran islanders did not make ganseys, but did only simple plain hosiery and crochet.

Mary and Margaret decided not to settle in America and returned to Ireland in 1908. Back home they blended their new knitting skills with what they saw sailors wearing and experimented with patterns. Other women on the islands took up gansey-knitting. At some later stage they stopped knitting in the round and changed to knitting flat pieces on two needles. Wools were imported from the mainland, and it was gradually discovered that the garments were saleable.

Mary's story bears the marks of truth and fits the other evidence with conviction. It is fairly well established that 'Aran jumpers' are a twentieth-century development of the basic guernsey.

Since 1936

This is borne out by Thomas Holmes Mason in *The Islands of Ireland* (1936). His photographs show none of the splendid cream sweaters, only very ordinary ganseys. He does not list knitting as an important handicraft of Aran, and he explicitly states that many years earlier the islanders used to buy their jerseys from shops.

By 1954, when David Thomson wrote *The People of the Sea*, a book about the legend of the seal-man, the dress of Aran men had become distinctive. He noted that the males of Inishmaan wore heavy jerseys of 'grey or blue, knitted in an intricate pattern'. That was the time when Gladys Thompson was studying the garments in the Dublin museum. Her careful descriptions of them in *Patterns for Guernseys and Jerseys* (1955) gave the definitive impetus to Aran knitting outside the island.

Yet Kiewe's perception of the ethnic quality of Aran knitting, matched by the popular acceptance of its uniqueness, is not to be underrated. In a short time in a small community (about 2500 in 1910 and 2000 in 1936), Aran knitting evolved to express a singular communal feeling for design. The folk art of a community does not lack authenticity simply because it has a short history.

The knitting has become emblematic. It belongs historically to the harsh world of famine and emigration, and to the hard life of the rocky islands. The patterns have a rough male Celtic beauty that needs no romanticizing, created by female skills. The women drew on levels of imagination that are earthier and more primitive than pseudo-religious allegories about the shapes of their patterns. Thomas Holmes Mason also wrote of Aran: 'There is a tradition that the knitting which is done after dark is always best: because the sheep are asleep.'

Sanquhar

The Ancient and Royal Burgh of Sanquhar is a proud little town in Dumfriesshire, set in the lovely valley of Nithsdale, which has long been an area of hosiery and tweed-making. A Sanquhar printer, Thomas Brown, issued *The Union Gazetteer for Great Britain and Ireland* in 1807, wherein he noted of his own town: 'The principal articles manufactured here are carpets, coarse serges, knitted stockings and mitts. The stocking trade is

141 Gloves with lined cuffs, knitted in pale grey-green and black to a Sanquhar recipe using the 'Duke' pattern, as published by the Scottish Women's Rural Institutes.

the oldest and was formerly more considerable than at present.' Miss Lambert in *The Handbook of Needlework* (1842) noted that the town was formerly celebrated for knitted stockings, but the industry was fatally checked at the beginning of the American war. Presumably she meant the American War of Independence (307). (See page 98.)

Dumfriesshire is a border county and Sanquhar barely 96 km (60 miles) from Carlisle. There are several points of contact between the history of Sanquhar gloves and the gloves knitted in Cumbria. Cumbrian knitted stockings likewise were sold to the army and to America.

One feature of good eighteenth-century stockings was that the customer's name or initials could be worked into the tops. This may be the origin of the Sanquhar practice of working a name or initials into the wrists of gloves. According to James Brown, writing *The History of Sanquhar* in 1891, the colours were for the most part simply black and white. He speaks of them as being 'woven on wires in a peculiar manner' in the early part of the nineteenth century, and 'sold in many quarters'. He deplored the failure of the town to develop this cottage industry at the time when he wrote.

James Brown also records how Charles Douglas, Duke of Queensberry and Dover (1698– 1778), a local benefactor, gave jointly with the Trustees for the Encouragement of Industry £40 a year to be distributed to promote stocking-making in the town. Much later, probably about 1880, ('quite recently', says Brown) the Duke of Buccleuch gave a large order for gloves – an occasion which may be the origin of the name 'Duke' for one of more popular fabric patterns.

The superiority of Sanquhar gloves for riding and driving was said by Brown to have been much promoted by a coursing judge named Hedley. Hedley was given a pair of the gloves and was 'more tickled with their appearance than impressed with their utility; till one day he was riding to hounds, when rain came on, and the reins kept slipping through his fingers, do what he might. In his dilemma he bethought him of the curious Sanquhar gloves which he happened to have in his pocket. These he exchanged for the leather, and to his surprise he was able to hold the reins quite

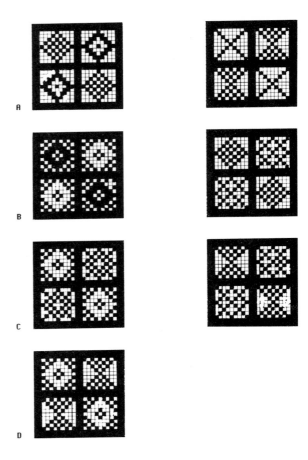

142 Dambrod designs from Sanquhar. A = Duke; B = Rose; C = Rose & trellis; D = Cornet & drum.

firmly, however 'soapy' they might become.'

Sanquharians were regarded as being distinctly anti-establishment. When the Duke of Buccleuch entertained the Prince of Wales to a shooting party on his Dumfriesshire lands in 1871, there were misgivings about the reception the townsfolk would give to the royal couple. In the event, floral arches were raised in the main street. The Prince and Princess were given a tumultuous welcome when they passed through the town during the morning, and an even more resounding one when they returned in the evening. It may have been on that occasion that another glove fabric pattern was named 'Prince of Wales'. It is sometimes called 'Prince of Wales's feather', but is in fact a miniature version of the traditional 'Shepherd's check' or 'Shepherd's plaid' and bears a close resemblance to part of the tweed pattern called 'Prince of Wales check'.

William Forsyth, once town clerk, recalled that when he was a student in Edinburgh about 1900 Sanquhar gloves were sold by a tailor in Prince's Street.

A few knitters kept the glove-knitting alive until 1933, when Miss Mary Forsyth, a Sanquharian, joined the homecraft department at Sanquhar Academy and began to teach glove-knitting in the school. During the 1939 war Hutchieson's Girls' Grammar School was evacuated from Glasgow to Sanquhar and Miss Forsyth taught the Glasgow girls. Before she retired in 1971, the pattern had thus become more widely known. Several patterns based on Sanquhar motifs were published in the Dundee weekly magazine *People's Friend* February – April 1955.

The patterns

In 1966 the Scottish Women's Rural Institutes published a Sanquhar glove pattern for the first time: the 'midge-and-fly'. This was followed by 'Duke' (undated) and by 'Shepherd's plaid' in 1976. The fourth, 'Prince of Wales', was issued about 1980 in mimeographed form. These patterns are admirably edited. They show the construction of fourchettes or quirks, made by decreasing some of the extra stitches cast on between the fingers to create a tiny triangular gusset. This feature gives the Sanquhar glove a comfortable fit and a long life, and is hard to find in glove patterns elsewhere. Some of the gloves also have wrist-linings knitted in.

The two-colour fabric designs are striking. The wrist designs, which are also used for stocking tops, are variations of black-and-white ribbing and broken ribbing. The palm designs fall into two groups: the dambrod and the check. The dambrod designs are not strictly chequerboard patterns (as 'dambrod' might imply) but a gridiron or graticule pattern of horizontal and vertical black lines, two stitches or two rows wide, over a white ground showing nine stitches and nine rows of white in

each graticule. The white squares are then filled with a black motif based on the diamond or saltire. In spite of their simplicity, these patterns can be richly satisfying when worked in the small scale of a glove in 3-ply yarn on needles size 2 mm or less. They can also be worked in reversed colours, white grid and motifs in a black ground. Names are given to the best designs: 'Duke', 'Rose', 'Rose and trellis', 'Cornet and drum'.

The checks are all variations of the traditional 'Shepherd's check', used in tweed-weaving. The typical design, known as 'Shepherd's plaid', is a diamond check in which horizontal rows of alternating black diamonds and white diamonds are interplaced with rows of speckled black-and-white diamonds. (The 'speckled' effect is very

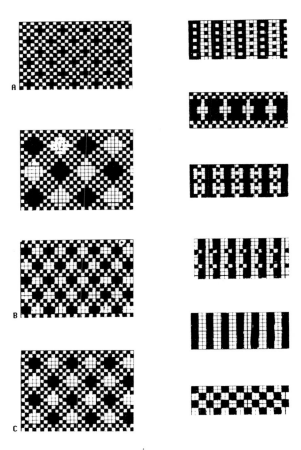

143 Sanquhar checks and cuffs. A = Midge and fly; B = Prince of Wales; C = Shepherd's Plaid; the right-hand column shows cuffs and edgings.

nearly an optical grey.) The diamonds are five rows high and five stitches wide. The diamond motif can be enlarged to seven rows high and seven stitches wide. The resulting bold check is more suitable for stockings than for gloves.

Direct reduction of knitted 'Shepherd's check' to diamonds of less than five stitches and five rows is mathematically impossible, because a diamond of three rows and three stitches makes a cross. The 'Prince of Wales' pattern, however, is essentially a check of the same family, an ingeniously contrived miniature.

'Midge and fly' or 'Midge and flea' is even more miniature. It is the finest possible knitted check: an overall speckling of alternate black and white stitches ('midges'), with a scattering of five-stitch black crosses ('flies'). Most of these check patterns can also be found in gloves from Cumberland, Westmorland and the Yorkshire Dales.

Sanquhar patterns all spring readily and naturally from the craftsmanship of the knitters. Although they lack flamboyance and have not exploited the possibilities and subtleties of colour, they have dignity and unpretentious beauty. It is not surprising that machine knitters, led by Mrs Thomson, wife of the present parish minister, have begun developing the Sanquhar tradition by using the Sanquhar fabrics for fully-fashioned hand-framed garments.

Maintaining the hand knitting tradition for the gloves has become difficult because 3 ply wool is little spun, and fine needles (British size 15 or 16, or under 2 mm) are no longer made. The short needles used for knitting fingers, about 13 cm (5 in) long, have not been obtainable for many years.

8 The Americas

South and Central America

Aboriginal knitting on hooked needles and on 'split' needles has been described in the section on technique (p 23). It is done in parts of Venezuela and Guyana, and appears to have no connection with Old World knitting. The only products of such work are narrow strips of fabric used as headbands or belts.

Yet there is a possibility that the hooked needles of the Warrau have a tenuous connection with the hooked needles used in Mexico, Honduras, Guatemala, Peru, Bolivia and Paraguay to knit bags, caps, sleeves, stockings, masks and even afghans. Anne-Marie Seiler-Baldinger gives a comprehensive list of American races and their knitted products in *Maschenstoffe in Süd- Und Mittelamerika* (1971). She accepts that this hooked-needle knitting was introduced into the continent by Spanish and Portuguese colonists. The method is essentially the same as that used to this day in some rural areas of Portugal, and being revived by young Portuguese who are conscious of their heritage, even in urban areas. The working yarn is carried round the nape of the neck; the needles are hooked at one end; stranded-colour knitting is purled, with the purl side facing the knitter.

Lila O'Neale gave more detailed descriptions of some of this peasant knitting in 'Textiles of Higher Guatemala', published by the Carnegie Institute of Washington in 1945. She described men's woollen carrying bags, about 28 cm (11 in.) square, with two woven handles, one a metre long and the other about 18 cm (7 in.). Most were knitted in black and white bands, squares and checks. Some had black and white stripes, some of the stripes bearing the words *matate nuevo*, 'new bag'. Some had horses in the contrasting colour, counterchanging with the colour of the stripes. Some bags had pale grey stripes on a white ground.

She described knitting techniques. One was the Portuguese method, throwing the yarn with the left hand, keeping the left-hand needle inert and activating the right-hand needle. She did not say whether or not knitting was always done in the round. The second technique was a laborious method of knitting in the round on three needles only. The needles were not used to make the loops, but merely as gauges and holding devices for the loops, which were created by pushing each loop off the needle and pushing the bight of the working yarn through it before placing it on the needle holding the new stitches. This is a primitive technique, which must look like a child struggling to form knitted loops.

European knitting is the norm for South American educated and urban classes.

The United States

Information about the history of hand knitting in the United States is hard to find. Milton Grass, a keen researcher, found barely enough for a few pages on the early stocking trade in the American colonies in his *History of Hosiery* (1955). The outline of his story reflects the history of knitting in Britain, though in 1775 an Act of Virginia Assembly encouraged the local production of stockings by offering subsidies in the form of

144 Bolivian Campesina women knitting. Altiplano, November 1984.

premiums for work produced. He suggests that the early colonists imported most of their hosiery from Europe. Framework-knitting began on the Atlantic seaboard in the middle of the eighteenth century.

Alice Morse Earle's *Two Centuries of Costume in America 1620 – 1820* (1903), a classic essay, scarcely offers more information about American hand knitting, though she is sure that early eighteenth-century references to 'knit waistcoats' and 'silk knit waistcoat-pieces' refer to hand-knitted work. She bases her diagnosis of handwork on advertisements by women willing to repair knit waistcoats by 'grafting'. This is scarcely conclusive: the knitted fabric could have been machine-made, and as likely imported as home-produced.

The Mrs Beresford who, according to Boswell, on 3 June 1784 irritated Dr Samuel Johnson by knitting in the post-coach from London to Oxford was the wife of an American congressman.

The westward expansion of America happened at a time when machine-made stockings were readily available and the life of a pioneer homestead probably left little time for women to do much knitting. In the older communities, however, knitting was certainly done. Catherine Fennelly in *The Garb of Country New Englanders 1790–1840* (1966) quotes the journal of one Ruth Henshaw on 20 January 1803: 'I finished a pair of shag mittens for Daddy, that is, a pair all over fringed, which is the new mode of knitting mittens'.

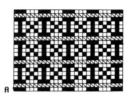 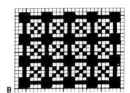

145 The Fox-and-Geese pattern of Maine mittens. A = 3 colours; B = 2 colours. This pattern is far richer than the chart of a small section suggests. A larger area will show the diagonals asserting themselves as interlacing diamonds. (Robin Hansen *Fox and Geese and Fences*)

Mittens and gloves are particularly interesting in the northeastern United States, Newfoundland and eastern Canada. Robin Hansen published her initial study of Maine mittens in *Fox and Geese and Fences* in 1985. They include many bicoloured or multicoloured patterns, some surprising mittens which are damped before donning, and 'drummed mitts', which have a lining of unspun wool ('drums' or 'thrums') knitted into them.

The patterns of the coloured mittens are related in name and shape to the patterns used in patchwork quilting. Their resemblance to European patterns suggests Scandinavian influence, and it is known that many of the fisherfolk of Newfoundland come from Channel Island stock.

An eccentric American tradition is recorded by Beverley Gordon in *Shaker Textile Arts* (1980). The Shakers are properly called the United Society of Believers in Christ's Second Appearing. They originated during a Quaker revival in England in 1747. In 1774 Anne Lee (1734–84) and eight others emigrated to New York state. They became known as Shakers, because their worship was ecstatic. They lived in isolated celibate communities of both sexes, and in the 1840s numbered nearly 6000, mostly in New England. After the Civil War their numbers declined. Only nine aged members survived in 1980.

Knitting was an integral part of the lives of Shaker sisters. They worked on fine needles, less than 2 mm (¹/12 in.) thick. They made circular rugs and chair-seat 'cushions' by sewing together flat spirals of tubular knitting. Mats usually had concentric colour-rings, 'cushions' had random colour patches. Chair seat covers could be trapezoidal in stockinet, bordered with a doubled strip of knitting. They also made the usual plain stockings, gloves, shawls, sweaters, 'gaiters' (actually a form of spats), men's neckties, afghans, and washcloths. The washcloths were circular, made of 16 segments of garter stitch, arranged in alternating colours. The rows ran radially, decreasing from the centre in alternate shortened rows. This was a favourite Victorian method of knitting a circular piece.

The nineteenth century

Several English knitting books were pirated in America during the middle years of the nineteenth century. I have seen no evidence of hand-knitting industry. Indeed, the export of stockings from the Yorkshire Dales to America suggests that Americans were not doing their own knitting. Perhaps there was something in American society that inhibited knitting on a large scale. Yet, like many crafts, knitting was done by Americans at neighbourly assemblies, from which came the expression 'knitting bee' and the earlier 'knitting frolic' noted by Henry Bradshaw Fearon, who visited America to explore the possibilities of immigration and recorded his impressions in *Sketches from America* (1818). He found that in Ohio 'religious females' were invited to the preacher's house to partake of a supper as a return for gifts of clothing, and even a goose, they had bestowed upon the minister. At that frolic they knitted clothes.

One remark in Ann S. Stephens *The Ladies' Complete Guide to Crochet, Fancy Knitting and Needlework*, published in New York in 1854, may

suggest lines for further investigation of the American story. She wrote: 'fashionable as this household accomplishment is getting among us, American ladies devote themselves less to needlework than those of almost any other nation'.

Twentieth-century writers

America's role in world knitting has, however, changed dramatically since 1970. Barbara Walker published her *A Treasury of Knitting Patterns* in 1968, the finest collection of fabric recipes thus far produced. In 1971 she followed it with *A Second Treasury of Knitting Patterns*. Smaller books were excerpted from these, but *Knitting from the Top* (1972), *Charted Knitting Designs* (1972), *Sampler Knitting* (1973) and *Mosaic Knitting* (1974) were new books and stimulated wide interest in knitting as a craft in which new things could be imagined and achieved. Mosaic knitting, a form of garter stitch or stockinet in two colours, changing the colour in alternate rounds or rows and using slipped stitches to produce a coloured pattern, was invented by Barbara Walker.

Elizabeth Zimmerman (1910–) was born in England and went to America when young. She is an exploratory knitter with an effervescent sense of humour. Her enthusiasm and common sense combine with the humour to produce books that have become influential on both sides of the Atlantic. *Knitting without Tears* (1971) is the most important, but *Elizabeth Zimmerman's Knitter's Almanac* (1974) and *Elizabeth Zimmerman's Knitting Workshop* (1981) extended its ideas and principles. Mrs Zimmerman has exploited garter-stitch with great success and has brought fresh thinking to the shaping of knitted garments. Periodical publications from her knitting supplies business at Babcock, Wisconsin, have done much to broaden knitters' horizons.

Influential in quite a different way has been Mary Walker Phillips. She published *Step by Step Knitting: A Complete Introduction to the Craft of Knitting* in 1967. Her major work is *Creative Knitting: A New Art Form* (1971) which has set her at the forefront of the movement to establish knitting as fine art rather than applied art. She has complete mastery of technique, and her work is to be found in several American art museums. It is elegant and has the distinction of creating forms from knitting, rather than creating forms in knitting that are derivative from other crafts or more natural to other crafts. The latter method produces artefacts that have a superficially more modern appearance, with forms reminiscent of abstract surrealism and 1960s pop art. The principal book on such art knitting is also American: Ferne Geller Cone *Knit Art* (1975).

American knitters are notably inventive. Lee Gilchrist in 1970 published *Twice-Knit Knitting*, describing a technique in which every loop is knitted twice, first with the loop to the right, then with that to the left. The resulting fabric is dense, of reduced elasticity and hard to ladder. Beverly Royce of Langdon, Kansas, in 1981 published the confusingly named *Notes on Double Knitting*, which gives instructions for knitting in the round on two needles only. She has even worked out how to do Anna Makarovna's hose-in-hose trick on two needles.

Cowichan knitting

Cowichan is a reserve for Canadian Indians of the Salish groups, near Duncan on Vancouver Island. The women there developed a type of knitting that spread to related groups of Indians in British Columbia and in the state of Washington. It still flourishes today.

Most of the early settlers and Hudson Bay Company employees on Vancouver Island came from the Scottish highlands and islands. The first sawmills were established in the 1860s. As there are clear memories of Indians knitting since the 1880s, it is likely that they learned the craft from the Scots in the very early days of the settlement.

For a generation or two they knitted only socks, but from a little before the First World War they began knitting knee-length underwear. This also was knitted in the round, starting from the bottom of the leg, and was heavy stuff, favoured by the local Japanese and Indian fishermen. It did not survive in use after the Second World War.

About the same time that underwear began to be made, the Cowichan Indians also began to make heavy sweaters. These too were made in the round on up to eight or nine needles. By 1950 cardigans, sleeveless pullovers, caps, gloves and mittens were also being made. The first sweaters were plain-coloured with turtle necks; but the typical Cowichan garment came to be the long-sleeved shawl-collar sweater decorated with bold designs in two-colour stranded knitting.

The wool was obtained from white farmers, then carded and spun by the Indian women. The needles were made by the men (usually husbands) from whale bone, deer bone, telephone wire or bamboo chopsticks. Eventually wood (dogwood,

146 Cowichan motifs.

ironwood, vine maple, ninebark or yellow cedar) became the standard material. The needles were double-ended, about 28 cm (11 in.) long and 6 mm (¼ in.) thick. They were said to have a working life of not more than a year. The process of making them was long and laborious. The fabric produced was stockinet at a tension varying from 14 to 20 stitches to 10 cm (4 in.).

The sweater was made in the round, beginning with a deep welt of two-and-two rib for the waistband. The body was then knitted in stockinet up to the scye. The front and back were divided and each was worked back and forth flat. A few stitches might be added under the arms. The armhole was generally not shaped, but a V-shaped neckline was made by decreases at the centre in the knit rows. The shoulder lines were decreased by binding off a third of the stitches in each of three successive knit rows. The shoulder lines were seamed together.

The stitches remaining at the back of the neck

147 Mrs Agnes Thorne, a Cowichan knitter. 1985.

were then knitted on in garter stitch, increasing at the beginning of every row, until the appropriate depth for the shawl collar had been reached. The back of the collar was then cast off. The edges of the collar were picked up across the ends of the rows and the collar knitted on in garter stitch to make the parts of the collar that extend down each side of the neck opening. After the first row, this part of the collar was shaped by decreasing a stitch at the outside edge of every row, till only one stitch remained at the base of the V. At the same time the last stitch of every row finishing at the neck edge end of the rows was knitted through the neck edge of the front body piece and thus attached to the neckline.

The stitches of the armholes were picked up on three needles, and the sleeve knitted in stockinet to the cuff, where a wristband of two-and-two rib was added to match the waistband. Apart from the shawl collar, the structure of the sweater is essentially a form of British seamen's gansey.

The yarn was used in two, occasionally three, natural colours – black, brown, grey, cream, in contrasting values. The ribbing, done always with one colour to the course, often had two to four stripes of colour contrasting with the background.

The stockinet parts of the sweater are patterned with stranded knitting in two colours. Some of the older designs were geometric and some were derived from aboriginal basketry motifs, but the knitters have long used graph paper to devise motifs taken from a wide variety of sources: oilcloth, linoleum, food and drink labels, blankets, magazines. The designs are used horizontally (as in Fair Isle knitting) and the design bands are usually matched on the sleeves.

Some large motifs, such as the eagle, occupy a band with a single motif, usually reproduced on back and front alike in the middle band. In geometric designs there are typically five bands with the largest in the middle. The collar usually has one or two narrow stripes of contrasting colour.

The non-geometric motifs are for the most part not from Indian sources. They include the firtree and maple leaf; bear, cat, fawn, horse, pig, deer, rabbit, squirrel, whale, eagle, goose, parrot, peacock, pelican, swallow, pheasant, butterfly and dragon. Because of their size and simplicity they often have a distinctively Indian flavour. On cardigans the two sides of the front are usually treated as separate units.

There are almost no floats of yarn across the back of the work. The floats are woven in. This produces a very dense, heavy, warm and hard-wearing fabric. Cowichan sweaters are an interesting example of aboriginal and colonial techniques fusing to produce a garment which is made by the aborigines but acceptable by wear for both communities. The structure of Cowichan sweaters comes from the Scottish settlers and the stranded colour motifs from Shetland knitting after the First World War, when Fair Isle sweaters were popular elsewhere.

Mary Maxim

Heavy outerwear promoted by the Canadian firm Mary Maxim drew its inspiration from Cowichan work. Miss Mary Maxim Ltd was incorporated in Dauphin, Manitoba in 1954, selling knitting prerequisites, patterns and wool. Heavy yarn of the Cowichan type was already being spun in Canada for Miss Mary Maxim. Large bright patterns for heavy sweaters were popular in Canada during the late 1950s. The firm had subsidiaries in Britain and the USA, and in Britain the vogue of Mary Maxim sweaters was at its height in 1961–3. After that it lost favour. An attempt to revive the patterns by Mailyarns of Syston in 1983 was a failure.

Mary Maxim patterns were realistic and included pictorial motifs, from a railway engine to a Friesian cow. There was also a wide range of designs for children. The latter have left a continuing influence.

9 Eastern knitting

The characteristics of eastern knitting

Mary Thomas first called attention to the distinctive qualities of eastern knitting in her *Knitting Book* (1938). Some of her information cannot be verified. For instance, her reference to 'a half-finished sock of the twelfth century found in a Turkish tomb' and worked on five needles (17) has eluded all who have tried to trace it.

Her description of the eastern and western methods of forming the four fundamental stitches (plain and purl, crossed and uncrossed) is classic (pp 50–7). She does not explain exactly where or when the eastern methods are used, though she assumes they are older. The fundamental difference of all 'eastern' stitches from 'western' stitches is that the loops of the eastern style lie on the needle with the left-hand side of the loop to the front. To knit plain, the right-hand needle must be put through the back of the loop and the yarn carried from the back over to the front of the needle before passing front to back between the needles. To purl, the right-hand needle must pass through the back of the loop and the yarn be thrown under the needle.

It is impossible to tell whether a piece of uncrossed stockinet has been made by the eastern or western method. Eastern crossed stockinet, sometimes found in round knitting from the Balkans, is distinguishable by the lie of the loops, left part crossed over the right.

Crossed stitches are made by inserting the right-hand needle through the front of the loop and throwing the yarn as for uncrossed eastern stitches. The western crossed stitch has the right-hand side of the loop crossing in front of the left. The eastern

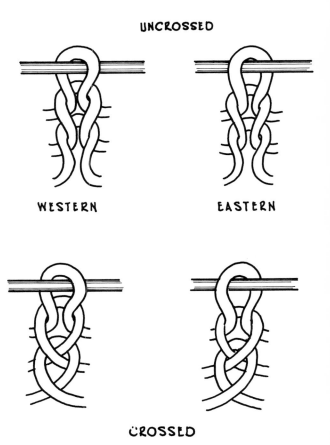

148 The fundamental stitches of Eastern and Western knitting.

crossed stitch has the left-hand side over the right, and in this respect resembles most nalbinding. It is probably related to carrying the yarn in the left hand and using hooked needles.

Mary Thomas also described a 'combined method' for flat stockinet, (in which the knit rows are worked in the western manner through the back of the loop, and purl rows in the eastern uncrossed method), as the accepted mode of knitting in Russia and the neighbouring Balkan States (p 55); and in *The Queen's Book of the Red Cross* (1939) she noted that 'sailors and many who have travelled east' prefer to knit in the eastern method.

A second characteristic of eastern knitting lies in the designs used for multi-coloured fabrics. Western designs are characterized by an emphatically horizontal structure, seen most clearly in the banded motifs of Shetland knitting; eastern designs, chiefly because they were developed on stockings, conceived as having a front and a back, and carried on four needles (in contrast to the western concept of a cylindrical stocking carried on three needles), are often markedly vertical in structure. Both traditions also have all-over patterns, but the linear features of east and west differ. The eight-pointed motif, whether star or rosette, is common to both, and all-over patterns are frequently diapered, but the eastern tradition is rich in simulated curves such as are rarely found in the west. The rectilinear grid on which all such knitting patterns are bound to be made causes the curved lines to be optical, not geometrical. Western taste has never developed the curlicues and twists that feature in Turkish knitting.

The third characteristic of eastern knitting is that footwear is made from the toe upwards.

These features are found from the Adriatic to China, from North Africa to Kashmir, roughly the area of Islamic cultural dominance.

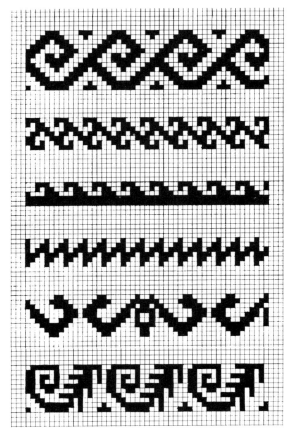

149 Turkish band motifs, showing the use of optically curving patterns.

Balkan knitting

At the beginning of the nineteenth century knitting was being done throughout the Balkan region, from Yugoslavia and Romania through Greece to the Greek Islands. The whole area shows a mingling of western and Islamic taste, as might be expected. In January 1944 the Royal Yugoslav Embassy held an exhibition of national art in London, in connection with which it published *Essays on National Art in Yugoslavia*, edited by Alec Brown. The short section on 'Yugoslav knitting and crochet' was written by Jane Koster and Margaret Murray. They wrote about the footwear, noting that the socks and slippers were knitted on five short copper needles, hooked at one end. They described five different forms of toe construction and two heels, claiming that the work was all done 'from the inside, so that the pattern-making is quite blind'. The fabric was stockinet, mostly uncrossed, but sometimes crossed, with gauges of from 20–80 stitches to 10 cm (4 in.).

They noticed the rich variety of fabrics that could be used in one sock or slipper. Parts might be crochet, parts knitted. Koster and Murray even described a stitch which they proposed to knit as one round of *slip a stitch purlwise, bring the yarn forward*, followed by a round of knitting two

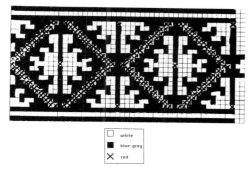

white
blue-grey
red

150 Nineteenth-century Serbian stocking pattern, partly Turkish in inspiration.

together all round, always working into the back of the stitches and taking the yarn over before the slipped stitch. This is a form of 'Tunisian' stitch. They may have been misled, for I have seen a fabric on Serbian slippers that is very similar to Tunisian stitch, but Serbian women have told me is actually worked with a single, eyed needle.

They classified the stockings according to decoration into four groups:

1 Soft flowery patterns, using as many as 14 different colours and 5 or 6 horizontal bands of pattern. Narrow patterns decorated the heels and toes of some socks, and others had cross stitch embroidery on the instep and round the top. Some of the wool used was mill-spun, with bright synthetic dyes. This type appears to have had urban, possibly western, connections.

2 Horizontal stripes of simple geometric patterns in red, blue, black, green and gold or yellow on a natural off-white ground.

3 Strong geometric patterns, a diamond predominating, in closely spun yarn of bright colours.

4 Slipper-socks with stiff anklets, in the 'Tunisian' fabric. Again the patterns were mainly diamond. Red predominated on a black ground, with white, orange, purple and green for contrast.

This classification, though interesting, is probably less useful than a geographically based system would be. Elements of a geographical classification can be obtained from Olive Lodge *Peasant Life in Jugoslavia* (1942), where knitting is described as a constant occupation of the women. Little girls begin to knit, even at the age of 3. Stockings, gloves and leggings, elaborately

patterned with roses and leaves and blue flowers, are mentioned as the chief knitted items (148). The same patterns are seen on dark calf-length stockings in a picture of a man from Šumadija (270). The men of Novi Pazar in the former Turkish central part have knitted sleeveless vests and patterned dark stockings (271). In Serbian areas to the south, in the Macedonian region, patterns are less floral and more brilliantly coloured, akin to what is seen in neighbouring Greece. In Bosnia, Muslim men themselves knit their long white stockings, and in the same area gaily patterned gloves are typical.

Bernard Newman in *Unknown Yugoslavia* (1960) shows a photograph of Macedonian men dancing in the white kilt called *fustanella*. Their dark knee-length stockings have bands of bright geometrical designs, about 15 cm (6 in.) deep, round the top. A beautiful plate of nine pairs of socks in Nikola Pantelić *Traditional arts and crafts of Yugoslavia* (1984) shows knitting from Serbia, Bosnia and Macedonia, chiefly either black or scarlet in colour, including a dark pair from an Albanian costume. The showiest are Macedonian bridal socks with patterns that look superficially like Fair Isle, in horizontal bands, but on closer examination prove to have stronger affinities with the motifs on Turkish woven rugs.

Pantelić also illustrates a pair of navy and red mittens that closely resemble a single mitten from Montenegro in the Mary Edith Durham collection at the Bankfield Museum, Halifax. The patterns of stranded-colour knitting are outlined with white beads and embroidered yellow chain-stitch, while the mittens are heavily hung with tassels of brown, blue and green yarns, and white beads on the thread ends of the tassels. Laura Start in her description of the Durham Collection (1939) noted that mittens of this sort were worn by old men in the winter, although such elaborate ones were already becoming uncommon by 1907.

Laura Start also stated that all over the Balkans both sexes of the peasant and hill tribes wore two pairs of thick knitted woollen socks, the outer pair elaborately decorated with appliqué and embroidery on top of the knitting, and forming a sort of slipper when the outdoor sandal was discarded on entering the house. In Yugoslavia these oversocks were called *opanke*, in Albania *opangi*, and in Romania *opinska*. E.F. Knight in *Albania* (1888) gave the Albanian word as *opunka*, and used it also of the oxhide outdoor slippers. The Durham collection, formed in 1900–14, includes several pairs of these slippers. One pair in violet wool, decorated with plaited silver braid and cord, has an inner sock in 'feather' or 'old shale' pattern.

Albania

It is a matter of luck if a travel-writer ever mentions knitted garments. A traveller who occasionally mentioned such things was Edward Lear. His *Journal of a Landscape Painter in Albania* (1851) describes a visit to Khimara in October 1848. He noticed the women's red worsted stockings, and the way two or three old crones retired into the obscurest shadows of the room, where they seemed to be knitting (276). His picture of 'a very handsome girl' is idyllic:

151 Two-colour design of the Montenegrin glove in Bankfield Museum. Design in navy on red with yellow spots in the stripes. Tree pattern on thumb. Most of the blue outlined in yellow chain stitch and covered with white beads.

. . . her raven tresses fell loose over her beautiful shoulders and neck, and her form from head to foot was majestic and graceful to perfection. Her dress, too: the short open Greek jacket or spencer, ornamented with red patterns, the many-folded petticoat, the scarlet-embroidered apron admirably became her. She was a model of perfect beauty as she stood knitting, hardly bending beneath the burden she was carrying – her fine face half in shade from a snowy handkerchief thrown negligently over her head. (251–2)

Albanian coloured motifs have been collected in Ikbal Mustafa *Albanian Popular Motives*, published by Tiranë University in 1959. The Turkish influence on these decorative designs for socks, stockings and cuffs is obvious. The eight-pointed star abounds, and frequently several colours are used in a row.

Greek stockings

The present national dress of the Greek male, the multi-gored white kilt called *fustanella*, originated in the Albanian and Macedonian mountains. It was adopted by some of the independence fighters against the Turks in the 1820s. As a sign of resistance the fustanella became popular through Roumeli, Thrace and Morea. Under the fustanella were worn breeches which met leggings gartered at the knee. The leggings were often highly ornamented with embroidery. This costume was the basis of the court dress devised by the romantic King Otto, who arrived from Germany in 1838.

The fustanella was originally as long as a Scottish kilt, but as it became more widely worn, it tended to become shorter. Sunday dress in some places, at least for young men, developed a very short fustanella, which became the model for the uniform of the evzones, the 'well-girded', the ceremonial guards of the royal court. The short fustanella looked well only if the breeches and leggings were replaced by long white stockings. The garters below the knee were retained as ornaments, usually black and tasselled.

Today the stockings of the evzones are machine-knitted. They are still leggings – footless stockings ending with shallow points over the ankle and

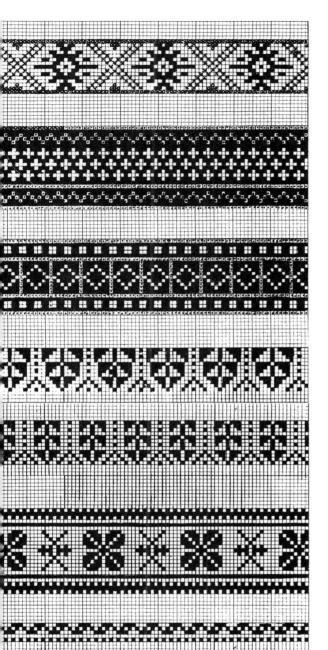

152 Albanian motifs after Ikbal Mustafa.

153 Evzones, Greek ceremonial guards, wearing machine-made leggings styled after the rural hand-knitted stockings or leggings.

Greek men in some places wear coloured stockings with the fustanella or with knee-length breeches. In parts of Thrace and Macedonia the stockings are black on weekdays and multi-coloured for festal wear. The Vlachs have white stockings with gold and coloured ornament. All these are patterned with horizontal bands of design. Ioanna Papantoniou has published excellent pictures in *Greek Costume* (2 volumes, 1973 and 1974).

Angeliki Hadzimichaelis in *The Greek Folk Costume* (1979) has pictures of women wearing similar stockings, especially from the Florina district. Most are red with horizontal bands of geometric design in black, red, yellow and white. Some of these bands show the familiar OXO pattern and include the eight-pointed star or cross. One pair from Boufi is black with bands of motifs in blue, yellow and shocking pink.

The Greek Islands

The Greek Islands have traditions in stocking knitting which are probably not essentially different from the tradition of the mainland. The islands have, however, been the object of learned

instep, fastened at the foot by an elastic strap under the sole. The tops of the stockings are attached to a suspender belt worn under the fustanella. The stockinet is cut and sewn, sometimes seamed up the inside of the leg, sometimes at the back.

Femme de l'île de Mycone.
dessinée par le Baron de Stackelberg.

154 A daintified picture of a Greek woman of the island of Mykonos in the Cyclades, wearing local dress and knitting a stocking. Drawn by Baron Otto Magnus von Stackelberg in 1811 and published in *Costumes et Usages de la Grèce Moderne* in 1825.

tourism for 300 years, with the result that we have some sketchy information for the history of their knitting, such as is not available for mainland Greece. There is even a picture of a woman of Mykonos standing and knitting a red stocking-cap, her ball of wool trailing on the ground. She wears a short white dress with wide sleeves. Her stockings and inner sleeves are blue, her inner bodice red and gold, her high-heeled mules white. Her large soft cap is red. She looks like anything but an island peasant woman. Yet that is what she is. The drawing was made by Baron Otto Magnus von Stackelberg in 1811, and published in his *Costumes et Usages de la Grèce Moderne* at Rome in 1825. It is a daintified version of the truth.

Marie-Gabriel Choiseul-Gouffier (1752–1817),

the French soldier and antiquary who was successively ambassador to Constantinople and Russia, published his *Voyage Pittoresque de la Grèce* in 1809, describing his observations of the 1790s. He said of the women of Kimolos that their costume was absurd, a mass of dirty white linen. They wore a short dress that left their legs showing, and they believed that the thicker their legs appeared, the more beautiful they would be. They wore several pairs of thick stockings at once and covered them with elaborately decorated socks. The Prussian diplomat Jacob Ludwig Bartholdy (1779–1825) gave a similar description from his journeys in 1803 and 1804, *Voyage en Grèce* (1807). Jacques Pitton de Tournefort (1656–1708), the great French botanist, visited the islands in 1700–2. *His Relation d'un voyage au Levant*, published posthumously in 1717, states laconically that the women of Kimolos do nothing but knit cotton stockings and make love. Earlier the Dutch scholar Olfert Dapper (1636–89), whose *Description exacte des Isles* was printed in Amsterdam in 1703, had described the dress of the women of Mykonos, including the cotton stockings, though he did not mention having seen the women knit.

155 Late nineteenth-century woman's stockings from Chios. White patterned with pink, blue, green, purple, red, black and other colours. Length of sole 22 cm (8 2/3 in.).

These constitute some of the few references discovered to knitting among the Greeks as early as the seventeenth century.

The stockings of the Greek islands are very varied in design. A late nineteenth-century pair in the Peloponnesian Folklore Museum at Nafplion has nine different patterns in bands on the leg, using ten bright colours. Some of the patterns may have come from Northern Europe, but two are outstanding: one of elaborate swans in red and green on a white ground, and another of horizontally barred lozenges in cream on a pink ground (fig. 155).

Balkan sleeves

Sleeves, coverings for the forearm, worn under the looser sleeves of cloth garments, are knitted in Macedonia, Albania and Greece. They are worn by both sexes, but most photographs show them being worn by women. Men certainly wore them in parts of Macedonia. They are patterned in a fashion similar to that of the stockings.

157 Gloves knitted by Sarakatzani, the transhumant pastoral people of northern Greece. The fingers are alternately black and mauve. Green and orange are used in the coloured pattern. Length 22 cm (8⅔ in.).

Ioanna Papantoniou also notes that on Chios young men wear knitted cotton bonnets.

The Ottoman Fez

Julia Pardoe (1806–62) was a voluminous and versatile historian, novelist and travel writer. In 1837 she published *The City of the Sultan*, an account of Istanbul, in which she described the imperial fez factory which Ömer Lufti Efendi had established in the suburb of Eyüp about 1832 (II 351;3). This was claimed by Miss Lambert in her *Handbook of Needlework* (1842) as evidence that the Turkish fez was knitted (305–6). Yet Miss Pardoe's evidence is uncharacteristically vague. She never saw a fez being knitted.

The fez was a new fashion in Turkey. Efforts to replace the splendid Turkish turban by this simplified little red cap had been made since the

156 Greek carved wooden knitting sheaths; (*c*) and (*d*) are believed to have come from the Ionian Islands; (*d*) is 33 cm long (13 in.), (*e*) 27 cm (10¾ in.).

beginning of the nineteenth century, but not until 1827 was the wearing of the fez ordered and accepted, as a thoroughly non-christian head-dress for men. At first the supply of crimson felt caps came from north Africa, chiefly from Tunis, though the town of Fez is in Morocco. The establishment of the imperial factory was sensible.

According to Miss Pardoe on her visit to Eyüp, 'about five hundred females were collected together in a vast hall, awaiting the delivery of the wool which they were to knit'. Three thousand workmen produced 1500 fezzes every month. She wrote:

> . . . the wool, having been spread over a stone-paved room on the ground floor, where it undergoes saturation with oil, is weighed out to the carders, and thence passes into the hands of the spinners, where it is worked into threads of greater or less size, according to the quality of the fez for which it is to be made available.

The women each took home six or a dozen balls of wool, each ball containing the quantity necessary for one cap. They were paid when they returned the caps.

The caps were washed with soap and water. After a complicated process of drying, dyeing, boiling, blocking on earthen moulds, and more drying, the nap was raised with the head of a bulrush, then sheared. They were pressed, and finally given the long purple tassel, before being packed. By that time the fez had 'no longer the slightest appearance of knitted wool, but all the effect of a fine close cloth.'

Nowhere does Julia Pardoe witness the knitting; nor is there any other evidence that fezzes were knitted. The Turkish word for 'to knit' can refer to other yarn processes, and Miss Pardoe may well have made a wrong translation. The conventional felt-making processes were certainly employed in Turkey. Until further evidence appears, we must at least treat as suspect Julia Pardoe's assertion that the Ottoman fez was knitted.

Turkish socks

The Turkish tradition differs from the Balkan so much that Turks regard Balkan designs as readily recognisable when they occur in Turkey. The Turks regard horizontally banded stockings as immigrant work; their own patterns are different.

Professor Kenan Özbel (1904–) is a Turkish teacher of art and crafts. In 1976 he published *Türk Köylü Çoraplari*, of which an English version appeared in 1981: *Knitted Stockings from Turkish Villages*. He claimed that these rustic socks had five functions: to identify the wearer's community; to express the wearer's social rank; to serve as gifts, sometimes as coded requests; to act as prophylactics and ward off the evil eye; and to commemorate natural disasters, violent events and great legends. Another book, published in Istanbul in 1981, is *Anatolian Knitting Designs* by Betsy Harrell. Mrs Harrell throws doubt on the value of Özbel's remarks on the symbolism of the patterns, in a way which forcibly reminds one of the

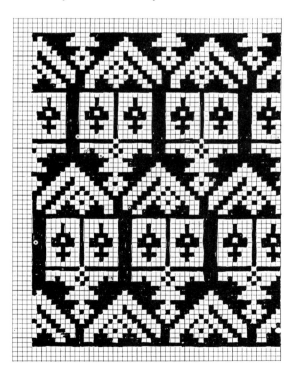

158 The 'almond' (*badam* or *boteh*) pattern on a Turkish sock.

demythologizing that has had to be done with Aran and Shetland patterns.

Özbel is more convincing when he classifies Turkish stockings in six categories according to their appearance: white stockings with openwork fabric in the leg section; black stockings worn with knee breeches by men in certain regions; multicoloured stockings for women, now scarcely to be seen; hennaed stockings, plain white with red henna staining on the toes and heels; undyed mohair stockings (which are placed inside a new loaf fresh from the oven to raise the fluffiness); and embroidered stockings, short for women and long for men. He says that the origins of Turkish knitting are unknown, but suggests that Anatolian knitted stockings go back to the seventeenth century. His book contains 192 diagrams and photographs, some in colour. Additional charts by Özbel were published in the brief section on knitting in Celal Esad Arseven *Les Arts Decoratifs Turcs* (no date, *c.*1946, Istanbul).

Betsy Harrell's book is in more modest format and contains 160 diagrams, with a description of

159 Turkish sock patterns showing derivation from carpet designs.

the technique for knitting the stockings. Her commentary is cautious and judicious. She makes a particular point of describing the patterns which are used for the soles of the stockings. Some features of the tradition become clear from a study of the two books together. The stockings are worked from the toe upwards in ordinary stockinet, and the triangular toe and the heel are pouches of the same shape. The colours are sometimes soft, but oftener bright, even lurid. Many colours may be used in one stocking, and often three or four colours, even up to eight colours, in a single round. The names of the patterns are not fixed and the same motif may have several names. These names are simple and homely: 'apple slice', 'sergeant's stripes', 'watch chain', 'earrings', 'beetle', 'nightingale', 'moth'. Many of the patterns, especially stars, hooked-edged diamonds and other large geometrical motifs, are taken from carpets and the woven rugs called kilim. The knitters have plain-pointed needles and carry the working yarn round the nape of the neck. The yarn is thrown with the left hand, and the hands are held over the needles.

Knitting beyond the Caucasus

Scènes, Paysages, Moeurs et Costume du Caucase (*c*.1850) is a collection of magnificent colour plates by Prince Gregor Gagarin with text by Count Ernst Stackelberg. Among the plates is one of a Tatar

The Levant

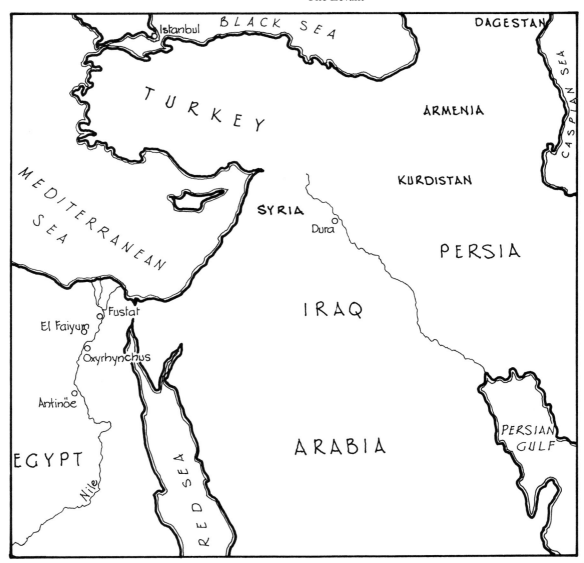

Beg wearing pink socks with narrow red vertical stripes. These socks were most likely knitted.

This is only one indication that footwear of the Turkish type was known further east. Armenia, Persia and Iraq formed an area of cultural interchange and mixture during the Ottoman period. Stockings might be worn far from the place where they were made, and knitters would learn patterns from places far away. Helen Grieg Souter and Mrs M. Sibbald in *More Dainty Work for Busy Fingers* (1920) proudly printed photographs of an Armenian stocking and sock in 'decidedly crude colouring', 'knitted by an Armenian woman of eighty winters'. The pattern on the sock is typically Turkish, with a motif that is common in carpets. The old lady may have learnt to knit that way in Turkey or some other part of the Turkish Empire. It was also an Armenian knitter, Aroosiag Mikaelian, who inspired Schiaparelli in the 1920s (with an unusual form of double-thread stockinet). (Fig. 108.)

In the 1980s stockings from Dagestan, on the western shore of the Caspian Sea, are on sale at tourist shops in Moscow. They are comparatively restrained in colour and ornamented with simple patterns, but they too are of the Turkish type. They have garter-stitch heels. The stockings of Persia are even more like the Turkish. In Jay Gluck *A Survey of Persian Handicrafts* (Tehran 1977) there are illustrations of socks with patterns like carpets, and the note: 'Every area has woollen socks, hats and gloves, each distinguishable by colour and design. Khurasan uses rich orange, blue, green and black, while Gilan has softer colours' (261–2).

The Indian department of the Victoria & Albert Museum possesses a cap from Persia. Acquired from Tehran in 1964, it is believed to have originated from New Julfa, the Armenian suburb of Isfahan. Although it appears round, its structure is strictly octagonal, with eight increases in each of the increase rounds of the crown. It is knitted from the crown outwards in silk stockinet of seven colours: dark red, navy blue, bright blue, gold, orange, green and white. The tree and flower designs have more in common with Kashmir knitting than with Turkish designs. An Armenian inscription surrounds it: *Nuer ar Hamazasp gtakd*, 'This cap is a present to Hamazasp'. (Colour plate 5.)

Kashmiri knitting

The Victoria & Albert Museum possesses several pieces of knitting from Kashmir. Some are in the textile department, but most in the Indian. It has generally been thought that knitting was introduced into India by Westerners. Postlethwayt's reference to knitting at Pulicat bears out this idea, as does the shape and style of a pair of socks in the museum, made of Chaddar floss rough silk in Shahpore jail in the mid-nineteenth century. They are knitted from top to toe and have grafting under the heel. In the western style, too, is a pair of white gloves with multicoloured wrist pieces added in the opposite direction. So is a pair of long white stockings patterned with floral sprigs in red, green and black. The toes are red; 20 cm (8 in.) clocks are grafted in at the ankles, and the heel is cast off underneath, much as some European heels were in the seventeenth century. The stockings are knitted from top to toe with a section added at the top, knitted in the opposite direction. In these items the shape is western, the fabric Indian.

Another pair of long stockings is red with black, yellow, white and green sprays. 'Knee guards' are attached to the front, pointing upwards. The knitting is done from toe to top. These appear to be entirely Indian. So do the red gloves, worked from the fingertips, ornamented with black, green and white scroll-work patterns.

With these pieces must be associated a pair of long gloves in the Ashmolean Museum at Oxford. They are 40 cm (16 in.) long and 10 cm (4 in.) wide at the wrist, knitted at a tension of about 10 stitches to the centimetre. They are white, with an all-over pattern of sprigs in red, navy blue and yellow. Blue bands with pink floral scrolls adorn the wrist, cuff and fingers. The finger-tips are red. The thumb has a neat gore, and stitches have been cast on to widen the palm above the thumb joint. These gloves are said to have belonged to Warren Hastings (1732–1818). He left India in 1784 and lived at Daylesford, near Stow-on-the-Wold, not far from Oxford, from 1788.

Both the Ashmolean and the Victoria & Albert also possess Indian gloves with very short wrists, covered with tiny motifs and decorated with bands of scroll-work. Though at first sight they look

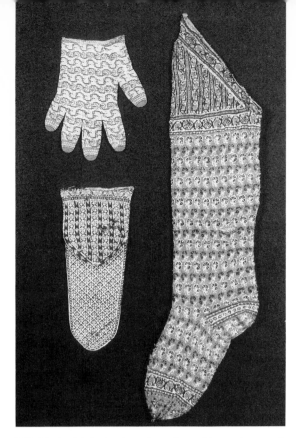

160 Kashmiri knitted sock and stocking, nineteenth century. The glove is not knitted.

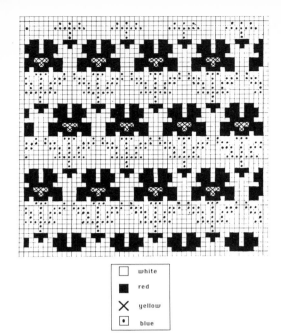

	white
	red
X	yellow
•	blue

161 A Kashmiri floral sprig pattern, related to shawl patterns. Most courses contain only two colours.

knitted, they do not have a knitted structure. They are probably crochet of the kind described by Peter Collingwood in *Textile and Weaving Structures* (1987, pp 34–9), where he illustrates artefacts from the Rann of Kutch and Afghanistan.

The Victoria & Albert Museum also possesses Indian knitted headwear. One tall white cap, covered with the typical *boteh* or 'Paisley' pattern well-known in Kashmir shawls, knitted in black, blue and red, is singularly beautiful. It is small – only 13 cm (5⅙ in.) in diameter, though 26 cm (10⅜ in.) high. The crown, in black, white, yellow and red, has a repeated floral motif that can be found also on slippers and on the Ashmolean gloves. Bands of flowers, in red, yellow, blue and green on a black ground, surround the rim and the crown. The other hat is a hood which has sprigs of red flowers with black stems, set on a golden yellow ground between broken diamond-shaped frames in black and light blue. The debt of both designs to Kashmir shawl-weaving is evident.

These two pieces are known to have come from Ludhiana in the Punjab, where a colony of Kashmiris settled in 1833 after they had left their homeland because of famine. They made Ludhiana an important centre for shawl-weaving.

Literary references

Literary references to Kashmir knitting are rare. Algernon Durand in *The Making of a Frontier* (1899) spoke of the 'gay-patterned knitted stockings which all Chitralis wore' in 1888 (61). In the following year he found that men's stockings in Hunza and Nagar were 'not knitted in such elaborate colours' (142).

Earlier, Sir Alexander Cunningham, the archaeologist, in *Ladak* (1854) spoke of woollen stockings and gloves in that city without mentioning the patterns (200). Godfrey Vigne, even earlier, in *Travels in Cashmir* (1835) mentioned gloves and socks manufactured from the shawl wool of the Kashmir goats. The best and clearest references are in the posthumously published notes of the adventurer and veterinary pioneer William Moorcroft, who visited Kashmir in 1820–2. In his *Travels in the Himalayan Provinces* (1841) we read of Ladakh:

> Both sexes wear stockings. They are of three kinds: of sheep's wool felted; of sheep's wool

knit; and goat's wool knit . . . The second sort is that most in use. The foot part is made by wearing, being very imperfectly shaped in the original . . . . One kind of stocking, made of shawl wool, is fancifully decorated and very showy. For summer wear half-stockings of cotton are imported from Kashmir and Kabul. (I 325)

Elizabeth Balneaves, visiting the region in 1961, met at Gupis, a village west of Gilgit, 'four lads of the village . . . handsome, cheery characters wearing home-knitted calf-length hose, dazzling in squares and diamonds of coloured wool' (169, 193). In the open-fronted shops of Chitral bazaar she noticed 'hand-knitted woollen socks of intricate and startling design'. She describes these and several other pieces of Indian knitting in *Mountains of the Murgha Zerin* (1972). (The *murgha zerin* is the beautiful Impeyan pheasant.)

In the same year a photograph was taken in the Leh bazaar street that was published in the *National Geographic Magazine* (123.5 [May 1963]:674–5). The picture shows a man leading a donkey and a *dzo* or yak-ox hybrid. The caption draws attention to 'knitted boots with turned-up

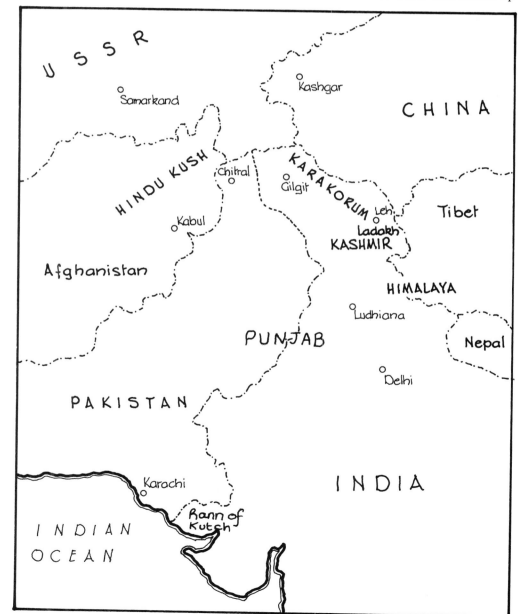

Kashmir

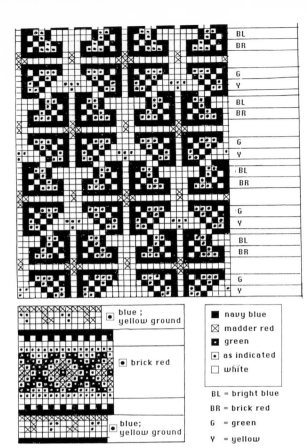

blue;
yellow ground

brick red

blue;
yellow ground

■ navy blue
⊠ madder red
▪ green
• as indicated
□ white

BL = bright blue
BR = brick red
G = green
Y = yellow

BL
BR

G
Y

BL
BR

G
Y

BL
BR

G
Y

BL
BR

G
Y

162 Multicoloured patterns from an Afghan sock. Bankfield Museum, received 1916 (1970/281 : 0.6774). Tension 6 sts = 1 cm. Uncrossed stocking stitch. Harsh wool. 158 sts at cast off. Width of folded sock 13 cm. Total length 28 cm: toe tip to heel tip = 26.8 cm (10¾ in.). Heel 5.5 cm (2⅙ in.).

toes'. They appear to be knitted slippers or socks like those in the Victoria & Albert Museum.

The patterns on these slippers can nearly all be found in the Turkish designs recorded by Betsy Harrell and Kenan Özbel. Though more finely knitted in soft shawl wool, they are almost indistinguishable from the Turkish socks. The turned-up toes in the Ladakh picture are merely the long triangular toes forced up by wear and walking. The Folk Art Museum at Santa Fe, New Mexico, has a pair of these slippers, described as Kurdish bridal socks. The floral sprig on them is the same as that on the Ashmolean gloves and the Ludhiana headdress. Two beautiful socks covered with a miniature pattern in red, white, yellow and dark and light blue, are kept in the Bankfield Museum at Halifax. They came from Afghanistan.

The whole picture is far from clear. Knitting has never been important to the people of India, but there seem to be traces of knitting traditions entering the sub-continent from the Middle East as well as from Europe. The elaborately coloured shawl-patterns reproduced in knitting, and the knitting of socks from the toe upwards are Eastern rather than Western elements (colour plate 6). If Mrs Rivers Turnbull is to be believed, the knitters of Kashmir were men (*Woman's library* II 1903; p 284).

This style even reached the northern boundary of China. On 1 December 1930 the missionaries Francesca French and Mildred Cable wrote a letter from Suchow, which was published in *A Desert Journal* (1934). They told of a journey eastward from Suchow on the Mongolian side of the Great Wall. As they approached the town of Maomu, they said:

> The guard was preparing its winter outfit, each man busily knitting a pair of stockings of homespun camel's hair yarn. Chinese fashion, they worked contrary to European ideas and began at the toe, working backwards. At our approach knitting needles were hastily laid aside and bayonets took their place. (151)

But, so far as we know, knitting was not much done in the Asian tradition on the Chinese side of the wall, except by Muslim men and women in Kansu. The soldiers' fashion of knitting was not Chinese, but Central Asian and Islamic.

North Africa

Information about knitting in northern Africa is hard to come by. A Coptic deacon tells me that both men and women in Egyptian villages knit coarse brown woollen skull caps on two hooked needles, with the yarn on the nape. Alfred Bel and Prosper Ricard have more to say in an article 'Le travail de la laine à Tlemcen' in *Les Industries Indigènes de l'Algerie* (1913). Tlemcen is an ancient Arab Islamic town near the Moroccan border, with an important wool trade. The authors describe the knitting that was done there in the round on five brass needles, each hooked at one end, 17–18 cm

(7 in.) long and 2–2.5 mm (1¹/₁₂ in.) thick.

In 1913 even the country Arabs were wearing European machine-made stockings, but formerly they had worn long hand-knit stockings, reaching above the knee. Mountain shepherds were still knitting brown woollen leggings for winter wear. The townspeople knitted socks, caps and trouser-girdles. The socks were coarsely made with double yarn (sometimes plyed) in stockinet with garter stitch heels. The toes were pointed like Turkish stocking-toes. The top was a picot hem, folded over a row of overs. Simple patterns of overs created openwork decoration for the stocking top.

The caps were for men. They had the same picot edge and consisted of a 7 cm (2³/₄ in.) high pill-box of open work finished with a flat top in which each decrease round had eight decreases, forming a cross, three stitches wide, across the crown.

The tasselled girdles were 3–4 cm (1¹/₄–1¹/₂ in.) across and 1.5 metres (5 ft) long. Six or eight stitches were cast on. Each row was worked *over, knit 2 together*. The description of the method is not clear, but appears to mean that the work was slid to the blunt end of the needle and worked off without turning – a simple method of knitting tubular cord. Earlier, true tubular girdles had been made in stockinet on five needles, using twenty stitches (five to each of four needles).

Bel and Ricard were not expert at describing knitting techniques. They say Algerian stockings resembled Turkish stockings, but do not say in what respect this was so. The general picture they give is of a diminishing and limited tradition.

China, Korea and Japan

The countries of East Asia have no native history of hand knitting. Though hand- and machine-knitting now flourish in all three lands, knitting has come to them all as part of the modernization process in the nineteenth and twentieth centuries.

Michael Harvey learned from Sakata Nobumasa, president of the Japan Knitting Technology Association, when he visited London in 1971, that there is some reason to believe the geishas of Nagasaki learned to knit during the Genroku period (1688–1704), though knitted garments had almost certainly reached Japan through Dutch and Portuguese traders earlier. Machine-knitted stockinet is to this day called *meriyasu* in Japan and Korea, and that word is derived from the Spanish *medias*, for stockings.

In 1960 seven pairs of old stockings were discovered in a Japanese temple. Three were silk and four cotton. All were hand-knitted with a gauge of seven or eight stitches to the inch. They appear to be of European origin, probably presented to Prince Mitokomon (1628–1700).

Korea was not fully opened to the West until the 1880s. Hand knitting was probably not taken up until after the annexation of the country by the Japanese in 1910. In the 1930s Korea was importing knitting wool from Patons' mill in Shanghai. From 1940 to 1970, little hand knitting was done in Korea, though industrial machine knitting flourished. From about 1980 onwards, with the developing economic prosperity of Korea hand knitting became more popular. Patterns and methods are dominated by Japanese practice, but knitting-books in Korean have begun to appear.

In 1983 the New China News Agency in Peking announced the discovery of some textiles in the tomb of a noblewoman, dating from the third century BC (the Warring States period) in Jiangling district, Hubei province, central China. These textiles included braids, with a knitted structure, attached to clothing.

Full descriptions of these braids have not yet become available in Europe. They may be of a type similar to those made by the Warrau and Taulipang in Guyana. They may not be knitted at all. The history of later Chinese knitting, learned from the West, is equally obscure. Patons established their Shanghai mill in 1932, in response to an already active market. Today in Shanghai women old and young can be seen knitting everywhere. They mostly use bamboo needles. Pattern books are easy to obtain, and, as in Korea, they show a notable Japanese influence. The Japanese influence is most obvious in the preference for diagrams rather than verbal instructions as the normal form of recipes. There are abundant signs that Europe and America too will increasingly adopt diagrammatic recipes.

Appendices

Historical glossary

Each term is given the date of its first known appearance in print. Since there are very few references to knitting before 1837 it must be remembered that a term dated 1840 or earlier may have been in use for a long time, even centuries, before the date given here. Where no reference to a printed source is given, the date noted is that recorded in the *Oxford English Dictionary* or its supplements. Where a reference is given, either the term (at least in the sense here in question) is not included in the dictionary or this glossary gives a date earlier than that in the *Dictionary*.

Abbreviations

CS	Caulfeild, Sophia and Saward, Blanche *Dictionary of needlework* 1882
EDD	*English dialect dictionary* 1900
EL	Lewis, E. *Wools and how to use them* 1884
FL	Lambert, F. *My knitting book* I 1844; II 1847, *Handbook of needlework* 1842
HEC	Cunnington, C.W. and P. *Handbook of English costume in the nineteenth century* 1970
HI	Hartley, M. and Ingilby, J. *The old handknitters of the Dales* 1951
MT	*Mary Thomas's knitting book* 1938 *Mary Thomas's book of knitting patterns* 1943
NE	*Natura exenterata* 1655
RC	Compton, R. *Complete book of guernsey and jersey knitting* 1985
WC	*Woolcraft* 2nd ed. c 1916
WG	*Workwoman's guide* 1838
WT	Watts, T. *The ladies' knitting and netting book* I 1837, II 1840 *Selections of knitting* 1844 *New illustrated knitting* 1845
WW	Watson, W. *Textile design and colour* 6th ed. 1912

ABB EDD 1757. Ultimately from the same root as *web*. Two qualities of short-staple wool; coarse and fine. Originally applied to wool for weaving. S. William Beck (1886) says the ten qualities of sorted wool are picklocks, prime, choice, super, head wool, downrights, seconds, abb, livery and short coarse (each taken from a different part of the fleece).

ABERGELDIE A castle about 2.4 km (1½ miles) east of Balmoral, leased in 1848 by the Prince Consort as a home for Albert, Prince of Wales (later Edward VII).

ACRYLIC 1853; but as knitting yarn in the 1950s. A synthetic fibre, manufactured chiefly from oil or coal.

AFGHAN 1833. A knitted or crochet rug or blanket, supposedly resembling something from Afghanistan.

ALLOA 1884. Another name for wheeling. From Paton's mill at Alloa, Clackmannanshire. EL

ANDALUSIAN 1882. A knitting yarn, usually 4 ply, comparable to Shetland; used for good quality stockings.

ANGOLA 1827. Incorrect form of Angora.

ANGORA 1833. Mohair. From the city of Ankara.

ARGYLE (Argyll) 1942. W.H. Wise & Co *Complete guide to modern knitting and crocheting* p 172: 'Argyle jerkin'. See Tartan.

ARRASENE 1881. A woollen yarn used like crewel wool but of a chenille type. From Arras, France.

AUTO HEEL A version of the Niantic heel in its simplest form, so named in *Woolcraft* c.1933. Possibly an abbreviation of *automatic*, since the heel reproduces a machine-knitted heel. See *Weldon's Practical stocking-knitter*, First series (*Practical Needlework* No. 11) 1886.

BACHELOR TEA-COSY 1893. *Leach's fancy workbasket* 1 Feb. p 173. A teacosy with openings for the handle and spout of the teapot, so that it need not be removed for pouring the tea.

BACK BAR A mistake produced by carrying a loop over two rows, leaving an unknitted loop at the back of the fabric. *Aunt Kate's knitting and crocket book c.* 1896

BACK STITCH A purl stitch. Gaugain 1840.

BAININ (BAWNEEN) Gaelic, from *ban* 'white'. Used in Ireland for 'whitish', and pronounced 'bawneen'. Originally used for the Aran man's jacket or waistcoat of woven stuff. Later (1958) applied to undyed wool for Aran knitting.

BALACLAVA HELMET 1881. (27 years after the battle), but 'Crimean helmet' in E.M. Corbould *The Lady's knitting book* Second Series (1876). A knitted helmet covering the ears and neck.

BARÈGE 1845. A form of intarsia knitting, imitating the fine woven wool fabrics of French Pyrenean villages such as Barèges, which was developed as a fashion fabric by Charles Rejaunier about 1823. FL *Handbook* 272.

BARROW (BARRY) 1878. A sleeveless covering for a tiny infant, precursor of the zipped carrybag. Usually of flannel, sometimes knitted. Also called *barrow-coat*.

BATE To decrease (derived from **ABATE**); 16th century, as in 'bate one's breath'. See *Merchant of Venice* III iii 32. MS knitting notes, Cornwall, early 20th century.

BATWING SLEEVE 1959. A dolman sleeve (loose sleeve cut or knitted in one piece with body of garment).

BEDOUIN A head-scarf or hood. *The Young Ladies Journal* Vo. 3, 1873.

BEIGE, BEGE 1858. French. Originally a fabric of undyed wool. Hence, the colour of such fabrics.

BERCEAUNETTE QUILT Pseudo-etymological perversion of *bassinette* 1854, meaning a cradle-basket or perambulator with a hood. From *basinet*, a helmet with a visor, not from *berceau*, a cradle. WT 1845, p 46.

BERET 1827. A flat knitted cap named after the headwear of Basque peasants.

BERLIN GLOVE 1836. A glove knitted of Berlin wool.

BERLIN WOOL 1842. A wool spun in Germany. A full, soft thread of brilliant colours and various plies, used also for embroidery. J. Gaugain *Lady's Assistant* II 345.

BERTHE, BERTHA 1848. A deep-falling collar attached to the top of a low-necked dress. Riego de la Branchardière *Winter book for 1848*.

BIKINI 1947. A scanty two piece swimsuit, originally for women. The name was later used for an equally scanty slip for men. From the Bikini Atoll in the Marshall Islands where the first atom bomb explosion test took place 30 June 1946.

BIND 1655. To complete a wale or wales by locking at the end. This term remains in use in the USA, but had been replaced by 'cast off' in Britain by the early 19th century. NE

BLACK STITCH 1938. A purl stitch, so called because it was indicated by a black square on a pattern chart. MT 52.

BOA 1836. Snake-like scarf.

BONNET A word of obscure history, doubtless from the French word meaning a cap, usually soft and brimless. It ceased to be used for such headgear in England during the 17th century, but was retained in this use in Scotland.

BONNETTING A soft cotton yarn – E.M.Corbould *The Lady's knitting book* 1st series 1874.

BOOT-HOSE, BOOT-STOCKING 1588. Stockings worn between fine stockings and boots to protect the former. In the early 17th century they had decorative tops that fell over the outside of the boot tops.

BOSOM FRIEND 1802. A man's chest-protector. As knitted, 1838 WG 275.

BOTANY 1882. Wool from Australia, named after Botany Bay. A fine merino yarn, fuller, softer and denser than typical worsted. WW 371.

BOUCLÉ 1895. From French: 'curly' or 'looped'. A yarn in which one ply is shorter than the other(s), producing loops along the whole of the yarn.

BOUT 1838. A round of knitting. WG; but used to mean 'a circuit' since the 16th century.

BRAD See *brod*.

BRIDAL SHIRT 1950. J. Norbury 'The knitter's craft'. According to Norbury, a Cornish term for an elaborately patterned fisher-gansey made by a bride for her groom to wear on the wedding day. See *Journal of Royal Society of Arts* 1951, 223.

BRIOCHE (*1*) 1844. A cake-shaped cushion in brioche fabric. FL 22.
(*2*) 1840. The knitted fabric also called Fisherman's Rib or (by Elizabeth Zimmerman) Prime Rib. WT 103. Rarely used for outerwear till the 1950s. See Fisherman's Rib.

BROD Middle English: a nail or spike. Sometimes used of a knitting needle in Scotland. See *prick*.

BUMP Very coarse undyed yarn, used in Westmorland and West Yorkshire in the 19th century. 1825 loosely twisted cotton used for candlewick fabrics and coarse sheets ('bump sheets') EDD. 1844. William Howitt *The Rural Life of England* (for wool).

BUMP CAP 1844. A stocking cap of bump, about a yard in length. Howitt.

BURNOUS(E) 1695 Arabic. A cloak (or cape) with a hood, sometimes with short sleeves, as in HEC 434.

CABLE 1844. The ornamental twisting of wales. FL 1844 p 54.

CANADIAN GLOVE 1875. A glove with thumb and bag for four fingers. A mitt. E.M. Corbould *The Lady's*

knitting book IV 14.

CANEZOU 1824 French. A shawl of lace or other material. Origin unknown, possibly Provençal. HEC 392.

CANION 1583. Men's thigh-coverings, attached to the trunks – the upper part of stockings, normally ornamented, and not knitted.

CANON (CANNON) Decorative stocking-tops, turned down over a garter worn below the knee. 1660: Pepys's diary, 24 May. Also called port cannons.

CAPELINE 1860s. Hood with small cape. HEC 478.

CAPOTE 1812. A long shaggy cloak or coat with a hood; a long mantle worn by women (from French).

CARDIGAN 1868. Knitted form of sleeved waistcoat. Named after the Earl of Cardigan (1797–1868).

CARDINAL 1858. A short cloak worn by ladies, originally of scarlet cloth with a hood. Later with sleeves.

CASAWECK 1847. Probably from French *casaque*. A short topcoat. HEC.

CASHMERE 1882. Yarn spun from the undercoat of the Kashmir goat. Also a yarn spun from fine short-stapled sheep's wool. CS.

CAST OFF 1838. WT p 111. See 'bind'.

CAST ON 1838 WT p 2. To start knitting by making the first course of loops. From 'cast' meaning 'to tie a knot'.

CEPHALINE 1844. The same as *sontag*; 'to be worn over the head on leaving heated rooms' WT 1840 p 84.

CHANCELIERE 1845. A footwarmer: a sac lined with fur into which both feet are put. FL *Handbook* 54.

CHEMISETTE (*1*) 1807. A form of blouse for a woman.
(*2*) 1844. A 'modesty vest' or false front worn in the neck opening of a dress.

CHINÉ 1858. An indistinct or mottled pattern achieved by printing the warp of a woven fabric in a supposedly Chinese style. The term is sometimes used to describe knitwear in mottled colours.

CIRCULAR NEEDLE 1924. A double-ended needle with a flexible centre. The flexible part was at first steel cable, but after WW II made of nylon. Advertisement in *Ladies' Field jumpers* Bk I.

CLEW An Anglo-Saxon/Old English word for a ball of thread or yarn, that has survived in dialect use.

CLOCK 1530. Ornament on the side of a stocking, probably originally to strengthen the ankle.

CLOUD 1877. A loose-knitted woollen scarf worn by ladies.

CORAL WOOL EL 1884. The meaning is not clear.

COURSE 1655. A row of stitches or loops across the width of a knitted fabric. NE 417.

CRAPE 1922. The middle part of a Shetland shawl when made in plain knitting. From the original use of 'crape' in the 18th century to mean a thin crisped material made of worsted. *The Queen* 30 12. 1922 p 869.

CUT 1632. A measure of yarn, a hank or skein. Scottish and N. English. 120 rounds of the legal reel; 228 cm (91 in.) long. 12 cuts made a slip.

DAMBROD 1779. Chequered. 'Board for the dame (queen) game'. Scottish dialect, used for small all-over check designs.

DAME WOOL EL 1884. The meaning is not clear.

DECREASE 1837. Knit two loops in one. WT.

DOILY 1678. A woollen stuff for summer wear, named after a linen-draper in the Strand, London, near Aldwych. By Jonathan Swift's time the stuff was used for doily-napkins at dessert; by the early 19th century 'lace doilies' were being put under sandwiches and other food. 1837 WT I.

DOLMAN 1585. A *dolaman*, or Turkish robe; 1883, the jacket of a hussar, worn as a cape; 1872, a woman's sleeveless mantle. 1934, *Dolman sleeve* (wider at body than at wrist).

DOUBLE KNITTING (*1*) 1837. Tubular knitting on two needles. WT 1837.
(*2*) 1911. A 4 ply yarn resembling 3 ply wheeling but stronger and softer, twice the weight of fingering. *Weldon's Practical Knitter* 310 p 11.

DOWN LOOP An error caused by knitting involuntarily through the loops of two rows at once in the same wale. Aunt Kate 1896.

DRUGGET 1792. A Scottish dialect word for wool mixed with cotton, flax or silk. EDD.

DRUM See Thrum (S.W. England: EDD).

DUTCH COMMON KNITTING 1838. 'German method' of knitting plain, with the yarn carried on the left forefinger. WG.

DUTCH CORN KNITTING 1882. The German method of carrying the yarn on the left hand. CS. Probably an error for the above.

ÉCHARPE 1772. From French: a scarf or sash originally worn from shoulder to waist obliquely. Synonymous with *peplum*.

EIDER 1884. A soft woollen-spun yarn. EL.

EIS WOOL 1882. Fine glossy 2 ply worsted. CS.

ENCHANTER See Fascinator.

ESTERHAZY *c.*1843. *Worktable and Embroidery Frame Companion.* A lady's handbag style. Esterhazy was the name of the Hungarian princely family, several members of which were diplomats for the Austrian empire.

FAGGOT 1931. A fabric pattern constructed of overs

and decreases to produce eyelets. Taken from faggoting in embroidery, which originally meant that a group of threads was tied in the middle like a faggot of twigs. Grey, (Mrs Robin) D.E., *Evelyn knitting book* p 10.

FALSE CLUE 1881. A ball of yarn so wound that it unwinds from the centre. 'An old-fashioned way of winding wool'. E.M.Corbould *The Lady's knitting book*.

FANCHON 1872. A diagonally folded square, often knitted, used as a head covering. (Diminutive of Françoise).

FASCINATOR 1878. A light, soft headcovering with scarf-like hanging appendages at both sides.

FEATHER PATTERN 1837. Old Shale pattern. WT.

FILIÈRE 1844. A gauge for measuring the thickness of knitting needles. FL 12, 108.

FINGERING 1681. Earlier 'fingram', possibly from French *fin grain*. A finely spun worsted yarn, contrasted with the woollen-spun 'wheeling'.

FISH 1928. A Cornish word for a knitting sheath, dating from the 1880s or earlier. S.W. Paynter, *Old St Ives*.

FISHERMAN'S RIB 1955. The same as brioche. *People's Friend* 2.4.1955 p 15.

FLEECY 1842. Woollen-spun yarn from English sheep, chiefly Leicestershire, in various plies and colours. FL 36.

FLOAT 1863. From weaving. The carrying of yarn across the back or front of the fabric without weaving or knitting it in. (Sometimes called 'loop' by industrial machine knitters.)

FLOSS Shetland Floss was 2 ply loose-spun worsted.

FRANKLIN 1862. Cornish name for seaman's jersey. Corah of Leicester's Price Lists 1862 and 1896.

FRILEUSE 1844. A frileuse or neck tippet: a very short scarf. FL 106.

FROCK 1811. As a knitted garment, a frock is a sweater or gansey, worn by sailors in lieu of a shirt. Not exclusively of knitted garments (see OED for 'duck frock' etc.).

FROLIC 1818. US. A knitting party was called a knitting frolic.

FULLY FASHIONED The shaping of knitted fabric as it is being knitted (without subsequent cutting). 'Fashioning' appeared in machine-wrought hosiery *c.*1850. 'Fully fashioned' is a hosiery term of 1923–4 and later.

GANSEY/GANSER 1868. Gansey is dialectal from Shetland, Yorkshire and Suffolk. EDD. 'Ganser' was used in Bedfordshire and other areas. See 'Guernsey'.

GARTER STITCH 1840. Probably so called because

it was used at the top edge of a stocking, to prevent the natural curling at the edge of stockinet fabric. Used for garters. J. Gaugain *Lady's Assistant* (or *Lady's book*) 1840 p 1.

GAUFFRE FANS 1840. Pieces for a quilt. WT 62.

GENEVIEVE 1837. A head-dress. WT 114.

GERMAN WOOL 1837. The same as Berlin wool. WT.

GRAFTING 1880. Darning two knitted pieces together so that the join is invisible.

GRUB STITCH 1896. A fabric knitted on an even number of stitches, 3 rows of K1 P1 followed by one row of P1 K1. *Weldon's Practical Needlework* Vol XI No 132 p 3.

GUERNSEY 1832 Guernsey frock; 1835 guernsey shirt; 1836 guernsey. A jumper usually worn by a seaman, so called from its knitted fabric, also called 'guernsey' since the 16th century.

HAMBURGH WOOL 1842. German worsted. FL 59.

HAP 1724. A covering. Used in Shetland for a small shoulder shawl.

HEATHER 1819 Speckled; 1883 a marl yarn (from "heather mixture"); E. Lewis *Directions for knitting socks and stockings* p 30.

HIT AND MISS Single rib.

HOGGER 1681. A footless stocking or gaiter.

HUCKABACK STITCH 1838. Moss stitch. WG.

HUG-ME-TIGHT 1860. A close-fitting sleeveless waistcoat for a woman. Originally US.

ICE WOOL See Eis wool.

IKAT 1931. Fabric woven from tie-dyed yarn in a manner that produces patterns in the weave (Malay, 'tie'). Introduced by G.P. Rouffaer *Die Batik-Kunst* 1899. The fabric has been imitated in knitting (using differently coloured yarns) by Kaffe Fassett 1983.

INTAKE Decreasing. Scottish. Aunt Kate 1896.

INTARSIA 1863. An Italian term for decorative wood inlay; 1957 applied to multicoloured flat knitting in which a separate strand is used for each colour area, the fabric being held together by twisting the two yarns at every colour change, without stranding or weaving on the wrong side of the fabric.

JACKET This word goes back to the 15th century, and seems always to have meant a short coat (not long enough for the hem to be sat on) with sleeves, and opening at the front.

JACQUARD 1897. A term sometimes used, especially by the French, as a synonym for Fair Isle, meaning stranded multicolour knitting. Joseph Marie Jacquard (1752–1834) of Lyons invented an apparatus for weaving figured fabrics, and his name was transferred to machines for knitting figured fabrics.

JAZZ 1919. A type of bold and brightly coloured design, especially popular during the 1920s and early 1930s.

JERSEY (*1*) 1587. Stockinet fabric, such as was knitted in Jersey.

(*2*) 1836. A jumper or sweater.

JERSEY OR GUERNSEY DRESS 1879. Clinging dress of knitted silk or wool, down to mid-thigh and there often swathed in a broad sash: worn over a trainless knitted skirt. Seamless, or invisibly fastened at back. Sometimes worn for tennis.

JOHN THOMAS A slang word originally used for a flunkey, then transferred to the male organ, and eventually to a wooden dowell such as is sometimes used in looped or pile knitting. 1984 S. McGregor *Complete book of traditional Scandinavian knitting* 37, 155.

JUMPER 18th century: short closed coat with sleeves. Dr Johnson equated it with 'waistcoat'. 1853 for sport and travel. US: a woman's pinafore dress.

KHAKI 1848. Urdu/Persian 'dusty'.

KNICKERBOCKER STOCKING 1859. Named from the clothing of the knickerbockers (Dutch immigrants) of New York state.

KNIT-AND-SEAM Ribbing. Cumberland. EDD.

KNITTING WW II sailors' slang for 'girls'. (Singular form: 'piece of knitting'.)

KNITTING BEE 1855. A knitting party. US.

KNITTING NEEDLE 1597. Florio's Italian dictionary.

KNITTING PIN 1580. Essex MS (C.W. & P. Cunnington *Handbook of English dress in the 16th century* p 88).

KNITTING PRICKS 1595. Knitting needles.

KNITTING SHEATH 1755.

KNOT (*1*) 1540. A measure of yarn; a hank. The length varied with the material.

(*2*) 1655. A purl stitch: used for counting purls. NE.

(*3*)1756. Any stitch. Richard Rolt *A new dictionary of trade*.

LADDER 1922. The effect of a dropped stitch in knitwear, which causes the wale to unlock its loops, producing a runged effect.

LADY BETTY WOOL 1843. A fine soft fleecy woollen yarn, originally in white only. The finest knitting yarn of the early 19th century. Possibly named after Lady Betty Germain (1680–1769) whose spinning wheels are still kept at Knole in Kent. FL79.

LAMB'S WOOL 1836. A soft, fine, woollen-spun yarn, not necessarily from the wool of lambs.

LOOP (*1*) 1837. An over. WT 110.

(*2*) 1756. A stitch. Richard Rolt *A new dictionary of trade*.

LOUGHRAM 1951. A long stocking without feet. Similar to Scottish *loag*. W. Yorkshire 19th cent. HI 33.

MADRAS YARN 1884. A wool/silk mixture. EL.

MAGYAR Late 19th century. Sleeve and body made in one piece.

MANCHETTE 1845. A detached sleeve. WT 77.

MARL 1892. A yarn of two or more plys of different colour, giving a mottled effect. From *marble(d)*.

MANTILLA 1886. Used by Mlle Riego of an elaborate cape. *Winter Book for 1886*.

MASK, MASH, MESH 1655. Stitch or loop. NE.

MASQUERADED 1678. An as yet unidentified coloured pattern, sometimes of stockings.

MATINÉE (COAT) (*1*) 1851. A woman's lingerie jacket.

(*2*) 1913. A baby's coat for outdoor wear. J.A. Fleming *Common-sense knitting* p 91; but not widely used before the late 1920s, when it first appeared in *Woolcraft* with the 8th edition.

MAZANIELLO CAP 1840. Masaniello (pronounced with a voiced *s*) was the nickname of Tommaso Niello (1620–47), who led a Neapolitan revolt against the Spaniards in 1647. A byword for boldness. The cap was vertically striped and cylindrical; with a high turned up rim, striped horizontally; and a round flat crown with a tassel. WT 15.

MAZARIN(E) 1689. A form of hood (later a shoulder cape) said to have been named after Hortense Mancini, Duchesse de Mazarin (1646–99).

MITRE 1882. A gusset, especially at the instep of a stocking.

MOGGAN, MOGGIN EDD Scotland, Staffordshire. A footless stocking; a stocking used as a purse. *Gardy-moggan*, a sleeve of the same shape.

MOHAIR 1570. Arabic *makhayyar*. The fleece of a Turkish goat.

MOSAIC KNITTING 1970. A fabric of garter stitch or stockinet, worked in two colours, using a single colour for each couple of rows, slipping stitches in the second colour so as to produce a two-coloured pattern on the right side of the fabric. Invented by Barbara Walker and described by her in *A treasury of knitting patterns* (1968), but not named until *A second treasury* (1970).

MOSS STITCH 1844. A fabric in which single plain and purl stitches alternate both vertically and horizontally. WT 52, 36.

MUFFATEE (*1*) 1707. A neck warmer (not knitted). (*2*) 1807. Knitted wrist warmers.

NAIL A measure of length for cloth: 6 cm (2¼ in. or the sixteenth part of a yard). Dating from 15th century at least and still occasionally used until about 1840. (1840 WG 2nd ed.)

NARROW 1837. To decrease. WT.

NIANTIC 1886. The Niantic were a small tribe of Algonquins in southwestern Rhode Island. After King Philip's War 1675–6, between English colonists and Philip, alias Metacomet, chief of the Wampanoags, the Niantic amalgamated with the surviving Narraganset, whose name they took. Their own name was given to a town in southern Connecticut. Niantic hose is machine-made, with similar pouches for seamless heel and toe. It has been imitated for hand knitting (*Weldon's Practical Stocking Knitter* First series Vol I No 11, 1886; *Weldon's Practical Knitter* 104th series Vol 32 No 381, 1917)

NIDDY-NODDY 1890. A T-shaped wooden instrument held in the hand for skeining and measuring wool.

NORFOLK 1866. A belted, loosely fitting jacket.

NYLON 1938. Synthetic polyamide yarn invented by Du Pont Co.

OPEN STITCH 1840. An over, or the eyelet created by it. J. Gaugain *Lady's assistant* I.

ORNÉ 1858. 'The Orné knitting ball consists of beautifully coloured threads of fine wool knotted at equal lengths, each knot terminating one row; and this, when knitted up, produces the . . . elegant design (of a bouquet of flowers)' *The Family Friend* 1858 p 16.

OSTRICH WOOL 1884. A yarn of silky appearance 'forming natural rings'. EL 9.

OUTLET *c*.1898. Increase. Scottish. Aunt Kate, 1896.

OVER (*1*) 1842. To turn over, or bring the yarn to the near-side of the work.
(*2*) 1915. Make one. Said by Mary Thomas 1938 to be the old term: derived from 'yarn over needle'. Klickmann *Modern knitting book* 1915 p 1.

PALETOT 1840. A short, loose-fitting coat, buttoned at the front. Nowadays, a loose overcoat. Origin unknown, but the word is French and associated with Middle English *pattok*.

PARTRIDGE 1882. Mottled in colour. CS.

PASHMINA 1880. Kashmir shawl-wool. From Persian *pashm*, wool.

PATENT KNITTING 1882. From a German name for brioche knitting. 'The old-fashioned name for brioche knitting'. CS.

PATTERN 1837. A pattern of stitches producing a particular kind of fabric. WT 98.
1837. A recipe for a garment. WT.

PATTI KNITTING 1881. Blackberry or Trinity stitch. Presumably named after one of two singers, the Hispano-English Adelina Patti 1843-1919 or the Italian Carlotta Patti 1835–89. E.M.Corbould *The Lady's knitting book* 3.50.

PEERIE Small (Shetland dialect).

PELERINE 1744. Various forms of mantle or cape, especially a tippet with ends coming down to a point in front.

PEPLUM 1893. From the Greek *peplos*, originally a shawl or scarf, synonymous with *écharpe*. By the 1890s it had come to mean a very short skirt or flounce attached to the lower edge of a coat or blouse.

PETTICOAT From the 15th century onwards the same thing as a waistcoat at that time: a short undercoat with sleeves and with or without a buttoned front, worn by both sexes. From the 17th century onwards 'petticoat' comes to mean an underskirt, made with or without a top. During the 18th century, both meanings can be found.

PETTICOAT FINGERING 1884. A soft worsted yarn developed about 1880. EL.

PICK UP 1655. To use loops of knitting already done as the first loops of new wales or courses. EN.

PICOT 1925. Picot knitting, a method of knitting coarse lace, is described as new in *Weldon's Practical Knitter* 147th series (No 475). Picot (French 'prick' or 'point') is recorded as a term in English needlework from 1882.

PIXIE HOOD 1938. A cap made by folding a rectangle of stuff in half and sewing together the two halves of one edge to make a simple pointed cap, usually tied under the chin by strings or tapes fastened at the two corners. Patons knitting pattern 1938.

PLAIN 1655. Stitch drawn through from the back to the front of the fabric, leaving the bight of the base loop to form a purl on the reverse side of the fabric. NE.

POINT NOUÉ 1875. A fabric pattern: from the lace of the same name. French 'knotted'. E.M.Corbould *The Lady's knitting book* Vol III p 50.

POLKA 1844. A woman's tight-fitting jacket, usually knitted. From the jacket worn for the Bohemian dance called a polka, introduced to London in 1842: originally danced in Prague in 1835. *Polka* is Czech 'half-step'.

PONCHO 1748. American-Spanish from Araucanian. A large square cloth with a hole in the middle, worn over the head. Used as a term in English 20th century fashion 1967.

PRANG 1985. Knitting needle (Devon). RC 40.

PRICK 1597. Knitting needle.

PULLED-BACK WOOL 1944. Previously knitted and unravelled yarn. *Stitchcraft* 1944 10-11. 1.

PULLOVER 1921. A casual jersey or sweater, usually with sleeves. The sleeveless form appeared in 1919 and became popular in the early 1930s, but the word was in common use for the sleeved form until the 1950s.

PURL, PEARL 1655. Stitch drawn through its base loop from front to back of the fabric, leaving the bight of the base loop on the front of the fabric as a raised purling. NE.

PYRENEAN WOOL 1847. Harsher but firmer than Shetland yarn. J. Gaugain; book title.

QUIRK 1547. The clock of a stocking. The word is English but is first known in Wales, where it survives as a term in knitting. Also used of the tiny gussets used in the construction of gloves.

RAGLAN 1857. Raglan cape, distinguished by the cut of the sleeve. (HEC 217.) Named after Lord Raglan (1788–1855). Described as a new style in knitting, *Needlework for all* 45 (December 1913) p 133.

RAISE (*1*) 1850. Increase by knitting twice into one stitch. Slater's *Ladies' worktable book*.

(*2*) 1896. Increase by raising a stitch in the row below that being knitted for the row in question. H.P. Ryder *Cycling and shooting knickerbocker stockings* p 6.

RAYON 1924. Regenerated cellulose.

RECEIPT Instruction or description for making a piece or garment. Earlier (from Chaucer's time) used in cooking and pharmacy. See 'recipe'. Occasionally used for knitting.

RECIPE See Receipt.

RHINEGRAVE *c*1660. Rhinegrave breeches or petticoat breeches were the beribboned trunks and/or knee length skirt popular in England *c*.1660–66; named after Karl Florentin, Rheingraf von Salm. Also the stockings (often with falling lace over the garters) worn with the breeches.

RIB (*1*) 1829. A wale of plain knitting against purl wales, or vice versa. See ribbed.

(*2*) 1838. A purl stitch. WT.

RIBBED 1789. A fabric composed of ribs.

RIG AND FUR (RIDGE AND FURROW) A dialect description of ribbing. EDD.

ROO 1612. To pluck wool from a sheep by running the fingers through its fleece.

ROUGHCAST STITCH 1838. Moss stitch. WG.

ROUND 1655. A course in round or tubular knitting. NE.

ROW 1800. A course in flat knitting (which is turned to work alternate courses). Marie Edgeworth *The parent's assistant* (ed 3) II.79.

RUN (*1*) 1878. A measure of woollen yarns: 1600 yards.

(*2*) 1878 To unravel, especially of a wale.

RUTLAND YARN 1884. Very fine, for hosiery. Doubtless originating in the county of Rutland. EL.

SCOGGER 1615. A footless stocking worn as a gaiter or on the forearm; also a stocking foot worn over a boot to prevent slipping on ice.

SCYE 1825. The armhole of a garment, into which the sleeve is inserted. (Of Scottish dialectical origin.)

SEAM 1655. Purl stitch. So called because a wale of purl stitches was used to simulate a seam up the back of a stocking. NE.

SEAMEN'S IRON 1985. Strong, dark blue 5 ply worsted yarn as used for making seamen's jerseys. RC 63.

SEMMIT 1456. An undershirt. By the nineteenth century principally a Scottish word.

SHANK 1546. A stocking, especially the leg part, while being knitted. Scottish. Hence 'shanker', a stockingmaker.

SHAWL 1662. From Persian *shal*. Originally a woven scarf used as a sash or turban by Muslims, especially in Kashmir. It was used in England as a drape by women in the later 18th century. Knitted shawls were being made by the time knitting books appeared in the late 1830s.

SHEATH 1753.

SHELL 1962. A miniature sleeveless sweater from America. The word was popular in Britain 1967–8 (See *Stitchcraft*.)

SHETLAND WOOL 1842. A 2ply soft-handling yarn, originally in natural colours only, finer than fingering, but thicker than Pyrenean. Not always from Shetland sheep. See WW 359. C. Mee *Manual of knitting* 93.

SHIRT The word is Old English. It originally meant a garment for the upper part of the body, worn next to the skin. The 'undershirt' or 'vest' developed in the 17th century and later. A knitted shirt is a 'waistcoat' or jumper, and the word appears in compound names for knitted outerwear such as 'bridal shirt' (said to be Cornish) and 'sea shirt' (said to be used in Aran).

SHRINK 1655. Knit two together. NE.

SICILIAN YARN 1884. EL.

SKIN WOOL 1792. Wool taken from the skin of a dead sheep. Redhead et al. *Observations on the different breeds*.

SLICKER 1884. Originally US, meaning a waterproof overcoat, usually orange or yellow. Used in UK for a knitted jacket without buttons in the 1960s.

SLIP (loop or stitch) 1837. To pass a loop from one needle to another without knitting it. WT.

SLIPOVER 1936. A sleeveless pullover. The most popular name for this garment from the 1960s onwards.

SLOPPY-JOE 1942. A loosely fitting sleeved jumper. US 1942; UK 1952.

SONTAG 1844. A head cloth, also called cephaline. From German 'Sunday'. A trapezoid shape with a white border, finished with ribbons and tassels. FL 27.

SPENCER 1803. A close-fitting jacket or bodice, commonly worn by women and children. From John George, second Earl Spencer (1758–1834), who wore a double-breasted overcoat, short waisted.

SPOTTED KNITTING 1882. A term sometimes used for Trinity stitch. CS.

SPOTTED FROCKS 1830. Two-coloured gansies, probably with single stitches alternating in colour both vertically and horizontally. See HI 119.

STIRRUP HOSE 1632. Long over-stockings or gaiters, without soles but with a strap or 'stirrup' under the foot. See C. Willett Cunnington & Phillis Cunnington *Handbook of English costume in the 17th century* 1966 p 65.

STITCH (*1*) 1599. A loop.

(*2*) 1624. A style or pattern in needlework generally.

STOCKINET (Stockingette, Stockinette) 1824. Stocking stitch fabric, plain one side and purl the other.

STRAITEN 1655. To decrease. NE.

SWEATER 1882. A jumper, jersey or gansey. Earlier used in plural for whole suit of clothes. Used for women's jerseys in US before 1896. *Knitter's circular and monthly record* December 1896.

SWIFT 1564. A rotating reel or wheel, usually of expandable diameter, used for winding yarn.

SWISS DARNING 1876. A. Floyer *Plain knitting and mending*. A classroom poster 1883 states that the method was known in English village schools before 1826. Originally a method of darning over worn parts of stockinet by duplicating the knitted structure; later used for decoration.

TACK 1903. Cornish. A flat oval piece of card or leather with two holes punched in it on the long axis. A tape is passed through these holes and tied round the waist so that the part of the tape across the centre of the tack is outside. The tack functions as a knitting sheath when a needle is thrust under this centre part of the tape and twisted to give it a holding tension. *The Woman's Library* II 299. From the earliest sense of the word, meaning 'attachment'. (Fig. 97.)

TAM-O'SHANTER 1840-50. A flat bonnet, like a beret but with a circumference about twice that of the head. Originally a Scottish labourer's bonnet. Named after the eponymous hero of a poem by Robert Burns written in 1790.

TANK TOP 1968. A pullover with a deep neck hole and narrow shoulder straps, popular in the 1960s and 1970s. From the earlier *tank suit*, an American word for a one-piece swimsuit with similar neck and armholes (1959).

TARTAN KNITTING 1886. *Catalogue of the International Exhibition of Industry, Science and Art* Edinburgh. 2017.

TEMPLAR CAP 1892. A balaclava helmet. C.T. Dent *Mountaineering* p 48.

TENSION (*1*) 1877. Tension device on a sewing machine.

(*2*) 1896. Paton's *Collection* mentions the principle of tension of the yarn controlling the size of the loop, but not the word. The principle is not commonly mentioned in patterns till the mid 1920s. See F. Klickman *Popular knitting book p 3* (1921).

THRUM 1535. Short ends of yarn, used for knitting into a fabric to produce a pile. Halliwell's dictionary 1847 equates the past participle with 'knitted'.

TIDY (*1*) 1828. A bag in which to keep scraps, odds-and-ends, small objects.

(*2*) 1850. An antimacassar.

TIPPEE 1985. A Yorkshire word for the Scottish 'wisker'. RC 63.

TOP 1949. A garment for the upper body, at first simple, informal and for women. Increasingly used from the 1960s.

TOPCROOK 1951. A metal ring, or half ring with a plate across the ends in which a hook or smaller ring was fastened to a swivel. It was used to attach the knitted work-in-progress to the body and relieve the weight on the needles. HI 35.

TOPSTRING 1951. An S-shaped hook used for the same purpose as a top crook. HI 17.

TRAILS 1985. Ribbed welts. RC 38.

TRICHINOPOLY WORK 1865. A form of gold or silver filigree work done at Tiruchirapalli in Madras State (formerly referred to as Trichinopoly), which sometimes produced the structure of a knitted fabric or knitted cord.

TUNISIAN STITCH A technique found in 19th-century Balkan footwear, making an over for every loop and slipping the loop in one row, knitting loop and over together in the next row. De Dillmont *Encyclopaedia of needlework c.1930*.

TURN (*1*) 1837. Two rows of knitting. WT 1837, 110.

(*2*) 1882. To turn the heel of a stocking.

(*3*) To turn the work before completing a row.

(*4*) 1838. To take the yarn between the needles.

TURNED STITCH 1655. A purl stitch. NE.

TWIN PIN A 'circular' (double-ended with flexible centre part) needle. Term in use by 1975.

TWINSET 1937. A woman's matching jumper and cardigan.

UHLAN CAP 1902. A type of Balaclava helmet. The Uhlan (ultimately from Turkish *oglan* 'a young man') was a light cavalryman in semi-oriental uniform, originally Polish, later used in the Prussian army. H. Warleigh *Ladies' work for sailors*.

UNDER 1837. To take under: knit into the back of the stitch. WT 111.

VAMPEY *c.*1225. An ankle-length stocking, or the foot part of a stocking. Also *vamp, vampany, vampy*.

VANDYKE *c.*1755. An edging with deeply cut triangular points, after the collars depicted in portraits by Sir Antony Vandyke (1599–1641).

VARENS 1784. Fisherman's blouse; 1872 jacket. Probably from French *vareuse* (1784). HEC 434.

VESEAT 1852. A shawl with tiny sleeves. From French *visite*.

VEST 1613. A robe or vest. In the 17th century meant a man's waistcoat. In 1851 it also means an undervest.

VEST WOOL 1884. Similar to Scotch fingering, but given a softer finish. EL.

VICTORIA WOOL 1882. Andalusian wool. CS.

VICTORINE 1849. A tippet, originally of fur, fastened at the throat with two pendant ends.

WAGER WELT or ALL FOOLS' WELT 1943. Garter stitch with one row in eight purled. MT 24. So called because it is difficult to guess how many rows are purled.

WAISTCOAT (*1*) 1519. A garment (with or without sleeves) covering the body above the waist. Usually of fine appearance and intended to be partly visible when worn. Not always open at the front. The same as a 'petticoat', shaped like a modern vest.

(*2*) 1711. A plain woollen garment, worn chiefly for extra warmth, and not necessarily visible. From 19th century always buttoned at the front and no longer like a modern vest.

WALE 1583. Originally a ridge or raised line on hose. In industrial machine knitting a vertical column of stitches, running perpendicular to the rows or rounds.

WATCHCAP 1911. A knitted close-fitting navy blue cap worn by enlisted men in the US navy in cold or storm.

WATCHET 1198. Light blue or sea-blue.

WELT (*1*) 1506. A strip used as binding, border or hem, whether knitted or not.

(*2*) 1838. A knitted welt. WG.

WHEELING 1808. A coarse woollen-spun yarn, usually 3 ply. See WW 359.

WHISK (WHISKER, WISKER) A horsehair-filled pad for anchoring the inert knitting-needle to a Shetlander's belt. Originally a bunch of straw. *Scottish studies* III pt 2 (1959) 223–5.

WHITE STITCH 1938. A plain stitch, so called because it was indicated by a white square on a pattern chart. MT 50.

WIRE 1774. Knitting needle. Chiefly Scottish, but also Northern English. Probably much older than 18th century.

WOOLLEN (SPUN) YARN 1886. Wool spun from fibres that have been combed but not carded. Soft, bulky, light yarn. S.W. Beck *Draper's dictionary* 373.

WOOLLY 1899. A knitted outer garment.

WORSTED (WASSIT, WORSET) 1455. Tightly spun, smooth yarn (from Worsted, Norfolk). The fibres are combed after being carded. Worsted yarn was being spun and woven by the 13th century. In the 19th century 'worsted' meant knitting yarn – a usage that continued among old people in country districts till the middle of the 20th century.

WYLIECOAT 1478. An undergarment or shirt. See waistcoat, petticoat. Scottish and northern.

YARN The word goes back to Old English, meaning a spun thread; but in the seventeenth and eighteenth centuries it was sometimes used to describe coarse or woollen spun yarn, in contrast to worsted. See Defoe *Everybody's business* (1725).

ZEPHYR (*1*) 1838. A soft shawl for a baby. WG 268. Also applied to various light articles of clothing during the 19th century, including an athlete's vest.

(*2*) 1845. Also Zephyr merino, Zephyr Germantown: soft, dense, 4 ply woollen yarn, mostly manufactured in Scotland to resemble Berlin wool. FL 52.

ZEPHYRINE 1838. 'A very convenient thing to lie over the head instead of a bonnet, especially in travelling and is generally knit of two colours'. An oblong of fabric, gathered at the ends and tied with ribbons under the chin. WG 267.

ZOUAVE 1848. Short jacket, usually embroidered. From the uniform of a French military corps originally raised from the Algerian tribe of Zouaoua (Zwawa).

English knitting literature

A check list of works published before 1910. The date given is of the first known impression. A second date indicates a significantly different edition. Most anonymous works are entered under the publishers' names (pub).

I Books and Cards

A'Beckett, Miss	*Companion to the Berlin Wool House* 1848
Anon	*A guide to knitting, netting and crochet* 1844
	Knitting and crochet lace edgings 1850?
	Knitter's notebook 1890
	Needlework panorama of knitting, etc 1852
	Swiss darning 1883
Aylott & James (pub)	*The knitted stocking and sock book* 2nd ed. 1847
Banks, Mrs G. Linnaeus	*The lace knitter's intelligible guide* 1st series 1847
Baynes, Mrs Godfrey John	*The knitted lace collar receipt book* 1846; second series 1846; third series 1847
	The album of fancy needlework parts I, II, & III 1847; part IV 1848
	The knitted lace chemisette & stomacher receipt book 1847
	The young mother's scrap book 1847
	The Berlin wool home and opera cap receipt book 1849
Beeton, Samuel Orchard	*Beeton's book of needlework* 1870
Bohn (pub)	*The ladies' worktable book* 1852 (see also Slater)
Brietzcke, Helen K. and Rooper, Emily F.	*A manual of collected lessons in plain needlework & knitting for use in elementary schools* 1885
Burrell, Mrs J.	*Knitted lace edgings* 1845; second series 1846; third series 1846
Butterick Publishing Co	*The art of knitting* 1892
	Fancy & practical knitting 1897
C, R.J. (See Cattlow, Rachel Jane)	
Carter, Mr W.	*The Royal Victoria knitting book* c.1851–2 (13 numbers)
	The Royal Exhibition knitting, netting & crochet book c.1852 (12 numbers?)
	The Princess Royal knitting and crochet book c.1852
Cassell (pub)	*The ladies' drawing-room book* 1852
	The ladies' work book (Part II of the above) 1852
Cattlow, Rachel Jane	*Directions for plain knitting for the working classes and schools* 1846
Caulfeild, S.F.A., & Saward, Blanche C.	*The dictionary of needlework* 1882
Chardin, Miss	*The lady's repository of receipts* c.1850
Clarke, H.G. (pub)	*The ladies' handbook of knitting, netting & crochet* 1842; 2nd series 1842
	The young ladies' worktable & embroidery frame manual 1843
Cooper, Marie Jane	*The new guide to knitting and crochet* 1847
Copley, Mrs Esther	*The comprehensive knitting book* 1849
Corbould, Elvina M. (EMC)	*The lady's knitting book* 1874; 2nd series 1875; 3rd series 1875; 4th series 1875.
	The lady's work book 1st series 1876
	Mother's knitter 1882
	The useful knitter Part I 1887; Part II 1887
	The knitter's note book 1890
	Directions for knitting drawers 1884
	The knitting teacher's assistant 1877
Cox & Co	*Victoria knitting cards* 1885

Cressy, Miss	*Instruction cards for knitting socks and stockings c.* 1880?
Cupples, Mrs George (Anne Jane)	*The stocking knitter's manual* 1867
	A knitting-book of counterpanes 1871
Curtis, A E	*Selfhelp knitting cards* 1884
Darton (pub)	*The ladies' worktable book* 1842 (3rd ed. 1846, 5th ed. 1848)
De Barras, E.	*Plain and fancy knitting* (Nutshell series) 1896
De La Hamelin, Rigolette	*The royal magazine of knitting, netting, crochet and fancy needlework* 1865?
Dillmont, Thérèse de	*Encyclopaedia of needlework* 1886
Dorinda	*Needlework for ladies for pleasure and profit* 1882
Dufour, Madame	*Ladies' album for the work table or gift book for 1849*
Edwards, Mrs M.A.	*The ladies' cabinet of knitted insertion lace and zephyr wool collars* 1846
	The lady's cabinet of French designs for insertion lace cuffs, edgings and collars 1846
Edwards, Mrs M.J.	*A new guide to knitting* (Birmingham) 1850?
Elliott, M.	*The book of hats and caps* 1890
Elise, Madame	*Madame Elise's crochet & knitting winter book* 1864
Fairfax knitting cards	See Cox & Co *Victoria knitting cards*
Faudel & Phillips (pub)	*Six Shetland shawls c.*1853
Finchley Manuals	*Finchley manual of industry III: Needlework* 1851?
Flohr, Apolline	*The German Christmas Eve* 1847
Floyer, Mrs A (or Mrs L.S.)	*Needle drill, position drill & knitting pin drill* (1881)
	Plain knitting and mending in six standards 1876
	Stocking knitting made easy 1899
Foster, J.	*Instructions for knitting a sock and stockings* 1884
Gaugain, Jane	(Unidentified patterns 1836 and 1837)
	The Lady's assistant 1840
	Appendix to the lady's assistant 1840
	The lady's assistant, second volume 1842
	Accompaniment to the second volume 1844
	The lady's assistant Vol III 1846?
	(*The lady's assistant* in 12 parts 1863; 1 volume 1875)
	Miniature knitting, netting and crochet book 1843
	The knitter's friend 1846
	Knitting book of Turkish, Pyrenees & Shetland shawls and scarfs 1847
	Knit polka book 1847
	Open knit d'oyley book No 1 1847
	Pyrenees & Shetland knits shawl and scarf book 1847
	Book of novelties in knitting and crochet 1849
	The book of knitted veils 1854
Giles, Mrs J.W.	*The gift netting, knitting and crochet book c.*1850
Gill, Thomas (pub. Easingwold)	*The handbook of knitting* 1845?
Girardin, Mme Marie, with Mrs Warren & Mrs Pullan	*Elegant work for delicate fingers* 1861
Gore, Mrs J.B.	*The Royal Shetland shawl, lace collar, Brighton slipper and China purse receipt book* 1846
Goubaud, Madame Adolphe	*Knitting and netting patterns* 1870
Goulden, C.	*Needlework and knitting drills* 1895
'Grandmother'	*Cottager's comforts and other recipes in knitting* 1887
Green, Agnes	*The knitted curtain receipt book* 1847
Hartree, Miss	*My knitted collar book* 1846
Hatchard, J., & Sons (pub)	*The knitting teacher's assistant* 1838 (new edition by E.M. Corbould 1877)
Head (pub)	*St Andrew's series c.*1900
	Highlander series n.d.
Heath, F.	*Invariable stocking scale* 1881

Herbert, Mrs	*The Christmas book of crochet, knitting & braid* 1848
Hope, Mr & Mrs George Curling	*The knitter's friend* 1842
	Book of babies' wardrobe in knitting & netting 1844
	The knitter's casket 1847
	Knitting book for polka dresses 1847
	The prize knitting book 1848
	The Ramsgate book of knitted lace edgings 1848
	The Ramsgate knitting book 1848
	My working friend 2nd ed.
Ingram, G.	*Ingram's Exhibition knitting & crochet book* 1854
Isobel	*Isobel's plain needlework* 1893
J., C.E.A.	*The floral knitting book . . . imitations of natural flowers* 1847
	Berries and fruit knitting book c.1848
Jackson, Mrs Elizabeth	*The practical companion to the work table* 1844
	The polka book 1849
James, T.M.	*Longman's complete course of needlework, knitting and cutting out* 1901
Jevons & Mellor (pub)	*No 3 knitting instructions* 1850?
Johnstone, Hunter (pub)	*The home knitter* 1876; 2nd series 1877 (See also Cupples)
Johnston, W. & A.K.	*Sewing and knitting designs* 1901
K., A.E.	*The Creeve knitting card* 1885/1895
Kate, Aunt	*Aunt Kate's knitting & crochet book* 1896
(Helen Greig Souter)	New and revised edition *c*.1901
	Aunt Kate's homework c.1907
Kelly, F.G.	*The lady's knitting book*, 4th ed 1848
Lady, A	*The knitter's cabinet* 1848
Lady, A	*The workwoman's guide* 1838
Lady, A	*The home knitter* (see Johnstone, Hunter)
Lady Manager, A	*The standard guide to knitting according to the code* (1870)
Lambert, Frances	*The hand-book of needlework* 1843; 2nd series 1845
	My knitting book 1843; 2nd series 1845
	The ladies' pocket book of knitting 1847
Lambton, Miss	*The ladies' pocket book of useful and ornamental knitting* 1847
Le Boutillier, E. & J.	*Third series of Parisian antimacassars* 1871
Lewis, E.	*Directions for knitting socks & stockings* 1883
	Wools and how to use them 1884
Loch, Miss Sophy	*The book of 'Hows'* 1900
	The second book of 'Hows' 1902
London Lace Paper & Valentine Company	*New series of Berlin patterns* c1880
Marsland (pub)	*The favourite crochet, knitting, netting & embroidery book* 1853
Mee, Cornelia	*Companion to the worktable* 1844
	Manual of knitting, netting and crochet 1842
	Exercises in knitting 1846
	Polka jackets in knitting and crochet 1848
	Comforts for the sick and wounded (Queen's winter book 2) 1869?
	Alliance book of knitting, netting and crochet 1856
	Manual of needlework 1854
Mee, Cornelia and Austin, Mary	*Worktable magazine* 1847
	Knitter's companion 1 1861
	Knitter's companion 2 1862
	Knitter's companion 3 (Queen's winter knitting book) 1862
	Knitter's companion 4 (Queen's winter knitting book) 1869

	Novelties in needlework 1 1869
	Novelties in needlework 2 1869
	Novelties in needlework 3 1870?
	Manual of knitting 1860
	Manual of knitting. 2nd series
	Bijou receipts for baby's wardrobe (2 series) 1869
	12 Bijou receipts for knitting and crochet 1875
Miland, John (pub)	*The ladies' knitting and netting book 1837* (by Miss Watts)
Missions to Seamen	*Ladies' work for sailors* 1902 (see Warleigh, H.)
Mitchell, C. (pub)	*The worktable & embroidery frame companion c.*1842
Myra (Mrs Matilda Browne)	*Myra's knitting books* 1889 etc.
	No 1 Myra's knitting lessons: rudiments
	No 2 Myra's knitting books: stocking knitting
National Society for Promoting the Education of the Poor	*Instructions on needlework* 1832
	The knitting teacher's assistant ?1838 (see Hatchard)
Owen, Mrs Henry	*The illuminated ladies' book of useful and ornamental needlework* 1844
	The handbook of knitting 1845
Parisian Lady, A	*The lady's cabinet of French designs* 1850?
Pullan, Mrs	*The lady's dictionary of needlework* 1856
Riego de la Branchardiere, Eleanore	*Knitting, crochet and netting* 1846
	The knitting book 1847
	The winter book for 1848
	Comforts for the Crimea or the fourth winter book 1854
	The child's winter knitting book 1857
	The winter knitting book for 1859
	The Andalusian knitting and netting book 1860
	The book of 12-ply Siberian wool 1860
	Mélange de laine for Siberian and Leviathan wools 1861
	The winter book for 1862
	The useful knitting book 1864
	The Abergeldie winter book 1867
	A new wool book 1869
	The winter book for 1886
	Selected works ed. Mrs Rivers Turnbull 1904–5
Ring, Mrs R.	*The Highbury handbook of useful and ornamental needlework* 1848
Rogers, Mrs Dresser	*The Regal knitted collar book* 1847
Ronaldson, Miss	*Gift book of useful and ornamental knitting . . .* 1885
	The lady's book of useful and ornamental knitting and netting work 1853
Rosevear, Elizabeth	*A textbook of needlework, knitting and cutting out: with methods of teaching* 1893, 1894, 1894, 1902, 1904
	Needlework, knitting and cutting out for older girls 1894
	A manual of needlework, knitting and cutting out for evening continuation schools 1894
Ryder, Miss E.	*How to knit socks* (4 cards) 1863; revised 1876
	How to knit stockings (4 cards) 1865
	How to knit spun-silk socks & stockings (4 cards) 1876
Ryder, Miss H.P.	*Children's comforts and how to knit them* 1866
	Winter comforts and how to knit them (4 cards) 1876
	How to knit the 'Richmond' glove
	Cycling and shooting knickerbocker stockings 1896
Savage, Mrs William	*The Winchester fancy needlework instructor* 1846; 3rd ed. 1847
	Gems of knitting and crochet 1847
	The knitted paletot 1850

	Polka jacket book 1850
Scrivenor, M. Elliott	*Paton's knitting and crocheting book* 1896
Shearman, Mrs	*Her Ladyship's knitting book* 1909
Slater (pub)	*The ladies' worktable book* 3rd ed. 1850
Smith, Elder (pub)	*The handbook of useful and ornamental amusements* 1845
Sylvia	*Book of designs in knitting* 1882
Symonds, J Henry (pub)	*The lady's book of knitting and crochet* 1875
T., M., and T., H.	*Pearsall's illustrated handbook for knitting in silks* 1899; (7th ed. 1906)
Thomson, C. & W.	*The knitted lace pattern book* 1850?
	The knitting and crochet work book 1st series
	The knitting and crochet work book 2nd series
Tranter and Adams	*Roumanian knitting cards* 1891
Valentine, Mrs	*The home book for young ladies*
Waite, M.	*Knitting cards for standards III and IV* 1891
Walker, Mrs	*The book of fancy knitting* 1860s?
	The book of knitted lace
	The cabinet of knitted lace
Wallis, Arthur	*The Brighton knitting book* 1846
	The new knitter 1868
	16 fancy-work designs 1869
	Treasures in needlework (with Mrs Pullan) 1855
Warleigh, Henrietta F.R.A.	*Knitting for everyone* 1880?
	Full directions and scales for knitting socks 1883
	Full directions and scales for knitting gloves 1883
	Full directions and scales for knitting edgings 1884?
	Full directions for knitting circles 1885
	Ladies' work for sailors 1902
Watts, Misses	*The ladies' knitting and netting book* 1837 (anonymous till fifth edition 1840. See Miland). Second series 1840; third series 1843
	Selections of knitting, netting and crochet work 1843
	The illustrated knitting, netting and crochet book 1845
Webb and Millington (pub)	*The handbook of plain and fancy knitting* 1860?
Weldon (pub)	*Weldon's practical shilling guide to needlework* c.1875
Wells, Mrs	*New knitting book* 1878
Wood, J.T. (pub)	*Knitting and crochet book for the million* 1852
'The Young Emigrant', Authoress of	*The industrial handbook Part II* 1853/1856
The Young Ladies' Journal	*Complete guide to the work table* 1884

II Periodical publications

Listed in chronological order of first knitting items.

The magazine of domestic economy: Feb 1843
The lady's newspaper and pictorial times 1847–1863
The worktable magazine (Mee & Austin) 1847
The ladies' needlework penny magazine 1848–9
The royal magazine (Rigolette de la Hamelin) 1848–9
The family friend (patterns by Warren and Pullan) 1849–
The lady's album of fancy work 1849–50 Grant & Griffith
The household friend 1849–
The ladies' companion and monthly magazine. Bradley 1851–7

The needle (Riego) 1852–4
The governess 1855–7 (patterns by Pullan)
The ladies' treasury 1859–95 (Mrs Warren)
The Queen 1861–
Weldon's practical needlework 1886
Leach's practical fancy work basket 1886
Leach's penny knitter 1892
Needlecraft practical journal 1903
Needlecraft monthly magazine 1907

The oldest extant English knitting pattern (see page 83)

'The order how to knit a hose' is printed in *Natura Exenterata: or Nature Unbowelled*, a medical compendium printed in London in 1655, 417–19. The original is printed as a single sentence, punctuated erratically with commas, and containing several errors. I have punctuated it into sentences and paragraphs, modernizing the spelling and italicizing the words and subtitles that I have added to the text.

The vocabulary includes 'mask' for stitch, and five words for purl: turned stitch, knot, knotted stitch, seam stitch and purl. The pattern is not skilfully recorded and would produce an ungainly stocking, though the clock is interesting. The mirror effect in paired decreases is well understood. The heel is made, as was often done in Tudor stockings, by folding the heel flap in half and casting off the two sides together so as to produce a short seam under the heel.

The recipe stops before reaching the toe. Presumably the pattern of the toe was omitted in error, or it may have been regarded as so well known as to be unnecessary. Or, since the recipe ends at the bottom of the page, the description of the toe may have been lost in the printing process.

The order how to knit a hose

First, in the top it must be six score and twelve stitches wide.

The leg

So work downward, and take in at every four purls, hard at the seam of the right-hand needle, one stitch; and of the left-hand needle leave a stitch between the seam and then take in. And so work down till you have made four purls.

And then begin the ham and work up straight. Neither widen nor straiten till you have made fourteen knots; and then widen out of both sides of your seam, as you did before, at every four purls, till you have wided seven

stitches at a side. Then work up plain. Neither widen nor straiten till you have made fourteen knots. Then take in at every fifth mask a stitch of each side, as you did before, till you have left but four and forty of every needle (which amounteth to six score and twelve). And if it chance in the working of your small that your ham rise somewhat round, you must take in somewhat faster than is appointed here, that your small be not too big.

And from your calf to the beginning of your clock amounteth unto seventy knots.

The clock

And so then divide your needles into three equal parts, allowing upon your two heel needles three stitches of each, more than upon your instep needle.

Round 1. And then at the beginning of the right-hand needle of the heel make two turned stitches, and so work plain till you come at the latter end of the left-hand needle to the instep-ward. And there make two turned stitches again; and then knit plain round till you come again to your heel-needle.

Round 3. Then make one purl at the beginning of your heel-needle. Then take up a stitch between the two purls and work it plain. Then the next stitch make a purl, and the next stitch work plain. Then shrink two stitches into *one* and work till you come to your left-hand needle. Then you must leave four stitches of your needle, and so shrink two together, then cast up your thread and make a knot, then widen a stitch and work it plain, and make a knot again.

And so then work your instep-needle. And so work plain one course round about, till you come to your right-hand heel needle.

Round 5. Then make at the first stitch one purl, and knit a plain stitch again; and then take up a stitch and work that plain. Next that cast up your thread and make a knotted stitch; and then work a plain stitch again, and take in two plain stitches into one, and so knit about till you come to the left-hand needle within five stitches. Then take two into one, then make a purl, then work a plain stitch, and take up a stitch and work it plain, and then work a purl.

And so then work your instep-needle, and then a plain course round about of all three needles.

Round 7. Then make your purl again when you come to your right-hand needle; and then two plain stitches; and then one purl; and so work till you come to your left-hand needle, within four stitches. Then make a purl stitch; two plain stitches; and one purl.

And so work your instep needle; and then a plain course about till you come to your right-hand needle again.

Round 9. Then make a turned stitch, then one plain stitch; then take up a stitch and make that a purl; then a plain stitch, then a purl, then a plain stitch; then take in two. And work about till you come to your left-hand needle, till you have left but six. Then shrink in two, then make a purl stitch; then knit plain again one stitch; then take up a stitch and make that a purl; then work a plain stitch; then make another purl.

And so to your instep needle, and knit a plain course round about.

Round 11. Then when you come at your right needle, make a purl; then a plain stitch, then a purl again; then a plain stitch again; then knit a *purl stitch; and then* plain again until you come at your left-hand needle, till you have left five stitches. Then you must make a purl stitch; then a plain stitch; then a purl stitch; then a plain stitch; then a purl stitch again.

And so to your instep needle; and then knit a plain course about until you come to your right-hand needle.

Round 13. Then a purl stitch, then a plain stitch, then a purl stitch; then take up a stitch and make that a purl, (and *thus* two purls together); then knit a plain stitch; and make a purl again, then a plain stitch, then knit two together. And so knit till you come to your left-hand needle, till you have but seven. Then take two into one, then a purl stitch, then a plain stitch, then a purl stitch; then take up a stitch and make that a purl (and so you shall have two purls together); then a plain stitch, then a purl again.

Then knit out your instep needle; then a course about plain.

Round 15. Then to your right-side needle, and at the first stitch make a purl; then a plain stitch, then two purls together; then a plain stitch; then a purl again. And so to your left-hand needle, till you come to six stitches. Then make a purl, then a plain stitch, then two purls together, then a plain stitch, then a purl again.

And so to your instep needle. And so a plain course, till you come to your right-hand needle.

Round 17. Then make a purl, then a plain stitch, then a purl; then take up a plain stitch, then make a purl again; then a plain stitch; then a purl; then a plain stitch; then a purl; and knit two together. Then knit to your left-hand needle till you have but eight stitches. Then take in two together; then make a purl; then a plain stitch; then a purl again; then take up one and make it a plain stitch; then knit a purl again; then a plain stitch again; then a purl.

And so to your instep needle. And so knit round about, neither widen nor straiten till there be ten purls on the side needles.

The heel

And take off your two side needles three stitches of each and put them on your instep needle. And then upon your two side needles knit up your heel till you have 54 purls, taking in at every four purls a stitch from the purl of the right side, and leave a stitch between the purl of the left side. And so take it in till you have but 28 stitches of each side.

Then upon your right-hand you must work off 12 stitches with the purls and all. Then take two stitches and loop one over another inward to the seam of your hose; and so work plain till you come within two stitches of your seam, and work them both into one stitch plain, as they lie, and then knit your seam stitch; and your other two stitches next your seam stitch must be looped outward from the seam. Then work till you have but 18 stitches of a needle, and knit two together.

And so must you take in and bind at every other course till your binding stitches do meet. If you chance to have any odd stitches of one needle more than of the other, bind on those stitches and not of the other. Then work till you come at your seam stitch, and so put both the right sides of your hose together of both your needles. And take a third needle and work both those needles together on the wrong side, looping one stitch over another as you do end a hose.

Then take two needles and take up all the knots on the wrong side, next to the edge stitch. And so knit one course plain round about your hose. And at the second upon your side needles you must at every fourth stitch take up a stitch. And so must you do of both sides of your side needles till you have seventy-six. And so take three at the point of your clock, at every course of stitch of both sides till you have done 10 purls. And these take in at every second course a stitch of each side till you have done twenty purls; and so at every third course till you have other twenty.

The clock pattern tabulated

Alternate rounds are knitted plain. The pattern below describes the working of the two needles for the heel only. The directions before the semicolon are for the first clock, those after the semicolon are for the second clock. Each row is then completed by knitting the third needle plain for the instep.

Round 1. P2, K to last 2: P2

Round 3. P1, pick up 1K, P1, K1, K2 tog; K to last 4: K2 tog, P1, pick up 1K, P1.

Round 5. P1, K1, pick up 1K, P1, K1, K2 tog; K to last 5: K2 tog, P1, K1, pick up 1K, P1.

Round 7.   P1, K2, P1; K to last 4: P1, K2, P1.

Round 9.   P1, K1, pick up 1P, K1, P1, K1, K2 tog; K to last 6: K2 tog, P1, K1, pick up 1P, K1, P1.

Round 11. P1, K1, P1, K1, P1; K to last 5: P1, K1, P1, K1, P1.

Round 13. P1, K1, P1, pick up 1P, K1, P1, K1, K2 tog; K to last 7: K2 tog, P1, K1, P1, pick up 1 P, K1, Pl.

Round 15. P1, 1K, P2, K1, P1; K to last 6: P1, K1, P2, K1, P1.

Round 17   P1, 1K, P1, pick up 1K, P1, K1, P1, K1, K2 tog; K to last 8: K2 tog, P1, K1, P1, pick up 1K, P1, K1, P1.

The heel explained

Distribute the stitches equally on three needles, 44 on each.

Work the 88 stitches on the two heel needles, back and forth in stocking stitch, for 64 (not 54) rows, maintaining the single purled stitch at the seam. In every fourth row, decrease one stitch on either side of the purl, making the decreased stitches lie symmetrically. At the end of the 64th row, 28 stitches will remain on each needle.

Knit 12 stitches off the first needle, knit a stitch and pass the previous (i.e. 12th) stitch over it. Continue the row, working the seam stitch and its decreases in alternate rows until 13 (not 18) stitches remain. Knit two together and turn. Purl across (knitting the seam stitch) until 11 stitches remain. Turn, knit one, pass the previous (the 11th) stitch over. Knit till 12 stitches remain, knit two together and turn.

Continue thus until the decreasings reach the edges of the heel flap. Work back to the seam stitch, put the two needles together with right sides facing each other, and join them by knitting together a stitch from each needle and casting off the stitches thus made.

Knit up 64 stitches on each side of the heel flap, knitting round the foot. In the second round increase by picking up a stitch after every fourth stitch on the sides. There will now be 76 stitches on each side needle and 44 across the instep. In each of the next 10 rounds knit 3 together at the end of each side needle near the instep. Decrease one stitch in the same place in the next 10 alternate rounds, thereafter in every third round 6 times.

end of _____ beginning of
second clock   first clock

□ knit
■ purl
⊞ pick up one knitwise
▪ pick up one purlwise
◩ knit two together in 1st clock
◪ knit two together in 2nd clock

163 The *Natura Exenterata* clock. Row 1, worked first, is the top of the clock.

Weldon's Practical Knitter

Weldon's Practical Knitter was published as a numbered series within the monthly comprehensive periodical publication of *Weldon's Practical Needlework*. Issues are undated until July 1915. Thenceforth the date appears in code on the cover thus: 7/15 = July 1915. The following table gives the year dates of the earlier issues.

Issue	Series	Year	Issue	Series	Year	Issue	Series	Year
Vol 1: No 1	1	1886	Vol 12: No 140	34	1897	Vol 22: No 253	67	1907
2	2		142	35		256	68	
4	3		Vol 13: 145	36	1898	264	69	
9	4		146	37		Vol 23: 267	70	1908
Vol 2: 17	5	1887	150	38		270	71	
24	6		152	39		273	72	
Vol 3: 25	7	1888	156	40		275	73	
35	8		Vol 14: 158	41	1899	Vol 24: 279	74	1909
36	9		161	42		283	75	
Vol 4: 41	10	1889	162	43		286	76	
46	11		165	44		288	77	
Vol 5: 49	12	1890	166	45		Vol 25: 293	78	1910
54	13		167	46		296	79	
55	14		Vol 15: 170	47	1900	298	80	
60	15		171	48		Vol 26: 301	81	1911
Vol 6: 62	16	1891	173	49		304	82	
64	17		175	50		309	83	
72	18		178	51		310	84	
Vol 7: 76	19	1892	Vol 16: 181	52	1901	Vol 27: 313	85	1912
82	20		189	53		317	86	
84	21		Vol 17: 203	54	1902	319	87	
Vol 8: 91	22	1893	Vol 18: 205	55	1903	324	88	
94	23		209	56		Vol 28: 326	89	1913
96	24		Vol 19: 217	57	1904	330	90	
Vol 9: 101	25	1894	218	58		333	91	
108	26		220	59		335	92	
Vol 10: 109	27	1895	225	60		Vol 29: 338	93	1914
114	28		Vol 20: 231	61	1905	341	94	
120	29		233	62		345	95	
Vol 11: 123	30	1896	238	63		347	96	
125	31		240	64		Vol 30: 349	97	1915
130	32		Vol 21: 246	65	1906	352	98	
132	33		251	66		355	99	

Select bibliography

Baker, Patricia. 'The fez in Turkey: a symbol of modernization?' *Costume* No 20, 1986, 73-85.

Barnes, Ishbel C M. 'The Aberdeen stocking trade', *Textile History* 8 1977, 77-98.

Beard, Charles R. 'Liturgical gloves in the collection of Mrs Philip Lehman', *The Connoisseur* XCIV. No 398 (October 1934) pp 226-30.

Beaulieu, Michèle. 'Les gants liturgiques en France au Moyen Âge', *Bulletin archéologique* Paris (N.S.4) 1969, 137-53.

Beckmann, Johann. *The history of inventions* (translated William Johnston) 1799, 1846.

Bellinger, Louisa. 'Patterned stockings: possibly Indian, found in Egypt' *Textile Museum Workshop Notes* 10 (1954).

Bennett, Helen M. *Scottish knitting* (Shire Album 164) 1986.

Bennett, Helen M. *The origins and development of the Scottish hand-knitting industry*, unpublished thesis: University of Edinburgh 1981.

Bohus Stickning. *Bohus stickning 1939-1969*, Göteborg 1980.

Brears, Peter C D. 'The knitting sheath' in *Folk life: a journal of ethnological studies* 20 Cardiff (1981-2), 16-40.

Buckland, Kirstie. 'The Monmouth cap', *Costume* xiii (1979), 23-37.

Buehler, Kristin. 'Classification of basic textile techniques', *Ciba Review* No 63 1948, 2295-2305.

Buehler-Oppenheim, Kristin and Alfred. *Katalog: Die Textiliensammlung Fritz-Iklé* Basel, Museum für Völkeskunde 1948.

Bültzingslowen, Regina Flury von, and Lehmann, Edgar. 'Nichtgewebte Textilien vor 1400' *Wirkerei-und Strickerei-Technik* Coburg, 1954 May 33-6; June 43-8; July 38-41; August 41-35; November 39-41; December 45-7. 1955 February 35-6; March 36-8; May 38-41. 1956 Feb 50-2.

Burnham, Dorothy K. 'Coptic knitting: an ancient technique', *Textile History* 3 (1972), 116-124.

Chapman, Stanley D. 'The Genesis of the British Hosiery Industry 1600-1750', *Textile History* 3 (1972), 7-50.

Ettinghausen, Richard. 'Kufesque in Byzantine Greece, the Latin West and the Muslim World', *A colloquium in memory of George Carpenter Miles* New York 1976, 28-47.

Geijer, Agnes. *Textile treasures of Uppsala cathedral* 1964.

Grass, Milton. 'Origins of the art of knitting', *Archaeology* 8.3. (Autumn 1955), 184-80.

Gudjonsson, Elsa. *Notes on knitting in Iceland* 1979, revised 1985.

Hartley, Marie and Ingilby, Joan. *The old handknitters of the Dales* Clapham, Yorkshire 1951.

Harvey, Michael. *Patons: a story of handknitting* 1985.

Hellman, Ruth P. 'Thérèse de Dillmont', *Bulletin of the Needle and Bobbin Club of New York* 59:1/2 (1976), 21-7.

Henshall, Audrey S, and others. 'Early textiles found in Scotland', *Proceedings of the Society of Antiquaries of Scotland*: 'I Locally made' LXXXVI (1951-2), 1-29; 'II Mediaeval imports' LXXXIX (1954-6), 22-39; 'Clothing and other articles from a late 17th century grave at Gunnister, Shetland' LXXXVI (1951-2), 30-42.

Johannson, Britta, and Nilsson, Kersti. *Binge: en halländsk sticktradition*, Stockholm 1986.

Lambert, A. 'Peasant textile art', *Ciba Review* No 66, 1948.

Lamm, Carl Johann. *Mediaeval textiles of the Near East* 1937.

Lane, Barbara S. 'The Cowichan knitting industry', *Anthropology in British Columbia* (1951) 2: 14-27.

Levey, Santina M. 'Illustrations of the history of knitting selected from the collection of the Victoria & Albert Museum', *Textile History* I Pt 2 (1969) 183-205.

Linthicum, M. Channing. *Costume in the drama of Shakespeare and his contemporaries* 1936.

Maillard, Elisa. 'Le point à l'aiguille au XIVe siècle', *Hyphé* (Geneva) 1946, 210-15.

Norbury, James. 'The knitter's craft', *Journal of the Royal Society of Arts* 26 January 1951, 216-28.

Norbury, James. 'A note on knitting and knitted fabrics', Singer, C., et al. *A history of technology* Vol III 1958, 181-6.

Norwick, Braham. 'The history of knitting', *Knitting Times* USA 10 May 1971, 26-31, 67.

Norwick, Braham. 'The origins of knitted fabrics', *The bulletin of the Needle and Bobbin Club* Vol 63 Nos 1 & 2 (1980), 36-51.

Özbel, Kenan. *Knitted stockings from Turkish villages* Istanbul 1981.

Pfister, Rudolf and Bellinger, Louisa. 'The textiles:

Knitting', Rostovtzeff, M.I., et al. *The excavations at Dura-Europos* Final Report IV, Part II. New Haven 1945, 54-5.

Pinchbeck, Ivy. *Women workers and the industrial revolution* (1750-1850) 1930 'Handknitting' 226-30.

Ponting, Kenneth G. 'In search of William Lee . . .' *Knitting International* December 1982.

Potter, Esther. 'English knitting and crochet books of the nineteenth century' *The Library: transactions of the Bibliographical Society*, March & June 1955.

Priaulx, T.F. and de Sausmarez, R. 'The Guernsey stocking export trade in the 17th century' *Transactions of the Société Guernsiaise* XVII (1962), 210-22.

Rath, Terence. 'The Tewkesbury hosiery industry' *Textile History* 7 1976, 140-53.

Reilly, Patrick. *Cornelia Mee 1815-1875*: a memoir. Privately printed. N.d. (1983).

Rowlands, Alexandra L. 'Machine knitted outerwear for adults from 1850 to 1939'. Part I. *Knitting International*. (March 1985) Vol 92 No. 1095, 29-31.

Sakata, Nobumasa, and Harvey, Michael. '400 years of knitting in Japan' in Michael Harvey *The history of knitting* (Patons Trade Services Publications No 2) n.d. (1974?).

Schmedding, Brigitta. *Mittelalterliche Textilien in Kirchen und Klöstern der Schweiz*. 1978, 90-2, 284-8.

Seiler-Baldinger, Annemarie. *Maschenstoffe in Süd- und Mittel-amerika* Basle 1971. Basler Beiträge zur Ethnologie Band 9.

Stuart, John. 'Notice of remains found in an ancient tomb recently opened in the cathedral church of Fortrose' *Proceedings of the Society of Antiquaries of Scotland*. I (1851-54), 281-4.

Thirsk, Joan. *The agrarian history of England and Wales IV 1500-1640* 1967.

Thirsk, Joan. 'The fantastical folly of fashion: the English stocking knitting industry 1500-1700', in N.B. Harte and K.G. Ponting edd. *Textile history and economic history: essays in honour of Julia de Lacey Mann* 1973, 50-73.

Thirsk, Joan. 'Industries in the countryside' Fisher, F.J. ed. *Essays in the economic and social history of Tudor and Stuart England* 1961 (p 70 for Dentdale).

Tibbott, S Minwel. 'Knitting stockings in Wales: a domestic craft', *Folk Life* St Fagans XVI (1978), 61-73.

Turnau, Irena. 'Aspects of the Russian artisan: the knitter of the seventeenth to the eighteenth century' *Textile History* 4, 1973.

Turnau, Irena. 'The diffusion of knitting in mediaeval Europe'. Harte, N.B. and Ponting, K.G. *Cloth and Clothing in mediaeval Europe* 1983, 19, 368-89.

Turnau, Irena. 'The history of peasant knitting in Europe: a framework for research' *Textile History*, 17 (2), 1986, 167-80.

Turnau, Irena. 'Stockings from the coffins of the Pomeranian princes preserved in the National Museum in Szczecin'. *Textile History* 8, 1977, 167-9.

Turnau, Irena and Ponting, Kenneth G. 'Knitted masterpieces' *Textile History* 7, 1976, 7-59.

Van Den Hurk, L.J.A.M. 'The tumuli from the Roman period of Esch, Province of North Brabant' *Overdruk uit Berichten van de Rijksdienst voor het Oudheidkundig Bodemonderzoek Jaargang* 23, 1973.

Walton, Penelope. 'An excavation in the Castle ditch, Newcastle-upon-Tyne 1974-6: The Textiles' *Archaeologia Aeliana* 5, IX, 1981, 200-1.

Wild, John Peter. *Textile manufacture in the northern Roman provinces* 1970.

Wright, Mary. *Cornish guernseys and knit-frocks* 1979.

Index

This index does not include references to the appendices.
*See also select bibliography, pp 243-4.